# Management, Organizations, and Paradoxes



Paradoxical tensions are persistently inevitable in today's complex organizational world. Therefore, managers should perceive them as a lens through which they see organizations and work through them. Reconciling paradoxes requires understanding their nature and appraising them. It also involves novelty and creativity in implemented tactics. Thus, to help managers navigate dualities and contradictions in their organizations, *Management, Organizations, and Paradoxes* presents a comprehensive overview of implementing the paradox theory from a distinct organizational standpoint in the Central and Eastern European (CEE) context. Beyond theoretical foundations, it integrates recent research findings and practical insights, providing rich knowledge for managing conflicting demands across diverse organizational dimensions. In addition, it unlocks new insights that can enrich academic discourse and guide practitioners in embracing a paradox mindset. It develops less-explored areas, such as paradox regarding sustainability in clusters, or digital and energy transition. It also explores paradox in human resource management, workplace learning, diversity, equity, and inclusion policy. It tests whether paradoxes have regional variation and provides insight from managerial practices in CEE. The authors prove that organizations embracing paradox can expand the scope of their opportunities and thrive.

This monograph can serve as a scholarly guide for managers, academics, and Ph.D students, encouraging them to analyze and manage organizations from a paradox angle.

**Malgorzata Rozkwitalska-Welenc** is a Professor of Economics specializing in Organizational Science and Organizational Behavior. She works at WSB Merito University in Gdansk, Poland.

**Agnieszka Zakrzewska-Bielawska** is a Professor of Strategic Management and the Head of Management and Quality Studies at Lodz University of Technology, Poland.

**Anna Maria Lis** is a Professor of Innovation Management, Inter-Organizational Cooperation, and Sustainable Development at Gdańsk University of Technology, Poland.

# Routledge Studies in Management, Organizations and Society

This series presents innovative work grounded in new realities, addressing issues crucial to an understanding of the contemporary world. This is the world of organized societies, where boundaries between formal and informal, public and private, local and global organizations have been displaced or have vanished, along with other nineteenth century dichotomies and oppositions. Management, apart from becoming a specialized profession for a growing number of people, is an everyday activity for most members of modern societies.

Similarly, at the level of enquiry, culture and technology, and literature and economics, can no longer be conceived as isolated intellectual fields; conventional canons and established mainstreams are contested. *Management, Organizations and Society* addresses these contemporary dynamics of transformation in a manner that transcends disciplinary boundaries, with books that will appeal to researchers, students and practitioners alike.

Recent titles in this series include:

**Evolution of Management in a Post-Pandemic World**
The Chameleon Paradigm
*Agnieszka Rzepka*

**Destructive Behaviors and Organizational Research**
A Comprehensive Overview
*Riann Singh and Shalini Ramdeo*

**The Ideology of Managerialism**
Fragments of a Future Theory
*Thomas Klikauer*

**Innovation and the Sharing Economy**
Employment, Human Capital, and the AI Revolution
*Edited by Pawan Kumar, Tanima Dutta, Sumesh Dadwal and Napinder Kaur*

**Management, Organizations, and Paradoxes**
Insights from the Central and Eastern European Region
*Edited by Malgorzata Rozkwitalska-Welenc, Agnieszka Zakrzewska-Bielawska, and Anna Maria Lis*

# Management, Organizations, and Paradoxes

## Insights from the Central and Eastern European Region

**Edited by Malgorzata Rozkwitalska-Welenc, Agnieszka Zakrzewska-Bielawska, and Anna Maria Lis**

Routledge
Taylor & Francis Group
NEW YORK AND LONDON

First published 2025
by Routledge
605 Third Avenue, New York, NY 10158

and by Routledge
4 Park Square, Milton Park, Abingdon, Oxon, OX14 4RN

*Routledge is an imprint of the Taylor & Francis Group, an informa business*



ISBN: 978-1-032-88349-6 (hbk)
ISBN: 978-1-032-89144-6 (pbk)
ISBN: 978-1-003-54139-4 (ebk)

DOI: 10.4324/9781003541394

Typeset in Times New Roman
by Deanta Global Publishing Services, Chennai, India

# Contents

# Figures

# Tables

# Contributors

**Damian Ciachorowski**, Gdansk University of Technology, Gdansk, Poland. Fields of Study: Digital Transformation, Sustainable Development, Strategic Management, and Organizational Studies.

**Joanna Czerska**, Gdansk University of Technology, Gdansk, Poland. Fields of Study: Lean Management, Lean Leadership, and Lean Didactics.

**Adrian Lis**, Collegium Civitas, Warsaw, Poland. Fields of Study: Interorganizational Cooperation, and Sustainable Development.

**Anna M. Lis**, Gdansk University of Technology, Gdansk, Poland. Fields of Study: Innovation Management, Interorganizational Cooperation, and Sustainable Development.

**Ewa Mariańska**, Gdansk University of Technology, Gdansk, Poland. Fields of Study: Quality Management, Lean Management, and Leadership.

**Agnieszka Miarecka**, WSB Merito University in Gdansk, Gdansk, Poland. Fields of Study: Strategic Aspects of Turnarounds, Life Cycle Issues, and Entrepreneurship.

**Elem Miranda**, University of Glasgow, Glasgow, Scotland. Fields of Study: Digital Entrepreneurship, Digital Scale-Ups, and Digital Start-Ups.

**Gabriela Misiura**, WSB Merito University in Gdansk, Gdansk, Poland. Fields of Study: Cross-Cultural Management, Human Capital Management, and Silver Generation at Work.

**Marcin Panek**, WSB Merito University in Gdansk, Poland. Fields of Study: Diversity and Inclusion Management, Sustainable Workplace Practices, Cross-Cultural Management, and Tourism and Hospitality.

**Malgorzata Rozkwitalska-Welenc**, WSB Merito University in Gdansk, Gdansk, Poland. Fields of Study: Organizational Behavior, Organizational Science, Human Resource Management, Cross-Cultural Management.

**Jacek Rybicki**, University of Gdansk, Gdansk, Poland. Fields of Study: Strategic Management, Business Models, Networks, and Philosophy of Science.

**Piotr Sycz**, Fahrenheit Universities: University of Gdańsk, Gdansk, Poland. Fields of Study: Lean Project Management, and Innovation Management.

**Dobrochna Sztajerska**, Cavalry Captain Witold Pilecki State University of Małopolska in Oświęcim, Oswiecim, Poland. Fields of Study: Quality Management, Process Optimization, Lean Management, Business Psychology, and Continuous Improvement Strategies.

**Candace TenBrink**, University of Houston, Huston, United States. Fields of Study: Strategic Aspects of Turnarounds, Life Cycle Issues, and Entrepreneurship.

**Elżbieta Wojnicka-Sycz**, Fahrenheit Universities: University of Gdansk and Gdansk University of Technology, Gdansk, Poland. Fields of Study: Innovation and Technology Transfer, Spatial Management from the Point of View of Innovation, and Regional Development.

**Chen Xiu**, Gdańsk University of Technology, Gdansk, Poland. Fields of Study: Interorganizational Cooperation, and Management in Energy Industry.

**Agnieszka Zakrzewska-Bielawska**, Lodz University of Technology, Lodz, Poland. Fields of Study: Strategic Management, Cooperation and Coopetition, and Knowledge Commercialization and Vaporization.

# Editors' Introduction

*Malgorzata Rozkwitalska-Welenc, Agnieszka Zakrzewska-Bielawska, and Anna Maria Lis*

In an increasingly complex, ambiguous, volatile, and uncertain contemporary business environment abundant in contradictions and conflicting demands, paradoxical tensions are inevitable. Managing these contradictions requires more than just resolving them; it requires adopting paradox as the lens through which organizational processes and systems are understood and handled. Given the current paradigm in organizational theory, managers should acknowledge competing demands and duality present in organizations' internal and external environments and "engage and navigate tensions rather than resolve them" (Carmine & Smith, 2021, p. 1). This assumption is the basis of the paradox theory in organizational science that emerged in the late 1970s and has significantly expanded through the pioneering contributions of W. K. Smith, S. Clegg, M. W. Lewis, M. Berti, A. Rego, and M. P. Cunha (e.g., Bednarek & Smith, 2024; Berti & Cunha, 2023; Gaim et al., 2019; Schad et al., 2019). The paradox theory in organizations continues its rapid development, and the monograph *Management, Organizations, and Paradoxes* provides an extensive overview of adopting the lens of the paradox theory from an organizational perspective.

The book explores paradox theory, focusing on the Central and Eastern European (CEE) region. The editors, Malgorzata Rozkwitalska-Welenc, Agnieszka Zakrzewska-Bielawska, and Anna Maria Lis, bring together various authors' theoretical insights and practical applications to address the dualities and tensions that managers face in today's organizations, i.e., paradoxes that "appear logical when seen separately but ludicrous and irrational when seen together" (Tekletsion et al., 2024, p. 2).

The distinguishing feature of this book is its contextual emphasis. On the one hand, we intend to emphasize the universality of paradoxes as constructs belonging to different contexts (including philosophical and logical ones). We focus on the organizational context, which provides an excellent lens for looking at economic actors and the socioeconomic environment in which these actors operate. On the other hand, our goal is to show the uniqueness of contemporary phenomena observed in Central and Eastern Europe, especially in Poland. While paradox theory has been extensively studied in Western contexts (e.g., in the United States, United Kingdom, Australia, Sweden, or Germany), more literature is needed to address its application in the CEE region. This volume fills

DOI: 10.4324/9781003541394-1

that gap, offering a multifaceted understanding of paradoxes within CEE countries' unique socioeconomic, political, and cultural realities. The book tackles less underexplored areas such as sustainability paradoxes in industrial clusters, the challenges of digital and energy transitions, and the complexities and contradictions of human resource management, workplace learning, diversity, equity, and inclusion policies. These areas are crucial to contemporary organizational practices but have not received adequate attention in existing paradox literature.

The relevance of this book exceeds university circles. The book incorporates empirical case studies from sectors such as hospitality and energy, local companies, and multinational enterprises and provides recommendations for managers struggling with contradictory demands. It demonstrates that embracing paradoxes requires a theoretical basis and a both-and approach for organizations seeking to survive and grow in the new normality. It proves, similarly to Lempiälä et al. (2023), the intertwined nature of various paradoxes organizations face. Furthermore, it examines whether paradoxes manifest differently in the CEE context than globally and offers valuable contributions to regional and international discussions on paradox theory.

The implications of this book are profound. First, as it provides a fresh perspective on managing organizational tensions, it can enrich the academic discourse on paradoxes. Second, it can also serve as a guide for practitioners, offering strategies for dealing with competing demands in different organizational environments in the CEE context. Third, it promotes a paradox mindset among managers and employees and encourages readers to view contradictions not as problems to be solved but as opportunities for learning, innovation, and growth. It is an essential resource for scholars, managers, and postgraduate students, offering new insights into how organizations can harness the power of paradox to manage the complexities of the modern business environment.

The monograph is divided into four main parts. The first part settles the theoretical and methodological foundations, and the remaining three parts address different dimensions of paradoxes in organizations in the CEE region.

## Chapter 1: Exploring the Complex Area of Organizational Paradoxes – Overcoming Methodological Obstacles

Adrian Lis addresses the methodological complexities of studying organizational paradoxes. The chapter provides tools for researchers and practitioners to explore how paradoxes operate within management contexts. It begins by analyzing the nature of paradoxes and their significance in management, introducing a classification framework to aid in selecting appropriate research methods and techniques. The focus then shifts to the methodological obstacles in paradox research, examining social science paradigms, particularly those within management studies, and presenting specific research methods and techniques. Emphasis is placed on the contexts in which these methods are applied, highlighting the methodological diversity in studying paradoxes. The chapter also summarizes the research approaches used throughout the monograph, underscoring their importance for understanding organizational paradoxes.

**Chapter 2: Organizational Paradox Theory – Managing Competing Demands Then and Now**

Authored by Jacek Rybicki, this chapter provides an overview of the evolution of paradox theory, tracing its origins from early debates to contemporary applications. The chapter introduces key concepts such as dialectics, dualities, and ambiguities and discusses the tripartite classification of paradoxes into learning, organizing, and belonging. It also explores the strategic management of paradoxes, offering a framework for understanding contradictions as sources of opportunity. The author presents and synthesizes two equilibrium concepts to handle strategic paradoxes.

**Chapter 3: Ambidexterity – A Strategic Approach to Overcoming Organizational Paradoxes**

Agnieszka Zakrzewska-Bielawska examines ambidexterity as a strategic and dynamic capability for addressing one of the most common paradoxes: the tension between exploration and exploitation. The chapter explores how organizations balance pursuing new opportunities while optimizing existing competencies, presenting various organizational perspectives on this paradox within ambidexterity research. She also points out a scarcity of studies from CEE.

Part II contains three chapters, focusing on paradox management from the human resources angle.

**Chapter 4: Human Resource Paradoxes in a Belgian Subsidiary of a Multinational Enterprise – An Ethnographic Case Study**

Gabriela Misiura uses ethnographic methods to explore paradoxes in human resource management, focusing on a Belgian subsidiary of a multinational corporation. This chapter uncovers contradictions, such as the expectation of managerial autonomy versus micromanagement, and provides insights into culturally sensitive HR practices in the CEE business context.

**Chapter 5: Homo Managerius – The Paradox of Leadership**

Ewa Mariańska, Joanna Czerska, and Dobrochna Sztajerska explore the paradoxes of leadership and their impact on expected leadership practices in Central and Eastern Europe, focusing on Poland. The study examines how leaders, nonleaders, and students perceive leadership styles and management challenges, offering insights into generational and professional perspectives. The authors underscore the importance of managing leadership paradoxes, such as balancing empowerment with emotional connection, to address the dynamic needs of modern organizations in CEE. The findings reveal critical variations in leadership expectations across professional and generational groups, contributing valuable insights to studying leadership in the CEE region.

### Chapter 6: Diversity, Equity, and Inclusion Policy Paradoxes – Insights from the Central and Eastern European Hospitality Sector

Marcin Panek explores diversity, equity, and inclusion (DEI) paradoxes, focusing on tensions between global standards and local cultural norms, particularly in traditionally homogeneous societies such as Poland. Through interviews with hotel staff in CEE, the author highlights effective strategies and areas when expectations clash with reality. This analysis deepens understanding of the challenges in implementing DEI policies in CEE and offers practical insights for fostering inclusive environments in the hospitality industry.

Part III delves into learning paradoxes and comprises two chapters.

### Chapter 7: Paradoxes in Innovation – Navigating the Duality of Closed vs. Open Innovation

Elzbieta Wojnicka-Sycz, Piotr Sycz, and Candace TenBrink explore the evolution of innovation theory from closed to open innovation, extending it to the interplay of business and non-profit innovation. They highlight a paradigm shift in the innovation theory, moving from reductionist approaches to holistic perspectives, with an increasing emphasis on improving quality of life over economic growth. Using panel regression and significance tests, the authors analyze data from the European Innovation Scoreboard, the Human Development Index database, and surveys of 2388 companies in Poland, CEE, and Western Europe (2014–2024). They reveal that CEE countries face barriers to adopting green innovation but are succeeding better than Western Europe in open innovation. The chapter highlights the need for innovation policies that consider regional differences and the dual goals of economic and social development.

### Chapter 8: Workplace Learning through Organizational and Leadership Paradoxes

Agnieszka Miarecka focuses on how organizational and leadership paradoxes foster workplace learning in multinational enterprises in CEE. The findings show that CEE's unique socio-political and economic context may influence how individuals handle paradoxes, leading to workplace learning and adverse effects like superficial learning and ethical issues. The study highlights the need for a paradox mindset and a learning culture that embraces complexity to leverage paradoxes effectively.

The final, fourth part centers around sustainability paradoxes and covers three topics.

### Chapter 9: Conflicting Demands of Sustainable Digital Transformation

Damian Ciachorowski and Elem Miranda examine the paradoxes involved in digital transformation, particularly the tension between technological innovation and sustainability. The study focuses on areas of digital transformation and shows which relationships between them can create paradoxical tensions. The chapter explores how companies in CEE can navigate the challenges of implementing digital initiatives that are both innovative and ethically sound. Despite the chapter taking a CEE and Western Europe perspective, the findings nevertheless appear universal for all countries implementing digital transformation.

### Chapter 10: Clusters in Reconciling Paradoxes in the Sustainability Pillars

Anna M. Lis and Malgorzata Rozkwitalska-Welenc focus on the role of industrial clusters in managing sustainability paradoxes. Using two case studies from CEE and one from Western Europe, this chapter explores how clusters can reconcile the conflicting demands of economic, social, and environmental sustainability. The study demonstrates that combining the goals and economic interests of different cluster entities enables the construction of a sustainable value chain that resolves paradoxical tensions in the intra-organizational environment.

### Chapter 11: Energy Transition Through Coastal Energy-Based Industrial Clusters – Paradoxes and Solutions

Authored by Chen Xiu, this chapter examines the pivotal role of energy-based industrial clusters in the global transition to renewable energy. It explores the paradoxical tensions inherent in this transformation, particularly the trade-offs between environmental sustainability and economic development. Focusing on three coastal energy clusters in the European Union, with particular attention to one of the Central and Eastern European countries, Poland, the chapter uncovers the challenges of balancing renewable energy goals with economic stability, such as potential unemployment in traditional energy sectors. By comparing regional experiences with broader European trends, the chapter highlights the opportunities and pitfalls of energy transition efforts.

Each monograph chapter identifies study limitations and provides well-grounded recommendations for future research, ensuring a roadmap for further exploration. Additionally, the chapters offer valuable theoretical insights that contribute to academic discourse, alongside practical applications that can guide policymakers, practitioners, and business leaders in addressing real-world paradoxes.

## References

Bednarek, R., & Smith, W. K. (2024). "What may be": Inspiration from Mary Parker Follett for paradox theory. *Strategic Organization*, *22*(3), 582–596. https://doi.org/10.1177/14761270231151734

Berti, M., & Cunha, M. P. E. (2023). Paradox, dialectics or trade-offs? A double loop model of paradox. *Journal of Management Studies*, *60*(4), 861–888. https://doi.org/10.1111/joms.12899

Carmine, S. & Smith, W. K. (2021). Organizational Paradox, Oxford Bibliographies in Management. https://doi.org/10.1093/obo/9780199846740-0201https://www.oxfordbibliographies.com/display/document/obo-9780199846740/obo-9780199846740-0201.xml

Gaim, M., Clegg, S., & Cunha, M. P. e. (2019). Managing impressions rather than emissions: Volkswagen and the false mastery of paradox. *Organization Studies*, *42*(6), 949–970. https://doi.org/10.1177/0170840619891199

Lempiälä, T., Tiitinen, S., & Vanharanta, O. (2023). Paradox as an interactional resource: An ethnomethodological analysis into the interconnectedness of organizational paradoxes. *Organization Studies*, *44*(11), 1825–1852. https://doi.org/10.1177/01708406221118671

Schad, J., Lewis, M. W., & Smith, W. K. (2019). Quo vadis, paradox? Centripetal and centrifugal forces in theory development. *Strategic Organization*, *17*(1), 107–119. https://doi.org/10.1177/1476127018786218

Tekletsion, B. F., Gomes, J. F. D. S., & Tefera, B. (2024). Organizational resilience as paradox management: A systematic review of the literature. *Journal of Contingencies and Crisis Management*, *32*(1), 1–12. https://doi.org/10.1111/1468-5973.12495

# Part I

# Introduction to Paradox Theory and Practice

# 1 Exploring the Complex Area of Organizational Paradoxes

## Overcoming Methodological Obstacles

*Adrian Lis*

### 1.1 Introduction

Today's organizations face increasingly complex and contradictory challenges due to the dynamic economic, social, and technological environment. Dilemmas such as the need to simultaneously foster innovation and maintain stability, the pursuit of short-term goals while considering long-range ambitions, or balancing individualism with collectivism are central themes in the management of contemporary organizations. This fact assumes particular importance in the case of companies that, as profit-oriented organizations, are particularly sensitive to the consequences of possible errors in decision-making processes.

The need to deal with actual or seemingly mutually exclusive challenges must have translated into the emergence of a distinct path of reflection and analysis, the central axis of which was to identify and understand the nature of the "contradictions" present in certain phenomena affecting organizations (but also individuals). A theory of paradoxes appeared to be the answer to this need. Although, as will be outlined in this chapter and, to varying degrees, in the rest of this book, the multiplicity of strands taken up in the reflection and research on paradoxes and the diversity of approaches of the various authors have not so far translated into the creation of a single coherent "theory of paradoxes." Instead of a unified picture of the whole, we have a collage of different materials so far.

The same is true of how researchers attempt to capture the specificity of paradoxes. The research methods and techniques used are far from homogeneous; however, in this case, it seems justified given the extremely wide range of phenomena termed "paradoxes" that remain in management science. The main aim of this chapter is to present and structure a set of methods that allow management researchers and practitioners to gain a deeper understanding of how paradoxes operate in organizations, what mechanisms influence their emergence, and how they can be effectively managed. Understanding these processes is crucial because paradoxes can both stimulate organizational development and pose a serious threat when they are not properly controlled and transformed into constructive elements.

This chapter is structured as follows: The general nature of paradoxes and their relationship to organizational management is discussed first, followed by

DOI: 10.4324/9781003541394-3

the methodological strands. The logic of thinking about empirical research will be preserved here, where the decision on the choice of specific research methods and techniques is preceded by a reflection on the paradigm in which the research reflection and the empirical research proper will be set. The chapter will conclude with a consideration of the main methods used in paradox research, the methodological challenges facing researchers engaged in paradox analysis in the management sciences, and the methodological approaches used in the remainder of this monograph.

## 1.2 Paradoxes in Management: Characteristics and Significance

Paradox is a phenomenon that has fascinated philosophers and scientists alike for centuries. In its simplest definition, paradox refers to a logical contradiction or seemingly irresolvable tension between two ideas that can both be true. In the context of the social sciences, paradox plays a heuristic role, forcing researchers to reflect on the complexity and ambiguity of social reality. Paradoxes are inherent in social and organizational phenomena, revealing tensions that often underpin processes of change and innovation. Contemporary interest in paradoxes stems from their role in describing and analyzing contradictions in complex systems such as organizations, political institutions, or societies. Paradoxes not only pose intellectual challenges but also provide tools to understand better phenomena that traditionally escape ambiguity and are difficult to grasp. Hampden-Turner (2021) notes that managing paradoxes is a key element of effectiveness in dynamic and unpredictable social environments.

The word "paradox" comes from the Greek parádoxon, meaning "contrary to expectation" or "contrary to popular opinion." In the Greek etymological sense of the word, "para" means "opposite" and "doxa" means "accepted opinion," paradoxes involve the juxtaposition of two incompatible and contradictory theses (Putnam, 1986; Statler et al., 2011; Stohl & Cheney, 2001). A paradox can also be viewed as contradictory but related elements that exist simultaneously and persist over time; they appear logical in isolation but are irrational, incoherent, and even absurd when simultaneously occurring (Smith & Lewis, 2011). Classical philosophy treated paradoxes as intellectual challenges that questioned logical assumptions or introduced doubt about the limits of human cognition. An example is *the Liar's Paradox*, attributed to Eubulides of Miletus, who stated: "This sentence is false." This sentence produces a logical contradiction, as it is impossible to determine whether it is true or false unequivocally.

In the philosophical tradition, paradoxes have been used as tools to test the limits of human reason. As summarized by Smith and Lewis (2011), Aristotle treated paradoxes as errors in logic that needed to be explained or resolved, while later philosophers such as Immanuel Kant regarded them as evidence of the limits of human cognitive capacity. In the *Critique of Pure Reason*, Kant pointed out that antinomies, a type of paradox, are inevitable in reflecting on the nature of the world and human experience. And because paradoxes are persistent, tensions are, in fact, never fully resolvable but can only be managed through mechanisms that recognize their permanence (Smith & Lewis, 2011).

The ancient philosophical concept of paradox was introduced into organizational research to analyze and explain organizational behavior in situations of dynamic change and increasing competition (Quinn & Cameron, 1988; Eisenhardt, 2000). The phenomenon of paradox is important for business practitioners because of its ability to make sense of tensions "embedded" in organizations or created by ongoing efforts to reconcile two or more contradictory, interrelated, and coexisting opposites (e.g., Smith & Lewis, 2011; Jarzabkowski et al., 2013). In such situations, it is not possible to act "zero-one," instead organizations and individuals need to develop "both-and" solutions that require dealing with the co-existence of the "two sides of the coin" and the resulting tensions (Lewis, 2000; Lewis & Smith, 2014).

Paradoxes in management can be divided into several categories, which help to understand their complexity and diversity. This chapter proposes the following division of paradoxes based on a comprehensive review of the literature in this area:

1. Organizational structures and processes – the contradictions between organizational flexibility and stability. On the one hand, organizations seek flexibility to respond quickly to changing market conditions; on the other hand, stability ensures consistency and predictability of operations.
2. Human resource management – the dilemma between individualism and collectivism in teams. Organizations need to balance employee autonomy with the need for collaboration and team action, which is key to achieving common goals.
3. Strategic objectives – paradoxes arise from the need to combine short-term and long-term goals. Organizations often have to choose between current financial performance and long-term investment in innovation.
4. Managing change and stability – the contradiction between the need to adapt and the need to maintain stability. On the one hand, organizations need to be ready for change; on the other hand, they need to maintain the structural stability that allows predictability and control.
5. Organizational values – a conflict of values, such as ethics versus pragmatism, where organizations have to balance the pursuit of profits with social responsibility and ethics.

Each of these paradoxes has its own peculiarities and a different impact on the organization's functioning, making the study and management require dedicated methods and analytical tools. Therefore, it is worth taking a closer look at each category highlighted.

### *1.2.1 Paradoxes Concerning Organizational Structure and Processes*

In management, organizational structures and processes underpin the functioning of an organization. Structure defines the formal organizational framework, such as hierarchy, division of roles, and power relationships, while organizational processes refer to the activities that implement this framework, such as decision-making processes, communication, and resource flows. Paradoxes in this area arise from the dynamic balance between the need for stability, predictability, and control and the desire for flexibility, innovation, and adaptability (Berti & Simpson, 2021). They are analyzed in the academic literature as unavoidable tensions that, if properly managed, can be a source of organizational growth and effectiveness.

- **Definitions and context of structural paradoxes**

Paradoxes regarding organizational structure arise when organizations attempt to balance the conflicting demands of maintaining hierarchy and formal procedures while promoting decentralization, autonomy, and flexibility. As Mintzberg (1993) notes, organizational structures allow consistency and predictability but can limit creativity and adaptability. Organizations face the challenge of reconciling these two requirements, which are contradictory and mutually reinforcing depending on the situation.

- **Stability versus flexibility**

The paradox of stability and flexibility is one of the most frequently analyzed in the context of organizational structures (Carmine & Smith, 2021). Organizational stability is based on predictable patterns of action, formal procedures, and clearly defined roles (Morgan, 2006). This provides an organization with the ability to control its actions and minimize risks. At the same time, flexibility requires the ability to react quickly to changing market conditions and adapt to new situations, which may require a move away from rigid structures and rules.

Lawrence and Lorsch (1967), in their classic work on organizational adaptability, emphasized that organizations operating in dynamic market environments need to combine elements of stability (e.g., clearly defined processes) with flexibility (e.g., the ability to respond quickly to change). The authors pointed out that the key challenge is to integrate these contradictions, allowing organizations to achieve long-term effectiveness.

- **Centralization versus decentralization**

Another important structural paradox is the tension between centralization and decentralization (Mintzberg, 1993; Gaim et al., 2022). Centralization allows an organization to concentrate power and decision-making at the highest level, promoting strategic coherence and resource control. Decentralization, on the other hand, allows for increased autonomy of individuals and teams, fostering innovation and increasing the organization's ability to adapt to local needs and conditions.

Research by Jarzabkowski et al. (2007) indicates that organizations often adopt a hybrid approach, which partially centralizes key strategic decisions while allowing autonomy in operational terms. Hybridizing these models allows strategic coherence and operational flexibility to be achieved simultaneously. Examples include multinational corporations that centralize key functions, such as financial management, while allowing autonomy to local subsidiaries to tailor products and services to specific local markets.

- **Paradoxes of organizational processes**

Organizational processes encompass activities that achieve organizational goals, including decision-making processes, work coordination, and resource management. Process paradoxes arise when organizations must maintain operational efficiency and foster innovation simultaneously.

- **Bureaucracy versus adaptation**

One of the key process paradoxes is the tension between bureaucracy and adaptation (Perrow, 1972). Bureaucracy, described by Max Weber as a model of rational management, is characterized by formal rules and hierarchies that enhance operational efficiency under predictable conditions. However, in a dynamic market environment, bureaucratic structures can hinder rapid action and innovation (Smith & Beretta, 2021).

Burns and Stalker (1961) introduced the concepts of "mechanistic systems" and "organic systems" as opposing organizational models. Mechanistic organizational systems, corresponding to bureaucratic structures, are effective under stable conditions, while organic systems, characterized by greater flexibility and fewer formal rules, perform better under volatile and unpredictable conditions. The paradox is that organizations often need to combine elements of both systems to balance efficiency and adaptability.

- **Control versus trust**

The paradox of control and trust is one of the most frequently studied in the context of organizational processes. Control encompasses oversight mechanisms, procedures, and monitoring systems to ensure compliance with established goals and norms. On the other hand, trust fosters collaboration and innovation by allowing employees more freedom and autonomy in decision-making (Keller & Sadler-Smith, 2019).

Research by Sitkin and Stickel (1996) indicates that organizations successfully managing this paradox adopt a "trust-based control" approach. In such a model, formal control mechanisms are complemented by building a culture based on mutual trust, which increases employee commitment and motivation. Examples include technology companies that employ flexible project management systems, combining formal oversight mechanisms with team autonomy.

Empirical research shows that organizations that can effectively manage structural and process paradoxes achieve higher organizational effectiveness, innovation, and adaptability levels. For example, according to He and Wang (2020), firms that effectively balance stability and flexibility in their structures are more resilient to crises and better able to cope with market uncertainty. Similarly, organizations that adopt hybrid governance models, combining control with trust, often report higher employee engagement and innovation (Sitkin & Stickel, 1996). An example of this can be found in the technology sector, where flexible project management structures, such as agile methodologies, enable rapid adaptation to market changes while maintaining consistency in organizational goals.

### *1.2.2 Paradoxes of Human Resource Management*

Human resource management (HRM) is a key area of an organization's operations that encompasses the processes involved in recruiting, developing, motivating, and retaining employees. The paradoxes in HRM arise from balancing conflicting demands, such as the need to individualize approaches to employees and foster collective collaboration or the pursuit of cost efficiency while investing in talent development (see also Chapter 4). These tensions are an inherent part of HRM. Research by Smith and Lewis (2011) suggests that these paradoxes arise from the dynamic relationship between organizations and employees, where different interests and values often conflict.

- **Individualism versus collectivism**

The paradox of individualism and collectivism in HRM refers to the tension between fostering employee autonomy and individual development, and building a team spirit of cooperation. Individualism promotes innovation and autonomy in decision-making, which can be particularly important in organizations that require creativity, such as the technology or marketing industries. On the other hand, collectivism based on common goals and mutual cooperation promotes the integration of activities and team cohesion.

Research by Liu et al. (2020) shows that leaders with a "paradox mentality" are able to effectively manage this tension by creating a work environment where individual autonomy is balanced with shared team values. An example of this is the hybrid working model, where employees have the flexibility to organize their own work but are also required to attend team meetings to maintain a shared vision regularly.

- **Control versus autonomy**

The paradox of control and autonomy refers to the contradiction between the need to monitor employees' activities and to foster their autonomy and responsibility for their performance. Control is traditionally seen as a key element of management that ensures compliance with organizational goals and minimizes risk. However, excessive control can lead to demotivation, reduced commitment, and declining innovation. In turn, autonomy, which allows employees more freedom in decision-making, fosters innovation and boosts team morale. Sitkin and Stickel (1996) point out that successfully managing this paradox requires building "trust-based control," which combines monitoring mechanisms with an organizational culture based on trust in employees' competence and intentions. An example of this approach is modern management systems based on performance indicators, which allow autonomy in executing tasks but still ensure that progress can be monitored.

- **Cost-effectiveness versus investing in talent development**

The paradox of cost-effectiveness and investing in talent development concerns the dilemma faced by organizations seeking to simultaneously minimize personnel costs and increase the value of their human resources through training, professional development, and the creation of attractive career paths. Cost-effectiveness is particularly relevant in organizations operating in a highly price-competitive environment, where reducing spending on human resources can be key to remaining competitive. On the other hand, investing in talent development is essential for maintaining a long-term competitive advantage, especially in sectors requiring high competence and innovation. Nayebpour and Sehhat's (2024) research indicates that organizations that successfully manage this paradox adopt a strategic approach that treats investment in employee development as part of building long-term organizational value. An example of this approach is flexible budgeting models that allow simultaneous investment in developing key talent and controlling operational costs.

- **Short-term performance versus long-term commitment**

The paradox of short-term productivity and long-term employee engagement is a significant challenge for organizations that need to achieve immediate results and build employee loyalty simultaneously. The drive to maximize productivity in the short term can lead to an overburdened workforce, which in turn negatively impacts employee engagement and performance in the long term.

Research by Cappelli and Tavis (2018) suggests that effectively managing this paradox requires implementing employee appraisal systems that combine short-term goals with long-term development strategies. Organizations such as Google and Microsoft use "periodic development conversations" systems that focus on current performance but, at the same time, take into account the long-term development needs of employees.

### *1.2.3 Paradoxes Regarding Strategic Objectives*

An organization's strategic objectives are the foundation of its long-term development and achievement of competitive advantage. However, strategy formulation and implementation involve balancing conflicting demands, such as short-term operational efficiency and long-term growth, exploration of new opportunities and exploitation of existing resources, or innovation and conservatism. These contradictions, or strategic goal paradoxes, are inevitable in a complex organizational environment and require special attention in management theory and practice. Strategic goal paradoxes are enduring tensions between conflicting priorities and strategic decisions an organization must make in a dynamically changing environment. Smith and Lewis (2011) point out that strategic paradoxes often arise from attempts to balance competing imperatives, such as the need for innovation and stability, which are inherent in an organization's operations.

- **Short-term results versus long-term development**

One of the most fundamental strategic paradoxes is the tension between short-term financial performance and long-term organizational development. Short-term performance pressures are often linked to the expectations of stakeholders, in particular investors and owners, who expect quick returns on investment. At the same time, long-term growth requires investment in research and development, human capital, and building lasting relationships with customers.

- **Exploration versus exploitation**

The paradox of exploration and exploitation refers to the tension between seeking new opportunities and maximizing value from existing resources and competencies. Exploration encompasses innovative activities, research and development, and investment in new business areas. Conversely, exploitation focuses on improving existing processes, products, and services to increase efficiency and profitability (see also Chapter 3).

March (1991), in his ground-breaking work, emphasized that organizations need to maintain a balance between exploration and exploitation, as excessive focus on one of these areas leads to risk. For example, organizations too focused on exploration may incur high costs and risk financial instability. In contrast, organizations focused solely on exploitation may lose their ability to innovate and adapt in a changing environment. A practical solution to this paradox may be to adopt an ambidextrous approach that allows exploration and exploitation activities to be developed simultaneously across different business units (O'Reilly & Tushman, 2013). For example, technology companies such as Google or Amazon create dedicated teams responsible for exploring new technologies, while other units optimize current products and services.

- **Innovation versus conservatism**

The paradox of innovation and conservatism relates to the need to balance the constant introduction of new solutions with the need to maintain stability and reduce risk. Innovation is a key success factor in many sectors, but an excessive focus on introducing novelty can lead to operational destabilization and increased costs.

As Cunha and Bednarek (2020) point out, organizations that successfully manage this paradox adopt an iterative approach that allows innovation to occur in a controlled manner. For example, new product launches can be phased, using pilots and market tests, which minimizes risk and allows for operational stability at the same time.

- **Localization versus globalization**

The paradox of localization and globalization is particularly evident in multinational corporations (see also Chapter 4), which must balance global consistency with local adaptation to specific markets. On the one hand, organizations seek to exploit economies of scale and standardization to reduce costs and increase efficiency. Alternatively, localization requires flexibility in adapting products, services, and marketing strategies to local cultural and market conditions.

Hampden-Turner's (2021) research suggests that successfully managing this paradox requires a "glocal" (*glocalization*) approach combining both strategies' advantages. McDonald's, for example, is introducing global quality and operational standards while adapting menus to local customer preferences, such as serving McVeggie in India or local burger variants in Japan.

### *1.2.4 Paradoxes of Change and Stability Management*

Managing change and stability is one of the key areas of management science, especially in the context of dynamically changing market and technological conditions. Paradoxes in this area arise from the tension between the need to adapt to changing external conditions and the need to maintain organizational stability, cohesion, and predictability. These contradictions are inevitable and require the simultaneous management of two seemingly contradictory imperatives: To innovate and change and to protect existing structures and processes. The paradoxes of change and stability are defined as the tensions arising from the need to simultaneously respond to new challenges and maintain order and operational continuity within an organization. Lewis and Smith (2014) emphasize that managing change requires a dynamic balance between innovation and conservatism, with both change and stability essential for long-term organizational success.

- **Flexibility versus structure**

The paradox of flexibility and structure refers to the tension between needing change and maintaining a stable organizational framework. Flexibility enables organizations to adapt to new conditions, for example, through rapid changes in strategy, processes, or business models. In contrast, structure provides organizations with predictability and consistency, which are key to operational efficiency.

Burns and Stalker (1961) introduced the concepts of "mechanistic" and "organic" management systems, emphasizing that mechanistic structures, based on rigid rules and hierarchy, are better suited to stable conditions, while organic structures, characterized by greater flexibility and decentralization, are more suitable in situations of dynamic change. The paradox is the need to combine these approaches to achieve stability and adaptability.

- **Implementing change versus protecting the status quo**

The paradox of implementing change and protecting the status quo is particularly evident in organizations that must introduce new processes or technologies and maintain existing operations simultaneously. Implementing change, such as digitalization or restructuring, is necessary for organizations to meet changing market expectations. At the same time, protecting the status quo maintains operational stability and minimizes risks.

Kotter et al. (2011), in his work on change management, emphasizes that organizations need to manage the change process effectively, creating a "sense of urgency" while ensuring that key operations and structures remain intact. This strategy, referred to as a two-pronged approach, enables the goals of change and stability to be pursued simultaneously.

- **Innovation versus operational sustainability**

The paradox of innovation and operational stability relates to the need to innovate in order to build a competitive advantage and maintain efficiency and consistency in daily operations. Innovation requires experimentation, creativity, and the ability to take risks, while operational stability is based on repetition, precision, and minimizing errors.

Research by Tushman and O'Reilly (1996) suggests that organizations can manage this paradox by introducing ambidextrous structures that allow innovation and operational activities to be supported simultaneously. For example, separate teams may be responsible for the experimentation and implementation of new products, while others focus on optimizing existing processes.

- **Stability of organizational culture versus change**

Organizational culture, defined as a set of shared values, norms, and beliefs, is key to organizational stability. At the same time, culture can become a barrier to change, especially if the prevailing norms and values conflict with the demands of the environment. The paradox of stability and cultural change lies in maintaining cultural consistency while adapting to new challenges.

Schein (2010) emphasizes that effective cultural change management requires a deep understanding of the existing culture and a conscious implementation of change in a way that is consistent with key organizational values. An example of such an approach is introducing new teamwork practices that do not undermine the core principles of collaboration and trust.

### *1.2.5 Paradoxes Concerning Organizational Values*

Organizational values form the basis of organizational culture and define what actions, attitudes, and goals are considered desirable in an organization. They are a key element of organizational identity and, at the same time, a source of contradictions that can arise when organizations attempt to simultaneously pursue different, often conflicting, priorities. Paradoxes of organizational values include the tensions between pursuing economic goals and realizing social values, between short-term profitability and long-term responsibility, or between individualism and collectivism. They refer to situations where organizations must simultaneously pursue conflicting goals or priorities based on different value systems. According to Badham et al. (2011), these paradoxes are particularly evident in organizations that attempt to balance the conflicting interests of their stakeholders – employees, customers, investors, and local communities.

As Smith and Lewis (2011) note, organizational values can be both a source of integration and cohesion and a source of conflict, which requires specific management to ensure that they do not disrupt the organization.

- **Economic versus social values**

One of the most fundamental paradoxes of organizational values is the tension between pursuing financial performance and the pursuit of a social mission. Economic values, such as cost efficiency, profitability, or revenue growth, are crucial for an organization's survival in a competitive market. At the same time, social values, such as social responsibility, sustainability, or an ethical approach to stakeholders, are becoming increasingly important in the face of increasing social and regulatory pressures.

Carroll and Shabana's (2010) research indicates that organizations can effectively manage this paradox by adopting an integrated approach that combines economic and social objectives within a sustainability strategy. An example is the Environmental, Social, Governance (ESG policy that simultaneously allows financial goals and social values to be achieved.

- **Short-term profitability versus long-term responsibility**

The paradox of short-term profitability and long-term responsibility is particularly apparent in organizations operating in sectors with high pressure on financial performance, such as the financial industry or the technology sector. Organizations must simultaneously satisfy investors' expectations of current financial performance and invest in long-term activities such as research and development, employee training, or social initiatives.

Epstein and Roy (2001) point out that organizations that successfully manage this paradox put in place strategic evaluation mechanisms that balance short-term goals with long-term ones. An example of this approach is the policy of Apple, which consistently invests in research and development even though such activities may initially reduce profitability.

- **Individualism versus collectivism**

The paradox of individualism and collectivism concerns the tension between promoting individual autonomy and fostering cooperation and shared team values. Individualist values, such as personal development and autonomy in decision-making, foster innovation and creativity. Collectivist values, on the other hand, such as solidarity, loyalty, and cooperation, enhance team cohesion and effectiveness.

Hofstede's (2001) research shows that organizations operating in collectivist cultures, such as Japan or South Korea, tend to promote team values, while organizations in individualist cultures, such as the US, focus on individual development. Managing this paradox effectively requires balancing both approaches, for example, by introducing appraisal systems that reward both individual and team achievements.

- **Conservatism versus innovation**

The paradox of conservatism and innovation in organizational values refers to balancing traditional norms and practices with openness to new ideas and solutions. In organizational values, such as attachment to traditions or procedures, conservatism provides stability and predictability but can hinder adaptation to changing conditions. In contrast, innovative values, such as openness to change or risk tolerance, foster creativity and the ability to transform.

March (1991) points out that successful organizations combine these two approaches, encouraging innovation in selected areas while maintaining stability in others. An example is Toyota, which is developing new technologies, such as hybrid vehicles, while maintaining traditional Kaizen values of continuous process improvement.

Each of the categories presented above for the division of paradoxes in management has a rich intrinsic specificity – not to mention that the different categories differ quite a lot. This means that besides the ontological diversity of the spheres of organizational reality, one should also consider their epistemological dissimilarity. Consequently – in addition to the multiplicity of forms in which the phenomenon of paradoxes in organizations manifests itself, one can also observe a multiplicity of ways of scientifically exploring and understanding them (and thus, for example, the methods and techniques used in empirical research).

## 1.3 Overview of Research Methods Used to Analyze Paradoxes

The study of paradoxes in the management sciences presents unique methodological challenges. Due to the complexity of paradoxes and their multidimensionality, traditional research methods often prove insufficient to capture organizational contradictions' full nature and dynamics. In recent years, researchers have developed a variety of methodological approaches that allow for a more comprehensive analysis of paradoxes. The key research methods used in analyzing paradoxes will be outlined below, along with examples of their application and potential for use in management research.

1. Ethnomethodological analysis

One approach used in the study of paradoxes is ethnomethodological analysis, which focuses on studying social interactions and everyday practices in organizations. This method enables researchers to analyze paradoxes as phenomena manifesting themselves in interpersonal relationships, team behavior, and organizational routines. An example of the application of this method is the study by Lempiälä et al. (2023), which demonstrates how paradoxes act as interactional resources and contribute to alleviating tensions in teams. The researchers showed that paradoxes can act as both conflict triggers and mechanisms to overcome conflict.

Ethnomethodological analysis provides a deeper understanding of how paradoxes function in everyday work and how employees construct and transform contradictions into constructive situations. It allows paradoxes to be examined from a micro-social perspective, focusing on how individuals interpret and manage them. This approach is an important complement to macro-organizational analyses, providing insights into the dynamic aspects of paradoxes at the individual level.

2. Fuzzy Delphi as a method for exploring paradoxes

The Fuzzy Delphi method, based on the classic Delphi technique, is an innovative approach to studying paradoxes, especially in the context of HRM and managerial competence. While researching paradoxes, the method enables the collection and analysis of expert opinions in an iterative manner, allowing the development of consensus on complex and multidimensional issues. In paradox management, the Fuzzy Delphi method has proved useful in studying managerial competencies and identifying key skills required to manage paradoxes, such as balancing employee and organizational interests (Nayebpour & Sehhat, 2024).

Using this method in paradox studies allows the uncertainty and complexity of the phenomena under study to be considered, which is crucial in the context of paradoxes. In the Fuzzy Delphi method, researchers use "fuzzy" assessments to better capture the complexity of perceptions of contradictions by different stakeholder groups. The results obtained in this way provide practical guidance for organizations that need to manage paradoxical challenges, especially in human resources and talent management.

3. Dynamic equilibrium model

The dynamic equilibrium model, also known as the "dissipative equilibrium model," is one of the more advanced research methods applied to studying organizational paradoxes (see also Chapter 1). This model assumes that organizations must constantly balance conflicting demands that may change over time. Unlike more static approaches, the dynamic equilibrium model recognizes that organizations operate in a state of constant change and must be able to adapt in response to new tensions and challenges.

Weiser and Laamanen (2022) further developed the dynamic equilibrium model by adding the concept of "dissipative equilibrium," which emphasizes that balancing paradoxes requires an organization to be constantly attentive and flexible. This model is particularly useful in sectors where market dynamics require an organization to respond quickly to changing conditions while maintaining operational stability. An example of this is the technology industry, where organizations must constantly adapt to innovations while ensuring the predictability of operational processes.

4. Luhmann's theory and the concept of deparadoxalization

Deparadoxalization theory, based on the ideas of Niklas Luhmann, is a different approach to the analysis of paradoxes, which emphasizes the management of contradictions by reinterpreting their meaning in an organization. Luhmann's theory suggests that paradoxes do not necessarily have to be "resolved" in the classical sense but can be managed by so-called "deparadoxalization," i.e., the transformation of paradoxical situations into decision-making resources. According to Luhmann's theory, paradoxes can stimulate innovation and enable organizations to generate new solutions in response to emerging challenges (Seidl et al., 2021).

Luhmann's approach is particularly interesting in managing paradoxes, as it sees contradictions as a natural part of social systems that do not need to be eliminated but can be adaptively transformed. Deparadoxalization assumes that organizations can create an interpretive framework that allows contradictory elements to be integrated to support their functionality and development. This method provides an alternative to traditional methods of managing conflict and contradiction, suggesting that paradoxes can be a source of inspiration and motivation for finding new solutions.

5. Interactional and micro-social perspectives

Research on paradoxes also often adopts a micro-social perspective, focusing on examining the interactions between members of an organization and analyzing how paradoxes manifest themselves in everyday practices and relationships. This approach focuses on the dynamics of contradictions at the individual and team level, allowing for a better understanding of how individuals experience and manage paradoxical tensions in their everyday actions.

An example of applying this approach is research on leaders' paradox mentality, which has shown that managing contradictions at the interpersonal level is crucial for developing innovation and organizational effectiveness (Liu et al., 2020). The micro-social perspective enables researchers to analyze subtle aspects of paradox dynamics, such as negotiation, compromise, and adaptive processes, which shape organizational culture and influence the effectiveness of teams. Specifically, research on leaders' paradoxical thinking and attitudes shows that managing paradoxes effectively requires acceptance of ambiguity and mental flexibility to manage better tensions arising from conflicts between different organizational values (Liu et al., 2020).

6. Quantitative approaches in paradox research

Although paradox research is usually based on qualitative methods, quantitative approaches are increasingly used to enable more objective analyses and comparisons. Quantitative methods, such as survey analysis (Hossain et al., 2024), experimental research, and statistical modeling (Andriopoulos & Gotsi, 2017), allow hypotheses about the impact of paradoxes on organizational performance to be tested. For example, research on the paradox of innovation and operational efficiency (Smith et al., 2017) indicates that organizations that are able to balance these two aspects perform better in the long term, which can be analyzed through statistical modeling of the correlation between innovation indicators and financial performance. Furthermore, moderation and mediation analysis (Schulte, 2022) allows for a more sophisticated analysis of the relationship between contradictions and their impact on different organizational aspects. In this research, quantitative methods provide a complementary tool to the qualitative analysis of paradoxes, allowing for a better understanding of their complexity and multifaceted nature (Henriksen et al., 2021).

7. Longitudinal studies and case studies

Research on paradoxes can also benefit from longitudinal and case study methods, which allow the observation of change over a long period of time and the analysis of specific organizational situations in which paradoxes play an important role. These methods enable researchers to track how organizations adapt to changing paradox tensions and modify their strategies in response to new challenges.

An example of such research is the analysis of organizations operating in the high-tech sector (Lin et al., 2020), which must constantly balance the demands of innovation and operational stability. Longitudinal studies can provide insights into adaptation processes and the ways in which organizations manage contradictions over time, which is particularly relevant in the context of dynamic economic sectors (Moschko et al., 2023).

8. Mixed methods in the study of paradoxes

In recent years, there has been growing interest in using mixed methods in paradox studies, which combine qualitative and quantitative approaches. Mixed methods allow for a comprehensive analysis of paradoxes, combining in-depth qualitative research with the statistical capabilities of quantitative approaches. In paradox research, the use of mixed methods allows for both broad and deep analysis, enabling a more holistic approach to contradiction management. For example, combining qualitative interviews with quantitative analysis of questionnaires can help researchers understand how employees perceive and experience paradoxes while also enabling them to test the relationship between employee attitudes and organizational performance. This approach is also used in research on innovation and performance paradoxes, where researchers analyze both qualitative aspects of organizational culture and quantitative performance indicators to understand better how organizations deal with conflicting demands.

The variety of research methods used to analyze management paradoxes reflects the phenomenon's complexity and multifaceted nature. Each approach discussed – from ethnomethodological analysis and the Fuzzy Delphi method to the dynamic equilibrium model and deparadoxalization theory – provides unique tools and perspectives that enable researchers to explore paradoxes in an organizational context. The choice of the appropriate method depends on the specific paradox under study, the organizational context, and the research objectives. However, as experience has shown, such a methodological choice is not straightforward, and numerous pitfalls and challenges will await the researcher/thinker in the process.

## 1.4 Methodological Challenges in Paradox Research

The study of paradoxes in management is an area of intensive exploration that makes important contributions to both management theory and organizational practice. Paradoxes – defined as coexisting, conflicting tendencies, and values that organizations must balance – require specific methodological approaches. However, the study of paradoxes presents a number of challenges, which include difficulties in defining, measuring, and modeling paradoxical tensions. A list of these challenges, i.e., the key methodological issues and barriers that researchers face in the analysis of paradoxes, as well as some possible ways to overcome them, are discussed in the following sections.

1. The problem of defining and conceptualizing paradoxes

One of the most serious challenges in studying paradoxes is their appropriate definition and conceptualization. Paradoxes can take various forms, from conflicting values within an organizational structure to individual tensions, making their identification difficult. The phenomenon's complexity often leads to divergent definitions and theoretical approaches, making it difficult to build a coherent body of knowledge. Clegg, Cunha, and Berti (2022) note that different approaches to the study of paradoxes result in a fragmentation of knowledge in the field, limiting the ability to compare research results. The solution to this problem is to develop a more harmonized conceptual framework that takes into account both the theoretical and practical diversity of paradoxes. An example of such an approach is the dynamic equilibrium model, which allows paradoxes to be studied as dynamic processes that adapt to changing conditions (Weiser & Laamanen, 2022). Conceptualizing paradoxes as adaptive rather than static phenomena allows for a more flexible research approach that better captures their multidimensional nature.

2. Difficulties in measuring paradoxes

Another methodological challenge in the study of paradoxes is the difficulty of measuring the phenomenon. Paradoxes, as contradictions that can coexist and reinforce each other, elude classical measurement tools. Paradoxes are often dynamic in nature, making it difficult to capture them with traditional, static measures. Even when using quantitative research methods such as survey analysis or statistical modeling, studying paradoxes requires methodological flexibility to account for variability over time. One possible solution to this problem is the use of mixed methods that combine qualitative and quantitative approaches, enabling a more comprehensive picture of the paradoxes under investigation. An example is Fuzzy Delphi analysis, which allows qualitative assessments to be obtained as fuzzy, flexible quantitative assessments. Nayebpour and Sehhat (2024) applied the Fuzzy Delphi method to study managerial competencies, enabling them to account for the complexity of perceptions of paradoxical tensions and their impact on HRM.

3. The problem of modeling paradoxes as dynamic processes

Paradoxes in organizations are characterized by high dynamics and variability over time, which poses a challenge when modeling this phenomenon. Traditional approaches to organizational analysis are often oriented toward static models that do not account for the evolution of paradoxical tensions in response to changing internal and external conditions. Researchers such as Weiser and Laamanen (2022) suggest that organizations operate in a dynamic equilibrium that requires constant adjustment and monitoring.

Dynamic models, such as the dissipative equilibrium model, allow a more precise grasp of the variability of paradoxes and their impact on the organization. These models are based on the idea that organizations must constantly balance between contradictions and respond to new tensions, which allows for a better understanding of the process of adaptation and adjustment in the face of paradoxical demands.

4. The challenge of integrating different levels of analysis

Paradoxes in management can occur at different organizational levels – from the individual to the team and the whole organization. Researchers often encounter difficulties in simultaneously analyzing paradoxes at different levels due to discrepancies in the methods and tools used to examine these levels. For example, micro-social research, such as ethnomethodological analysis, enables understanding paradoxes in everyday interactions between employees but may not be sufficient to scrutinize structural paradoxes at the macro-organizational level (Lempiälä et al., 2023).

Integrating different levels of analysis is possible through mixed methods, which combine micro- and macro-organizational analyses. An example is the combination of ethnomethodology and quantitative methods, which enables understanding how paradoxes manifest themselves at both the individual and structural levels. This approach allows researchers to understand better how contradictions within an organization affect its structure and culture.

5. Difficulties in interpreting results and generalizing

Paradoxes are an extremely complex and multidimensional phenomenon, making the interpretation of research results challenging. Diverse organizational contexts and the individual experiences of employees influence how paradoxes are perceived and managed. Interpreting research results on paradoxes often requires considering the specificities of a particular context, which can make it difficult to generalize the results and apply them to different organizations.

One way of dealing with this challenge is through the use of grounded theory, which facilitates the generation of theory based on empirical data from a given context, which can provide more relevant conclusions for a specific organization. An example of this approach is a study by Cunha and Bednarek (2020), which showed how paradoxes could be seen as simultaneously a source of novelty and absurdity, depending on the organizational context.

6. The ethical and practical challenge in the study of paradoxes

The study of paradoxes also raises ethical and practical concerns. Paradoxes often involve contradictory values, such as financial efficiency versus social responsibility, which can create employee tensions and conflicts. Researchers must be particularly sensitive to these aspects and aware that paradox analysis can affect morale and team dynamics. In addition, implementing paradox research findings can be problematic in organizational practice, especially when they indicate the need to manage conflicting values that may seem irreconcilable. For example, organizations may find it difficult to simultaneously seek to maximize profits and meet high ethical and social standards. In such situations, managing paradoxes becomes a theoretical challenge and a practical dilemma that requires compromises and negotiation skills.

The solution to this challenge may lie in engaging organizational leaders in the research process and using the results to promote transparency and reinforce an ethical approach to managing contradictions. Gaim et al. (2022) suggest that a "paradoxical mindset" approach can support leaders in accepting tensions and finding creative ways to manage them rather than seeking to resolve them completely, which in many cases is impossible.

7. Problems of applicability and translation of research results into practice

One of the key challenges in paradox research is to transform research findings into practical guidelines that can be implemented in the day-to-day management of organizations. As complex and multi-level phenomena, paradoxes are often difficult to capture within simple recommendations and standard procedures. Organizations that operate in a volatile market environment may find it difficult to adopt paradox management strategies that are too theoretical or complex to apply.

To overcome this challenge, researchers can adopt a collaborative approach with practitioners so that the research process considers organizational needs and the realities of everyday management. Action research methods that combine theoretical analysis with practical implementation can be particularly useful here. In this type of research, it is important that the research findings not only enrich theory but are also adapted to organizational reality and can be easily applied by managers.

8. Difficulties arising from the multi-contextual nature of paradoxes

Organizational paradoxes may have different meanings depending on the cultural, social, or industry context, which raises another challenge in researching them. International research shows that paradoxes can be interpreted and managed differently depending on organizational and national culture. For example, paradoxes may create stronger tensions and the need to resolve them quickly in cultures with a low tolerance for ambiguity. Conversely, in cultures where acceptance of contradictions is higher, paradoxes may be seen as a natural part of management and present a less stressful challenge for employees.

Therefore, researchers should take into account the multicontextuality of paradoxes and analyze them in various settings to better understand their specificities and dynamics in the context of different cultures and industries. An approach to the study of paradoxes that considers these variables can provide more universal lessons and contribute to the development of management practices tailored to the specific requirements of local markets.

9. The challenge of educating and preparing researchers to work with paradoxes

The final identified challenge in paradox research is the education and preparation of the researchers themselves to work with the phenomenon. Paradoxes require a specific interdisciplinary approach and the ability to integrate different research methods and tools. This requires researchers to have theoretical knowledge, methodological flexibility, and the ability to work with various data.

One way to address this problem is to promote interdisciplinarity in researcher education, enabling them to develop skills in various research methods, such as qualitative analysis, statistical models, and mixed methods. In addition, young researchers must have the opportunity to develop practical skills, for example, by working with organizations in action research or research internships. Such experiences allow them to better understand the complexity of the paradoxes and challenges organizations face and effectively apply the knowledge they have gained in practice.

The challenges presented above in undertaking both theoretical reflection and empirical research and analysis in the area of paradoxes made visible within organizations of different types seem to have another common denominator – besides the specific, "contradictory" nature of the phenomenon of "paradox" itself: It is the lack of in-depth reflection by researchers on the ontological and epistemological side of the reality under study. One can conjecture that at least part of the problems experienced by researchers and thinkers dealing with the issue of paradoxes is because they "jump" immediately from the choice of the research problem of interest to the choice of method (and further, research technique), without reflecting on the broader perspective and context in which they want to place their considerations. In doing so, they skip over a key stage in the design of the research process – the choice of paradigm.

## 1.5 The Essence of a Paradigm in Science: Paradigms of Management Science

A paradigm, introduced into the philosophy of science by Kuhn (1962), denotes a set of basic concepts, theories, and philosophical assumptions that form the foundations of a given scientific discipline. It is a conceptual scheme recognized by the majority of scholars in a given field, which serves as a model for solving problems and interpreting phenomena. Kuhn defines a paradigm as a "widely recognized scientific achievement" that provides research patterns and theoretical solutions for the scientific community. The paradigm encompasses both ontological assumptions, which define the nature of reality, and epistemological assumptions, which concern how we come to know and study the world. In addition, it combines methodological and cultural elements, providing a framework for the accumulation of knowledge, the formulation of hypotheses, and the interpretation of research results. In this way, it provides a normative reference point for researchers, setting out directions for research, types of acceptable experiments, and criteria for evaluating their results.

However, neither in science is it understood as a whole nor in its individual disciplines is there a situation in which there is one and only one paradigm as a dogmatic point of view of reality and a way of studying it. Although there are periods in which one paradigm gains more importance and popularity than others, this is neither an unconditional dominance nor indefinite nor absolute. Moreover, in many disciplines of science (especially the humanities in the broadest sense), it is a natural state of affairs that several paradigms coexist at the same time, and the choice of one of them is determined by the researchers' worldview, which coincides with the ontological-epistemological assumptions of the given paradigm. However, it is necessary to add at this point that a different role will be played by paradigms within the natural sciences and a different one within the social sciences: In the area of natural sciences, a paradigm will most often be a reflection of the current state of knowledge in terms of the laws governing a particular dimension of reality (without having any feedback effect on this reality itself), whereas, in the context of the broader social sciences, a paradigm is a manifestation of the researcher's views on social reality, strongly influencing this reality as an object of study (if only due to the choice of research methods and techniques as a consequence of the choice of paradigm). The social sciences cannot discover exceptionless laws (as is the case, e.g., in biology, chemistry, and physics), so they will naturally have more concepts concerning the ontology and epistemology of their area of interest.

Within the social sciences, it is worth mentioning the achievements of sociology in this field, as the findings of this scientific discipline have had, and continue to have, the greatest influence on the formation of paradigms within the management sciences. Thus, beginning with the dawn of modern sociology, Auguste Comte postulated the creation of a science of society based on the methodology of the natural sciences (Comte, 1830). His conception of positivism became the foundation for many later theories. Comte divided the development of human thought into three stages: Theological, metaphysical, and positivist, pointing out that the use of empirical research methods characterizes the last of these. Durkheim (1897), on the other hand, introduced the concept of social facts to be studied by sociology. His research on suicide showed that social phenomena could be analyzed objectively, identifying the relationships between social structures and the behavior of individuals. The structural paradigm that Durkheim proposed focuses on studying social structures and their impact on the individual.

An important contribution to the division of paradigms in the social sciences has been the distinction between macro- and micro-approaches. In the sociological literature, macro-paradigms include structural-functional theories, conflict theories, and world systems, while micro-approaches include symbolic interactionism, ethnomethodology, and phenomenology. Macro-structural approaches include structural functionalism, of which Parsons (1951) was one of the main representatives. In his social systems theory, he pointed out that society consists of interrelated parts forming an integrated whole. Central to this theory is the concept of social equilibrium, which assumes that society strives for stability by fulfilling basic functions. Conflict theories, put forward by Marx (1867) and later developed by authors such as Mills (1956), focus in turn on social inequalities arising from the distribution of resources and class struggle as a driving force for social change, while Immanuel Wallerstein's world systems theory (1974) analyses globalization processes and the interrelationships between center, periphery, and semi-periphery countries, extending the macro-structural perspective to the analysis of international socioeconomic systems.

Micro-social approaches include, among others, symbolic interactionism. Mead (1934) and Blumer (1969) laid the foundations for this approach, which focuses on the study of human interaction and the role of symbols in meaning-making. Blumer coined the term "symbolic interactionism" and emphasized that social reality is constructed through interaction. Garfinkel (1967), in turn, proposed ethnomethodology, which is the study of everyday practices and ways in which people make sense of social reality, and Schütz (1932) proposed phenomenology, which examines the subjective experiences of individuals by paying attention to how people make sense of their actions in the social world. Phenomenology inspired later research on social consciousness and identity.

Although the work of Kuhn (1962), already mentioned in this text, focused mainly on the natural sciences, his theory of scientific revolutions was also applied to sociology and other social sciences. Kuhn argued that the development of science is not a linear process but proceeds through sudden paradigm shifts. As a complex and interdisciplinary discipline, sociology was particularly vulnerable to such changes. An example of a sociological paradigmatic revolution was the emergence of critical theories, such as the Frankfurt School, which introduced new ways of analyzing society by combining philosophy, psychology, and the social sciences. Horkheimer (1947), Adorno (1944), and Habermas (1981) contributed to the development of this approach by emphasizing the importance of critical reflection on society and its structures.

Contemporary sociology and other social sciences face the challenges of integrating different paradigms and developing new theoretical approaches. For example, postmodern theories, such as the concepts of Michel Foucault (1975), have challenged traditional divisions between macro- and micro-approaches, pointing to the multidimensionality of power and knowledge in society. At the same time, the development of social network theory and big data analysis has opened up new research possibilities that require a redefinition of traditional paradigms.

Echoes of sociological reflections on paradigms have been reflected in other social sciences, including management science. From the classification proposed by Burrell and Morgan (1979; 2019) (proposing a dichotomous division in terms of the nature of science: Objective versus subjective, and the nature of society: Radical change versus regulation), through its modification by Hatch (2018), which linked paradigms such as classical, modernist, interpretative-symbolic, and postmodern to philosophical orientations and selected representatives of management science, to the inclusion of concepts based on positivism, neopositivism, conventionalism, and pragmatism by Johnson and Duberley (2000).

A relatively new approach to the question of paradigms in management is that proposed by Sułkowski (2002), which integrates previous approaches while taking into account the new contemporary specificities of the social sciences. Sułkowski considers four basic paradigms:

1. Neopositivist-functionalist-systemic paradigm (NFS)
2. Interpretative-symbolic paradigm (IS)
3. The paradigm of radical structuralism (critical current)
4. The paradigm of radical humanism (postmodern current)

Each of these paradigms represents a different way of understanding organizational reality, research approach, and management practice. Below is a detailed analysis of each.

### *1.5.1 The Description of Paradigms*

1. The NFS paradigm

The positivist paradigm in management has its roots in the classical positivist philosophy of Auguste Comte and developed from the neo-positivism of the 20th century. It is based on the assumptions of objectivity, rationality, and the universality of scientific principles. In the context of management, positivism focuses on identifying universal principles for effective management and their application in different organizations. Within this paradigm, organizations are seen as mechanical systems that operate predictably and determinedly. Researchers assume organizations can be studied using quantitative methods such as statistics, mathematical models, and controlled experiments. The key objective is to maximize efficiency and productivity while minimizing risk.

This paradigm's limitations become apparent in analyzing dynamic, unpredictable organizational, cultural, and social processes. Operating within the NFS paradigm can lead to reductionism and oversimplification prevalent in classic positivist approaches. However, the NFS paradigm can be useful in analyzing formal and structural aspects of organizations, such as decision-making processes, resource allocation, or operational optimization.

2. The IS paradigm

The interpretivist paradigm, an alternative to positivism, comes from hermeneutics, phenomenology, and symbolic interactionism traditions. It focuses on the subjective meanings and interpretations that organizational actors give to their actions and experiences within organizational structures. In this approach, the organization is conceived as a social construct shaped by language, symbols, and interpersonal interactions. Research in the interpretive paradigm is based on qualitative methods such as interviews, participant observation, and narrative analysis.

The IS paradigm is particularly useful for analyzing organizational culture, emphasizing the importance of symbols, myths, and rituals in the formation of organizational identity (where culture is seen as a dynamic process of negotiating meanings between members of an organization). Organizations are places where business goals are pursued and where people co-create and share common values, norms, and beliefs. The interpretivist approach also applies to HRM, emphasizing the role of dialogue, mutual understanding, and individual employee narratives in building commitment and motivation. Unlike the positivist paradigm, interpretivism emphasizes the importance of the cultural and social contexts that determine how organizations operate.

3. The critical paradigm

The critical paradigm, strongly rooted in the tradition of Marxism, critical theory, and neo-Marxist social philosophy, emphasizes issues of power, domination, and emancipation in organizations. It analyzes mechanisms of control and subordination in organizational structures and points to their role in reproducing social inequalities. The critical paradigm treats the organization as an arena for conflicts of interest between different social groups. Researchers in this strand emphasize that formal organizational structures often serve as tools of hegemony that maintain the dominance of the management elite over the rest of the organization. Hence, there is a need for critical reflection on management practices that can lead to marginalization and exclusion of workers.

Within this paradigm, it is important to reveal inequalities and identify possible ways to overcome them. The importance of emancipating employees by fostering diversity, inclusivity, and co-determination in organizational processes is emphasized.

4. The postmodern paradigm

Postmodernism, the newest of the paradigms, emerged in response to the limitations of modernist approaches to organization. The postmodern paradigm rejects universal theories and objective truths, focusing instead on fragmentation, pluralism, and relativism. Organizations in this paradigm are seen as collections of multidimensional narratives in which each organizational actor has their own perspective. Research is based on exploring local contexts and subjective experiences, leading to deconstructing traditional organizational hierarchies and structures. The nature of contemporary change necessitates a critical look at dominant management narratives, such as the constant need for growth, efficiency, or standardization. Instead, it emphasizes the importance of cultural diversity and the changing expectations of employees and customers globally. Postmodernism also enables a more complex and holistic view of organizations as social phenomena.

Each paradigm presented offers a different perspective on organizations, their functioning, and management processes, allowing for more comprehensive and multidimensional analyses. Positivism, interpretivism, critique, and postmodernism are alternative approaches and complementary perspectives to better understand contemporary organizations' complexity.

### *1.5.2 Paradigm Choice versus Choice of Research Methods and Techniques*

Selecting an appropriate research paradigm is a fundamental step in the design of empirical research. Paradigms, as sets of epistemological and ontological assumptions, determine not only the nature of the research but also its aims, methods, and ways of interpreting the results. In the social and management sciences, paradigms such as positivist, interpretivist, critical, and postmodern allow researchers to choose the approach best suited to the specifics of the phenomena under study. As Burrell and Morgan (1979; 2019) note, the choice of paradigm determines the way in which research reality is perceived and the methodological tools used. As Guba (1990) points out, inconsistencies between these elements can lead to discrepancies in the interpretation of research results. For example, positivism, which assumes the objective nature of reality, promotes the use of quantitative methods such as experiments or statistical analysis. In contrast, interpretivism, focusing on the subjective experiences of individuals, favors qualitative approaches such as in-depth interviews or narrative analysis. However, the choice of paradigm is not just a technical issue. As Lincoln and Guba (1985) notes, it also reflects the values and beliefs of the researcher, which influence the interpretation of results and the formulation of conclusions. In the context of management science, Sułkowski (2002) argues that the choice of paradigm determines how key concepts such as power, organizational culture, or change are understood.

The division of methods for studying paradoxes in management according to the paradigms distinguished by Sułkowski (functionalist, interpretivist, critical, postmodern) can be carried out on the basis of their epistemological and ontological assumptions. The result of such a juxtaposition will be a ready-made list of methods that researchers dealing with the issue of paradoxes will be able to apply when choosing one paradigm variant rather than another. It is worth emphasizing that the methods of studying paradoxes presented earlier constituted a certain fragment of all possible, methodologically sanctioned ways of empirically studying reality, and the following list – although it contains more – cannot be treated as fully exhaustive either. The acceptable research perspectives are too numerous to list them all. Hence, the limitation is here to those chosen most often and raising the least methodological questions in the field of paradox research.

The following attribution is therefore proposed:

1. The neo-positivist-functionalist-systemic (NFS) paradigm

Main assumptions: Organizational reality is objective, and research aims to explain and control phenomena. Functionalism focuses on measuring and modeling phenomena to increase efficiency.

**Research methods:**

- **Fuzzy Delphi analysis**: An expert-based method used to identify and measure the managerial competencies needed to manage paradoxes (Nayebpour & Sehhat, 2024).
  - Justification: Functionalism, despite its qualitative elements, considers Fuzzy Delphi analysis is a quantitative method, as it relies on mathematical data processing models such as fuzzy logic to systematically quantify expert opinion in order to produce objective and measurable results (which is the essence of the NFS paradigm).
- **Dynamic equilibrium model**: A model that examines how organizations adapt to conflicting demands while maintaining operational balance (Weiser & Laamanen, 2022).
  - Justification: Functionalism because it focuses on anticipating and optimizing paradox management strategies.
- **Quantitative research**: surveys, statistical modeling, moderation, and mediation analysis.
  - Justification: Functionalism, because these tools allow objective measurement of phenomena related to paradoxes.

2. The interpretative-symbolic (IS) paradigm

Main assumptions: Based on a subjective understanding of phenomena, interpretivism examines the meaning that organizational participants attribute to contradictions. It emphasizes the role of context and interaction.

**Research methods:**

- **Ethnomethodological analysis**: exploring the interactions and meanings associated with paradoxes in the everyday work of organizations (Lempiälä et al., 2023).
  - Rationale: Interpretivism because it focuses on everyday practices and subjective interpretations of paradoxes by participants.
- **Case studies (Case Study)**: Analysis of specific organizations to understand how they manage paradoxes, e.g., exploring the tension between globalization and localization (Hampden-Turner, 2021).
  - Rationale: Interpretivism, as this method enables an in-depth analysis of the specific contexts and meanings attributed to paradoxes.
- **Grounded theory**: Creating theory from data collected in a specific context.
  - Rationale: Interpretivism because it considers research participants' subjective perceptions of paradoxes.

3. The paradigm of radical structuralism (critical current)

Main assumptions: Focuses on uncovering hidden power tensions, inequalities, and conflicts in organizations. Identifies systemic sources of paradoxes and opportunities for their transformation.

**Research methods:**

- **Deparadoxalization theory**: Interpreting paradoxes as elements that support decision-making processes by reinterpreting them (Seidl et al., 2021).
  - Justification: Criticism because the method takes systemic tensions and tries to turn them into sources of innovation.
- **Values conflict analysis**: Exploring paradoxes in nongovernmental organizations that need to balance ethical and operational goals (Simon, 2022).
  - Justification: Criticism, as the method, reveals tensions arising from conflicts of interest and values within organizational structures.
- **Critical narrative analysis**: Exploring how organizational narratives represent contradictions and tensions, e.g., in crisis management (Hampden-Turner, 2021).
  - Justification: Criticism as it analyzes power and inequality in constructing narratives.

4. The paradigm of radical humanism (postmodern current)

Main assumptions: Emphasizes the complexity and ambiguity of contemporary organizations, accepting paradoxes as a natural part of reality that does not require elimination but creative management.

**Research methods:**

- **A multi-contextual perspective**: Exploring differences in the perception and management of paradoxes across cultures and industries (Gaim et al., 2022).
  - Justification: Postmodernism, as this method recognizes that paradoxes have multiple meanings depending on the context.
- **Analysis of paradoxes as elements of organizational complexity:** Research indicates that paradoxes are inevitable and part of organizational complexity (Cunha & Bednarek, 2020).
  - Justification: Postmodernism, as this method, considers paradoxes as an integral part of the organization and focuses on accepting them rather than resolving them.
- **A storytelling approach**: Analysis of organizational narratives that highlight contradictions as a source of innovation.

- Justification: Postmodernism, as this method takes into account the multiple narratives and meanings attributed to paradoxes.

It is worth emphasizing again that the methods used in the above list do not exhaust the list of methods that can be used in empirical research on paradoxes. It is only the author's proposal based, on the one hand, on the frequency with which researchers choose particular methods and, on the other hand, on their usefulness in describing and/or explaining events and phenomena related to paradoxes perceived through particular paradigms. It should also be noted that in contemporary research approaches, the so-called triangulation of data, i.e., the procedure of using data of different origins or applying different methods within one research process (to obtain the fullest possible picture of the studied reality), plays an increasing role. This means that in some empirical studies, researchers adopt a multidimensional paradigmatic perspective and use different research methods.

## 1.6 Conclusions and Discussion of the Content of the Individual Chapters

As an intrinsic part of contemporary management, paradoxes pose particular challenges but simultaneously offer significant potential for developing organizational theory and practice. This chapter aimed to examine methodological approaches to studying paradoxes in management and present their role in shaping contemporary organizational practices. These considerations indicate that both the nature of paradoxes and their effective management require a sophisticated and multidimensional approach that includes both the phenomenon's dynamism and complexity. Paradoxes are an extremely valuable heuristic tool for understanding tensions arising from organizational dynamics, such as the balance between exploration and exploitation, operational efficiency and innovation, or economic interests and social values. Incorporating paradox theory into organizational analyses enables a better grasp of the nature of these tensions and allows organizations to develop strategies that not only reduce the risks associated with these contradictions but also transform them into a source of innovation and growth. A key element of successful paradox management is adopting a dynamic equilibrium perspective that enables organizations to adapt to changing external and internal conditions. Models such as "dissipative equilibrium" or methods such as grounded theory or Fuzzy Delphi are particularly useful in paradox research, as they allow for integrating micro- and macro-social perspectives and analyzing tensions in the context of time and place. At the same time, qualitative research and case studies provide a valuable contribution to understanding paradoxical phenomena, especially concerning local, sectoral, and cultural contexts.

Practically, the effective management of paradoxes requires organizational leaders to be particularly sensitive to their dynamic and multi-level nature.

Paradoxical thinking, an essential element of leadership, enables leaders to integrate seemingly contradictory goals and values into a coherent management system. Practices such as decentralization combined with centralization of key strategic functions or the simultaneous promotion of innovation and stability are effective tools for managing paradoxes. Examples from organizations such as Google, Toyota, and Amazon indicate that adopting an ambidextrous approach, allowing simultaneous management of exploration and exploitation, can be the key to achieving sustainable competitive advantage.

However, it should be noted that paradox research still faces a number of methodological challenges. One of these is the lack of a coherent theoretical framework to capture the phenomenon in different contexts comprehensively. In addition, the dynamics and complexity of paradoxes require the ongoing development of analytical tools to measure, model, and analyze them in real time. In this context, developing mixed methods and interdisciplinary research approaches that integrate different theoretical and practical perspectives is particularly important. Paradoxes in management are not just an academic challenge but are central to organizational practice. Managing them requires the right theoretical tools and practical skills, such as the ability to integrate conflicting goals, build trust within an organization or flexibly adapt strategies to changing conditions. Organizations that can effectively manage paradoxes minimize the risks associated with conflicts and tensions and enhance their ability to innovate, adapt, and build long-term value for their stakeholders.

This multifaceted and complex nature of paradoxes themselves, and how they can be studied and analyzed, can be seen in the different sections of this book. The following chapters tackle the problem of paradoxes from different perspectives: They draw on different areas of organizational functioning, define different research problems, and harness different methods to address them (and some of them put theoretical considerations within the chosen issue to work). This is the strength of this publication.

Chapter 1 (Organizational Paradox Theory: Managing Competing Demand Then and Now), a non-empirical chapter, used a systematic literature review as a research method, a typical procedure in theoretical and conceptual analyses. This approach aimed to synthesize existing concepts in paradox theory and their classification and clarify the key dynamics and mechanisms of paradox management. The author draws attention to the constant tensions and contradictions present in organizations and postulates that the solution to such tensions is to navigate them and move toward dynamic equilibrium rather than eliminate them. This fits in with the concept of paradoxes as dynamic interdependent structures, as mentioned by, among others, Smith and Lewis' (2011) theory, highlighted in both the analysis and analysis paper.

Chapter 3 (Ambidexterity: A Strategic Approach to Overcoming Exploration and Exploitation Paradox) uses a narrative literature review as a research method. The aim is to present the concept of ambidexterity as a strategic approach to managing the exploration and exploitation paradox. The chapter analyzes the theoretical literature and empirical research in this area, identifying the main streams of research and types of ambidexterity, such as structural, contextual, temporal, and leadership. The analysis emphasizes the need to manage tensions sustainably rather than eliminate them. In addition, contextual and structural approaches to ambidexterity point to a constructivist perspective (interpretivist-symbolic paradigm), which involves the influence of multiple stakeholders and contexts on how tensions are managed.

Chapter 4 (Human Resource Paradoxes in a Belgian Subsidiary of a Multinational Enterprise: An Ethnographic Case Study) describes a study conducted using an ethnographic method, specifically in the form of covert participant observation. The study's author, being part of the organization under study (Belgian Production Company – BPC), collected data from daily interactions, documentation, and interviews with employees at different levels. The use of autoethnography made it possible to capture both emic (internal) and etic (external) perspectives. The analysis in Chapter 4 fits into an interpretivist-symbolic (constructivist) perspective, which aligns with qualitative and ethnographic approaches. The constructivist perspective is based on examining social reality from the participant's point of view, which is important for capturing the paradoxical nature of HRM in international organizations.

Chapter 5 (Homo Managerius: The Paradox of Leadership) used a quantitative method based on statistical analysis; in particular, the Leadership Practices Inventory was used. A survey was conducted with three groups of respondents (leaders, non-leaders, and students) to identify differences in perceptions of leadership styles and paradoxes. Statistical analysis included Kruskal-Wallis tests and Principal Components Analysis, which allowed a precise understanding of the differences between the groups. Leaders manifested characteristics consistent with the paradoxical leadership approach, which integrates contradictions and uses tensions to drive innovation and adaptation. The analysis links leadership theories (e.g., Waldman et al., ROK) with regional realities, highlighting the importance of adopting a structural-functional perspective, where tensions between different leadership dimensions are treated as strategic tools.

Chapter 6 (Diversity, Equity, and Inclusion Policy Paradoxes: Insights from the Central and Eastern European Hospitality Sector) uses case studies as the main research method to provide an in-depth analysis of diversity, equity, and inclusion (DEI) policy implementation practices in the Central and Eastern European Hospitality Sector. The author examines specific cases of leading hotels in detail, using a qualitative method to identify the key paradoxes these organizations face. The approach combines the analysis of empirical data with a theoretical framework for the study of paradoxes. It shows that paradoxes are not a problem to be solved but are a key element of management in a complex social and cultural environment.

Chapter 7 (Paradoxes in Innovation: Navigating the Duality of Closed versus Open Innovation and Business versus Non-profit Innovations) uses a mixed-methods approach based on quantitative and qualitative analysis. This includes bibliometric analysis, based on Web of Science data, to capture the evolution of innovation paradigms from mechanistic to postmaterialist. Alongside this, panel regression and statistical tests have also been applied to explore the impact of open and closed innovation on economic development and social indicators, such as the Human Development Index, in European Union countries. The last is a survey of 2,388 companies in Poland and Europe between 2014 and 2024, allowing us to capture differences between business and non-profit innovation. The authors point out that the shift from a mechanistic to a holistic paradigm reflects changing priorities in science and innovation policy. At the same time, paradoxes in management are unsolvable but can be managed by integrating contradictions. Conflicts between closed and open innovation or technological and social goals are inevitable but can lead to synergies within the postmaterialist paradigm.

Chapter 8 (Workplace Learning through Organizational and Leadership Paradoxes: Insights from Multinational Enterprises in Central and Eastern Europe) uses a qualitative approach based on grounded theory. The study is based on semi-structured interviews with 26 employees from Central and Eastern European countries representing multinational enterprises. The aim was to capture how employees perceive, manage, and learn in the context of organizational and leadership paradoxes in their workplace. The approach uncovered contextual and dynamic aspects of management paradoxes in a region with a specific historical and sociopolitical background. The study is primarily embedded in a constructivist (interpretivist-symbolic) perspective, which allows us to understand how individual experiences and contexts shape the perception and management of paradoxes in a multicultural environment.

Chapter 9 (Conflicting Demands of Sustainable Digital Transformation) applies a qualitative methodology based on semi-structured interviews with 10 experts from different European countries with experience in digital transformation. Data analysis was carried out in three stages: transcription and deductive coding (based on a previous literature review), followed by the identification of paradoxical tensions. The study's main objective was to identify the relationships between the areas involved in the process of sustainable digital transformation and how these interactions lead to paradoxes. The study points to the need to accept tensions as a permanent part of transformation processes rather than trying to eliminate them. A constructivist perspective is evident in the analysis, where the influence of diverse stakeholders (employees, leaders, regulation) on the dynamics of transformation is considered.

Chapter 10 (Energy Clusters in Reconciling Paradoxes in Corporate Sustainability) uses a multiple case study method, analyzing three energy clusters in Europe: two from Central and Eastern Europe (Romania and Hungary) and one from Western Europe (Germany). Data was collected over several years (2017, 2020, 2022) through interviews with cluster coordinators, document analysis, and observations. The study identified paradoxical tensions in sustainability management in green energy clusters and provided insights into coping practices. The study fits into the dynamic equilibrium perspective, which assumes that paradoxes are inevitable in complex systems such as green energy clusters. Managing them involves recognizing, accepting, and using them to create sustainable practices that combine conflicting goals. In addition, the findings allude to a constructivist perspective (the IS paradigm), where different stakeholder groups contribute to building a shared vision of sustainability.

Chapter 11 (Energy Transition Through the Energy-based Industrial Clusters: Paradoxes and Their Solutions) uses a qualitative approach with exploratory case studies within energy-based industrial clusters (EBICs). The study focuses on identifying and analyzing paradoxical tensions in energy transition processes, with a particular focus on sustainability. A key methodological aspect was the qualitative analysis of the structural and operational factors influencing the development of clusters and their ability to cope with environmental and economic paradoxes. EBICs are analyzed as complex systems in which conflicting environmental and economic objectives are balanced dynamically. This perspective also involves a constructivist aspect, in which energy transition is interpreted as a negotiation process between diverse stakeholders in industrial clusters.

## References

Adorno, T. W. (1944). *Dialectic of Enlightenment*. New York: Social Science Publishers.

Andriopoulos, C., & Gotsi, M. (2017). Methods of paradox. In W. K. Smith, M. W. Lewis, P. Jarzabkowski, & A. Langley (Eds.), *The Oxford Handbook of Paradox* (pp. 513–529). Oxford: Oxford University Press.

Badham, R., Claydon, R., & Down, S. (2011). The ambivalence paradox in cultural change. In W. D. Boje, B. Burnes, & J. Hassard (Red.), *The Routledge Companion to Organizational Change* (s. 407–424). New York: Routledge.

Berti, M., & Simpson, A. V. (2021). The dark side of organizational paradoxes: The dynamics of disempowerment. *Academy of Management Review*, *46*(3), 469–490.

Blumer, H. (1969). *Symbolic Interactionism: Perspective and Method*. Englewood Cliffs, NJ: Prentice-Hall.

Burns, T., & Stalker, G. M. (1961). Mechanistic and organic systems. *Classics of Organizational Theory*, *10*(2), 209–214.

Burrell, G., & Morgan, G. (1979). *Sociological Paradigms and Organizational Analysis*. London: Heinemann.

Burrell, G., & Morgan, G. (2019). *Sociological Paradigms and Organisational Analysis: Elements of the Sociology of Corporate Life*. Florence: Routledge.

Cappelli, P., & Tavis, A. (2018). HR goes agile. *Harvard Business Review*, *96*(2), 46–52.

Carmine, S., & Smith, W. K. (2021). Organizational paradox. Oxford Bibliographies in Management.

Carroll, A. & Shabana, K. (2010). The business case for corporate social responsibility: A review of concepts, research and practice. *International Journal of Management Reviews, 12*(1), 85–102. 10.1111/j.1468-2370.2009.00275.x

Comte, A. (1830). *Cours de philosophie positive*. Paris: Rouen Frères.

Cunha, M. P. E., & Bednarek, R. (2020). A source of novelty and/or absurdity: The paradoxes of management. *International Journal of Business Environment, 11*(1), 69–79.

Durkheim, E. (1897). *Le Suicide: Étude de sociologie*. Paris: Félix Alcan.

Eisenhardt, K. M. (2000). Paradox, spirals, ambivalence: The new language of change and pluralism. *Academy of Management Review, 25*(4), 703–705.

Epstein, M. & Roy, M-J. (2001). Sustainability in action: Identifying and measuring the key performance drivers. *Long Range Planning, 34*(5), 585–604.

Foucault, M. (1975). *Surveiller et punir: Naissance de la prison*. Paris: Gallimard.

Gaim, M., Clegg, S., e Cunha, M. P., & Berti, M. (2022). *Organizational Paradox*. Cambridge University Press.

Garfinkel, H. (1967). *Studies in Ethnomethodology*. Englewood Cliffs, NJ: Prentice-Hall.

Guba, E. G. (1990). *The Paradigm Dialog*. Newbury Park, CA: SAGE Publications.

Habermas, J. (1981). *The Theory of Communicative Action*. Boston, MA: Beacon Press.

Hampden-Turner, C. (2021). Commentary: Paradoxes of social structure. In *Interdisciplinary Dialogues on Organizational Paradox: Investigating Social Structures and Human Expression, Part B* (pp. 87–98). Bingley: Emerald Publishing Limited.

Hatch, M. J. (2018). *Organization Theory: Modern, Symbolic, and Postmodern Perspectives*. Oxford: Oxford University Press.

He, L., & Wang, Q. (2020). Do Chinese corporate foundations enhance civil society? In L. Roza S. Bethmann, L. Meijs, & G. von Schnurbein (Eds.), *Handbook on Corporate Foundation* (pp. 125–147). Cham: Springer. https://link.springer.com/chapter/10.1007%2F978-3-030-25759-0_7

Henriksen, T. D., Nielsen, R. K., Vikkelsø, S., & Bévort, F. (2021). A paradox rarely comes alone: A quantitative approach to investigating knotted leadership paradoxes in SMEs. *Scandinavian Journal of Management*, 37(1), 101135.

Hofstede, G. (2001). *Culture's Consequences: Comparing Values, Behaviors, Institutions, and Organizations across Nations*, 2nd ed. Thousand Oaks, CA: Sage.

Horkheimer, M. (1947). *Eclipse of Reason*. Oxford: Oxford University Press.

Hossain, M. I., Kumar, J., & Islam, M. T. (2024). The interplay among paradoxical leadership, organizational ambidexterity, and strategic flexibility. *European Business Review*.

Jarzabkowski, P., Balogun, J., & Seidl, D. (2007). Strategizing: The challenges of a practice perspective. *Human Relations, 60*(1), 5–27.

Jarzabkowski, P., Le, J. K. & Van de Ven, A. H. (2013). Responding to competing strategic demands: How organizing, belonging, and performing paradoxes coevolve. Strategic Organization, *11*(3), pp. 245–280. doi: 10.1177/1476127013481016

Johnson, P., Duberley, J. (2000). *Understanding Management Research: An Introduction to Epistemology*. London: Sage Publications.

Keller, J., & Sadler-Smith, E. (2019). Paradoxes and dual processes: A review and synthesis. *International Journal of Management Reviews, 21*(2), 121–144.

Kuhn, T. S. (1962). *The Structure of Scientific Revolutions*. Chicago, IL: University of Chicago Press.

Lawrence, P., & Lorsch, J. (1967). Organizations and environment: Managing differentiation and integration. Homewood, IL: Irwin.

Lempiälä, T., Tiitinen, S., & Vanharanta, O. (2023). Paradox as an interactional resource: An ethnomethodological analysis into the interconnectedness of organizational paradoxes. *Organization Studies, 44*(11), 1825–1852.

Lewis, M. W. (2000). Exploring paradox: Toward a more comprehensive guide. *Academy of Management Review, 25*, 760–776.

Lewis, M. W., & Smith, W. K. (2014). Paradox as a Metatheoretical Perspective: Sharpening the Focus and Widening the Scope. *The Journal of Applied Behavioral Science, 50*(2), 127–149.

Lin, H., Qu, T., Li, L., & Tian, Y. (2020). The paradox of stability and change: A case study. *Chinese Management Studies*.

Liu, Y., Xu, S., & Zhang, B. (2020). Thriving at work: How a paradox mindset influences innovative work behavior. *The Journal of Applied Behavioral Science, 56*(3), 347–366.

March, J. (1991). Exploration and exploitation in organizational learning. *Organization Science, 2*, 71–87.

Marx, K. (1867). *Das Kapital*. Hamburg: Verlag von Otto Meissner.

Mead, G. H. (1934). *Mind, Self, and Society*. Chicago: University of Chicago Press.

Mills, C. W. (1956). *The Power Elite*. New York: Oxford University Press.

Mintzberg, H. (1993). *Structure in Fives: Designing Effective Organizations*. Englewood Cliffs: Prentice-Hall, Inc.

Morgan, G. (2006). *Images of Organization*. Thousand Oaks, CA: Sage Publications.

Moschko, L., Blazevic, V., & Piller, F. T. (2023). Paradoxes of implementing digital manufacturing systems: A longitudinal study of digital innovation projects for disruptive change. *Journal of Product Innovation Management, 40*(4), 506–529.

Nayebpour, H., & Sehhat, S. (2024). Designing the competency model of human resource managers based on paradox theory (case study: information and communication technology industry). *International Journal of Organizational Analysis, 32*(7), 1181–1203.

O'Reilly III, C. A., & Tushman, M. L. (2013). Organizational ambidexterity: Past, present, and future. *Academy of management Perspectives, 27*(4), 324–338.

Parsons, T. (1951). *The Social System*. Glencoe, IL: The Free Press.

Perrow, C. (1972). *Complex Organizations: A Critical Essay*. Glenview, IL: Scott, Foresman.

Putnam, L. (1986). Contradictions and paradoxes in organizations. In L. Thayer (Ed.), *Organization communications: Emerging Perspectives* (pp. 151–167). Norwood, NJ: Ablex.

Quinn, R. E., & Cameron, K. S. (Eds.). (1988). *Paradox and Transformation: Toward a Theory of Change in Organization and Management*. Cambridge, MA: Ballinger Publishing Co/Harper & Row Publishers.

Schein, E. H. (2010). *Organizational Culture and Leadership*. Hoboken, NJ: John Wiley & Sons.

Schulte, L. (2022). Integrating immediate gains with sustainable performance: Systematic review of paradox. *Management Review Quarterly*, *72*(2), 121–140.
Schütz, A. (1932). *Der sinnhafte Aufbau der sozialen Welt: Eine Einleitung in die verstehende Soziologie*. Vienna: Springer.
Seidl, D., Lê, J., & Jarzabkowski, P. (2021). The generative potential of Luhmann's theorizing for paradox research: Decision paradox and deparadoxization. In R. Bednarek, M. Pina e Cunha, J. Schad, & W. K. Smith (Eds.), *Interdisciplinary Dialogues on Organizational Paradox: Investigating Social Structures and Human Expression, Part B* (Vol. 73, pp. 49–64). Emerald Publishing Limited.
Simon, A. F. (2022). Paradox in leading a human rights funder network. *Journal of Nonprofit Education & Leadership*, *12*(3), 99–116.
Sitkin, S. B., & Stickel, D. (1996). The road to hell: The dynamics of distrust in an era of quality. *Trust in Organizations: Frontiers of Theory and Research*, *196*, 215.
Smith, P., & Beretta, M. (2021). The Gordian knot of practicing digital transformation: Coping with emergent paradoxes in ambidextrous organizing structures. *Journal of Product Innovation Management*, *38*(5), 603–621.
Smith, W. K., & Lewis, M. W. (2011). Toward a theory of paradox: A dynamic equilibrium model of organizing. *Academy of Management Review*, *36*, 381–403.
Smith, W. K., Erez, M., & Jarvenpaa, S. (2017). Paradoxes and dualities of innovation and change. *Organization Studies*, *38*(3), 303–324.
Statler, M., Heracleous, L., & Jacobs, C. D. (2011). Serious play as a practice of paradox. *The Journal of Applied Behavioral Science*, *47*(2), 236–256.
Stohl, C., & Cheney, G. (2001). Participatory processes/paradoxical practices: Communication and the dilemmas of organizational democracy. *Management Communication Quarterly*, *14*(3), 349–407.
Tushman, M., & O'Reilly, C. (1996). Organizations. *California Management Review*, *38*(4), 8–30.
Wallerstein, I. (1974). *The Modern World-System I: Capitalist Agriculture and the Origins of the European World-Economy in the Sixteenth Century*. New York: Academic Press.
Weiser, A. K., & Laamanen, T. (2022). Extending the dynamic equilibrium model of paradox: Unveiling the dissipative dynamics in organizations. *Organization Theory*, *3*(3), 26317877221090317.

# 2 Organizational Paradox Theory

## Managing Competing Demand Then and Now

*Jacek Rybicki*

### 2.1 Introduction

The word *paradox* generally refers to a construct that belongs to philosophical, logical, and organizational contexts (Cameron & Quinn, 1988; Smith & Lewis, 2011; Poole & Van de Ven, 1989). Nevertheless, it is emphasized that it is possible to link paradoxes to three main classes: Rhetorical paradoxes, logical paradoxes, and social paradoxes (De Toni et al., 2023). In the first class, paradoxes are stimuli that spark the reader's attention or challenge rigid truths, subsequently expanding the horizons of understanding or laying the groundwork for innovation and creativity. In the second class, paradoxes are dealt with in the field of logic, where, starting with Aristotle's *Metaphysics*, attempts have been made to suppress paradox, that is, to impose the concept by which a statement cannot be true and not true at the same time *the law of excluded middle* (Chen, 2002). The third class is the most important one in terms of this study. The social paradox is identified not as a logical contradiction but as a form of tension between incompatible positions and tendencies. On an organizational level, this paradox emerges as a paradoxical situation in which individuals and groups are surrounded by a field of tensions (De Toni et al., 2023). Social paradoxes include organizational and strategic paradoxes, creating dualisms, contradictions, and oppositions. Dualisms and oppositions are natural and do not cause problems in decision-making processes as long as managers find clear premises in specific situations that support adopting one of the solutions. However, if both opposing elements become important for the organization and begin competing, tensions arise, and dualism becomes a paradox (Schad et al., 2016; Kaleta et al., 2024).

Paradox traces back to deep theoretical roots, with rich foundations in philosophy and psychology, including the works of Aristotle, Confucius, Freud, Hegel, Jung, Kierkegaard, Lao Tzu, Hampden-Turner, Harris, Smith, and Berg. Even as these ideas emerge from ancient roots, paradoxes intensify as contemporary reality (Schad et al., 2017). Ancient philosophers such as Buddha, Lao Tzu, and Plato argued that paradoxes made up of opposites exist as a unified whole. In Chinese philosophy, the symbol yin-yang refers to special interconnections in which movement from one side significantly affects the other. These observations show us that the phenomena around us cannot exist without their opposite.

DOI: 10.4324/9781003541394-4

More modern philosophy, particularly dialectical and existential approaches, blends Eastern and Western understandings of interdependent contradictions. The introduction drew from rich insights across a variety of disciplines, including Eastern philosophy (Taoism, Confucianism), Western philosophies (Hegel, Heraclitus), psychodynamics (Adler, Frankel), psychology (Schneider, Watzlawick), political science (Marx, Engel), communications and sociology (Taylor, Bateson), and negotiations and conflict resolution (Follett). More recent work has advanced foundational building blocks toward a theory of paradox. Buddhist, Hindu, and Taoist teachings assume that the interdependence between oppositional elements is permanent. They suggest that one should strive not so much to resolve the paradox as to understand it. The Western philosophical foundations of paradox emerged in ancient Greece (Heraclitus), as reflected in the splitting of the term into two parts: *Para* (despite, in contrast to) and *doxa* (opinion, praise). Greek philosophers presented paradox in terms of both contradiction and interdependence. They valued rhetorical paradoxes that seemed absurd and irrational. They were intended to inspire the mind and ultimately foster greater rationality and logical analysis. In fundamental philosophical and psychological concepts, they find three principles of paradoxes: The unity of opposites, the concept of balance, and the principle of holism (Schad et al., 2016).

The unity of opposites is at the heart of Hegel's dialectics since thesis and antithesis are mutually constituted. The persistence of the paradoxical structure means we constantly seek a balance between opposing poles. The *doctrine of the mean* appears in both Eastern and Western thought. In Aristotelian ethics, balance refers to the search for the *golden mean* between extremes. Confucius also created a doctrine of achieving harmony by avoiding extremes. On the other hand, Hegel referred to Socratic and Kantian philosophy and presented the dialectics theory as an alternative path to dynamic equilibrium (Schad et al., 2016).

Organizational paradox offers a theory of the nature and management of competing demands. Historically, the dominant paradigm in organizational theory depicted competing demands as trade-offs or dilemmas that could be resolved by choosing one option. In the late 1960s, scholars such as Woodward, Lawrence, and Lorsch introduced contingency theory, suggesting that individuals resolve these tensions by considering the context and environment. Paradox theory offers an alternative approach, suggesting that these tensions cannot be resolved. It argues that managers must accept, engage, and navigate tensions rather than *resolve* them. These philosophical and psychological foundations inspired early organizational theorists to define paradox and sharpen this lens for management science (Lewis, 2000; Poole & Van de Ven, 1989; Quinn, 1988). Western philosophers and academics built a theory of the organizational paradox and, based on their inquiries, developed it by relating the paradox to organizational issues, including strategic ones.

Over the past decade, paradox theory has developed impressively. Such advances have been fueled by a rising collective experience of paradoxes, such as change, scarcity, and plurality, intensifying awareness of conflicting, interdependent, and persistent forces. Interdisciplinary and cross-cultural influences have additionally made paradox theory simultaneously fragmented and complex. Therefore, this chapter bridges an identified research gap of scattered knowledge on contemporary paradox theory. There is a strong need to synthesize existing concepts on paradoxes (e.g., organizational and strategic paradoxes). It is also valuable to analyze the equilibrium issue in a tension synthesis situation and synthesize the main paradox management concepts, namely navigating the paradoxes.

Chapter 1 contains the following subsections: The research methodology, the elements of paradox theory in the management field, the categorization of organizational and strategic paradoxes, the analysis of paradoxes regarding the balance between tensions (search for optimal solutions), and conclusions.

## 2.2 Methodology

The study of organizational and strategic paradoxes has gained considerable attention in the past two decades due to the business context's dynamic and complex nature. Therefore, a qualitative systematic review method was adopted to synthesize the abundant literature. The research method of the literature review included three stages. Stage one involved analyzing publications with keywords from Web of Science, Scopus, Google Scholar, and Wiley. Stage two involved screening abstracts of the selected publications. At this research stage, citation frequency was used as a criterion for article selection. Stage three involved analyzing and synthesizing the content of the previously selected publications.

A total of 885 selected articles were analyzed, of which 41 literature items were reviewed in this chapter. The extended keywords used in the research were as follows: Dilemma in paradox theory, trade-off as paradox, dialectic contradictory, organizational ambiguities, duality in management, paradox theory, organizational paradox, strategic paradox, and paradox dynamic equilibrium.

All records reviewed involve opposite but interrelated demands or paradox elements in their processual conceptualization of paradoxes, suggesting a view of the process as paradox management. The number of cited articles by keyword is presented in Table 2.1.

The research used a qualitative systematic review. It is best to review and synthesize studies to draw broad theoretical conclusions about literature, linking theory to evidence and evidence to theory (Siddaway et al., 2019). A systematic review of the literature can be conducted to confirm or refute whether current practice is based on adequate evidence, to determine the quality of that

*Table 2.1* The Number of the Found and Cited Publications by Keyword

| *No.* | *Keywords* | *Items Generated by Abstract* | *Cited Publication* | *Percentage (%)* |
|---|---|---|---|---|
| 1 | Dilemma in paradox theory | 0 | 0 | 0 |
| 2 | Trade-off as paradox | 96 | 2 | 4.9 |
| 3 | Dialectic contradictory | 0 | 0 | 0 |
| 4 | Organizational ambiguities | 49 | 3 | 7.3 |
| 6 | Duality in management | 126 | 2 | 4.9 |
| 7 | Paradox theory | 238 | 10 | 24.4 |
| 8 | Organizational paradox | 285 | 16 | 39.0 |
| 9 | Strategic paradox | 91 | 8 | 19.5 |
| 10 | Paradox dynamic equilibrium | 0 | 0 | 0 |
| | Total | 885 | 41 | 100 |

*Table 2.2* The Number of the Found and Cited Publications by the Database

| *No.* | *Database* | *Items Generated by Abstract* | *Cited Publication* | *Percentage (%)* |
|---|---|---|---|---|
| 1 | Web of Science | 357 | 15 | 36.6 |
| 2 | Scopus | 328 | 8 | 19.5 |
| 3 | Google Scholar | 190 | 15 | 36.6 |
| 4 | Wiley | 10 | 3 | 7.3 |
| | Total | 885 | 41 | 100 |

evidence, and to resolve any uncertainties or differences in practice that may arise. Such differences in practice may arise from conflicting evidence, and a systematic review should resolve such conflicts. Conducting a systematic review can also identify gaps, shortcomings, and trends in current evidence and help build on and inform future research in this area. Systematic reviews can be used to create statements to guide organizational and strategic decision-making processes. The number of publications found and cited by the database is presented in Table 2.2.

Selected literature showed that paradoxes have been studied in many scientific disciplines, such as medicine, philosophy, technical sciences, economics, management, sociology, ecology, psychology, and more. Articles from these scientific disciplines were not selected; only articles from the management field were considered. The analysis and synthesis of the investigated publications can be considered as a method for drawing conclusions.

## 2.3 Elements of the Paradox Theory in Management Science

Paradox was introduced into the management and organization literature in the late 1980s (Cameron & Quinn, 1988; Poole & Van de Ven, 1989). In 2000, the paradox was defined as contradictory but related elements that appear logical in isolation but absurd and irrational when they occur together (Lewis, 2000). The paradox research in management and organization studies encompasses a rich variety of theoretical perspectives and methods. They focus on how organizations experience persistent tensions between seemingly irreconcilable conflicting elements and which strategies could manage them (Clegg et al., 2002; Lewis, 2000; Lewis & Smith, 2014; Smith & Lewis, 2011).

Paradox is also defined as contradictory, interdependent, and persistent tensions, noting their dynamic, ever-changing, and cyclical nature. Some Western scholars describe the origins of paradox as inherent within systems, while others highlight their social construction through cognition, dialogue, and rationality. Still, other academics explore the relationship between tensions' inherent and socially constructed nature. Moreover, some scholars focus more on understanding the dimensions of paradox, while others depict the ongoing dynamic interaction and evolution. Scholars have added complexity as paradox theory grows and expands, emphasizing paradoxes as nested across levels and as knotted and interwoven across various tensions. These tensions also consider power dynamics, uncertainty, plurality, and scarcity of systems within which paradoxes emerge (Lewis, 2000, Lewis & Smith, 2014).

A paradox may be defined as the persistent contradiction between interdependent elements (Lewis, 2000). This definition identifies two core characteristics of paradox: Contradiction and interdependence. The contradiction lies at the heart of paradoxical tensions. Early philosophers and psychologists explained that contradictions emerge as oppositional elements that foster a tug-of-war experience. According to Cameron and Quinn (1988), the key characteristic of paradox is the simultaneous presence of contradictory, even mutually exclusive elements. As Lewis (2000) mentioned, the conflicting demands seem logical in isolation but absurd and irrational when appearing simultaneously. Similarly, Poole and Van de Ven (1989) described paradoxes as interesting tensions, oppositions, and contradictions between theories that create conceptual difficulties.

As paradoxical dynamics become more salient in contemporary organizations, scholars increasingly explore their nature, approaches, and impact. Many academics posit definitions, constructs, and relationships to build theory on paradox (Smith & Lewis, 2011). Others explore paradoxical relationships applied to specific phenomena (Hahn et al., 2014; Polowczyk, 2014). Academics also use paradox as a tool for theorizing (Dameron & Torset, 2014). This versatility of applications renders paradox a metatheory (Lewis & Smith, 2014), applying a set of key constructs and principles across phenomena, contexts, and theories. Thus, today, paradox theory represents an overarching theoretical perspective.

It defines general principles that will help study and theorize various phenomena. Paradox as a metatheory concerns the principles of the emergence, but the management of paradoxical tensions is in a variety of contexts, concepts, and methodological approaches (Lewis & Smith, 2014). Metatheory complements and can create bridges between more specific, earlier theories (Poole & Van de Ven, 1989). As such, it becomes a tool for meta-theorizing across management theories. Its potential is revealed in describing paradoxes in diverse research areas in management sciences, such as corporate governance, leadership, or transformation and strategy. Paradox as a metatheory offers a powerful lens for management science, providing a deeper understanding of constructs, relationships, and dynamics surrounding organizational tensions (Schad et al., 2017) while enriching extant theories and processes of theorizing.

Many fundamental insights opened up a space for a solid and valuable dialogue and debate on the definition of paradox and its relationship to other concepts, such as dialectics, dualism, and dichotomy. Another milestone in developing paradox theory is The Oxford Handbook of Organizational Paradox (Smith et al. 2017), which introduces and offers theoretical and practical tools for researchers wishing to study organizational paradoxes.

Nowadays, the functioning of organizations is associated with the tensions that accompany the decision-making process in the context of conflicting choices: Flexibility vs. tight control, exploration vs. exploitation, autocracy vs. democracy, achieving social goals vs. financial goals, global vs. local actions, etc. For many years, researchers specializing in strategic management have been attached to the contingency (situational) theory, seeking answers to questions such as: Under what conditions should managers choose A or B? Are we entering a new geographical market X or not? Are we starting production of a new product Y or not? In turn, the contingency perspective identifies the conditions under which companies should pursue different, opposing goals, e.g., when they have to focus on exploration and exploitation or when to favor mechanistic and organic structures in companies. In the literature on strategic management, there is no terminological coherence regarding these contradictions; they are named and defined, among others, as contradictions, dualities, dichotomies, or dialectics (Smith & Lewis, 2011). Their common denominator is the occurrence of a few essentially opposing elements: Perspectives, approaches, requirements, identities, goals, or practices (Lewis, 2000). Simplified dialectical thinking based on the triad is presented in Figure 2.1.

Thesis and antithesis change, creating a synthesis that becomes a new thesis for a new antithesis. Dialectical philosophers such as Hegel posit a natural conflict between opposing elements (thesis and antithesis). Leveraging logic, this approach envisions a progressive process whereby the conflict enables resolution (synthesis). Such a resolution serves as a new assertion (thesis) that spawns its alternative (antithesis), fostering a new solution (synthesis) and fueling a never-ending search for greater truth (Clegg, et al., 2002).

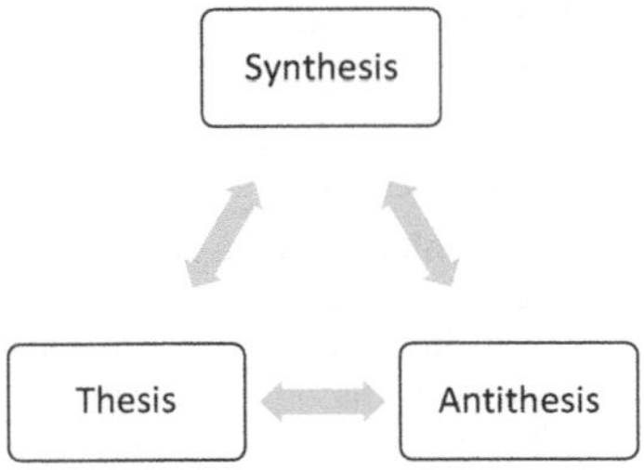


*Figure 2.1* The Basic Triad of Dialectical Thinking.

As a result of the findings of paradox research, Western scholars have developed the foundational building blocks of the theory, definitions, assumptions, and boundaries (Smith & Lewis 2011). They propose a theory that addresses how paradoxical tensions exist as latent tensions in systems that become salient through social construction or conditions of change, scarcity, and pluralism. They further argue that tensions exist in a dynamic interactive state that they describe as dynamic equilibrium – *solution of the paradox*.

Fundamental differences between opposite perspectives change research expectations. From a situational perspective, tensions are treated as problems that *must be solved* using rational analysis and formal logic. On the other hand, the paradoxical perspective assumes the need for a holistic understanding of tensions and how cognitive and social elements affect the decision-making process (Polowczyk, 2023; Andriopoulos, 2003; Berti et al., 2023). Moreover, every significant technological invention or organizational innovation causes the expansion of this space by adding a new, previously unknown dimension (Corbett et al., 1993). Multidimensional analysis should identify the best elements for a dynamic equilibrium from an organizational point of view.

In the paradox theory, synonymous concepts are characterized by subtle situational differences presented in Table 2.3. All situations are based on dialectical thinking, from binary through continuum thinking to paradox thinking.

The next section discusses various paradoxes identified in the management science literature.

## 2.4 Categorizing Organizational and Strategic Paradoxes

Today's world is multidimensional, multipolar, and multipurpose, and increasingly, classic management challenges such as leadership vs. management, exploitation vs. exploration, virtual vs. physical presence, economic sustainability vs. environmental sustainability, localization vs. globalization, etc., assume the characteristics of paradoxes rather than problems or dilemmas (Nielsen et al., 2023).

*Table 2.3* From Dilemma to the Paradox Situation

| *Situation* | *Description* |
|---|---|
| Dilemma | An impossible choice – dichotomy (side A or side B) |
| Trade-off | Possible solutions on a continuum |
| Dialectic contradictory | Elements that can be resolved through integration |
| Ambiguities | Two self-consistent but mutually incompatible frames |
| Irony | Situations or dialogues in which the apparent meaning of a statement or action is inconsistent with its intended meaning |
| Duality | Contradictory and complementary demands |
| Paradox | The simultaneous presence of contradictory demands that persist over time |

When organizations face tensions, they often lean toward one pole and emphasize either perspective (Ghemawat & Costa, 1993). Much of the management literature, particularly earlier research, uses the contingency argument (e.g., Smith & Lewis, 2011), emphasizing the existing context perspective. Contingency theory describes organizational behavior in which competing options are chosen to achieve a short-term goal. If the competing solution is viewed as a dilemma, the management approach to resolving the tension would be to consider the pros and cons of each side and then prioritize one pole over the other. Three fundamental characteristics limit the issue of resolving paradoxes:

- Irrationalism – organizational elements that seem logical in isolation but absurd and irrational when combined (Lewis, 2000).
- Interdependence – these opposing elements must be inextricably linked; they must be dual (Lewis, 2000).
- Persistence – these tensions cannot be definitively resolved because they *persist over time* (Smith & Lewis, 2011).

Scholars have used the concept of paradox to explore a variety of issues because the paradox theory is a theoretical lens that can offer useful insights into various organizational phenomena (Lewis & Smith, 2014), such as change (Luscher & Lewis, 2008), hybridity, identity, innovation, and ambidexterity (Andriopoulos & Lewis, 2009; O'Reilly & Tushman, 1996 and 2008), and leadership (Lewis et al., 2014). Constructing opposing elements as dialectic triggers an integrative response (Smith & Lewis, 2011), developing a new alternative through the integration (synthesis) of thesis and antithesis. This concept encompasses the widely acknowledged categorizations of paradoxes prevalent in literature, emphasizing (Lewis, 2000) tripartite classification, i.e., learning, organizing, and belonging

– and Smith and Lewis' (2011) extension to include performing. Smith and Lewis (2011) created a fairly coherent and complete catalog of organizational tensions containing four groups, namely:

- Belonging tensions, e.g., individual vs. collective, competition vs. cooperation.
- Learning tensions, e.g., stability vs. change, long-term vs. short-term perspective.
- Organizing tensions, e.g., efficiency vs. flexibility.
- Performance tensions, e.g., financial goals vs. corporate social responsibility.

In addition to the tensions and paradoxes occurring within the distinguished groups, they indicate the possibility of tensions between elements belonging to different categories, e.g., efficiency vs. flexibility (belonging to the groups related to results and organizing). Paradoxical behavior is counter-intuitive. The need to apply opposing solutions simultaneously creates tensions that managers manage differently through strategies using two contradictory options. These are synthesis, simultaneous deepening of both options, the duality of managerial competencies, and searching for a third solution or separating two contradictory options within one organization so they do not directly conflict with each other. Relations among organizational paradoxes are presented in Figure 2.2.

This all creates the conditions for categorizing organizational paradoxes. The categorization of organizational paradoxes is presented in Table 2.4.

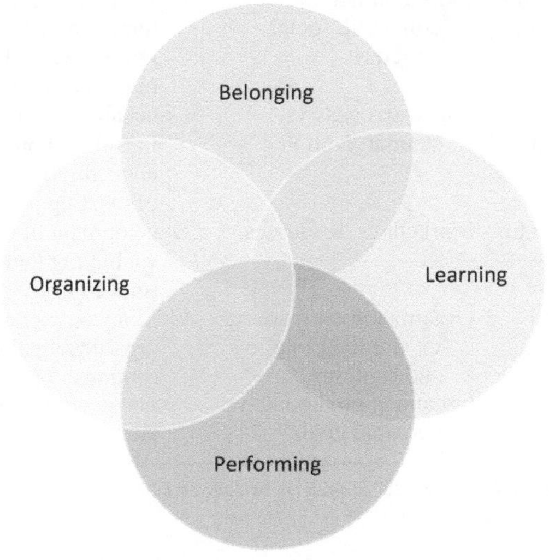


*Figure 2.2* Relations among Organizational Paradoxes.

*Table 2.4* Type and Example of Organizational Paradoxes

| *No.* | *Type of Paradox* | *Example of Paradox* | *Tensions Perspective* |
|---|---|---|---|
| 1 | Learning | Exploration vs. exploitation | Focusing on the development of the existing product vs. focusing on searching for new, convertible solutions |
| 2 | Organizing | Emergent vs. planned | Changes implementation one by one vs. batch changes and implementation of a few changes simultaneously |
| 3 | Belonging | Centralization vs. decentralization | Emphasis putting (in the case of the serial product) on the solution searching inside the company vs. emphasis putting (in the case of the serial product) on the solution searching outside the company |
| 4 | Performing | Autonomy vs. accountability | Additional tasks avoidance and focusing on the basic responsibilities vs. acceptance of additional tasks, keeping in mind the common good |
| 5 | Learning and Belonging | Knowledge sharing vs. knowledge protection | Widely discussing results of changes vs. informing about results of changes only the most interested people |
| 6 | Performing and Organizing | Individualistic vs. collective social structure | Investing in training to build human potential vs. investing in innovative technologies to build market advantage |
| 7 | Learning and performing | Innovativeness vs. standardization | Concentration on new products introduced on the market vs. concentration on standardization of existing products |
| 8 | Organizing and belonging | Markets vs. resources | Development of own resources vs. buying them on the market (make or buy) |
| 9 | Learning and Organizing | Organizational learning vs. dominant logic and routine | Flexible and agile outcomes vs. organizational capabilities and routines |
| 10 | Performing and belonging | Organizational goals vs. personal goals | Focus on corporate goals vs. focus on managerial goals |

*Source:* Based on Smith & Lewis (2011) and Tryczak et al. (2023).

Types of organizational paradoxes and the network of their relationships should be complemented by a categorization of strategic paradoxes.

Meyer and de Wit (1998) create and categorize strategic paradoxes. They distinguish four basic ways of analyzing strategy. This classification includes the theory of strategic paradoxes and tensions. These are the puzzle, the dilemma, the trade-off, and the paradox. A puzzle is a problem that requires mental effort and has only one correct solution. Puzzles can be complicated or difficult to investigate, but there is always the best way to analyze them. Strategic tension can be treated as a puzzle. The opposites that create it often seem completely incompatible. There is only one way to solve the puzzle, but to learn it, it is first necessary to analyze the problem thoroughly.

In strategic management, the dilemma already mentioned is considered an uncomfortable problem that has two equally valid solutions, but from a logical point of view, neither is ideal. Both options have advantages and disadvantages, but neither is clearly better. Strategic tensions can also be viewed as dilemmas. By adopting this approach, the strategist accepts the incompatibility of opposites and must choose one of them. For example, the manager decides to compete or cooperate (de Wit and Meyer, 1998).

The trade-off also previously addressed a problem in which many different solutions are possible – each of them considers competing options in different proportions. In this situation, each solution has its pros and cons. Strategic tension can also be seen as a trade-off. In this approach, the strategist accepts the conflict between contradictions and constantly strives to maintain the proportions between them, depending on the changes in the situation. The problem, in the form of a paradox, has no real solution, as there is no possibility of logical integration of two opposites into an internally coherent way of understanding the problem.

Paradox, therefore, causes the strategists to face the challenging task of struggling with the problem without any chance of finding a final solution. The best thing that can be done in this situation is to constantly look for temporary (changing) solutions, trying to mitigate the force of the individual contradictions as much as possible. Therefore, strategic tension can also be viewed as a paradox. Strategists accept the conflict between two opposing positions but at the same time try to mitigate them in some way. They constantly look for new ideas for applying both truths simultaneously. In such a situation, strategists combine the best two contradictory elements.

De Wit and Meyer listed ten fields of strategic paradoxes, ranging from strategic thinking through strategic levels and context of action to organizational purpose (Figure 2.3).

Two more fields of analysis are considered in this concept, which means the process of corporate strategy formulation and strategic change. Fields of paradoxes correspond to tension situations. In this case, paradox management aims to minimize the tension between two contradictions. The different fields of

*Figure 2.3* Ten Fields of Strategic Paradoxes.

analysis of strategic paradoxes correspond to the types of tensions creating the relevant paradox, thus:

- Strategic thinking corresponds to logic vs. creativity.
- Strategy formulation corresponds to deliberate vs. emergent.
- Strategic change corresponds to revolution vs. evolution.
- Business-level strategy corresponds to markets vs. resources.
- Corporate-level strategy corresponds to responsiveness vs. synergy.
- Network-level strategy corresponds to competition vs. cooperation.
- The industry context corresponds to compliance vs. choice.
- The organizational context corresponds to control vs. chaos.
- The international context corresponds to globalization vs. localization.
- And organizational purpose corresponds to profitability vs. responsibility.

Figure 2.4 shows ten tensions accompanying each of the presented fields of paradoxes.

The ten tensions correspond to the ten perspectives of strategic paradox analysis, thus:

- Logic vs. creativity should be analyzed by rational thinking vs. generative thinking.

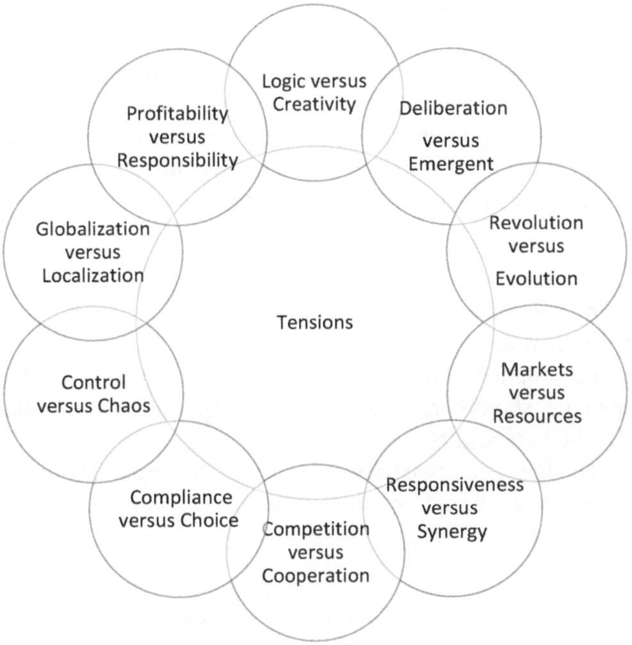


*Figure 2.4* Ten Tensions of Strategic Paradoxes.

- Deliberate vs. emergent strategy formulation should be analyzed by planning vs. incrementalism perspectives.
- Revolution vs. evolution should be analyzed by correspondence to discontinuous vs. continuous changes.
- Markets vs. resources should be analyzed by outside – in vs. inside – out perspectives.
- Responsiveness vs. synergy should be analyzed by Strategic Business Unit portfolio vs. core competencies.
- Competition vs. cooperation should be analyzed by discrete organization vs. embedded organization.
- Compliance vs. choice should be analyzed by an industry evolution vs. industry creation perspective.
- Control vs. chaos should be analyzed by organizational leadership vs. organizational dynamics.
- Globalization vs. localization should be analyzed by global convergence vs. international diversity perspectives.

- And profitability vs. responsibility should be analyzed from the shareholder value vs. stakeholder value perspective.

The strategy formulation process can be broken down into its component parts according to different criteria. The process, according to de Wit and Meyer (1998), can be broken down into three partially overlapping issues – each of which involves the manager having to make a specific choice and, as a result, is subject to lively discussion and disagreement in three areas:

- Strategic thinking – this issue revolves around the strategist. It boils down to how a manager should think and analyze business reality for the strategic thinking process to deliver the best results.
- Strategy formulation – this issue centers around strategy. It boils down to how a manager should organize activities for the strategy formulation process to deliver the best results.
- Strategic change – this issue revolves around the organization. It boils down to how a manager should organize change so that the strategic renewal process yields the best results.

De Wit and Meyer (1998) see paradoxes in strategic thinking, the strategy formulation process, and strategic change as a process of adapting to changing operating conditions. The paradoxes they mention address many issues related to the strategy formulation process. They force academics and managers to think creatively to resolve paradoxes based on taking the best of the thesis side and the best of the antithesis side in a given decision-making situation or strategic decision-making process. Thus, it is useful to analyze strategic paradoxes through different cognitive perspectives. de Wit and Meyer propose ten such perspectives. Figure 2.5. presents ten perspectives on analyzing strategic paradoxes corresponding to the tensions presented in Figure 2.4.

To sum up, Cameron and Quinn's (1988) understanding of the definition of paradox was central to the concepts of Smith and Lewis (2011) and de Wit and Mayer (1998). All concepts are the basis for explaining the ability to analyze and manage paradoxes. Schmit and Lewis' (2011) perspective describes organizational paradoxes, while de Wit and Meyer (1998) limit themselves to strategic paradoxes. Paradox theory replaces the choice between competing demands from contingency theory with the insight that these demands are often interrelated in a persistent relationship over time. For example, exploration creates capabilities that later can be exploited, whereas exploitation creates the resources necessary to fund exploration. Accordingly, choosing between competing demands is impossible. Instead, a dynamic equilibrium (Smith & Lewis, 2011) between the opposing poles of a paradox is required to create long-term

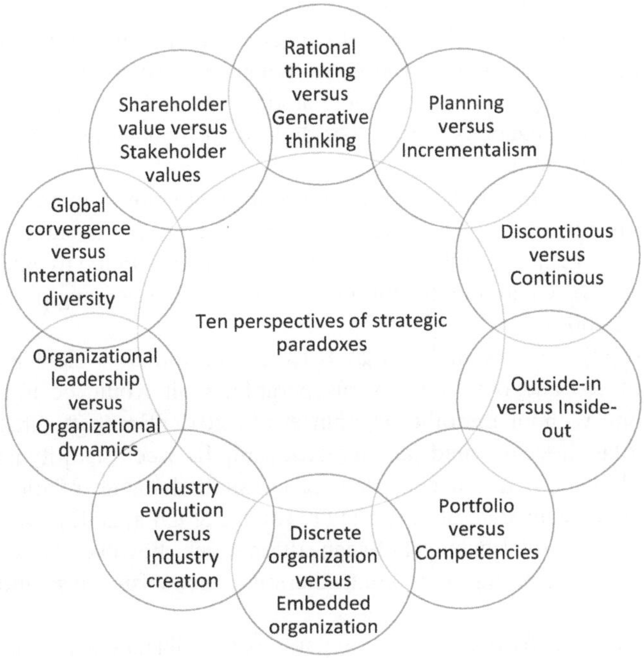


*Figure 2.5* Strategy Perspectives of Paradoxes.

viability (Boemelburg et al., 2023). In this situation, managers seek ways to find a strategically changing equilibrium.

## 2.5 Analysis of Paradoxes – In Search of Sub-Optimal Equilibrium

Paradox scholars diverge from dialectical tradition when the new synthesis renders the underlying tension (Gaim et al., 2018). In dialectics, the synthesis meets a newly emerging antithesis, while the tension in paradox persists. Dialectics prove paradoxical when a new synthesis sustains the initial thesis and antithesis in relation to one another (Clegg, 2002; Langley & Sloan, 2011). These tensions can be resolved by making choices between alternative outcomes. Dialectics emphasizes contradictory and interrelated elements but assume these relationships change over time. Thesis and antithesis change, creating a synthesis that becomes a new thesis for a new antithesis. This process never ends and makes the solutions to the paradox dynamic in nature. In contrast, paradoxes emphasize the enduring, underlying tension between opposing forces that cannot be resolved but must be accepted and the tension minimized. This is the resolution of the paradox. In organizational systems, tensions persist between present and future and between individuals and collectivities, or integration and differentiation. Assuming that the solution to the paradox can be an equilibrium between tensions, this equilibrium is dynamic. Its dynamics are determined by the conditions of action in a particular situation. Paradoxes must be viewed as a dialectical process, and organizations must adopt dialectical logic instead of binary logic (for instance, dilemma).

In business practice, paradoxes are not analyzed theoretically but require concrete, consistent actions. These actions are embedded in a dynamic context. In this situation, a change in the context implies a change in the dynamic equilibrium of paradox. Changing the optimum of action is an ongoing process (Smith &Tushman, 2005).

Many scholars stress the interplay between contradictory elements as mutually constituted and ontologically inseparable, so it would be impossible to describe one without the other (Quinn et al., 2012; Smith & Graetz, 2006). These scholars have detailed such a relationship between stability and change. Duality scholars focus on changing, processual, dynamic relationships that remain in a constant state of becoming (Tsoukas & Chia, 2002). Duality scholars highlight the relationship between alternatives; however, they place less stress on understanding their contradictions, inconsistencies, and conflicts (Schad et al., 2017).

There are currently two concepts of paradox equilibrium in the literature: The first is the conception of dynamic equilibrium, and the second is the concept of dissipative equilibrium. The dynamic equilibrium model (Smith & Lewis, 2011) suggests that depending on managers' acceptance of paradox and dynamics of paradox play out as either vicious or virtuous cycles. Based on psychological and cognitive research, the model holds that managers prefer consistency and react defensively to contradictory demands. Managers may seek to resolve their discomfort by supporting only one side of a paradox. Such behavior can, however, spur vicious cycles of escalating efforts toward one extreme or another (Lewis, 2000). Hence, the behavioral model argues that management's ability to overcome bias and support both poles of a paradox is key to long-term success and provides a vital foundation for virtuous cycles (Lewis & Smith, 2014; Smith & Lewis, 2011). Once a paradox has been accepted, the paradoxical resolution requires management to constantly shift between alternative strategic options to support competing demands and inequal amounts (Weiser & Laamanen, 2022). The behavioral model assumes that paradoxes can be subsumed under management's control once managers can overcome their own biases. Hence, the dynamic equilibrium model tends to treat *paradoxes as things* to be solved or controlled (Cunha & Putnam, 2019), ignoring the inherent complexity and instability associated with them. The organizational reality is, however, chaotic, complex, fluid, sometimes random, frequently messy, and often surprising (Weiser & Laamanen, 2022). Even when senior management can overcome its biases and support both poles of the paradox in a consistently inconsistent manner, it is impossible for them to account for the biases of all other organizational members and anticipate the consequences of their everyday decisions, actions, and interactions. Hence, while the dynamic equilibrium model represents *the concept of order,* the continuously evolving reality may be better described through *the concept of disorder* (Weiser & Laamanen, 2022).

Instead of focusing on ways to reach equilibrium, we need theories on how to deal with dis-equilibrium states (Cunha & Putnam, 2019). Although Smith and Lewis (2011) also note that when managers engage in paradox resolution, the threat of vicious cycles persists, requiring managers to remain vigilant. Instead, they conclude that managing paradoxical tensions via dynamic, purposeful, and ongoing strategies of acceptance and resolution fosters sustainability (Weiser & Laamanen, 2022).

Consequently, the dynamics of the equilibrium model tend to treat paradoxes as things to be solved or controlled (Cunha & Putnam, 2019), ignoring the inherent complexity and instability of the programs associated with them (Gaim et al., 2018). This dynamic equilibrium model represents the *concept of order*.

The dissipative equilibrium model differs in its assumptions regarding the following:

- The nature of the equilibrium – the balance is more unstable than previously suggested due to unexpected external chance events and different types of internal drift that continuously threaten the temporary balance.
- The role of managerial agency – previously accepted paradoxes appear in new, unexpected manifestations that are often difficult for management to recognize and preemptively control.
- The role of tensions – the pull of the different poles of paradox is unequal and changes continuously.
- The dynamics of paradox management – management must invest energy and be vigilant in recognizing different types of drift and developing corrective interventions to rebalance the organization.
- Longer-term outcomes – acceptance, paradox resolution, and embedding the paradox into structures, systems, and processes do not yet ensure longer-term sustainability. Thus, virtuous cycles may be more difficult to achieve than prior research has suggested (e.g., Lewis & Smith, 2014; Smith & Lewis, 2011).

The dissipative equilibrium model of paradox contributes to developing a more realistic understanding of paradox management's organizational challenges and longer-term outcomes (De Toni et al., 2023). This model conceptualizes equilibrium maintenance under organizational tensions as continuous balancing. Building on recent theoretical work that has challenged the dynamic equilibrium model due to its lack of process sensitivity (Cunha & Putnam, 2019), the focus has been on how paradox dynamics play out beyond the *steady state of dynamic equilibrium* (Gaim et al., 2018; Weller & Ran, 2020). Based on the analysis, the dissipative equilibrium model is presented to capture better the temporary nature of equilibrium and the ongoing attention and interventions management needs to (re)balance the organization (Weiser & Laamanen, 2022).

In this case, management's role is to impose constraints on local activities and observe the results of the system by changing the bonds, all the while increasing or decreasing the amount of energy injected into the dissipative structure they manage (Anderson, 1999). The comparison of theoretical frameworks, i.e., the two concepts of equilibrium and synthesis of them, is shown in Table 2.5.

Both equilibrium models have been synthesized by treating them as thesis and antithesis. It can be said that these concepts paradoxically describe paradox equilibrium in terms of its solving.

## 2.6 Conclusions

Managing paradoxes represents an interesting way of reasoning and analyzing processes in managerial practice. Although they have a long history, paradox theory continues to be developed as a metatheory. The author developed different forms of synthesis through theoretical ways of defining paradoxes. Ways of minimizing tensions are ongoing, where synthesis is the new thesis, and its opposite is the antithesis. Thus, paradoxes should be managed through a dynamic/dissipative equilibrium (or its synthesis) that momentarily represents a fit with the changing conditions of action, i.e., the context of the paradox.

The analysis of the concept of strategic paradox according to de Wit and Meyer and the concept of organizational paradox by Schmit and Levis was presented. It was concluded that the solution to the organizational and strategic paradoxes does not exist. One can only navigate or manage the paradox, searching for temporary equilibrium.

The contribution of this chapter to the knowledge of paradox theory are the four research results:

1. New synthesis of the concept of paradoxes according to de Wit and Meyer and Smith and Lewis.
2. Visualizing the permeation of four organizational paradoxes in the concept introduced by Schmit and Lewis.
3. Presenting a new perspective on the analysis and synthesis of paradoxes in the Schmit and Lewis' model.
4. Paradoxical synthesis of dynamic and dissipative equilibrium.

The chapter has several limitations. Only ten articles with the highest citations were taken for the literature survey. Paradoxes were presented from the

*Table 2.5* Paradox Equilibrium: Comparison and Synthesis of Theoretical Frameworks

| *Framework Feature* | *Dynamic Equilibrium (Thesis)* | *Dissipative Equilibrium (Antithesis)* |
|---|---|---|
| Nature of equilibrium | A stable state of dynamic balance based on ongoing behavioral shifts to accommodate the continuous and equal pull by opposing forces | An unstable state of dynamic balance in which the organization is constantly pulled away from equilibrium and must be rebalanced in response |
| Synthesis | A relatively stable state of dynamic equilibrium based on constant oscillations of behaviors to adapt to constant change and to minimize the effects of being constantly thrown out of equilibrium | |
| Role of managerial agency | Paradoxical tensions can be subordinated through the management practices of acceptance and resolution | Paradoxical tensions remain beyond managerial control since independent forces cause the organization to drift out of balance |
| Synthesis | Paradoxical tensions can be accepted and resolved in business practice.<br>However, to some extent, they are beyond the manager's control, and the organization could lose its balance | |
| Role of paradoxical tensions | The different poles of the paradox exert a continuous and equal pull in opposing directions | The pull of the different poles of the paradox is unequal and changes continuously |
| Synthesis | The dynamics of the contradiction causes the tensions of the paradox to exert attraction and repulsion in different directions<br>The constant attraction and repulsion of the tensions of the paradox change over time | |
| Dynamics of paradox management | Acceptance of paradox is followed by continuous shifting between competing demands to support the different sides of a paradox | Acceptance of paradox is followed by continuous vigilance and mindful interventions to rebalance the organization in response to organizational drifting |
| Synthesis | Once the paradox is accepted, there is a constant shift between competing demands and conscious interventions to rebalance the organization in response to organizational drift | |
| Outcomes of paradox management | Acceptance and paradox resolution lead to self-reinforcing virtuous cycles of peak performance and sustainability | Paradox management allows the organization to maintain a paradoxical state at the "edge of chaos" |
| Synthesis | Accepting and resolving paradoxes leads to self-perpetuating sustainability cycles, but at the same time, it remains on the "edge of chaos" | |

*Source:* Based on Weiser & Laamanen (2022).

perspective of general management and strategic management theory. Paradoxes in specific organizational and strategic contexts were not examined. The chapter does not analyze paradoxes in relation to certain fields of human resource management and strategic management. The limitations of the research are due to the method used in the article selection process (a substantial number of articles on paradox theory and only seven articles synthesizing the existing knowledge on organizational and strategic paradox theory that can be found in the databases).

Despite extensive research on paradox theory, new research should be conducted as longitudinal studies. It is necessary to examine the transition between different *dynamic/dissipative equilibria* in order to identify the complex mechanisms that drive or constrain dialectical shifts.

Considering complementary ways paradoxes become enacted helps bridge different ways to conceptualize tensions. This means shifting attention from trivial categorizing pursuits (i.e., deciding whether a phenomenon is a real paradox or not), acknowledging instead the fluidity of tensions and the different causal powers that influence the relation between different ontological domains of tensions. As the research reminded by Lewis and Smith (2011), "navigating paradox is paradoxical" and searching for paradox equilibrium is also paradoxical. This effort may be fraught with difficulties and will require further refinement. It is necessary that the paradox perspective can evolve into a new paradigm, conceptualizing organizations not just as the result of the rational creation of stable arrangements but as ongoing efforts to achieve a precarious balance between order and disorder (Berti et al., 2023).

## References

Anderson, P. (1999). Complexity theory and organization science. *Organization Science, 10*(3), 216–232. https://doi.org/10.1287/orsc.10.3.216

Andriopoulos, C. (2003). Six paradoxes in managing creativity: An embracing act, long range, planning, pergamon, *36*(4), 375–388. https://doi.org/10.1016/S0024-6301(03)00071-2

Andriopoulos, C., & Lewis, M. W. (2009). Exploitation-exploration tensions and organizational ambidexterity: Managing paradoxes of innovation. *Organization Science, 20*(4), 696–717. https://psycnet.apa.org/doi/10.1287/orsc.1080.0406

Berti, M., Pina, E., & Cunha, M. (2023). Paradox, dialectics or trade-offs. A doble loop model of paradox. *Journal of Management Studies, 60*(4), 861–888. https://doi.org/10.1111/joms12899

Boemelburg, R., Zimmermann, A., & Palmie, M. (2023), How paradoxical leaders guide their followers to embrace paradox: Cognitive and behavioral mechanisms of paradox mindset development. *Long Range Planning, 56*(4), 102319. https://doi.org/10.1016/j.lrp.2023.102319

Cameron, K. S., & Quinn, R. E. (1988). Organizational paradox and transformation. In R. E. Quinn & K. S. Cameron (Eds.), *Paradox and Transformation: Toward a Theory of Change in Organization and Management*(pp. 1–18). Cambridge, MA: Ballinger.

Chen, M. J. (2002). Transcending paradox: The Chinese 'Middle Way' perspective, Asia Pacific. *Journal of Management, 19*(2/3), 179–199. https://doi.org/10.1023/A:1016235517735

Clegg, S. R. (2002). General introduction. In S. R. Clegg (Ed.), *Management and Organization Paradoxes.* Amsterdam: John Benjamins. https://doi.org/10.1075/aios.9

Clegg, S. R., da Cunha, J. V., & da Cunha, M. P. (2002). Management paradoxes: A relational view. *Human Relations, 55*(5), 483–503. https://doi.org/10.1177/0018726702555001

Corbett, Ch., & Van Wassenhove, L. (1993). Trade-offs? What -trade-offs? Competences and competitiveness in manufacturing strategy. *California Management Review, 35*(4), 107–122. https://doi.org/10.2307/41166757

Cunha, M., & Putnam, L. (2019). Paradox theory and paradox of success. *Strategic Organization, 17*(1), 95–106. https://doi.org/10.1177/1476127017739536

Dameron, S., & Torset, C. (2014). The discursive construction of strategists' subjectivities: Towards a paradox lens on strategy. *Journal of Management Studies, 51*(2), 291–319. https://doi.org/10.1111/joms.12072

De Toni., Zollo G., & De Zan A. (2023). Organizational paradoxes and metamorphosis in collective action. *Systems, 11*(5), 241. https://doi.org/10.3390/systems11050241

de Wit, B., & Meyer, R. (1998). *Strategy: Process, Content, Context: An International Perspective.* London: International Thomson Business Press.

Gaim M., Wahlin N., Cunha M., & Clegg S. (2018). Analyzing competing demands in organizations: A systematic comparison. *Journal of Organizational Design, 7*(6), 1–16. https://doi.org/10.1186/s41469-018-0030-9

Ghemawat, P., & Costa, J. (1993). The organizational tension between static and dynamic efficiency. *Strategic Management Journal, 14,* 59–73. https://www.jstor.org/stable/2486497

Hahn, T., Preuss, L., Pinkse, J., & Figge, F. (2014). Cognitive frames in corporate sustainability: Managerial sensemaking with paradoxical and business case frames. *Academy of Management*, 39(4), 463–487. http://dx.doi.org/10.5465/amr.2012.0341

Kaleta, A., Witek-Crabb, A., Lichtarski, J., M., Ignac,y J., & Rojek-Nowosielska, M. (2024). Perspektywa paradoksów w zarzadzaniu strategicznym, Przegląd Organizacji, nr. 985 DOI: 10.33141/po.2022.02.02

Langley, A., & Sloan, P. (2011). *Organizational Change and Dialectic Processes.* Abingdon, UK: Routledge.

Lewis, M. (2000). Exploring paradox: Toward a more comprehensive guide. *Academy of Management Review, 25*(4), 760–776. https://doi.org/10.2307/259204

Lewis M., & Smith K., (2014). Paradox as a metatheoretical perspective: Sharpening the focus and widening the scope. *The Journal of Applied Behavioral Science,* 127–149. http://dx.doi.org/10.1177/0021886314522322

Luscher, L., & Lewis, M. (2008). Organizational change and managerial sensemaking: Working through paradox. *Academy of Management Journal, 51*(2), 221–240. https://www.jstor.org/stable/20159506

Nielsen, R., K., Bevort, F., Henriksen, T., Hjalager, A., & Lyngard, D. (2023). *Navigating Leadership Paradox: Engaging Paradoxical Thinking in Practice*. Berlin/Boston: de Gruyter. DOI.10.1515/9783110788877

O'Reilly, C., & Tushman, M. (2008). Ambidexterity as a dynamic capability: Resolving the innovator's dilemma. *Research in Organizational Behavior*, *28*, 185–206. https://doi.org/10.1016/j.riob.2008.06.002

Polowczyk, J. (2014). Zarządzanie strategiczne jako wielowymiarowa przestrzeń paradoksów, *Studia Oeconomica Posnaniensia*, No.2.

Polowczyk, J. (2023), Taksonomia paradoksów w zarzadzaniu strategicznym, Szkoła Główna Handlowa, Zeszyt naukowy 194. https://doi.org/10.33119/sip.2023.194.3

Poole, M. S., & Van de Ven, A. (1989). Using paradox to build management and organizational theory. *Academy of Management Review*, *14*, 562–578. https://doi.org/10.2307/258559

Quinn, R. E. (1988). *Beyond Rational Management: Mastering the Paradoxes and Competing Demands of High Performance*. San Francisco, CA: Jossey-Bass.

Quinn J., Donaldson L., & Luo N. (2012). The benefits of persisting with paradigms in organizational research. *Academy of Management Research*, 26(1), 93–104. https://www.jstor.org/stable/23208287

Schad, J., Lewis, M., Raisch, S., & Smith, W., K. (2016). Paradox research in management science: Looking back to move forward. *Academy of Management Annals*, *10*(1), 5–64. 10.1080/19416520.2016.1162422

Siddawey, A., Wood, A. M., & Hedges L., V., (2019). How to do systematic review: A best practice guide for conducting and reporting narrative reviews, meta-analyzes and meta-synthesis. *Annual Review of Psychology*, *70*(1), 747–770. DOI: 10.1146/annurey-psych-010418 – 102803

Smith A., & Graetz F., (2006). Organizing dualities and strategizing for change. *Strategic Change*, *15*(5), 231–239. https://doi.org/10.1002/jsc.760

Smith, W. K., & Lewis, M. W. (2011). Toward a theory of paradox: A dynamic equilibrium model of organizing. *The Academy of Management Review*, *36*(2), 381–403. http://dx.doi.org/10.5465/AMR.2011.59330958

Smith, W., K., Lewis, M., W., Jarzabkowski, P., & Langley, A., (Eds.) (2017). *The Oxford Handbook of Organizational Paradox*. Oxford University Press. https://doi.org/10.1093/oxfordhb/9780198754428.001.0001

Smith, W. K & Tushman, M. L. (2005). Managing strategic contradictions: A top management model for managing innovation streams. *Organization Science*, *16*(5), 522–536. https://www.jstor.org/stable/25145990

Tryczak, J., Lis, A., & Ziemiański, P. (2023). Paradoxes in the engineering change management process. *Scientific Papers of Silesian University of Technology Publishing House*, *185*, 511–527.

Tsoukas, H., & Chia, R, (2002). An organizational becoming: Rethinking organizational change. *Organization Science*, *13*(5), 567–582. http://dx.doi.org/10.1287/orsc.13.5.567.7810

Tushman, M., & O'Reilly, C., (1996). Ambidextrous organizations: Managing evolutionary and revolutionary change. *California Management Review*, *38*(4), 8–30. https://doi.org/10.2307/41165852

Weiser, A., & Laamanen, T., (2022). Extending the dynamic equilibrium model of paradox: Unveiling the dissipative dynamics in organizations. *Organization Theory*, 3. https://doi.org/10.1177/26317877221090317

Weller, S., & Ran, B., (2020). Social entrepreneurship: The logic of paradox. *Sustainability*, *12*(24), 10624. https://doi.org/10.3390/su122410642

# 3 Ambidexterity

## A Strategic Approach to Overcoming Exploration and Exploitation Paradox

*Agnieszka Zakrzewska-Bielawska*

### 3.1 Introduction

Modern management increasingly revolves around paradoxes, which are becoming more pervasive and heightening the need for a management approach that equips researchers and practitioners to effectively address them (Clegg et al., 2002). Managers now recognize that organizations' paradoxical characteristics are not necessarily indicators of dysfunction; rather, they reflect organizational pluralism and complexity (Berti et al., 2021). As a result, managers are developing a paradox mindset rooted in integrative thinking – a willingness to view opposition as a normal and constructive aspect of organizational life (e Cunha et al., 2023) that helps them to manage organizations in a more effective way. Given the prevalence of paradoxes, managers must navigate the contradictions, oppositions, and tensions they create (Dameron & Torset, 2014; Farjoun, 2017). The question that arises, however, is how to do so effectively. A relatively new concept, ambidexterity, offers a potential solution. This concept equips managers to handle the tensions arising from exploratory and exploitative activities, enabling them to seek a balance between the two. Although these activities are inherently contradictory, they are essential for organizational growth and competitive advantage.

In management studies, ambidexterity has been intensively studied over the past two decades (e.g., Chakma, Paul, & Dhir, 2024; Junni et al., 2013; Saleh et al., 2023; Wenke et al., 2021). Researchers have explored the phenomenon from diverse perspectives and management domains. While this proliferation of studies has broadened and deepened our understanding of ambidexterity, it has also created ambiguity around how to resolve tensions between exploration and exploitation, achieve a balance, and assess its impact on corporate performance. Moreover, existing research has primarily focused on ambidexterity in companies operating in the United States, United Kingdom, and other Western European countries (Chakma et al., 2024; Roth & Corsi, 2023). However, there is a notable lack of studies, or only a limited number of works, investigating the paradox of exploration and exploitation in enterprises from Central and Eastern European (CEE) countries (e.g., Dodourova et al., 2023; Vogl et al., 2024; Zakrzewska-Bielawska, 2021). This creates a *research gap*. Therefore, a review

DOI: 10.4324/9781003541394-5

and synthesis of existing research from highly developed countries focused on understanding the management of the exploration-exploitation paradox through a strategic ambidexterity approach could inspire CEE researchers to conduct empirical studies in this area. Such efforts would help bridge the gap and further enrich the global body of knowledge on ambidexterity.

The purpose of this chapter is to identify the specificity and complexity of ambidexterity as a strategic approach that enables managers to cope with the exploration-exploitation paradox. To achieve this, a narrative review of the literature was conducted. This type of review provides a broad overview of research on a specific topic, synthesizing existing findings while highlighting overarching trends and debates. Although it adopts an unsystematic approach to selecting studies, often relying on the author's expertise or familiarity with the literature, it offers a high-level perspective on the state of knowledge (Byrne, 2016; Juntunen & Lehenkari, 2021; Zhou et al., 2017). However, it may not involve comprehensive searches of all relevant databases or the application of strict inclusion/exclusion criteria.

The chapter begins by explaining the paradox of exploration and exploitation. It then discusses ambidexterity as a strategic approach and identifies ways for balancing these two activities (various types of ambidexterity). The final section explores the tensions this paradox creates in different areas of organizational management and evaluates the impact of ambidexterity on corporate performance.

## 3.2 Exploration and Exploitation Paradox

Paradoxes in modern management involve contradictory yet interrelated elements that coexist simultaneously and persist over time (Cameron & Quinn, 1988; Smith & Lewis, 2011). These paradoxes often manifest as conflicting demands, opposing perspectives, or seemingly illogical findings that remain prevalent in organizational contexts (Berti & Cunha, 2023; Gaim & Wåhlin, 2016; Lewis, 2000; Smith & Tracey, 2016). Organizational paradoxes are also understood as manifestations of tensions, defined as "cognitively and/or socially constructed polarities that obscure the interrelatedness of the contradictions" (Lewis, 2000). Additionally, they are linked to dilemmas, which are described as forced choices between equally attractive or unattractive options (Putnam et al., 2016). Consequently, paradoxes serve as an "umbrella concept that encompasses the conceptual map for all organizational tensions and contradictions" (Cunha & Putnam, 2019). However, this broad conceptualization can sometimes lead to confusion (Berti & Cunha, 2023).

The dual nature of paradoxes makes them prevalent in organizational management, with one of the most extensively discussed being the paradox of exploration and exploitation. This paradox refers to the challenge organizations face in balancing the need to explore new opportunities (exploration) with the need to exploit existing capabilities and resources (exploitation). This balance is crucial for innovation and long-term success but inherently involves tensions and trade-offs (Andriopoulos & Lewis, 2009; Zakrzewska-Bielawska, 2021).

The terms *exploration* and *exploitation* were first introduced by Schumpeter (1934) and later popularized by March (1991). Exploration expresses search, variation, risk-taking, experimentation, play, flexibility, discovery, and innovation (March, 1991). These activities facilitate the creation of new knowledge, helping firms navigate uncharted territories and capitalize on emerging opportunities (Levinthal & March, 1993). Exploration also fosters the development of social capital by enabling collaborations, networking, and trust-building within and beyond organizational boundaries (Benitez et al., 2018; Lavie et al., 2011). By challenging existing market norms and paradigms, exploration opens pathways for firms to identify and address unmet customer needs and to pioneer innovative products or services with unique benefits (Sirén et al., 2012; Smith & Tushman, 2005; Wenke et al., 2021). Firms adopting exploratory strategies aim to anticipate market demands, often seeking to shape rather than simply respond to customer preferences. These strategies are closely tied to disruptive innovation, which involves creating entirely new markets or significantly altering existing ones through transformative offerings (O'Cass et al., 2014). Activities associated with exploration are typically research-and-development-driven, focusing on developing breakthrough technologies, processes, or business models. They allow firms to remain competitive by staying ahead of industry trends and seizing first-mover advantages. Exploration capabilities are inherently long-term in nature and represent a departure from a firm's prior routines and competencies (Moreira, Navaia, & Ribau, 2022).

However, exploration is not without its challenges. It is inherently associated with high levels of uncertainty and risk, as the outcomes of exploratory efforts are unpredictable and often take significant time to materialize. These activities can lead to resource strain, as they require sustained investment with no immediate returns. Additionally, the experimental nature of exploration involves a high probability of failure, necessitating resilience and adaptability within organizations (Clauss et al., 2021). To successfully engage in exploration, organizations must embrace flexible and organic structures. Such structures facilitate decentralized decision-making, reduce rigid standardization, and enable adaptive responses to rapidly changing environments (Zhang & Sun, 2023). Employees need to exhibit a strong tolerance for failure, viewing setbacks as learning opportunities rather than obstacles (Ireland & Webb, 2009). Visionary leadership is crucial in this context, as it inspires teams to think beyond conventional boundaries and fosters a shared commitment to bold, innovative goals. Moreover, an organizational culture that values creativity, encourages experimentation, and is open to novel ideas is critical for sustaining exploratory activities (Zakrzewska-Bielawska, 2021). Exploration also benefits from external partnerships and networks, which can provide access to complementary knowledge, technological expertise, and market insights. Through collaborative ventures such as alliances, joint ventures, and open innovation initiatives, firms can enhance their exploratory efforts while sharing risks (Majid et al., 2021; Zahoor et al., 2024). Additionally, the integration of advanced analytics and digital technologies can support exploration by enabling data-driven decision-making and uncovering patterns that might otherwise go unnoticed (Liu et al., 2023b).

The key characteristics of exploration are illustrated in Figure 3.1, emphasizing its core meanings and terms as well as the organizational factors that enable it.

In summary, exploration is a vital activity for organizations aiming to drive long-term growth through radical innovation, despite its inherent risks and uncertainties. By fostering a supportive culture, structures, and leadership, firms can position themselves to thrive in an ever-changing business environment.

In contrast, exploitation involves activities such as refinement, choice, production, efficiency, selection, implementation, and execution (March, 1991). It focuses on optimizing and utilizing existing knowledge and resources to maximize output and achieve stability (Levinthal & March, 1993). This approach often relies on established relationships and well-defined processes, as organizations tend to replicate successful partnerships from the past, particularly those aligned in industry and organizational size (Lavie et al., 2011). Such collaborations emphasize trust, predictability, and familiarity, fostering open channels for knowledge sharing and creating environments characterized by routine and standardization. These qualities enable firms to maintain a consistent operational rhythm, leveraging proven systems to achieve predictable outcomes. Additionally, exploitation builds on strong operational competencies that facilitate efficiency in repetitive tasks such as production, financial operations, and commerce. This alignment with routinized, bureaucratic systems and tightly integrated processes supports seamless execution and enhances productivity (He & Wong, 2004; Koryak et al., 2018). It encourages a structured approach,

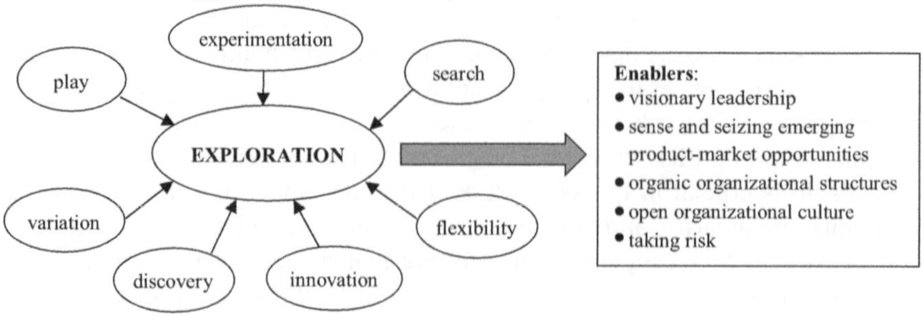


*Figure 3.1* Core Characteristics of Exploration.

wherein established practices and institutional knowledge play a pivotal role in driving operational excellence.

Deeply rooted in a firm's existing market presence and strategic goals, exploitation typically follows a path of incremental progress along established trajectories (Wenke et al., 2021). Rather than venturing into uncharted territories, this approach focuses on refining current products and services, improving quality, or achieving cost efficiencies. By concentrating on gradual improvements, firms can secure reliable, short-term performance outcomes, such as enhanced profitability or customer satisfaction (Sirén et al., 2012; Smith & Tushman, 2005; Gupta et al., 2006; O'Cass et al., 2014). This predictability often makes exploitation an attractive strategy, particularly for risk-averse organizations that prioritize operational stability and incremental gains. Exploitative activities are underpinned by disciplined, routine-based behaviors that emphasize resource efficiency and process optimization (Moreira et al., 2022). Through minor but consistent modifications to existing routines, technologies, and product offerings, firms can adapt to market demands while minimizing resource waste. This approach enhances competitiveness and reduces operational risks by relying on tried-and-true methods (Kohtamäki et al., 2010). By focusing on refining their core expertise, organizations ensure that their existing capabilities remain relevant and effective in addressing customer needs (O'Cass et al., 2014).

To succeed with an exploitation-driven approach, organizations often adopt specific structural and cultural characteristics. These include a hierarchical, top-down leadership style, which reinforces clarity in decision-making, and mechanistic structures that prioritize order and efficiency. Additionally, a conservative organizational culture underpins these activities, emphasizing adherence to established practices and fostering an environment where incremental improvements are valued over radical changes (Zakrzewska-Bielawska, 2021).

By relying on these foundations, firms engaging in exploitation can sustain long-term competitiveness through the systematic enhancement of existing resources and processes, aligning their operations closely with market demands while mitigating risks associated with innovation or change. The key characteristics of exploitation are illustrated in Figure 3.2, emphasizing its core meanings and terms as well as the organizational factors that enable it.

Compared to exploration, which thrives on flexibility and broadening horizons, exploitation is grounded in specialization and deep expertise in targeted domains. It benefits from standardized and formalized processes, which ensure the efficient application of this focused knowledge (Ireland & Webb, 2009). This strategy drives employees to commit to well-defined, short-term goals, aligning their efforts with the organization's immediate priorities. While exploration fosters adaptability and innovation, exploitation emphasizes continual improvement, efficiency, and refinement across the organizational landscape (Hu & Chen, 2016).

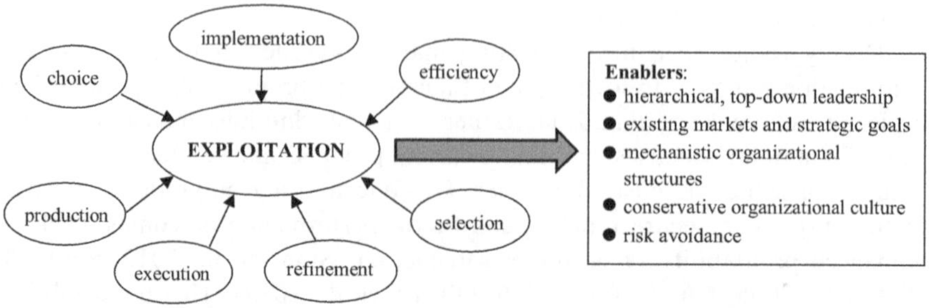


*Figure 3.2* Core Characteristics of Exploitation.

Organizations to persist, grow, and achieve a competitive advantage require both exploration and exploitation. These activities create a paradoxical relationship, imposing significantly different demands on organizational architectures, processes, and capabilities (Paredes & Olander Roese, 2024). Due to their inherently distinct nature, they generate ongoing and often conflicting demands within an organization, leading to various tensions. The prevailing view on the exploration-exploitation paradox emphasizes its generative character. This perspective highlights how persistent, conflicting demands and tensions can be harnessed as a driving force for change, renewal, and competitive advantage (e Cunha et al., 2023). Nonetheless, this paradox also encompasses pragmatic dimensions, particularly in how top management addresses and resolves these conflicting demands (Bao et al., 2022). Resolving organizational paradoxes requires a multifaceted approach that involves accepting and leveraging the paradox, clarifying and separating levels of analysis, temporally managing conflicting elements, and introducing new concepts (Cunha & Putnam, 2019; Smith & Lewis, 2011). In the case of the exploration-exploitation paradox, scholars propose solutions that either separate or integrate the conflicting demands. Central to this discussion is the concept of ambidexterity, which enables organizations to navigate and balance these tensions effectively.

## 3.3 Ambidexterity: Navigating the Contradictions of Exploration and Exploitation

The pursuit of addressing the paradox of exploration and exploitation has been widely studied and debated, leading to the concept of ambidexterity. The vast majority of scholars define ambidexterity as a strategic capability (e.g., Kortmann et al., 2014; O'Reilly & Tushman, 2013; Ramachandran et al., 2019; Zahoor et al., 2024) that enables a firm to execute inherently paradoxical strategies. These strategies embody and manifest two main objectives, exploration and exploitation, that carry tensions, trade-offs, and performance dilemmas (Han

& Celly, 2008). A significant body of research also considers ambidexterity to be a dynamic capability (e.g., O'Reilly & Tushman, 2008; Popadiuk et al., 2018; Weiss & Kanbach, 2022), as firms must reconfigure their competencies to balance exploration and exploitation. In this view, ambidexterity is seen as a set of actions (or routines) taken by top management to identify opportunities and reconfigure resources to capitalize on them (Kriz et al., 2014). Therefore, we define ambidexterity as the dynamic and strategic capability of an organization to explore new competencies while exploiting existing ones. This capability is expressed through the combination of the scale of activities related to paradoxical in nature exploration and exploitation, as well as the pursuit of a relative balance between them.

The strategic nature of ambidexterity has led to this phenomenon being studied not only from diverse theoretical perspectives but also across different levels of the organization and its environment. The contribution of ambidexterity to the field of organizational studies can be categorized into four evolutionary stages (Audretsch & Guerrero, 2023; Birkinshaw& Gupta, 2013; Guerrero, 2021) as (1) the initial stage (1995–2005), highlighting its importance and foundational concepts; (2) the expansion stage (2006–2009), marked by growth in definitions, antecedents, and consequences; (3) the consolidation stage (2010–2019), focused on identifying multiple tensions; and (4) the rejuvenation stage (2020–2023), characterized by an emerging re-focus on the concept. Their short characteristics are presented in Table 3.1.

Despite the extensive research on ambidexterity, there is still no consensus on how to navigate the contradictions between exploration and exploitation. As the field has evolved, individual proposals have emerged, reflecting diverse perspectives. Researchers have suggested various approaches to addressing this paradox, differing based on the dimensions of time and space, the level of analysis, or the theoretical perspective adopted.

Initially, the time dimension – understood as the extent to which ambidexterity is pursued simultaneously or sequentially over time – was a key focus of discussion. Early on, temporal ambidexterity was introduced, highlighting the sequential nature of exploration and exploitation. This approach, also referred to as sequential ambidexterity, involves organizations focusing on one activity at a time, alternating between periods of exploration and periods of exploitation to maintain balance over the long term (Lavie & Rosenkopf, 2006). It treats the two activities as mutually exclusive, positioning them as ends of a single continuum. Consequently, the pursuit of balance between these activities, particularly regarding their impact on an organization's long-term effectiveness, is often conceptualized through the lens of an inverted U-shaped relationship (Gupta, Smith, & Shalley, 2006).

As organizational demands grew more complex, the concept of simultaneous ambidexterity emerged. While exploration generates new knowledge and exploitation applies it, each activity drives the need for the other. Managing both

*Table 3.1* Evolution of Ambidexterity Studies

| *Stage* | *Characteristics* | *Major References* |
|---|---|---|
| Initial (1995–2005) | • Conceptualization of ambidexterity<br>• Focus on organizational structures<br>• Characteristics of ambidextrous organizations<br>• Link to innovation and performance<br><br>Concentration on understanding ambidexterity as a mechanism for balancing innovation and performance through dual structures. Organizations were seen as needing specific structures to facilitate innovation, combining separation, and integration to meet diverse needs. Key traits of ambidextrous organizations included higher performance, stability without disruptive changes, overcoming inertia, and proactive adaptation to external changes. This stage emphasized the link between ambidexterity, innovation, and sustained performance but did not yet explore connections with entrepreneurship | Spender & Kessler (1995)<br>Tushman & O'Reilly (1996)<br>Benner & Tushman (2003)<br>Birkinshaw & Gibson (2004)<br>He & Wong (2004)<br>O'Reilly & Tushman (2004)<br>Van Looy et al. (2005) |
| Expansion (2006–2009) | • Exploration vs. exploitation tension<br>• Resource allocation focus<br>• Dynamic capabilities perspective<br>• Different conceptual and empirical approaches<br>• Emergence of strategic ambidexterity<br><br>Focus on balancing exploration and exploitation to improve performance, addressing tensions like integration vs. diversification and static vs. dynamic forces. Key influences included March's view on resource allocation and Teece et al.'s emphasis on dynamic capabilities. Research explored ambidexterity through different lenses, including knowledge management, strategic management, and organizational behavior. This period also saw the emergence of strategic ambidexterity, focusing on individual, and team decision-making in balancing operational activities. However, the connection between ambidexterity, innovation, and entrepreneurship was still overlooked | Lubatkin et al. (2006)<br>Vinekar et al. (2006)<br>Jansen et al. (2008)<br>Li et al. (2008)<br>Raisch & Birkinshaw (2008)<br>Cao et al. (2009)<br>Carmeli & Halevi (2009)<br>Chang et al. (2009)<br>Jansen et al. (2009)<br>Mom et al., (2009)<br>Raisch et al. (2009)<br>Simsek (2009) |

(*Continued*)

*Table 3.1* (*Continued*)

| *Stage* | *Characteristics* | *Major References* |
|---|---|---|
| Consolidation (2010–2019) | • Proliferation of theoretical frameworks<br>• Expansion of empirical research focusing on new structural and contextual tensions<br>• Emergence of new forms of ambidexterity<br>• Consolidation in innovation ambidexterity<br>• Ambidexterity in entrepreneurship<br>• Growing number of literature reviews, meta-analyses, and co-citation analyses<br><br>Focus on a proliferation of theoretical frameworks across diverse disciplines, such as psychology, anthropology, contingency management, agency theory, corporate social performance, human resource management, big data, conflict management, etc. Empirical studies expanded to explore new structural and contextual tensions, including alignment vs. adaptiveness in projects, insourcing vs. outsourcing in clusters, etc. New forms of ambidexterity emerged, e.g., employee ambidexterity, service-sales ambidexterity, and ambidextrous leadership, while innovation ambidexterity research became more prominent in large organizations. Entrepreneurship-focused ambidexterity concepts, such as venturing and entrepreneurial university ambidexterity, also gained attention, reflecting a broadening and deepening of the field | Rosing et al. (2011)<br>Bot (2012)<br>Jansen et al. (2012)<br>Nosella et al. (2012)<br>Birkinshaw & Gupta (2013)<br>O'Reilly & Tushman (2013)<br>Turner & Lee-Kelley (2013)<br>Wei et al. (2014)<br>Kao & Chen (2016)<br>D'Souza et al. (2017)<br>Zhou et al. (2018)<br>Adler et al. (2019)<br>Martin et al. (2019) |
| Rejuvenation (2020–2023) | • Expansion to new geographic and social contexts<br>• Exploration of ambidexterity during challenging times (e.g., crises, resilience)<br>• Investigation of new tensions and paradoxes<br>• Integration of the ecosystem perspective<br>• Focus on technological disruptions<br><br>This stage is marked by exponential publication growth and novel advancements reflecting changing socioeconomic and technological contexts. It explores new geographic and social settings, examines resilience and public policy during crises, and investigates emerging tensions like public vs. private dynamics, rival vs. collaborators, or diversity vs. meritocracy. An ecosystem perspective gains prominence, emphasizing inter-organizational configurations and collaborative platforms. Technological disruptions, including chatbots, blockchain, and big data, also significantly broaden the scope and relevance of ambidexterity studies | Iborra et al. (2020)<br>Wu et al. (2020)<br>Benzidia et al. (2021)<br>De Silva et al. (2022)<br>Doblinger et al. (2022)<br>Khan et al. (2022)<br>Priyanka et al. (2022)<br>Yu et al. (2022)<br>Fan et al. (2023)<br>Roth & Corsi (2023) |

simultaneously is challenging yet essential, as they are not opposing but coexisting activities (Farjoun, 2002). Therefore, exploration and exploitation should be viewed as orthogonal activities that interact, coexist, and complement each other (Gupta et al., 2006). Scholars, however, hold differing views on how to achieve a balance between them. Some researchers argue for a balance between the two activities (He & Wong, 2004), while others advocate for an unequal emphasis, suggesting prioritizing either exploration (Levinthal & March, 1993) or exploitation (Nagji & Tuff, 2012), depending on the organization's capabilities and environmental conditions (D'Souza et al., 2017; Uotila et al., 2009). Meanwhile, others recommend maximizing both activities simultaneously (Cao, Gedajlovic, & Zhang, 2009).

Considering the space dimension – which captures whether ambidexterity occurs within independent or interdependent organizational units – two approaches have been distinguished: Structural separation (differentiation) and integration (Raisch et al., 2009). The first approach, known as structural ambidexterity, involves deploying exploration and exploitation activities in separate organizational units, with these activities carried out simultaneously (Huang & Kim, 2013; Kang & Snell, 2009; O'Reilly & Tushman, 2004). Top management plays a crucial role in coordinating them, enabling the use of distinct strategies, structures, and processes (Jansen et al., 2008). The second approach, referred to as harmonic ambidexterity, entails the simultaneous pursuit of exploration and exploitation within the same entity (Kassotaki, 2022). This approach presents significant challenges as exploration and exploitation activities compete for limited resources, often resulting in conflict, contradictions, and inconsistencies.

As attention shifted to the level of analysis – macro (organization-wide) vs. micro (individual level) – contextual ambidexterity was introduced (Gibson & Birkinshaw, 2004; Möller et al., 2022). This approach focuses on the behavioral ability of employees and managers to simultaneously engage in exploration and exploitation within their roles. Unlike structural ambidexterity at the macro level, which often separates these activities, contextual ambidexterity emphasizes their integration within the same context. It recognizes that individuals frequently face both demands in their daily work, requiring them to make their own judgments about how to allocate time between conflicting priorities. This perspective highlights the critical role of organizational context and culture in enabling employees to balance these competing demands effectively (Kang & Snell, 2009; Rao & Mattarelli, 2024; Wang & Rafiq, 2014).

The role of leadership in balancing exploration and exploitation activities resulted in the emergence of leadership ambidexterity (Carmeli & Halevi, 2009; Lawrence et al., 2022). This view highlighted the importance of managers in navigating the contradictions between exploration and exploitation. Leaders were seen as pivotal in integrating these opposing activities, overcoming structural or organizational barriers, and fostering alignment with the company's strategic objectives (Boumgarden et al., 2012). Leadership ambidexterity focuses on managerial skills to ensure the coexistence of innovation and efficiency within the organization. It is examined not only from the organizational level but also through the lens of contextual ambidexterity (Carmeli & Halevi, 2009; van Assen, 2020).

There are also studies that examine more than one dimension of balancing exploration and exploitation. Based on them, scholars have proposed their own typologies, which further categorize approaches to ambidexterity. For example, reciprocal ambidexterity refers to the synergistic fusion of complementary exploration and exploitation activities that occur in sequence and are spatially separated (Simsek, 2009). Another example is peripatric ambidexterity, which is achieved at the individual level in a sequential manner (Prange & Schlegelmilch, 2009).

More recently, ambidexterity has combined different methods of balancing exploration and exploitation across organizational levels. This perspective recognizes that organizations can employ structural separation at the corporate level, contextual integration at the unit level, and sequential adjustments at the project level, tailoring their approach to specific circumstances. By dynamically adapting methods to meet organizational needs and external conditions, companies can achieve greater flexibility and effectiveness. This approach is referred to as dynamic ambidexterity (Chen, 2017). Similarly, relative ambidexterity assumes that different methods of balancing exploration and exploitation are context-dependent, with the optimal balance varying by industry and strategic group. This perspective emphasizes that organizations should consider their specific environments, resources, and competitive landscapes when determining how to balance these activities (D'Souza et al., 2017).

Lastly, a more recent advance in paradox research has introduced another possibility: A curvilinear link between exploration and exploitation. This possibility includes this link in the same space and at the same time, resulting in both partial trade-offs and partial synergies in a nonlinear pattern. It reframes the exploration-exploitation paradox as a duality, both partially conflicting (for partial trade-off) and partially complementary (for partial synergy), and is called yin-yang balancing (Li, 2014; Schad et al., 2016). This approach examines how opposites interact within a system. At a given time or space, one opposite plays a dominant role while the other is subordinate, creating an asymmetrical balance. Over time, their roles shift through a transitional phase, marked by a tipping point. The relationship between opposites follows a U-shaped curve: At low levels, they are least complementary and most conflicting, but at moderate levels, they complement each other best, resulting in synergy and minimal conflict. The most effective balance occurs when the dominant opposite is moderately high, and the subordinate is moderately low, ensuring harmony and optimal interaction (Li et al., 2023). In summary, yin-yang balancing suggests that exploration and exploitation can – and should – be balanced simultaneously in an interactive manner. This is particularly true when viewed as a duality that involves both

*Table 3.2* Dealing with the Exploration-Exploitation Paradox: Ambidexterity Types

| *Dimension* | *Types of Ambidexterity* |
|---|---|
| Time<br>(sequentiality vs. simultaneity) | • temporal ambidexterity<br>• sequential ambidexterity<br>○ balance dimension of exploration and exploitation<br>○ combined dimension of exploration and exploitation |
| Space<br>(independently or interdependently) | • structural separation<br>• integration |
| Level of analysis<br>(macro vs. micro) | • structural ambidexterity<br>• contextual ambidexterity |
| Leadership | • leadership ambidexterity on an organizational level<br>• leadership ambidexterity on a contextual level |
| Time & space | • harmonic ambidexterity<br>• partitional (structural) ambidexterity<br>• cyclical (punctuated) ambidexterity<br>• reciprocal ambidexterity |
| Time and level of analysis | • punctuated ambidexterity<br>• structural ambidexterity<br>• contextual ambidexterity<br>• peripatric ambidexterity |
| Different methods of balancing exploration and exploitation across organizational levels | • dynamic ambidexterity<br>• relative ambidexterity |
| Duality<br>(trade-off vs. synergy) | • linear models (mentioned above)<br>• yin-yang balancing |

partial trade-offs and partial synergies, achieved through mechanisms of partial separation and partial integration.

Table 3.2 synthesizes the discussed types of ambidexterity, illustrating how to navigate the contradictions between exploration and exploitation.

Overall, the evolution of ambidexterity reflects a growing recognition of its complexity and the need for diverse, multi-level, and adaptive strategies. Early approaches focused on separating exploration and exploitation through time or structure. Later perspectives increasingly highlighted integration, leadership, and the role of context, while the most recent approach emphasizes yin-yang balancing, enabling organizations to navigate these tensions more holistically. The challenge of overcoming the exploration and exploitation paradox through ambidexterity has been studied extensively by researchers from both theoretical and empirical perspectives. Therefore, the next chapter provides a brief review of the major studies.

## 3.4 Paradoxes in Research from an Ambidexterity Perspective

The paradox of exploration and exploitation emerges across various areas of organizational management. Scholars have conducted reviews of existing studies, grouping them by theoretical perspectives and analyzing them across different domains. For example, Papachroni, Heracleous, and Paroutis (2015) explored a variety of literature, encompassing areas such as organizational learning, technological innovation, organizational design, innovation, and strategic management.

Zakrzewska-Bielawska (2021), using a systematic literature review, classified ambidexterity studies into eleven key management domains, including general management, strategic management, knowledge management/organizational learning, innovation management, project management, human resources management, organizational design, leadership, organizational culture, alliances/partnerships/networks, and performance. Snehvrat et al. (2018) analyzed the proliferation of ambidexterity research within the management field, categorizing studies into eight areas: Human resources, leadership and behavioral sciences, information systems, innovation/technology/research and development/engineering/project management, marketing, operations/TQM/supply chain management, organization, and strategy. In turn, Saleh, Durugbo, and Almahamid (2023), through a systematic review, identified seven key fields of ambidexterity research: Process mechanisms, organizational learning, leadership styles, technology investments, organizational contexts, environmental uncertainties, and institutional pressures. While Chakma, Paul, and Dhir (2024), in a hybrid and integrative review, grouped ambidexterity studies according to theoretical approaches, including behavioral integration, the paradoxical view, organizational learning, the attention-based view, contingency theory, upper echelon theory, the knowledge-based view, and dynamic capabilities.

Taking into account overview papers and considering that ambidexterity has been examined across many diverse areas of management. Table 3.3 highlights the most frequent and commonly studied management domains. It includes the paradox of exploration-exploitation in particular areas and tensions associated with them from the lens of ambidexterity research.

The paradox of exploration and exploitation in organizational management manifests differently across various organizational fields. It is a natural and ubiquitous aspect of organizational operations, often triggering tensions that managers must address. These tensions can be particularly challenging, requiring managers to remain both aware and flexible while developing the organization's strategic and dynamic capabilities to effectively explore and exploit. This necessity underscores the importance of shaping ambidexterity. Organizations may adopt linear models of ambidexterity or embrace yin-yang balancing, depending on their resources, context, and external conditions. Successfully balancing

*Table 3.3* Paradox of Exploration-Exploitation with Associated Tensions in Management Studies

| *Domain of Management* | *Paradox* | | *Tension* |
|---|---|---|---|
| | *Exploration* | *Exploitation* | |
| Organizational learning | New knowledge<br>Double-loop learning<br>Tacit knowledge<br>Routines | Old knowledge<br>Single-loop learning<br>Explicit knowledge<br>Experimentation | Search vs. refinement<br>Variation vs. implementation |
| Innovation | Radical/discontinuous innovation | Incremental innovation | Change vs. continuity<br>Chaos vs. inertia<br>Rigidity vs. capability |
| Strategic management | Build on new competencies<br>Deliberate strategy<br>New product – market domains<br>Proactive market orientation<br>Dynamic efficiency | Build on existing competencies<br>Emergent strategy<br>Existing product-market domains<br>Reactive market orientation<br>Static efficiency | Leverage vs. stretch<br>Chaos vs. control<br>Creativity vs. logic<br>Creativity vs. profitability |
| Organizational design | Organic structures<br>Decentralization<br>Autonomy<br>Non-routine tasks<br>Informalization | Mechanistic structures<br>Centralization<br>Hierarchy<br>Routine tasks<br>Formalization | Flexibility vs. efficiency |
| Organizational context | Social support<br>Support<br>Trust | Performance management<br>Discipline<br>Strech | Adaptation vs. alignment |
| Leadership | Transformational leadership<br>Opening leader behaviors | Transactional leadership<br>Closing leader behaviors | Empowerment vs. control bottom-up vs. top-down |

exploration and exploitation through ambidexterity allows organizations to gain a competitive advantage and enhance performance. Overemphasis on existing competencies can lead to a "success trap," where organizational inertia hinders adaptation to changing environmental conditions, resulting in poor performance. Conversely, prioritizing exploratory innovation excessively may result in a "failure trap" (Levinthal & March, 1993). Firms capable of integrating exploitation and exploration simultaneously are better positioned to survive and achieve higher profitability and sustained growth (Koryak et al., 2018).

Many researchers have studied how ambidexterity enables firm survival, competitive advantage, and performance gains. Analyzing recent review papers on the state of ambidexterity research (Chakma et al., 2024; Kassotaki, 2022; Papachroni et al., 2015; Saleh, Durugbo, & Almahamid, 2023; Snehvrat et al., 2018; Zakrzewska-Bielawska, 2021), it is evident that a significant majority demonstrate a positive relationship. Ambidexterity has been shown to positively impact various performance metrics, including sales growth, innovation, profitability, transition to scale, return on investment, cash flows, market share, short-term and long-term firm performance, and market valuation. Additionally, it enhances subjectively perceived performance indicators such as company reputation, employee satisfaction, and organizational survival.

The relationship between ambidexterity and firm performance has been examined across various contexts, including mergers and acquisitions, manufacturing firms, high-tech companies, multinational enterprises, small and medium-sized firms, and corporate ventures. Additionally, it has been studied at multiple levels, such as the firm level, business unit level, project and team levels, and the individual level. Researchers have expressed opposing views on the impact of ambidexterity on companies' performance. Therefore, this relationship should be further explored using different methods, indicators, influencing factors, and levels of analysis.

Although most studies report a positive relationship between ambidexterity and performance, some indicate that ambidexterity has no effect on it (Vrontis et al., 2017) or even a negative relationship (Lavie et al., 2011). Boumgarden et al. (2012), in turn, identify ambiguities in ambidexterity theory, specifically regarding how exploration, exploitation, and firm performance are related. They suggest that ambidextrous organizations achieve high performance by maintaining a balance between exploration and exploitation. In contrast, imbalances or mismatched design elements reduce performance and survival chances. Organizations tend to gravitate toward optimal configurations of exploration and exploitation, with deviations leading to performance declines. Similarly, Riccaboni and Moliterni (2009) argue that firms balancing these activities effectively gain stability, a competitive advantage, and central positions within their networks.

A key contribution in this area is the work of Junni et al. (2013), who conducted a meta-analysis to define the relationship between organizational ambidexterity and performance. They explored this relationship through various contextual and methodological moderators, including how ambidexterity and company performance are measured, the levels of analysis, data collection approaches, and the operational sectors of the studied enterprises. Their findings highlighted the significance of these moderators and their impact on the strength of the ambidexterity-performance relationship. The analysis revealed that studies using diverse methods and cross-sectional data demonstrate a stronger relationship between ambidexterity and company performance than those relying on archival data. Additionally, subjective measures of company performance show stronger effects than objective measures. Combined ambidexterity was found to have a stronger relationship with company performance than balanced ambidexterity. The relationship between ambidexterity and performance is also stronger at higher levels of analysis, such as at the company or alliance level. Finally, the impact of ambidexterity on performance is weaker in the manufacturing sector.

Considering the region and country, the most impactful research, with the highest number of citations, originated from the United States and the United Kingdom (UK), followed by China. Other productive countries included Canada and Taiwan. Research from Europe constitutes the largest group overall, with significant contributions, beyond the UK, coming from Italy, Switzerland, the Netherlands, Spain, and Austria. Other European countries are represented by only a few or single articles, highlighting a distinct shortage of studies from CEE (Chakma et al., 2024; Roth & Corsi, 2023). For example, Zakrzewska-Bielawska (2021) examined the strategic choices of Polish companies from an ambidexterity perspective, considering environmental, resource, structural, process, and cultural factors. Vogl et al. (2024) investigated ambidexterity within the context of CEE by studying an internationalizing SME in the Czech Republic. Dodourova, Zhao, and Harzing (2023) adopted a micro-foundations approach to study eleven multinational corporations in Bulgaria's software development industry, focusing on local research and development projects. Their research identified four types of ambidexterity: Global knowledge differentiator, global-local knowledge integrator, emerging local-global integrator, and local knowledge integrator. Additionally, Popadić, Černe, and Milohnić (2015) analyzed the impact of exploration, exploitation, and ambidexterity on innovation performance in Bulgarian, the Czech Republic, Estonian, Romanian, and Slovakian firms. Despite these contributions, research on ambidexterity in the CEE region remains insufficient, often addressing narrow, isolated issues that limit the identification of patterns characteristic of this region. This underscores and reinforces the need for further studies on the paradox of exploration-exploitation in the CEE context.

Extensive research on ambidexterity demonstrates that the paradox of exploration and exploitation remains a central theme in organizational management, with significant implications for both theory and practice. The diverse body of research highlights the complexity of balancing these two activities across various domains, such as innovation, strategic management, human resources, and organizational design. Studies show that achieving this balance through ambidexterity can enhance competitive advantage and foster long-term success. However, the relationship between ambidexterity and performance is complex, with outcomes varying depending on organizational context, design, and external factors.

## 3.5 Conclusion

In conclusion, the exploration and exploitation paradox represents a critical challenge for modern organizations seeking to innovate while maintaining operational efficiency. The tension between exploration – focused on risk, flexibility, and long-term innovation – and exploitation centered on optimization, efficiency, and short-term stability – requires organizations to manage contradictory demands simultaneously. Both strategies are essential for a firm's growth and competitiveness, but their inherent conflicts can create organizational stress and complexity. Rather than viewing these paradoxes as detrimental, however, modern management embraces them as opportunities for dynamic change, fostering resilience, and enabling a continuous competitive advantage.

Over time, the concept of ambidexterity has evolved, reflecting a growing understanding of its complexity and the diverse ways in which organizations can balance these contradictory activities. Early approaches focused on separating exploration and exploitation temporally or structurally. As the field matured, a more integrated view emerged, recognizing that exploration and exploitation are not mutually exclusive but complementary when managed effectively. More recent advancements, such as yin-yang balancing, offer a nuanced perspective, suggesting that exploration and exploitation can coexist and interact dynamically, with partial trade-offs and synergies emerging at different times and in various contexts. Overall, the evolution of ambidexterity highlights its increasing importance as a mechanism for sustaining long-term organizational success. However, the relationship between ambidexterity and firm performance is complex, with varying outcomes depending on contextual factors.

Many studies underscore the importance of adopting ambidexterity to navigate the tensions inherent in the exploration-exploitation paradox. Future studies should continue to explore the conditions under which ambidexterity produces positive outcomes and investigate the mechanisms that help firms adapt to changing circumstances, particularly in the CEE region. By refining our understanding of ambidexterity and its impact, organizations can better leverage this concept to foster innovation, improve operational efficiency, and sustain competitive advantage.

## References

Adler, R., Hiromoto, T., & Suzuki, H. (2019). Amoeba management and organizational ambidexterity: Similarities, differences, and implications for organizational fit and success. *International Journal of Productivity and Performance Management, 69*(2), 405–427.

Andriopoulos, C., & Lewis, M. W. (2009). Exploitation-exploration tensions and organizational ambidexterity: Managing paradoxes of innovation. *Organization Science, 20*(4), 696–717.

Audretsch, D. B., & Guerrero, M. (2023). Is ambidexterity the missing link between entrepreneurship, management, and innovation? *The Journal of Technology Transfer, 48*(6), 1891–1918.

Bao, Y., Yuan, W., Bao, Y., & Olson, B. (2022). Does more CEO ambivalence lead to higher organizational ambidexterity? A paradoxical perspective. *IEEE Transactions on Engineering Management, 69*, 2386–2398.

Benitez, J., Castillo, A., Llorens, J., & Braojos, J. (2018). IT-enabled knowledge ambidexterity and innovation performance in small US firms: The moderator role of social media capability. *Information & Management, 55*(1), 131–143.

Benner, M. J., & Tushman, M. L. (2003). Exploitation, exploration, and process management: The productivity dilemma revisited. *Academy of Management Review, 28*(2), 238–256.

Benzidia, S., Makaoui, N., & Subramanian, N. (2021). Impact of ambidexterity of blockchain technology and social factors on new product development: A supply chain and Industry 4.0 perspective. *Technological Forecasting and Social Change, 169*, 120819.

Berti, M., & Cunha, M. P. E. (2023). Paradox, dialectics or trade-offs? A double loop model of paradox. *Journal of Management Studies, 60*(4), 861–888.

Berti, M., Simpson, A., Cunha, M. P., & Clegg, S. R. (2021). *Elgar Introduction to Organizational Paradox Theory*. Cheltenham: Edward Elgar Publishing.

Birkinshaw, J., & Gibson, C. (2004). Building ambidexterity into an organization. *MIT Sloan Management Review, 45*, 47–55.

Birkinshaw, J., & Gupta, K. (2013). Clarifying the distinctive contribution of ambidexterity to the field of organization studies. *Academy of Management Perspectives, 27*(4), 287–298.

Bot, S. D. (2012). Process ambidexterity for entrepreneurial firms. *Technology Innovation Management Review, 2*(4), 21–27.

Boumgarden, P., Nickerson, J., & Zenger, T. R. (2012). Sailing into the wind: Exploring the relationships among ambidexterity, vacillation, and organizational performance. *Strategic Management Journal, 33*(6), 587–610.

Byrne, J. A. (2016). Improving the peer review of narrative literature reviews. *Research Integrity and Peer Review, 1*, 1–4.

Cameron, K. S., & Quinn, R. E. (1988). Organizational paradox and transformation. In Quinn, R. E., & Cameron, K. S. (Eds.), *Paradox and Transformation: Toward a Theory of Change in Organization and Management* (pp. 1–14). Cambridge, MA: Ballinger Publishing Co/Harper & Row Publishers.

Cao, Q., Gedajlovic, E., & Zhang, H. (2009). Unpacking organizational ambidexterity: Dimensions, contin- gencies, and synergistic effects. *Organization Science, 20*(4), 781–796.

Carmeli, A., & Halevi, M. Y. (2009). How top management team behavioral integration and behavioral complexity enable organizational ambidexterity: The moderating role of contextual ambidexterity. *The Leadership Quarterly*, *20*(2), 207–218.

Chakma, R., Paul, J., & Dhir, S. (2024). Organizational ambidexterity: A review and research agenda. *IEEE Transactions on Engineering Management*, *71*, 121–137.

Chang, Y. C., Yang, P. Y., & Chen, M. H. (2009). The determinants of academic research commercial performance: Towards an organizational ambidexterity perspective. *Research Policy*, *38*(6), 936–946.

Chen, Y. (2017). Dynamic ambidexterity: How innovators manage exploration and exploitation. *Business Horizons*, *60*(3), 385–394.

Clauss, T., Kraus, S., Kallinger, F. L., Bican, P. M., Brem, A., & Kailer, N. (2021). Organizational ambidexterity and competitive advantage: The role of strategic agility in the exploration-exploitation paradox. *Journal of Innovation & Knowledge*, *6*(4), 203–213.

Clegg, S. R., da Cunha, J. V., & e Cunha, M. P. (2002). Management paradoxes: A relational view. *Human Relations*, *55*(5), 483–503.

Cunha, M. P. E., & Putnam, L. L. (2019). Paradox theory and the paradox of success. *Strategic Organization*, *17*(1), 95–106.

Dameron, S., & Torset, C. (2014). The discursive construction of strategists' subjectivities: Towards a paradox lens on strategy. *Journal of Management Studies*, *51*(2), 291–319.

D'Souza, D. E., Sigdyal, P., & Struckell, E. (2017). Relative ambidexterity: A measure and a versatile framework. *Academy of Management Perspectives*, *31*(2), 124–136.

De Silva, M., Howells, J., Khan, Z., & Meyer, M. (2022). Innovation ambidexterity and public innovation intermediaries: The mediating role of capabilities. *Journal of Business Research*, *149*, 14–29.

Doblinger, C., Wales, W., & Zimmermann, A. (2022). Stemming the downturn: How ambidexterity and public policy influence firm performance stability during economic crises. *European Management Journal*, *40*(2), 163–174.

Dodourova, M., Zhao, S., & Harzing, A. W. (2023). Ambidexterity in MNC knowledge sourcing in emerging economies: A microfoundational perspective. *International Business Review*, *32*(2), 101854.

e Cunha, M. P., Rego, A., Berti, M., & Simpson, A. V. (2023). Understanding pragmatic paradoxes: When contradictions become paralyzing and what to do about it. *Business Horizons*, *66*(4), 453–462.

Fan, H., Gao, W., & Han, B. (2023). Are AI chatbots a cure-all? The relative effectiveness of chatbot ambidexterity in crafting hedonic and cognitive smart experiences. *Journal of Business Research*, *156*, 113526.

Farjoun, M. (2002). Towards an organic perspective on strategy. *Strategic Management Journal*, *23*(7), 561–594.

Farjoun, M. (2017). Contradictions, dialectics, and paradoxes. In A. Langley & H. Tsoukas (Eds.), *The Sage Handbook of Process Organization Studies* (pp. 87–109). Los Angeles, CA: Sage.

Gaim, M., & Wåhlin, N. (2016). In search of a creative space: A conceptual framework of synthesizing paradoxical tensions. *Scandinavian Journal of Management*, *32*(1), 33–44.

Gibson, C. B., & Birkinshaw, J. (2004). The antecedents, consequences and mediating role of organizational ambidexterity. *Academy of Management Journal, 47*(2), 209–226.

Guerrero, M. (2021). Ambidexterity and entrepreneurship studies: A literature review and research agenda. *Foundations and Trends® in Entrepreneurship, 17*(5–6), 436–650.

Gupta, A. K., Smith, K. G., & Shalley, C. E. (2006). The interplay between exploration and exploitation. *Academy of Management Journal, 49*(4), 693–706.

Han, M., & Celly, N. (2008). Strategic ambidexterity and performance in international new ventures. *Canadian Journal of Administrative Sciences, 25*(4), 335–349.

He, Z. L., & Wong, P. K. (2004). Exploration vs. exploitation: An empirical test of the ambidexterity hypothesis. *Organization Science, 15*(4), 481–494.

Hu, B., & Chen, W. (2016). Business model ambidexterity and technological performance: Evidence from China. *Technology Analysis and Strategic Management, 28*(5), 583–600.

Huang, J., & Kim, H. J. (2013). Conceptualizing structural ambidexterity into the innovation of human resource management architecture: The case of LG Electronics. *The International Journal of Human Resource Management, 24*(5), 922–943.

Iborra, M., Safón, V., & Dolz, C. (2020). What explains the resilience of SMEs? Ambidexterity capability and strategic consistency. *Long Range Planning, 53*(6), 101947.

Ireland, R. D., & Webb, J. W. (2009). Crossing the great divide of strategic entrepreneurship: Transitioning between exploration and exploitation. *Business Horizons, 52*(5), 469–479.

Jansen, J. J., George, G., Van den Bosch, F. A., & Volberda, H. W. (2008). Senior team attributes and organizational ambidexterity: The moderating role of transformational leadership. *Journal of Management Studies, 45*(5), 982–1007.

Jansen, J. J., Simsek, Z., & Cao, Q. (2012). Ambidexterity and performance in multiunit contexts: Cross- level moderating effects of structural and resource attributes. *Strategic Management Journal, 33*(11), 1286–1303.

Jansen, J. J., Tempelaar, M. P., Van den Bosch, F. A., & Volberda, H. W. (2009). Structural differentiation and ambidexterity: The mediating role of integration mechanisms. *Organization Science, 20*(4), 797–811.

Junni, P., Sarala, R. M., Taras, V. A. S., & Tarba, S. Y. (2013). Organizational ambidexterity and performance: A meta-analysis. *Academy of Management Perspectives, 27*(4), 299–312.

Juntunen, M., & Lehenkari, M. (2021). A narrative literature review process for an academic business research thesis. *Studies in Higher Education, 46*(2), 330–342.

Kang, S., & Snell, S. (2009). Intellectual capital architectures and ambidextrous learning: A framework for human resource management. *Journal of Management Studies, 46*(1), 65–92.

Kao, Y. L., & Chen, C. F. (2016). Antecedents, consequences and moderators of ambidextrous behaviours among frontline employees. *Management Decision, 54*(8), 1846–1860.

Kassotaki, O. (2022). Review of organizational ambidexterity research. *Sage Open, 12*(1).

Khan, Z., Amankwah-Amoah, J., Lew, Y. K., Puthusserry, P., & Czinkota, M. (2022). Strategic ambidexterity and its performance implications for emerging economies multinationals. *International Business Review, 31*(3), 101762.

Kohtamäki, M., Kautonen, T., & Kraus, S. (2010). Strategic planning and small business performance: An examination of the mediating role of exploration and exploitation behaviours. *The International Journal of Entrepreneurship and Innovation, 11*(3), 221–229.

Kortmann, S., Gelhard, C., Zimmermann, C., & Piller, F. (2014). Linking strategic flexibility and operational efficiency: The mediating role of ambidextrous operational capabilities. *Journal of Operations Management, 32*, 475–490.

Koryak, O., Lockett, A., Hayton, J., Nicolaou, N., & Mole, K. (2018). Disentangling the antecedents of ambidexterity: Exploration and exploitation. *Research Policy, 47*(2), 413–427.

Kriz, A., Voola, R., & Yuksel, U. (2014). The dynamic capability of ambidexterity in hypercompetition: Qualitative insights. *Journal of Strategic Marketing, 22*(4), 287–299.

Lavie, D., Kang, J., & Rosenkopf, L. (2011). Balance within and across domains: The performance implications of exploration and exploitation in alliances. *Organization Science, 22*(6), 1517–1538.

Lavie, D., & Rosenkopf, L. (2006). Balancing exploration and exploitation in alliance formation. *Academy of Management Journal, 49*(4), 797–818.

Lawrence, E. T., Tworoger, L., Ruppel, C. P., & Yurova, Y. (2022). TMT leadership ambidexterity: Balancing exploration and exploitation behaviors for innovation. *European Journal of Innovation Management, 25*(3), 703–719.

Levinthal, D. A., & March, J. G. (1993). The myopia of learning. *Strategic Management Journal, 14*(S2), 95–112.

Lewis, M. (2000). Exploring paradox: Toward a more comprehensive guide. *Academy of Management Review, 25*(4), 760–776.

Li, P. P. (2014). The unique value of Yin-Yang balancing: A critical response. *Management and Organization Review, 10*(2), 321–332.

Li, C. R., Lin, C. J., & Chu, C. P. (2008). The nature of market orientation and the ambidexterity of innovations. *Management Decision, 46*(7), 1002–1026.

Liu, Q. R., Liu, J. M., & He, Z. P. (2023b). Digital transformation ambidexterity and business performance. *Journal of Enterprise Information Management, 36*(5), 1402–1420.

Lubatkin, M. H., Simsek, Z., Ling, Y., & Veiga, J. F. (2006). Ambidexterity and performance in small- to medium-sized firms: The pivotal role of top management team behavioral integration. *Journal of Management, 32*(5), 646–672.

Majid, A., Yasir, M., Yasir, M., & Yousaf, Z. (2021). Network capability and strategic performance in SMEs: The role of strategic flexibility and organizational ambidexterity. *Eurasian Business Review, 11*(4), 587–610.

March, J. G. (1991). Exploration and exploitation in organizational learning. *Organization Science, 2*(1), 71–87.

Martin, A., Keller, A., & Fortwengel, J. (2019). Introducing conflict as the microfoundation of organizational ambidexterity. *Strategic Organization, 17*(1), 38–61.

Möller, K., Schmid, F., Seehofer, T. M., & Wenig, P. (2022). How the design of an organizational context helps to attain contextual ambidexterity. *Schmalenbach Journal of Business Research, 74*(4), 603–629.

Mom, T. J., Van Den Bosch, F. A., & Volberda, H. W. (2009). Understanding variation in managers' ambidexterity: Investigating direct and interaction effects of formal structural and personal coordination mechanisms. *Organization Science*, *20*(4), 812–828.

Moreira, A. C., Navaia, E. C., & Ribau, C. (2022). The importance of exploration and exploitation innovation in emerging economies. *Journal of Open Innovation: Technology, Market, and Complexity*, *8*(3), 140.

Nagji, B., & Tuff, G. (2012). Managing your innovation portfolio. *Harvard Business Review*, *90*(5), 66–74.

Nosella, A., Cantarello, S., & Filippini, R. (2012). The intellectual structure of organizational ambidexterity: A bibliographic investigation into the state of the art. *Strategic Organization*, *10*(4), 450–465.

O'Reilly, C. A., & Tushman, M. L. (2004). The ambidextrous organization. *Harvard Business Review*, *82*(4), 74–81.

O'Reilly, C. A., & Tushman, M. L. (2008). Ambidexterity as a dynamic capability: Resolving the innovator's dilemma. *Research in Organizational Behavior*, *28*, 185–206.

O'Reilly, C. A., III., & Tushman, M. L. (2013). Organizational ambidexterity: Past, present, and future. *Academy of Management Perspectives*, *27*(4), 324–338.

O'Cass, A., Heirati, N., & Ngo, L. V. (2014). Achieving new product success via the synchronization of exploration and exploitation across multiple levels and functional areas. *Industrial Marketing Management*, *43*(5), 862–872.

Papachroni, A., Heracleous, L., & Paroutis, S. (2015). Organizational ambidexterity through the lens of paradox theory: Building a novel research agenda. *The Journal of Applied Behavioral Science*, *51*(1), 71–93.

Paredes, K. M. B., & Olander Roese, M. (2024). Towards innovation capability in retail services: managing the tensions of exploration and exploitation. *The International Review of Retail, Distribution and Consumer Research*, *34*(3), 1–20. https://doi.org/10.1080/09593969.2024.2312892

Popadić, M., Černe, M., & Milohnić, I. (2015). Organizational ambidexterity, exploration, exploitation and firms innovation performance. *Organizacija*, *48*(2), 112–119.

Popadiuk, S., Luz, A. R. S., & Kretschmer, C. (2018). Dynamic capabilities and ambidexterity: how are these concepts related?. *Revista de Administração Contemporânea*, *22*(5), 639–660.

Prange, C., & Schlegelmilch, B. B. (2009). The role of ambidexterity in marketing strategy implementation: Resolving the exploration-exploration dilemma. *Business Research* (früher: BuR - Business Research), *2*(2), 215–240. https://doi.org/10.1007/BF03342712

Priyanka, L., Jain, M., & Dhir, S. (2022). Antecedents of organization ambidexterity: A comparative study of public and private sector organizations. *Technology in Society*, *70*, 102046.

Putnam, L. L., Fairhurst, G. T., & Banghart, S. (2016). Contradictions, dialectics, and paradoxes in organizations: A constitutive approach. *Academy of Management Annals*, *10*(1), 65–171.

Raisch, S., & Birkinshaw, J. (2008). Organizational ambidexterity: Antecedents, outcomes, and moderators. *Journal of Management*, *34*(3), 375–409.

Raisch, S., Birkinshaw, J., Probst, G., & Tushman, M. L. (2009). Organizational ambidexterity: Balancing exploitation and exploration for sustained performance. *Organization Science*, *20*(4), 685–695.

Ramachandran, I., Lengnick-Hall, C. A., & Badrinarayanan, V. (2019). Enabling and leveraging ambidexterity: influence of strategic orientations and knowledge stock. *Journal of Knowledge Management*, *23*(6), 1136–1156.

Rao, A., & Mattarelli, E. (2024). Reacting to the ambidexterity mandate: How experienced tensions and cognitive dissonance influence innovative behaviors in a global organization. *Strategic Organization*, *22*(2), 297–329.

Riccaboni, M., & Moliterni, R. (2009). Managing technological transitions through R&D alliances. *R&D Management*, *39*(2), 124–135.

Rosing, K., Frese, M., & Bausch, A. (2011). Explaining the heterogeneity of the leadership-innovation relationship: Ambidextrous leadership. *The Leadership Quarterly*, *22*(5), 956–974.

Roth, L., & Corsi, S. (2023). Ambidexterity in a geographic context: A systematic literature review on international exploration and exploitation of knowledge. *Technovation*, *124*, 102744.

Saleh, R. H., Durugbo, C. M., & Almahamid, S. M. (2023). What makes innovation ambidexterity manageable: A systematic review, multi-level model and future challenges. *Review of Managerial Science*, *17*(8), 3013–3056.

Schad, J., Lewis, M. W., Raisch, S., & Smith, W. K. (2016). Paradox research in management science: Looking back to move forward. *Academy of Management Annals*, *10*(1), 5–64.

Schumpeter, J. A. (1934). *The Theory of Economic Development.* Cambridge: MIT Press.

Simsek, Z. (2009). Organizational ambidexterity: Towards a multilevel understanding. *Journal of Management Studies*, *46*(4), 597–624.

Sirén, C. A., Kohtamäki, M., & Kuckertz, A. (2012). Exploration and exploitation strategies, profit performance, and the mediating role of strategic learning: Escaping the exploitation trap. *Strategic Entrepreneurship Journal*, *6*(1), 18–41.

Smith, W. K., & Lewis, M. W. (2011). Toward a theory of paradox: A dynamic equilibrium model of organizing. *Academy of Management Review*, *36*(2), 381–403.

Smith, W., & Tracey, P. (2016). Institutional complexity and paradox theory: Complementarities of competing demands. *Strategic Organization*, *14*(4), 455–466.

Smith, W. K., & Tushman, M. L. (2005). Managing strategic contradictions: A top management model for managing innovation streams. *Organization Science*, *16*(5), 522–536.

Snehvrat, S., Kumar, A., Kumar, R., & Dutta, S. (2018). The state of ambidexterity research: A data mining approach. *International Journal of Organizational Analysis*, *26*(2), 343–367.

Spender, J. C., & Kessler, E. H. (1995). Managing the uncertainties of innovation: Extending Thompson. *Human Relations*, *48*(1), 35–56.

Turner, N., & Lee-Kelley, L. (2013). Unpacking the theory on ambidexterity: An illustrative case on the managerial architectures, mechanisms and dynamics. *Management Learning*, *44*(2), 179–196.

Tushman, M. L., & O'Reilly, C. A. (1996). Ambidextrous organizations: Managing evolutionary and revolutionary change. *California Management Review*, *38*(4), 8–30.

Uotila, J., Maula, M., Keil, T., & Zahra, S. A. (2009). Exploration, exploitation, and financial performance: Analysis of S&P 500 corporations. *Strategic Management Journal*, *30*(2), 221–231.

Van Assen, M. F. (2020). Empowering leadership and contextual ambidexterity–The mediating role of committed leadership for continuous improvement. *European Management Journal*, *38*(3), 435–449.

Van Looy, B., Martens, T., & Debackere, K. (2005). Organizing for continuous innovation: On the sustainability of ambidextrous organizations. *Creativity and Innovation Management*, *14*(3), 208–221.

Vinekar, V., Slinkman, C. W., & Nerur, S. (2006). Can agile and traditional systems development approaches coexist? An ambidextrous view. *Information Systems Management*, *23*(3), 31–42.

Vogl, M., Schumacher, C., & Maas, P. (2024). Building and Managing an Ambidextrous SME in Central and Eastern Europe. *JEEMS Journal of East European Management Studies*, *28*(4), 664–697.

Vrontis, D., Thrassou, A., Santoro, G., & Papa, A. (2017). Ambidexterity, external knowledge and performance in knowledge-intensive firms. *The Journal of Technology Transfer*, *42*, 374–388.

Wang, C. L., & Rafiq, M. (2014). Ambidextrous organizational culture, contextual ambidexterity and new product innovation: A comparative study of UK and Chinese high-tech firms. *British Journal of Management*, *25*(1), 58–76.

Wei, Z., Zhao, J., & Zhang, C. (2014). Organizational ambidexterity, market orientation, and firm performance. *Journal of Engineering and Technology Management*, *33*, 134–153.

Weiss, L., & K. Kanbach, D. (2022). Toward an integrated framework of corporate venturing for organizational ambidexterity as a dynamic capability. *Management Review Quarterly*, *72*(4), 1129–1170.

Wenke, K., Zapkau, F. B., & Schwens, C. (2021). Too small to do it all? A meta-analysis on the relative relationships of exploration, exploitation, and ambidexterity with SME performance. *Journal of Business Research*, *132*, 653–665.

Wu, J., Wood, G., Chen, X., Meyer, M., & Liu, Z. (2020). Strategic ambidexterity and innovation in Chinese multinational vs. indigenous firms: The role of managerial capability. *International Business Review*, *29*(6), 101652.

Yu, C., Yang, H., Sun, H., & Lin, Z. (2022). Rivals or collaborators? Relational ambidexterity and absorption speed. *Journal of Management*, *48*(7), 1918–1947.

Zahoor, N., Khan, Z., Marinova, S., & Cui, L. (2024). Ambidexterity in strategic alliances: An integrative review of the literature. *International Journal of Management Reviews*, *26*(1), 82–109.

Zakrzewska-Bielawska, A. (2021). *Ambidextrous Strategy: Antecedents, Strategic Choices, and Performance*. London: Routledge.

Zhang, Q., & Sun, X. (2023). How incentive synergy and organizational structures shape innovation ambidexterity. *Journal of Knowledge Management*, *27*(1), 156–177.

Zhou, J., Bi, G., Liu, H., Fang, Y., & Hua, Z. (2018). Understanding employee competence, operational IS alignment, and organizational agility – An ambidexterity perspective. *Information and Management*, *55*(6), 695–708.

Zhou, J., Shafique, M. N., Adeel, A., Nawaz, S., & Kumar, P. (2017). What is theoretical contribution? A narrative review. *Sarhad Journal of Management Sciences*, *3*(2), 261–271.

# Part II

# Paradoxes in Managing People

# 4 Human Resource Paradoxes in a Belgian Subsidiary of a Multinational Enterprise

## An Ethnographic Case Study

*Gabriela Misiura*

### 4.1 Introduction

*What I am saying now is a lie* is a statement attributed by historians to Eubulides of Miletus, a philosopher who lived around 400 BC. The statement is one of the most famous logical problems, sometimes called the "Liar paradox" (Martinez-Fernandez & Oms, 2024). Philosophers and other experts dealing with logic have been pondering this utterance to this day. If the articulated sentence is true, then, according to its content, it is a lie. If, however, it is a lie, that means it is not true that it is a lie, it should then be assumed that the statement is true.

The concept of paradoxes has been present parallelly in the East and the West, with the East using it to analyze and explain the existing world, for example as referred to the Ying-Yang model (Schad et al., 2016). According to this outlook, everything has its opposite, and these opposites coexist in harmony. Therefore, the East considers reality as "both one and the other" while the West regards it as "either-or" (Zhang et al., 2015). The concept of paradoxes in the West dates back to ancient times, to Socrates, Plato, and Aristotle. More contemporarily, it may be connected with such thinkers and their concepts as Georg Wilhelm Friedrich Hegel and antithesis and their natural conflict; Søren Kierkegaard – finiteness, understood as norms or limitations, and infinity that can also be understood as exploration and uncertainty; Carl Gustav Jung – conscious and unconscious, and Albert Einstein – objects are simultaneously in motion and at rest (Schad et al., 2016).

While the notion of a paradox was imported from the world of philosophy, psychology, and sociology by researchers analyzing the functioning of organizations, one needs to admit that researchers most often focus on issues such as leadership, strategic decision-making, or innovations and much more rarely on areas close to human resources management (Aust et al., 2017). The paradox theory has been applied in this chapter to analyze the tensions that were identified in human resource management (HRM) practices at a Belgian Production Company (BPC). There has been a reference to the country-of-origin (COO) effect in the above-mentioned analysis that in itself is quite an innovative view on the problem of paradoxes in management and in HRM in particular. Owing to the analysis performed from the angle of the COO, it was possible to consider

DOI: 10.4324/9781003541394-7

the researched areas from an institutional and cultural perspective. This work also extends the current knowledge about the operation of Belgian corporations in Poland and thus about the management where Polish and Belgian cultures correlate. Ethnocentrism, both individual and organizational, as well as an attempt to examine its role in the paradoxes identified in the organization, has been an important theme raised in the course of the research. The study of the organization was designed and conducted (mainly because of its subject) along the principle of ethnographic research that more fully reflected the context of everyday life of the organization (Ciuk et al., 2018).

## 4.2 Literature Review

### *4.2.1 Paradoxes in Management*

#### *4.2.1.1 The Essence of Management Paradoxes*

The concept of paradox in management sciences has been defined as involving "contradictory yet interrelated elements that exist simultaneously and persist over time" (Smith & Lewis, 2011, p. 382) or a "persistent contradiction between interdependent elements" (Schad et al., 2016, p.10). As mentioned above, such an understanding of paradox is typical of Western cultures. Contradiction, i.e., the Western understanding of paradox, in consequence, leads to tensions (Schad et al., 2016), mainly because both parts of the paradox analyzed separately seem to make sense, but when combined they are completely illogical. The said tensions constitute the basis for initiating change while impeding this change at the same time. Paradoxes may concern areas such as:

- Belonging (*belonging tensions*), e.g., individual vs. collective perspective, cooperation vs. competition.
- Learning (*learning tensions*), e.g., stability vs. change, long-term vs. short-term objectives.
- Organizing (*organizing tensions*), e.g., efficiency vs. flexibility.
- Performance (*performing tensions*), e.g., financial goals vs. Company Social Responsibility (CSR) (Smith & Lewis, 2011).

*The belonging paradox* is particularly important in the processes of restructuring because at that time loyalty to the organization is disrupted. It also hurts the level of trust in employees. On the one hand, one wants to trust the developed solutions leading to change, but on the other hand, there is a constant need for control because the change takes place at a time when there are no established rules of operation and patterns – these are the ones that are the subject of change. The paradox occurs when employees identify with two different organizational units that pursue goals at two opposing Poles of the paradox

(Jarzabkowski et al., 2013). In turn, *the paradox of learning* is the tension between the old and the new, or the tension caused by the need to choose between stabilization and change (Schad et al., 2016). The groundbreaking work of James Gardner March has referred to the paradox of learning. It indicates that performance-related activities are treated as operational, while strategic activities as exploratory. According to this theory, operation constitutes an improvement of any of the existing reality, the use of existing resources, while exploration is searching for new knowledge and possibilities and experimentation. Therefore, operational activities are more certain than exploration activities, which are largely unknown (Beletskiy & Fey, 2021). Balancing or ambidexterity is extremely important in companies that want to be treated on the market as innovative entities. In companies, this can be especially evident in research and development departments, where the expectations of creativity need to be reconciled with an insufficient budget, or where creative thinking needs to pair with scrupulous implementation of the plan and meeting deadlines (Andriopoulos & Lewis, 2010). *The paradox of organizing* is the tension between differentiation and integration, control and delegation of powers, and, as the paradox of belonging, it is very important in restructuring processes. The most striking example can be the specializations of individual departments that have their roles and tasks but which collectively should cooperate toward one common company-wide goal (Jarzabkowski et al., 2013). The paradoxes of organizing include

- Flexibility – formalization.
- Centralization – decentralization.
- Delegation of authority – increased control.
- Increase in the complexity of the organization – striving for simplification.
- Cooperation – control (Lewis, 2000; Smith & Lewis, 2011).

The final category of identified paradoxes relates to performance. *Performing paradoxes* primarily arise where there are many stakeholders, and the fact in turn leads to the creation of various, often competing goals (Smith & Lewis, 2011).

Skillful navigation in the world of paradoxes is the hallmark of good leaders. This duality, ambiguity, and the related tensions in managing a subordinate team are manifested, especially where it is necessary to:

- Combine focusing on one's actions with focusing on the actions of others.
- Maintain both the appropriate distance and proximity.
- Treat subordinates equally while trying to approach each of them individually.
- Enforce compliance with laws and regulations while ensuring flexibility.
- Maintain control over decisions while giving autonomy in making decisions to subordinates (Zhang et al., 2015).

This raises the question:

RQ1: What tensions occurred in the studied BPC organization in management, and how did they manifest themselves?

#### *4.2.1.2 Human Responses to Paradoxes*

Tensions resulting from paradoxes cause a feeling of anxiety in an individual because, according to Freud's psychology, they threaten the ego. As a result, the response to tension is a defensive attitude that initially reduces anxiety, but ultimately the defensive action increases the pressure from the other party, leading to the creation of a "strange loop" (Lewis, 2000). In the same work, Marianne Lewis points out three possible ways of reacting to paradoxes: Acceptance, confrontation, and transcendence, i.e., searching for a way out of a paradoxical situation through totally unconventional solutions. In the literature, one can also find solutions that deeply penetrate the anatomy of paradox and its components:

- Acceptance of the fact that a paradox exists, and translating it into constructive use instead of ignoring it.
- Spatial separation of two opposing Poles (in the organization and at the level of individuals).
- Temporary separation of the components of the paradox (it is assumed that one component of the paradox occurs at a certain time, and the other at another time).
- New proposal for solving the paradox (Poole & Van de Ven, 1989).

In response to strong tensions, a paradoxical situation is often ridiculed and met with humorous statements and jokes (Jarzabkowski & Lê, 2017). Therefore, concerning the above, the question arises:

RQ2: What was the reaction of Polish employees to the tensions at BPC?

### *4.2.2 Paradoxes in HRM*

#### *4.2.2.1 The Essence of HRM Paradoxes*

The role of an employee in the human resources department inherently includes ambiguity, conflict, contradiction, or duality (Cayrat & Boxall, 2023). The expectation of effective implementation of both strategic and operational tasks strongly impacts human resources departments and their operations that involve strategic HRM strongly rooted in labor process theory. More tensions are perceived in strategic human resources management where a large number of stakeholders with different, and sometimes contradictory, goals and expectations are involved (Keegan et al., 2019). The above is synonymous with the organizing paradox (Smith & Lewis, 2011) where strong institutional requirements occur while the external and internal ones do not match. In turn, the labor process theory emphasizes the stark discrepancy between production capacity and what can be understood as the "human experience of work" (Keegan et al., 2019) that also relates to the internal dualism and tensions of the HR function, i.e., "soft" and "hard" HR (Arrowsmith & Parker, 2013) and is also reflected in the performing paradox. Increasing efficiency, i.e., faster pace of work, emphasis on greater involvement in performed activities, adhering to deadlines, clash with other activities, such as training and development, and as a result with a high rate of employee satisfaction that can often be an indicator of the work quality of the HR department.

Tensions occurring in the organization cause stress, anxiety, and discomfort in employees or dysfunction in organizational behavior, including decision-making (Putnam et al., 2016). Long-term stress culminates in burnout (Edú-Valsania et al., 2022) with all its negative effects on the employees and the organization, including an increase in the employee turnover rate. The role of the HR department is so much more important in this situation since the department becomes a kind of reducer of various organizational tensions. One of the main indicators of effective operation for every HR department in every organization will be minimizing fluctuations. This will be particularly important, however, for a company that wants to be innovative and, consequently, gain a competitive advantage. Such an organization must care for the expansion and retention of knowledge that directly translates into tasks for the HR department, i.e., activities aimed at keeping knowledge workers within the organization (Mabey & Zhao, 2017). HR staff is also subject to the dichotomy between working with company management and being a "spokesperson" for employees, and this mixed loyalty and the constant balancing act between the different areas also generate significant tension. Another issue concerns the dilemma of whether tasks should be delegated to line managers or employees of particular teams, and if so which tasks that would be, or whether they should be left, either in part or as a whole, within the HR department (Cayrat & Boxall, 2023; Benett et al., 2023). All the above raises the question:

RQ3: What tensions were observed in the operation of the HR department at BPC?

#### *4.2.2.2 The Country-of-Origin Effect and HRM Paradoxes*

The theory of paradoxes is deeply embedded in the DNA of the organization and operation of HR departments in multinational corporations (MNCs). As part of an international business venture, the HR department must run by the strategy of the parent company, but when operating as part of a local business in the country where the branch is located, it must also operate in specific economic, legal, and cultural conditions of the country hosting the MNC. Therefore, the department is subject to the impact of two forces, i.e., global integration and local adaptation (Pudelko & Harzing, 2007), and such a situation, of course, causes constant tensions, which create a paradox (Beletskiy & Fey, 2021). This is therefore a relevant part of the discussion on the issue of the so-called country-of-origin (COO) effect in management, and specifically on issues related to the internationalization of enterprises. The analysis of the process of internationalization of a company is performed to examine to what extent the practices of branches of international corporations are subject to global corporate standardization and to what extent they are locally adapted to the conditions dictated by the host country. These considerations can be carried out in two ways: Based on institutional theory and the cultural basis, arising from, for example, anthropology and research on individual cultures. The first theory assumes that the company's operations are influenced by institutions, and these institutions have been shaped in a given country for years and are broadly understood as the sum of historical, geographical, religious, philosophical, legal, economic, and cultural experiences constituting the external environment of the organization. The second approach follows how Geert Hofstede understood culture, i.e., as a state of collective programming of the group mind (Hofstede et al., 2010), which means as software that programs a human being in the socialization process within a specific cultural environment. When confronted with another culture in a business environment, managers must determine the position of their culture to the foreign one. Ethnocentrism defined as the belief that the ethnic group to which we belong is better than others is one of such relevant attitudes. This perspective is reflected in *Bakairi*, the language of a Brazilian tribe, where the word "kura" means both "we" and "good," and the word "kura-pa" means "not we" and "bad" (Bizumic et al., 2009). How managers think about doing business abroad and where they place their culture toward other cultures was defined in the late 1960s by Howard Perlmutter. In his EPRG model, he pointed to a specific evolution of the approach to other cultures: From ethnocentrism, through regiocentrism and polycentrism to geocentrism (Barmeyer, 2021). As understood by Perlmutter, ethnocentrism is of an organizational nature, and its idea is to impose on subsidiaries the activities that are identical to those applied by the parent company. The above is based on the belief in the priority role of one's own culture. If, in turn, the behavior or attitudes of a specific person undoubtedly show the superiority of one culture while discriminating against another, one may call it *individual ethnocentrism* (Khan & Jin 2024). Thus, the question arises:

RQ4: Was ethnocentric behavior in the organization (individual or organizational) observed as a likely source of tension?

## 4.3 Methodology

### *4.3.1 Research Strategy*

The presented research results were carried out in the spirit of constructivism, applying a *case study* as a *qualitative method* (Noor, 2008). The research matches the ethnographic trend, whose advantage is that the study work is conducted in real life and not in an experimental environment that the scientist may somehow control (Whitehead, 2005) and predict possible events. This real-life unpredictability poses a challenge to the researcher. The data may be collected in several ways, i.e., by observations from outside the research environment, without the researcher's participation in the studied phenomena, in a passive manner, in a moderate way, or fully. The last method involves the researcher observing the research environment from within and fully participating in the culture being studied (Oswald & Dainty, 2020). Such was the case of data collection at BPC.

Ethnographic research tries to answer the questions "why?" or "how?" although most often it does not provide grounds for generalizations (Abell & Engel, 2023). The following work is based on observations made inside the organization by the researcher who has also been an employee of the organization. Therefore, it can be described as *an auto-ethnographic study* in the genre of *personal experience narratives* (Denzin, 1989). Owing to the selection of such a method, phenomena may be observed from both the *emic* (internal) and *etic* (external) perspectives (Mostowlansky & Rota, 2020). Emic experiences of reality are those that can only be examined by a member of the studied community and refer to human behavior within this single studied community, while etic experiences are those that are observable by the researcher and are subject to objective analysis. Unfortunately, there is currently a tendency to perceive emic and etic perspectives, i.e., *Insider* vs. *Outsider* ones, as methods that are opposing and not complementary (Beals et al., 2020). Therefore, as it can be seen, a paradox is present in this work even at the level of methodology and is unveiled in the form of tension between the imposed etic of the academic world and the emic point of view of the researcher (Beals et al., 2020). It should be mentioned that this auto-ethnographic study is also descriptive and retrospective in nature, which means that at the time the experiences or described interactions occurred, there was no open research project in progress, and therefore no data collection for any research may have been considered (Edwards, 2020).

### *4.3.2 Empirical Setting: Belgian Production Company*

The empirical environment involved the premises of a subsidiary of BPC, located in Poland, where the role of HR business partner (HRBP) was implemented in October 2022. The CEO, employed in August 2022, and also new to the organization, was the initiator of the new position in the company structure. His decision was based on the belief that such a role was necessary to effectively and safely guide the company through the process of reorganization and the ownership change, planned over the next few years. The one year from October 2022 to October 2023 was considered for the study.

The examined organization was BPC, which had two owners: The private owner (50% of shares and 1 share) and the corporate owner (50% of shares less 1 share). This was the only joint business venture of both owners in Poland. The company's value in the last year before the planned transaction was significant in relation to the final sum for which the corporate owner would finally buy out the company from the private owner. Therefore, the main goal for both parties, namely the ultimate change of ownership from private to corporate owner, was the same; however, the parties had completely different goals regarding the company's value. These opposing objectives were reflected in the different expectations of the CEO and the Co-CEO regarding operational activities and, consequently, the HR department.

During the research period, there were approximately 100 people employed in the factory in Poland, and the company's person in charge was a Polish manager holding the position of Chief Executive Officer (CEO), associated with the private owner. The representative of the Belgian Corporate Owner, the Co-CEO[1], cooperated with the Polish CEO. The substantive and managerial areas of responsibility were divided between both CEOs (Figure 4.1). The person in the position of CEO changed three times within 1.5 years.

### *4.3.3 Data Collection*

The data were collected as a result of hidden participatory observation, document analysis, and a survey as well as interviews with employees.

#### *4.3.3.1 Hidden Participatory Observation*

Due to the self-retrospective method of the study, it should be assumed that the conducted observation was decidedly participatory. Since collecting the research material did not constitute the basis for the observations and no member of the organization had been informed about the observation taking place, the observation therefore was of a hidden nature. The study remarks made were written down several months after the termination of the researcher's interaction with the organization.

#### *4.3.3.2 Documentation Analysis*

The researcher happened to operate in the very center of the researched areas, thanks to which she had access to the documentation (regulations, e-mails, formal and informal guidelines), and she also participated in the creation of many of the documents herself.

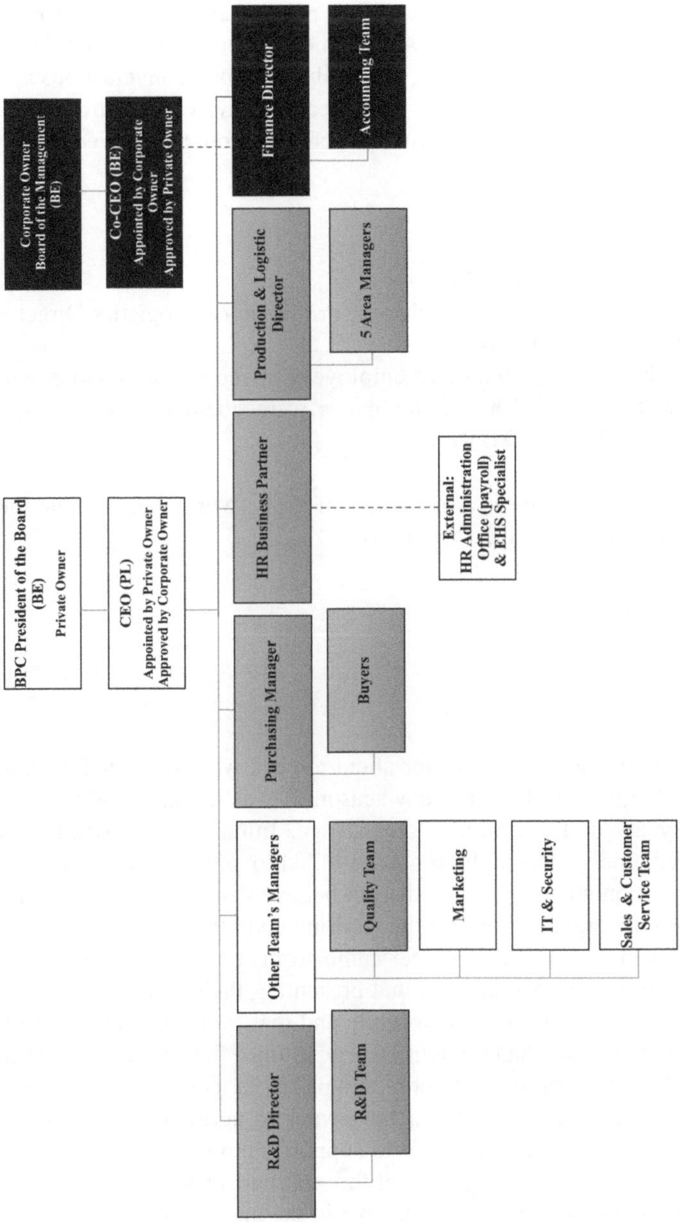


*Figure 4.1* Simplified Organizational Chart of BPC.

*Note*: Separate colors signify positions of loyalty or positions united around a common goal.

#### *4.3.3.3 Interviews with People from Different Levels of the Organization during Daily Interactions*

As part of the job description, the position of the researcher, i.e., the key post in the HR department, involved working with people and, therefore, human interaction at every level of the organization, primarily including conversations and the exchange of key data. Thus, in a self-retrospective way, a lot of information as well as many statements were successfully recreated from the conversations:

- With the private owner (PO).
- With the corporate owner (CO).
- With the Co-CEO, coded as CCEO.
- With key managers of individual divisions: Production & Logistics Director (PLD), Chief Accountant (ChA).
- During in-depth interviews with five employees of the research and development department, in which the employees were guaranteed anonymity: R&D1, R&D2, R&D3, R&D4, R&D5.
- With the CEO.
- With some line employees in the course of daily work, i.e., Production Worker (PW) and Logistic Specialist (LS).

*Research on satisfaction*

a) *Satisfaction Survey*

The anonymous online survey lasting for about a week was conducted in June 2023, before the beginning of the holiday season. It was the first study of this type in several years of the company's existence. Initially, large skepticism could be observed among the employees, who failed to understand the purpose of this type of questionnaire, since they did not believe that their opinion would have an impact on the organization and the working conditions in the company. The biggest enthusiasm about the project came from the white collars (WC) who had learned from other workplaces that presenting their point of view and being a part of a change was worth their while and that every opinion counted. A group of blue collars (BC) had thought otherwise since they believed that the idea might have been interesting, but not in this particular company. According to them, nothing would have convinced the owner to agree to the necessary changes in the operation of the factory or to support a thorough reconstruction of the organizational culture. A large part of the staff had such a limited trust in the BPC management that they did not believe in the anonymity of the survey and were afraid to write about what they thought and felt and what changes they expected honestly.

b) *Anonymized Interview Intelligence with the Employees of the Research and Development (R&D) Department (SI)*

Due to the major crisis that affected the team, the employees of the R&D department were asked to participate in an in-depth study. It consisted of a direct one-on-one conversation with HRBP, where they provided answers to a prepared set of questions (identical for all employees). The report from each conversation was anonymous, i.e., the management board did not receive the information about who was the author of a specific statement. The conversations were quite long, and the employees expressed their problems, complaints, and feelings in a fairly open manner. They were not afraid to talk about their frustrations, giving the impression of people who had nothing to lose.

### *4.3.4 Analysis and Interpretation*

At the time related to this research, the HRBP had no intention to collect materials for the study, since there was no intention to conduct it. What constituted experience in the course of the daily work was recorded approximately eight months after the cooperation of the HRBP with BPC had terminated. Moreover, the results of the satisfaction survey, in the part specifying, for example the number of respondents, have been approximated because the researcher did not have access to the original document summarizing the survey once the cooperation with the company terminated.

Following the methodology of qualitative research, the collected material was coded to organize and categorize the gathered information which then allowed for the interpretation of the data (Graue, 2015). Coding was performed in a hybrid manner. It was based on two contrasting approaches: Deductive and inductive. Part of the codes had been created earlier, based on literature studies (deduction), whereas the other part emerged during the analysis of the collected material, as the response to the lack of appropriate codes related to what had just been identified (Swain, 2018). During the coding process, the code lists were created for:

- The people – whose oral or written statements (survey) were used in the study.
- The sources of obtaining the research material (surveys, in-depth interviews, everyday interactions, documents).
- The studied phenomena (learning, belonging, performing, organizing, paradoxes in the operation of the HR department, ethnocentrism).

The interpretation of the research material consisted of categorization followed by abductive reasoning (abduction), i.e., comparing the material obtained in the field with the existing theoretical patterns. This is the so-called flexible pattern-matching technique (Bouncken et al., 2021). The use of numerous methods, as well as obtaining information from various levels and positions within the organization provided for the research triangulation. The long period of observations and collection of the remaining data also proved important in this context.

## 4.4 Findings

As presented below, a number of paradoxes were identified. The employees' reactions to occurring tensions were also observed and the identified behavior of the ethnocentric character was described.

### *4.4.1 Belonging Tensions*

The greatest tensions occurred between the Polish and Belgian sides, and this dissonance generated a dividing line within the teams and paralyzed the work of many of them, although the BPC case was slightly more complex. Polish employees working at BPC had their Polish CEO, who started the strenuous process of changes and the reconstruction of the organizational structure, preparing the company for the complete takeover by the Belgian corporate owner. Meanwhile, the decisions of the local CEO were repeatedly questioned or altered by either the private Belgian owner or the corporate owner, who became more involved in the company's current affairs after another increase in the company's capital. As a result, local Polish staff had a major problem with defining their affiliation and loyalty. *Should I follow the path set out by the Polish manager of the company that employs me here in Poland, or should I go along the path of his superior, i.e. the Belgian private owner, who is currently the majority owner? Or maybe I should invest in loyalty to the future owner, i.e. the corporation?* (R&D2, SI).

Belgian Production Company employees would say, somewhat facetiously, *Let us hurry to love the CEOs, they leave so quickly* (PW, DI). This was a paraphrase of a poem, popular in Poland, by priest Jan Twardowski: *Let us hurry to love people they depart so quickly.*[2] To the employees of the Polish factory, the high turnover in this position was not only a source of jokes. Frequent changes in the position responsible for taking numerous key decisions made the staff tired of constant replacements and unwilling to get involved in restructuring projects since the employees were convinced that the person in this position would change in a few months anyway. This attitude of employees, although understandable due to what had happened in the past, was a significant obstacle to the implementation of the projects planned by the new CEO. Paradoxically, in the eyes of the staff, especially those with the longest work experience, the person identified as a permanent and reliable element in the situation appeared to be the Belgian private manager – a person repeatedly exhibiting a lack of respect and trust toward employees and never appreciating the work they did. Two groups of workers could be perceived here: The first group included "old employees" who ignored the owner's outbursts of fury, his cries of *This is Africa* or *donkey people* and used to say *he may be crazy, but he is ours and we already know him* (PW, DI); the second group consisted of "new" employees, with shorter experience, who had not experience burnt-out yet, who still believed in changes, and therefore in the vision of the CEO, and who verbally presented their lack of acceptance of the working conditions, the instability of the situation in the company and the owner's behavior. They would say *This is not some Congo!* (PLD, DI) and *if nothing changes, I am going to leave, I won't be treated like this* (ChA, DI). One of them was the CEO who, during one of the conversations, bluntly stated to the Belgian owner *Don't treat me like this! I'm not your slave!* (CEO, DI). The majority private owner expected the Polish CEO employed in Poland to be independent and "provident" in his approach, repeatedly saying *You are the boss* or *This is your decision* (PO, DI), while constantly personally interfering in such insignificant details as a single piece of scrap on the production floor spotted by cameras to which he had access in real-time, or criticizing *post factum* the decisions made by the CEO.

### *4.4.2 Learning Tensions*

Due to the constant rotation in the position of the CEO, BPC gave the impression of a company that cared about changes, and employing new people in the position of the CEO was because the predecessors were not able to lead the company through the necessary restructuring. However, striving for change seemed superficial because the Belgian private owner seemed to sabotage every project proposed in the company that would disrupt the status quo. There was a tension between the need for change in the organization and the need to maintain stability (Table 4.1).

In their humorous way, the employees provided comments concerning this scuffle related to projects, and one of the most popular slogans was *Someone who worked at BPC won't laugh in a circus* (LS, DI).

The most spectacular example, however, was how the company reacted to the results of the satisfaction survey, which was supposed to provide an answer to the question of the main cause of employee dissatisfaction and to provide clues regarding the changes that should have been introduced to improve the atmosphere within the staff and prepare the company for a big change. The main conclusion from the survey was that the permanent micromanagement of the Belgian private owner and his chaotic changes in decisions, not consulted with anyone, had the greatest negative impact on the employees' sense of security and job satisfaction. HRBP conducted an in-depth satisfaction survey in the R&D department. The department was the second one, after the production and logistics department, to feel the effects of such activities. Employees gave an example of a product being withdrawn from the catalog following one phone call or an email. Such an impromptu decision resulted in hours or days of work, engaging several IT programs, only to have the removed product brought back

*Table 4.1* Changes and Innovations Introduced in BPC

| *Project* | *Area* | *The Process of Change* | | |
|---|---|---|---|---|
| | | *Maintained in Its Original Form* | *Changed/Fractionally Maintained* | *Discarded or the Old Solution Restored* |
| Creation of backup positions for the previously singular post of the Purchasing Manager | Structure/ organization | | | X |
| Employing a professional to manage a specialized assembly department | Structure/ organization | | | X |
| HRBP position | Structure/ organization | | X | |
| Employee benefits (medical care, small benefits cafeteria) | Motivation/HR | | | X |
| Bonus based on KPIs | Motivation/ management | | | X |
| Hybrid work and task system for managers | Work organization/ motivating | | X | |
| Initiation of lean manufacturing project | Production | | | X |
| Change of the ERP system | Work organization/ tools | X | | |
| Cooperation with the local vocational school | CSR | | | X |
| Integration meetings | Motivation | | | X |
| Hiring a security company | Administration | | | X |
| Self-service (independent organization of own trips by Belgians) | Administration | | | X |
| Lean raw materials management system | Production logistics | | X | |
| Employing a production planner | Production planning | X | | |
| Staff induction system (a series of training sessions) | HR | | | X |
| Fleet policy | Administration | X | | |

a few days later following a laconic message. The staff would say *Our work is not respected* (R&D1, SI), *No one asks us for our opinion* (R&D3, SI), and *Instead of doing some creative work, we keep modifying the catalog* (R&D5, SI). The situation in this department became tense to such an extent that the most experienced employees threatened to leave. About 70% of employees declared in the survey that they wanted to leave within the next year, and about half of them within the next few months. The corporate owner stepped in then, assuring everyone (employees, management staff, and the CEO) that the Belgian private owner would refrain from the manual control of either the production or the R&D departments. The problem was that this change, yet again, was only apparent, and after a few weeks, the situation returned to its previous state.

### *4.4.3 Organizing Tensions*

At the organizational level of the company, tensions were visible at the interface between the operations of certain departments:

- Finance vs. Purchasing.
- Maintenance vs. Finance.
- HR vs. Finance.
- Maintenance/Technical vs. Production.
- Production vs. Quality.
- R&D vs. Production.

The delegation of powers was another thorny issue, especially for the private owner. He expected every smallest decision to be at least presented to him, and preferably consulted beforehand, with his opinion taken into account. A certain problem was noticed related to the acceptance of the CEO's autonomous decisions taken within the operational area of the company (production, logistics, maintenance, quality, HR), since the CEO considered himself a perfectly experienced and competent person. It was also significant that when preparing the company's budget, the Co-CEO and the private owner did not deem it appropriate to talk to managers of individual departments about the issue, therefore they did not provide them with an opportunity to argue the substantiation of particular expenses. Thus, except for the mandatory training and the training required by law regulations, virtually all other training was eliminated in the HR department, particularly affecting the department that needed to keep abreast with the latest knowledge and trends, i.e., the R&D department. This action deprived Polish employees of the right to express their opinions on the budget. The only Polish representatives at the budget meeting were the Financial Director and the CEO. However, their voice was not to be taken into account.

It is also noteworthy that the private owner made frequent visits to the Polish manufacturing plant. His visits took place every two weeks and lasted from two to four days, triggering cooperation-control paradoxes. The employees, referring to the promotional campaigns of the Lidl store chain, called every week when the owner was present in the company the *Belgian week* (PW, DI). There was an atmosphere of anticipation and concern in the company related to issues that would make the owner dissatisfied and to speculations as to who would be the *mascot of the week* (PW, DI), i.e., the person would have to justify his or her decisions in the course of long forced conversations with the owner. Blue-collar employees reported to the HR department that they were constantly "followed" by cameras and that every minute of their work was scrutinized, including their lunch breaks in the employee dining room. Once, the department foreman and two machine operators were talking about repeated failures of a machine and they were looking for a solution together, standing in the production hall near the machine. The owner demanded that they be punished for unproductive small talk while working, a situation that sparked great outrage among the employees. Since the CCTV camera only provided images, he could not know what the conversation was actually about. Such situations demotivated employees who preferred to move unproductively around the hall at a fast pace to appear very busy when watched by the cameras. The employees also raised the issue of lack of trust in the company by saying *If the company doesn't trust us, we don't trust the company* (ChA, DI). The owner sent, primarily to the CEO, dozens of videos documenting, in his opinion, the laziness and incompetence of the employees, as well as their management at various levels. The videos resulted in the CEO's frustration and a sense of helplessness and distracted him from the issues that were more important from a business point of view. This was one of the reasons for the clear diminishing of his motivation which was expressed by him in many conversations with HRBP.

### *4.4.4 Performing Tensions*

The main paradox of the BPC's performance was created by several stakeholders with entirely different goals. There was a visible discrepancy between the goals of the private owner striving for high company value and the corporate owner anxious for the company to have a low value, balancing on the verge of profitability, just above the break-even point. The Polish CEO tried to find the golden mean, a kind of "third way" that would reconcile the interests of both owners and that would also take into account the CEO's idea for the reorganization of the company with regard to the local socio-cultural conditions. However, this multitude of tendencies gave rise to another paradox, mentioned earlier, namely the paradox of belonging.

The very clear tension in the area of results was demonstrated by the dilemma between the results and the employer branding. In the case of BPC, the divergence was decidedly in favor of the results. For unknown reasons, the studied company and its Belgian management did not seem to notice its strongly negative image on the local labor market. They did not react to the repeated messages about the unfavorable perception by the employees of the employee referral program implemented by HRBP. Despite the promised attractive financial reward for bringing new staff to the company, not a single CV was obtained. None of BPC's employees would recommend to anyone this manufacturing plant as a place to work. The staff expressed this in their statements, such as *I like my neighbor and I won't get him into this mess* (PW, DI). Also, the advertisements published on external recruitment portals, both nationally and locally, resulted in dramatically low interest in the form of applications from candidates, and the quality of skills included in CVs suggested people with no professional experience or very desperate to get any job after many months of searching for employment in the labor market. Both internal and external employer branding was very weak. Information about yet another employee leaving, including, for example, a key specialist in a given field, was received with a comment from the private owner (PO_DI) *If not this one, then there will be another one. He was not suitable for the job,* a statement indicating a complete lack of reflection on the management methods adopted. He considered spending on motivational activities (integration, benefits, and medical care) a whim or a fancy, saying *I guess we pay them for their work? Isn't that enough?*

Human Resource business partner tried to change the employer's brand image and initiate corporate social responsibility-related activities by establishing cooperation with local technical colleges, by attempting to sign a partnership agreement with one of the business universities, or by opening a path for executing an industrial PhD program within the company. The actions were appreciated by the Polish CEO but completely ignored by the Belgian side. On the other hand, there was clear pressure for efficiency and unwillingness to increase salaries or implement bonuses. Curiously, an increase in productivity was expected without the implementation of any motivational tools. The CEO and HRBP had to convince the management board to implement a bonus based on key indicators rather than the completely ineffective, unfair, and not motivating discretionary bonus, the amount of which depended on the subjective assessment of an employee's work by his or her superior.

## 4.5 Discussion

As a result of the observations, it was possible to identify several paradoxes that fall into the four categories indicated in the literature (Smith & Lewis, 2011), and their significant reflection on the functioning of HRM in BPC was also noticed.

Human Resource business partner operated within the examined organization like any other representative of this profession, i.e., in the world of paradoxes that could be considered natural for this position: Hard HR vs. soft HR, interests of owners vs. interests of employees, and strategy vs. operations. In BPC, however, these paradoxes were reinforced by pathologies such as individual and organizational ethnocentrism and pathologically accumulated tensions. Two paradoxes were particularly visible, namely incompatible financial goals of both owners and the problem of micromanagement of the private owner, who tried to force solutions identical to those used in his Belgian company, even though he openly pointed to the local CEO as the creator and maker of decisions. HRBP's attempt to oppose the implementation of a given solution, for example, due to the specificity of the Polish legal environment, was received with misunderstanding and was treated as bad will. What is also extremely important, both the private and corporate owners were not interested in learning about local conditions (cultural or institutional). There were no questions asked about what problems the employees had with the organization of work, what feelings they experienced, what they thought about their work, and the reasons for leaving were not analyzed (the departure was treated as evidence that Poles were not loyal or that those leaving were weak individuals unworthy of any attention). In other words, everything was analyzed through the prism of preconceived reasoning concerning Poles and the Polish factory created by Belgians and originating in Belgium that would confirm organizational ethnocentrism. In this situation, the actions taken by HRBP were a kind of tilting at windmills, and in practice, it was exhausting work that mainly included looking for opportunities to meet the sometimes contradictory expectations of various parties.

Poles, at least those who experience life in communist times, are a nation that knows a lot about life in a world of paradoxes.[3] One of the viral humorous memes appearing online shows this perfectly:

"In the Polish People's Republic:

- Everyone had a job.
- Even though everyone had a job, no one worked.
- Even though no one worked, the plan was always completed in more than 100%.
- Even though the plan was always completed in more than 100% completed, nothing could be bought.
- Even though one could not buy anything, everyone had everything…" (Pinterest).

Many Poles remember that period in the country's history as tragic, therefore the above summary of those times indicates an approach that ridicules paradoxes, tensions, and difficult situations and is something that can be pointed to as an element of the Polish national character. The Polish national pride that sometimes borders on nationalism, visible during patriotic celebrations, is another characteristic of Poles. In the Polish mentality, there is a natural polarization into "We" and "They," e.g., employees vs. management. Additionally, since they are suspicious by nature, Poles disregard arguments that are not supported by what they feel about a given topic. This, of course, stems from the difficult history of the nation. All of the above makes it difficult to build trust in the authorities and in change for Poles who are motivated by rewards and positive incentives rather than punishment. This nation can be very resilient in an atmosphere of fear and threat, and it can also cope with an authoritarian style. On the one hand, hierarchy is accepted, on the other hand, strong authoritarianism is very negatively perceived because it is associated with the past regime. Manifesting authoritarianism in Polish enterprises makes employees lose respect for authority (Nasierowski & Mikula, 1998). The above-mentioned characteristics were also visible in BPC. Therefore, it seems that although accustomed to living in a world of paradoxes, Poles will be sensitive to their occurrence within organizations. Attention should be paid to the belonging paradox (WE vs. THEY), the learning paradox (high index of uncertainty avoidance and therefore reluctance to change, according to Geert Hofstede), and the organizing paradox (excessive control and sanctions). These paradoxes particularly affect this nation, and if there is a strong deviation of the paradox in one direction, the members of the nation will feel it severely. As for the paradox of results, Poles will react similarly to other nations, although it can also be assumed that in the Polish understanding, the different stakeholders will be perceived and treated as one category called "They." The choice of loyalty between various stakeholders may appear to them as a choice "between the plague and cholera," as bluntly expressed in a Polish saying that describes a choice between two unfavorable options (PAN).

The collected research material was, therefore, analyzed in the context of the previously posed research questions.

### *4.5.1 Research Question 1*

The first research question concerned the tensions that occurred in BPC in the area of management and how they manifested themselves. The analysis carried out in the reality of BPC showed all four types of paradoxes mentioned by Smith and Lewis (2011). The researcher found two issues particularly interesting. The first was that the dilemmas and tensions could occur not only between two opposing elements but, as in the case of BPC, between three (Figure 1), i.e., the private owner, the corporate owner, and the CEO and the departments loyal to them respectively. BPC employees had to choose which stakeholders they sympathized with and which goals they supported. The second issue concerned the superiority of the performing paradox over others. The performing paradox, strongly correlated with the multitude of stakeholders and the divergent goals, was the dominant paradox that was the basis for emerging tensions in other areas. Assuming that the private owner cared about high company value while the corporation cared about low company value, as on the date of sale (therefore the goal vectors were opposite), then the parties to the deal would take opposite positions as related to the other paradoxes. Additionally, the role of the CEO should be mentioned again, whose actions simultaneously indicated following the direction set by the corporate owner (e.g., replacing the Enterprise Resource Planning (ERP) system) and following the path of the private owner (striving to obtain the best possible result in terms of increasing the company value).

The performing paradox seemed to be central and predominant in the analyzed company. The enterprise that was focused on results lost sight of its people to the detriment of its internal and external employer branding. The employees were treated subjectively and not objectively and HRBP, despite not having tools and means, desperately tried to change both the internal and external perception of BPC.

### *4.5.2 Research Question 2*

Unceasing, chaotic changes in the position of the CEO, in the company's organizational structure, and related to its goals resulted in huge demotivation of employees and a decline in their trust in the company, as well as uncertainty that the actions initiated in one month would be continued in the next. With the low level of or the lack of trust in the company, it would be difficult to talk about conditions for innovative activities (Bylok & Kuceba, 2021, Dovey, 2009). The permanent control indicating the company's lack of trust also increased the reciprocity of similar feelings among employees. The employees' behavior demonstrated all three possible reactions to the perceived paradoxes (Lewis, 2000):

- *Acceptance* – employees with the longest experience, those who accepted their fate and felt resignation. Most often, these were blue-collar workers, from small towns, who saw no other alternative.
- *Contestation/conflict* – employees with shorter experience, mainly specialists and managers, people with experience from other organizations.
- *Transcendence* – some managers were aware of the existence of tensions related to the fully divergent goals of both ownership parties. These people were looking for a point at which the conflicting positions could somehow be reconciled (CEO, HRBP, R&D Director, Production Director, Quality Manager) ultimately led to the consolidation of common resistance of the private and corporate owners and resulted in the dismissal or voluntary departure of the demotivated and frustrated representatives of the third type of reaction to the perceived paradoxes – the transcendence. As shown in the example, choosing the third option did not necessarily bring a positive outcome in the form of creating a completely innovative solution.

It was also noticed that in an environment full of paradoxes, employees also coped with harsh reality by ridiculing absurdities that, as a result of enormous tensions, appeared daily (Jarzabkowski & Lê, 2017).[4]

### *4.5.3 Research Question 3*

The third question concerned the identified paradoxes that were visible in the functioning of the HR department and the work of the HRBP.

#### *4.5.3.1 Turnover and Recruitment*

Employees from every level of BPC were open to new job offers, which of course increased the turnover rate. This was due to many issues including

- Loss of trust due to excessive control (organizing tension).
- Unfair treatment of Polish and Belgian employees, unequal division of labor (belonging tension reinforced by ethnocentric attitudes).
- Lack of a sense of consistency and stability – changes introduced superficially or temporarily, frequent changes of the CEO, no guarantee that the change would be permanent and would consistently result in further steps (learning tension).
- The image of an employer, a company that treated employees subjectively, an enterprise not to be associated with for long by some employees who had been developing their careers and their brand (performing tensions).

A high turnover rate provoked demanding behavior since the employees saw the company in a critical situation. High turnover, of course, also meant numerous recruitment projects that took up time that could have been used in other HR areas.

#### *4.5.3.2 Perception of the Role of HR*

The role of HRBP was also perceived in different ways that impacted the delegated tasks and expectations that the stakeholders expressed toward the HR department:

- The CEO – expected operational support from HRBP, and needed a partner who would assist him in carrying out key changes during the arduous process of restructuring the company and its ultimate sale. He was aware of the fact that the subject of "soft HR" was non-existent in the company, that the processes were in disarray, and that the employees were not treated objectively in any way. He wanted to invest in employees and build a team that would feel important to the organization and its owners. He expected the creation of new solutions in the field of HRM, but for this to happen, the commitment from the owners was also necessary, as well as consistency, and changes in human mentality, and habits, building trust and a platform for cooperation – and that required a lot of time and support from the entire organization.

- Private owner – wondered *what HRBP actually did after the 5th of each month, when salaries had already been paid*, a thought that he expressed in the form of a question at the Management board meeting. The only thing he expected was reporting of absences with the related costs and the rate of accidents split among departments, therefore these were activities characterizing partial controlling of personnel. In turn, he approached the results of the satisfaction survey in a very personal way. He seemed offended by the results, and when reading quotes from the interviews with anonymous employees of the R&D department, he actually screamed. He did not understand at all what was wrong with his behavior and why his right to make decisions was being questioned at all. He referred to many years of his own experience and his expert knowledge. He boycotted or publicly pointed out as unimportant, the attempts of HRBP to introduce changes, even though this was one of the critical areas in the company that needed them.
- Corporate owner – approached the position of HRBP quite neutrally, expected actions that would result in increased commitment and satisfaction, but at the lowest possible financial costs. He was interested in a satisfaction survey and initially agreed to finance the expected benefits and change the organization of some departments. However, he reacted quite nervously to the results of the study, which clearly outlined the allegations addressed to the company's management. The employees pointed out that there was a clear difference in the treatment of Belgians and Poles in the company, especially Polish engineers from the R&D department, who matched the competencies of their Belgian colleagues, did not receive tasks requiring creativity but tedious administrative work and paperwork that could be entrusted to university graduates. If the corporate owner expected changes, it would be with the least amount of financial resources – which in most cases was simply impossible. Sometimes the decisions were completely at odds with the operation of HRBP and contrary to the messages the company conveyed to employees. For example, the CEO together with HRBP announced the payment of additional funds under the so-called Christmas bonus, which had been previously communicated to private and corporate owners with appropriate funds allocated in the department's budget. The bonus was to be paid with the November salary, i.e., at the beginning of December, thus supporting the household budgets of the employees at a time when the expenses related to the festive season were the highest. Meanwhile, due to the company's financial needs, it was decided that the bonus would be paid as late as January of the following year. This was, of course, met with a negative reception by the employees, albeit without any surprise since they suspected that the company would once again betray their trust. This decision also undermined the authority of the CEO and HRBP, newly hired a few months earlier. Once again, the company confirmed that it wanted changes, but changes were introduced in such a way that nothing

would have to be altered in the operation of the company and the behavior of the key figures in the organization.

This different perception of the role, tasks, and priorities by the three decision-makers in the company meant that also HRBP was confronted with the necessity to implement tasks and meet the expectations that were at times completely contradictory.

#### *4.5.3.3 Lack of Trust*

All documents regarding, for example, the purchase of services for HR or arranging a power of attorney for an external employee who was dealing with payroll and who was responsible for contacts with state offices required the signing of documents by members of the management board A and the members of the management board B (out of four people, three were Belgians). The local Polish CEO did not have the authority in this regard. Perhaps this was because the company was aware of the short-term cooperation with each successive CEO. Regardless of the reason, the circulation of documents was very complex. In addition to the process of obtaining signatures from the Belgian management board members, time was required in order to translate Polish official forms into English, and to substantiate the need to grant a power of attorney to an officer of an outsourced company administering employee and payroll documentation to contact the Social Insurance Institution. As a result, all these processes were increasingly time-consuming.

The inability of the HR department to manage its own budget fully caused tensions between HRBP and employees. Several times, due to the lack of possibility to use its own resources, the HR department failed to execute the planned tasks that had already been communicated to the staff.

### *4.5.4 Research Question 4*

It was observed that the country-of-origin effect had a likely impact on the identified organizational paradoxes. Although HR practices were not subject to convergence in BPC, and the local HRBP was theoretically at liberty to choose methods and tools, as well as to achieve goals, the Belgian (corporate) side had a major influence on the shape and functioning of the HR department. The limitations in the operation of the HRM area resulted from the authority to make financial decisions vested only in Belgians and depended on their assessment of the situation. If the course of action of the CEO and HRBP did not seem reasonable to the financial decision-makers, they would simply deny specific expenses, as shown in the example of the budget construction described above. Therefore, no implementation of corporate *best practices* took place and it was the Belgians who decided what would happen in the HR area in the coming months. Decisions regarding finances are an unalienable right of the company owner, but the complete lack of consultation with the local management – both the CEO and HRBP – would indicate some kind of ethnocentric bias. Also, the competencies of Polish engineers in the R&D department were questioned, which meant that they were given less significant and more tedious tasks, surely well below their knowledge and qualifications. In the researched company, ethnocentrism occurred both in individual and organizational forms (Khan & Jin, 2024), and, as could be seen, it accompanied the emerging tensions identified in this work. It can be seen in the statements quoted above and in the recorded situations as well as in the described organizational models, e.g., the R&D department and the division of the work within.

### *4.5.5 Contributions, Limitations, and Future Research*

The carried-out analysis constitutes a significant contribution to the literature on the issue of paradoxes in the area of HRM, especially in the context of multinational corporations. It also points to the impact of ethnocentric attitudes and behavior on paradoxes in management, which is an issue poorly researched to date. Thanks to the conducted research, it was possible to identify tensions leading to paradoxes in HRM and also to demonstrate, using the example of the indicated behavior of BPC employees, how paradoxes in management were perceived in Polish culture.

The study offers practical implications for improving organizational effectiveness and adapting MNCs to the specific cultural conditions of other countries like Poland in Central and Eastern Europe. It urges managers to raise awareness of the tensions since it can promote innovation and organizational adaptability, enabling faster responses to changing market conditions. It also prevents the occurrence of costly cultural barriers. As a result, MNCs can compete more effectively in the marketplace, increasing their stability and loyalty among employees and customers.

Since there was no intention to conduct research during the observation period, the material collected after a few months may be incomplete and inaccurate. Because the researcher was also an "actor" of the described events, there is a risk of unconscious or subconscious subjectivity (Van Maanen, 2010) in the interpretation of the observed phenomena. Due to the adopted method, the study does not include in-depth interviews, which would have enriched the material, had the research been conducted openly.

Based on the analysis, possible areas for further research were outlined that could provide more information on:

- The impact of ethnocentrism on paradoxes in management, including HRM.
- Whether the occurrence of one paradox results in the occurrence of others in other areas.

- What the effects of choosing transcendence are – how organizations respond to non-standard behavior, going beyond the two possible Poles of the paradox.

These issues could become a field for further in-depth research, especially since this work based on a case study cannot be the basis for building generalized theories.

## Notes

1 Such terminology related to both functions is unusual. The Cambridge English Dictionary defines Co-CEO as *the title given to each of two people who share the job of chief executive in a company*. This was not the case in BPC, most likely due to the fact that it would have caused difficulties in the recruitment for the position that demonstrated a high level of rotation anyway (3 CEOs within the period of 1.5 years).

2 This is a fragment of a poem called "Let us hurry" that the author dedicated to Anna Kamienska. Priest Jan Twardowski had been a member of the Home Army (Armia Krajowa) and participated in the Warsaw Uprising. As a result of his war experiences, he decided to become a priest. Polish source: https://agencja-informacyjna.com/spieszmy-sie-kochac-ludzi-wierszem-roku-2020/, accessed on: 28.08.2024.

3 The researcher focuses her work on Poland, but it is reasonable to assume that due to the shared post-Soviet reality, certain cultural traits Poles may share with citizens of other countries in the Central and Eastern European region. Wherever there was a Soviet sphere of influence there was also a specific, centralized economic model, which implied specific labor relations and culture.

4 This also seems to be a certain characteristic of Poles, who in the time of the German Nazi occupation during WWII would sing humorous folk songs with lyrics adapted to ridicule the Nazis and their oppressive practices involving street round-ups. "Axe, hoe, ball and drinking glass…" songs, penalized by Germans, would remain the patriotic protest songs of the occupied Poland helping Poles survive the time of oppression.

## References

Abell, P., & Engel, O. (2023). Ethnographic Causality. Groningen: University of Groningen Press.

Andriopoulos, C., & Lewis, M. W. (2010). Managing innovation paradoxes: Ambidexterity lessons from leading product design companies. *Long Range Planning*, *43*(1), 104–122.

Arrowsmith, J., & Parker, J. (2013). The meaning of 'employee engagement' for the values and roles of the HRM function. *The International Journal of Human Resource Management*, *24*(14), 2692–2712.

Aust, I., Brandl, J., Keegan, A., & Lensges, M. (2017). Tensions in managing human resources. Introducing a paradox framework. In K. S. Wendy, W. L. Marianne, J. Paula, & L. Ann (Eds.), *The Oxford Handbook of Organizational Paradox* (pp. 413–433). Oxford: Oxford University Press.

Barmeyer, C., Bausch, M., & Mayrhofer, U. (2021). Constructive Intercultural Management: Integrating Cultural Differences Successfully. Cheltenham (UK), Northampton (USA): Edward Elgar Publishing.

Beals, F., Kidman, J., & Funaki, H. (2020). Insider and outsider research: Negotiating self at the edge of the emic/etic divide. *Qualitative Inquiry, 26*(4), 593–601.

Beletskiy, A., & Fey, C. F. (2021). HR ambidexterity and absorptive capacities: A paradox-based approach to HRM capabilities and practice adoption in MNC subsidiaries. *Human Resource Management, 60*(1), 863–883.

Benett, H., McCracken, M., O'Kane, P., & Brown, T. (2023). The elusiveness of strategic HR partnering: Using paradox theory to understand tensions surrounding the HR business partnering role. *Human Resource Management Journal, 34*(4), 1–18.

Bizumic, B., Duckitt, J., Popadic, D., Dru, V., & Krauss, S. (2009). A cross-cultural investigation into a reconceptualization of ethnocentrism. *European Journal of Social Psychology, 39*(6), 871–899.

Bouncken, R. B., Qiu, Y., Sinkovics, N., & Kürsten , W. (2021). Qualitative research: Extending the range with flexible pattern matching. *Review of Managerial Science, 15*, 251–273.

Bylok, F., & Kuceba, R. (2021). The impact of trust on the creation of knowledge and innovation in enterprises. Virtual Conference Hosted by Coventry University. *Proceedings of the 22nd European Conference on Knowledge Management* (pp. 130–137). Reading: Academic Conferences and Publishing International Limited.

Cayrat, C., & Boxall, P. (2023). The roles of the HR function: A systematic review of tensions, continuity and change. *Human Resource Management Review, 33*(4), 1–26.

Ciuk, S., Koning, J., & Kostera, M. (2018). Organizational ethnographies. In C. Cassell, A. L. Cunliffe, & G. Grandy (Eds.), *The SAGE Handbook of Qualitative Business and Management Research Methods: History and Traditions* (pp. 270–285). London: SAGE Publications.

Denzin, N. K. (1989). *Interpretive Biography*. London: Sage Publication.

Dovey, K. (2009). The role of trust in innovation. *The Learning Organization, 16*(4), 311–325.

Edú-Valsania, S., Laguia, A., & Moriano, J. A. (2022). Burnout: A review of theory and measurement. *International Journal of Environmental Research and Public Health, 19*(3), 1–27.

Edwards, J. (2020). Ethical Autoethnography: Is it possible? *International Journal of Qualitative Methods, 20*(3), 1–6.

Graue, C. (2015). Qualitative data analysis. *International Journal of Sales, Retailing & Marketing, 9*, 5–14.

Hofstede, G., Hofstede, G. J., & Minkov, M. (2010). *Cultures and Organizations: Software of the Mind*. New York: McGraw-Hill.

Jarzabkowski, P., Lê, J. K., & Van de Ven, A. H. (2013). Responding to competing strategic demands: How organizing, belonging, and performing paradoxes coevolve. *Strategic Organization, 11*(3), 245–280.

Jarzabkowski, P. A., & Lê, J. K. (2017). We have to do this and that? You must be joking: Constructing and responding to paradox through humor. *Organization studies, 38*(3-4), 433–462.

Keegan, A., Brandl, J., & Aust, I. (2019). Handling tensions in human resource management: Insights from paradox theory. *German Journal of Human Resource Management, 33*(2), 79–95.

Lewis, M. W. (2000). Exploring paradox: Toward a more comprehensive guide. Academy of Management Review, *25*(4), 760–776.

Mabey, C., & Zhao, S. (2017). Managing five paradoxes of knowledge exchange in networked organizations: New priorities for HRM? *Human Resource Management Journal, 27*(1), 39–57.

Martinez-Fernandez, J., & Oms, S. (2024). The many faces of the liar paradox. Principia: An International Journal of Epistemology, *28*(1), 15–21.

Khan, M. H., & Jin, J. (2024). The relationship between ethnocentric behaviour and workforce localisation success: The mediating role of knowledge sharing tendency. *European Research on Management and Business Economics, 30*(2), 100245.

Mostowlansky, T., & Rota, A. (2020). Emic and etic. The Cambridge Encyclopedia of Anthropology, 1–16.

Nasierowski, W., & Mikula, B. (1998). Culture dimensions of Polish managers: Hofstede's indices. *Organization Studies, 19*(3), 495–509.

Noor, K. B. (2008). Case study: A strategic research methodology. *American Journal of Applied Sciences, 5*(11), 1602–1604.

Oswald, D., & Dainty, A. (2020). Ethnographic research in the construction industry: A critical review. *Journal of Construction Engineering and Management, 146*(10), 03120003.

PAN, https://wsjp.pl/haslo/podglad/44410/ktos-wybiera-miedzypomiedzy-dzuma-ai-cholera. Accessed on 02.09.2024

Pinterest, https://ie.pinterest.com/pin/727542514776387171/, accessed on: 01.09.2024

Poole, M. S., & Van de Ven, A. H. (1989). Using paradox to build management and organizational theories. *Academy of Management Review, 14*(4), 562–578.

Pudelko, M., & Harzing, A.-W. (2007). Country-of-origin, localization, or dominance effect? An empirical investigation of HRM practices in foreign subsidiaries. *Journal of Human Resource Management, 46*(4), 535–559.

Putnam, L. L., Fairhurst, G. T., & Banghart, S. (2016). Contradictions, dialectics, and paradoxes in organizations: A constitutive approach. *The Academy of Management Annals, 10*(1), 65–171.

Schad, J., Lewis, M. W., Raisch, S., & Smith, W. K. (2016). Paradox research in management science: Looking back to move forward. *Academy of Management Annals, 10*(1), 5–64.

Smith, W. K., & Lewis, M. W. (2011). Toward a theory of paradox: A dynamic equilibrium model of organizing. *Academy of Management Review*, 36(2), 381–403.

Swain, J. (2018). *A Hybrid Approach to Thematic Analysis in Qualitative Research: Using a Practical Example*. London: Sage research methods.

Van Maanen, J. (2010). Ethnography as work: Some rules of engagement. *Journal of Management Studies, 48*(1), 218–234.

Whitehead, T. L. (2005). Basic classical ethnographic research methods. *Cultural Ecology of Health and Change, 1*(1), 1–29.

Zhang, Y., Waldman, D. A., Han, Y.-L., & Li, X.-B. (2015). Paradoxical leader behaviors in people management: Antecedents and consequences. *Academy of Management Journal, 58*(2), 538–566.

# 5 Homo Managerius

## The Paradox of Leadership

*Ewa Marjańska, Joanna Czerska, and Dobrochna Sztajerska*

### 5.1 Introduction

Leadership is a critical area of research within management sciences and presents a considerable challenge for practitioners in diverse organizational contexts. The increasing complexity of contemporary organizational structures, coupled with dynamic market conditions, requires leaders to navigate a range of paradoxes. Richard Feynman, Nobel Prize winner in physics, said: "A paradox is not a conflict within reality. It is a conflict between reality and your feeling of what reality ought to be" (Feynman, 1965, p.18). In management studies, paradoxes are understood as enduring conflicts between interdependent elements that demand approaches that acknowledge and skillfully manage these ongoing tensions. This might mean, for example, balancing between empowering team members and maintaining control or between acting decisively and being flexible and open to feedback (Schad et al., 2016). Paradox is an inherent feature of organizational change that leaders face daily.

Leaders today are navigating an environment defined by rapid and ongoing change. According to a report by Harvard Business Publishing, the current business climate is marked by volatility, uncertainty, complexity, and ambiguity (VUCA), which requires leaders to adapt continually to these dynamic conditions (Axon et al., 2019). In other words, leaders operate in paradoxical conditions daily.

In Central and Eastern European (CEE) countries, educational systems have traditionally centered on principles of certainty and absolutism, mirroring the region's broader social and political structures. This approach stems from a history of centralized authority and strict social hierarchies (Dakin, 1991). The legacy of serfdom and the dominance of the aristocracy further shaped education to uphold existing social orders. This influence is evident in how curricula were structured to maintain the status quo, limiting independent thinking and fostering a sense of inevitability around established power dynamics (Radice, 2004). As a result, absolutism and certainty are now deeply ingrained and often perceived as essential qualities within educational and societal expectations in CEE countries. This historical influence has left a lasting imprint, making certainty and rigid structure appear preferable and required in teaching and learning

DOI: 10.4324/9781003541394-8

processes. This might mean that operating in changing conditions in CEE countries might be very stressful for leaders.

Having learned a deeply rooted need for certainty and absolutism on the one hand and the fast-paced, constantly shifting business world on the other, agility in leadership might be considered a critical capability for navigating change effectively. Agility is the capacity to lead successfully in the face of swift changes and increasing complexity, and agile leaders are uniquely prepared to anticipate and adapt to evolving environments, thereby driving innovation and building resilience within their organizations (Joiner & Josephs, 2007). Leaders with a paradox mindset are better equipped to handle complexities. This approach encourages accepting contradictions rather than immediately seeking to resolve them, promoting an environment that values both/and thinking over either/or thinking (Miron-Spektor et al., 2011). Effective communication is essential for managing paradoxes. Leaders need to cultivate a culture that supports open discussions about conflicting tensions, enabling teams to collaboratively develop solutions and unite around common objectives (Fairhurst, 2001). Thus, it can be said that agile leaders use paradoxical leadership. This term entails balancing conflicting demands and harnessing their tension to enhance organizational performance (Lüscher & Lewis, 2008). However, while paradoxical leadership is increasingly recognized as critical in managing modern organizational challenges, limited empirical research explores its practical implementation and impact across diverse countries. Addressing this gap is crucial to understanding how leaders can effectively develop and sustain paradoxical thinking in real-world settings. The following research question was posed: Are there different expectations of leaders, non-leaders, and non-working students, leading to leadership paradoxes?

This chapter seeks to deepen our understanding of leadership paradoxes, enduring conflicts between interdependent elements that demand approaches to acknowledging and skillfully managing these ongoing tensions. It explores how different professional and generational groups perceive management challenges and their preferred leadership styles. The study was conducted within three groups: Leaders, non-leaders, and students in Poland. It examines how these groups view management challenges and their preferred leadership approaches. The research, conducted in Poland, provides insights that may be particularly valuable for understanding leadership dynamics in CEE countries, where cultural and historical factors shape unique management perspectives. The study might contribute to a broader understanding of leadership in diverse socioeconomic contexts by addressing these regional specificities.

This chapter addresses key research questions exploring how leaders, non-leaders, and students in Poland perceive management challenges and their preferred leadership styles. It also investigates the critical differences in perceptions of leadership paradoxes across professional groups. It examines the impact of cultural and historical factors unique to Central and Eastern Europe, represented here by Poland, on leadership approaches.

## 5.2 Literature Overview and Theoretical Framework

### *5.2.1 Selected Leadership Paradoxes*

The literature describes many models of paradoxes in leadership. Below is a selection of three of these. The common element linking these models is one paradox related to maintaining the right balance of leadership between Confidence and Humility. Waldman and Bowen (2016) outline that leaders frequently face four central paradoxes: Confidence vs. humility, control vs. letting go, consistency vs. change, and consistency vs. change paradox. These are discussed in Table 5.1.

The Confidence vs. Humility Paradox is also mentioned among the eleven paradoxes identified by Hill and Lineback (2011) (Table 5.2). According to

*Table 5.1* Leadership Paradoxes Proposed by Waldman and Bowen (2016)

| *No.* | *Paradox* | *Description* |
|---|---|---|
| 1. | Confidence vs. Humility | Leaders need to display confidence to inspire trust and make decisive choices while balancing it with humility to remain open-minded and avoid arrogance. Humility enables leaders to recognize their limits, seek others' input, and continue learning, fostering approachability, stronger relationships, and better decision-making. |
| 2. | Control vs. Letting Go | Leaders need to establish the balance between maintaining control over processes and outcomes and empowering others through autonomy. While control ensures alignment with organizational goals, letting go enables employees to take ownership, make independent decisions, and foster innovation. Influential leaders strike a middle ground, establishing clear expectations while allowing employees the freedom to make choices and learn from experiences. |
| 3. | Consistency vs. Change | Leaders need to balance stability with the need to adapt. Consistency builds reliability and supports long-term goals, creating stability for employees and stakeholders. Nevertheless, in a changing world, leaders must remain agile and ready to adjust strategies to stay competitive. Achieving this balance helps leaders maintain a strong foundation while responding to new challenges and opportunities. |
| 4. | Profitability vs. Social Responsibility | Leaders need to balance financial performance with ethical responsibilities. While leaders face pressure to prioritize profits, the growing emphasis on corporate social responsibility (CSR) encourages consideration of societal and environmental impacts. Managing this balance allows leaders to achieve sustainable growth by integrating CSR into their business models, aligning profitability with positive social impact. |

*Table 5.2* Leadership Paradoxes Proposed by Hill and Lineback (2011)

| *No.* | *Paradox* | *Description* |
|---|---|---|
| 1. | Confidence vs. Humility | Leaders need to exude confidence to build trust but remain humble to accept feedback and acknowledge areas for improvement. This balance strengthens credibility and openness to learning. |
| 2. | Authority vs. Influence | Leaders must balance using formal authority to make decisions with influencing those outside their direct control. Mastering this balance helps inspire cooperation and commitment throughout the organization. |
| 3. | Focus on Tasks vs. Focus on People | While driving tasks to completion, leaders also need to build strong relationships. Balancing these priorities maintains productivity and keeps team morale high. |
| 4. | Individual Accountability vs. Team Accountability | Leaders hold individuals responsible for their contributions while cultivating a shared sense of accountability within the team. This dual focus strengthens personal growth and teamwork. |
| 5. | Short-Term Results vs. Long-Term Goals | Leaders need to deliver immediate results to show progress while keeping sight of long-term strategies aligned with the organization's future vision. This balance is critical to achieving lasting success. |
| 6. | Consistency vs. Flexibility | Consistency fosters trust and reliability, whereas flexibility allows leaders to adapt to new challenges. Balancing the two enables a steady yet responsive leadership approach. |
| 7. | Directive Leadership vs. Participative Leadership | Leaders sometimes need to provide direction and benefit from involving the team in decision-making. Balancing these approaches empowers the team while enabling decisive leadership. |
| 8. | Control vs. Delegation | Maintaining control helps leaders uphold standards, but delegation encourages team ownership and development. Leaders who delegate effectively empower others while safeguarding quality. |
| 9. | Stability vs. Change | Stability provides a sense of security, yet change drives progress. Leaders must balance these forces to foster a steady foundation while guiding teams through adaptation. |
| 10. | Internal Focus vs. External Focus | Leaders must improve internal operations while staying aware of external opportunities and threats. This balanced focus ensures both operational efficiency and market responsiveness. |
| 11. | Personal Life vs. Professional Life | Leaders must often balance professional demands with personal well-being. Striking this balance supports sustained productivity and well-being, benefiting both the leader and the team. |

these authors, this paradox regards the need for leaders to exude confidence to build trust but remain humble in accepting feedback and acknowledging areas for improvement. This balance strengthens credibility and openness to learning.

Tim Elmore proposes a slightly different approach to leadership paradoxes (Elmore, 2021). This author defines eight paradoxes of great leadership, including the previously mentioned Confidence vs. Humility paradox (Table 5.3).

According to Elmore (2021), leadership approaches have significantly changed over the last seventy years, and what we are facing now is the "Poet-Gardener" type of leadership. Elmore lists ten characteristics of the "Poet-Gardener" leader:

*Table 5.3* Leadership Paradoxes Proposed by Tim Elmor (2021)

| *No.* | *Paradox* | *Description* |
|---|---|---|
| 1. | Confidence and Humility | Great leaders exhibit the right mix of confidence to lead decisively and humility to listen and learn from others. This combination builds trust and openness within the team. |
| 2. | Visibility and Invisibility | Leaders need to be present and visible to guide and inspire, yet step back to allow others to shine. This approach empowers team members and strengthens their self-reliance. |
| 3. | Stubbornness and Open-Mindedness | Effective leaders stay committed to their vision while remaining receptive to fresh ideas. This balance enables them to hold firm to their goals while adapting to new perspectives. |
| 4. | High Standards and Generosity | Leaders should drive excellence with high expectations but balance this with empathy and patience. This approach pushes teams to improve while providing necessary support. |
| 5. | Personal Confidence and Team Dependence | Leaders need self-confidence to make decisions but also rely on their teams, valuing collaborative input. This encourages a strong sense of teamwork and shared purpose. |
| 6. | Visionary Thinking and Detail Orientation | Leaders think ahead with a strategic vision while also paying attention to crucial details. This balance ensures that ambitious ideas are both achievable and actionable. |
| 7. | Teaching and Learning | While leaders guide and teach, they remain open to learning from others. This mindset demonstrates humility and a commitment to growth. |
| 8. | Leading and Serving | True leadership involves both guiding others and serving their needs. This balanced approach fosters respect and loyalty by showing support and dedication to the team's success. |

1. Is highly rational.
2. Interprets culture well.
3. Is emotionally secure.
4. Shares ownership freely.
5. Empowers others.
6. Is comfortable with uncertainty.
7. Listens and fosters self-discovery.
8. Embraces the role of mentor.
9. Is less formal in structure.
10. Is driven by service more than ego.

"Poet-Gardener" leaders are very aware and usually read situations before they lead them. As a result, they practice paradoxical leadership as a norm. Elmore's approach to leadership paradoxes was adopted in analyzing the results obtained in the research section of this chapter.

Perceptions of leadership paradoxes and preferences for leadership styles can differ significantly based on individuals' professional experiences, generational perspectives, and gender, further complicating leadership dynamics. Contemporary leadership research increasingly highlights that individuals in different organizational roles, such as leaders, non-leader employees, and those without professional experience, often hold varying expectations of leaders and may prefer distinct leadership styles (Gabriel, 2015; Sauer, 2011). Additionally, generational differences are recognized as a significant factor in shaping leadership expectations, with each generation influenced by unique experiences in the labor market, organizational cultures, and evolving technologies (Dat & Nam, 2023; Bertsch et al., 2022; Gabrielova & Buchko, 2021).

### *5.2.2 Leadership in Central and Eastern European Countries*

In CEE countries, the educational systems have historically emphasized principles of certainty and absolutism, reflecting the region's broader social and political frameworks. This approach is rooted in a history marked by centralized authority and rigid social hierarchies, which shaped governance and societal values and practices (Dakin, 1991). The legacy of feudal systems, characterized by serfdom and the dominance of aristocratic structures, influenced educational institutions to reinforce the prevailing social order. This hierarchical influence manifested in curricula prioritizing obedience and conformity over critical thinking and innovation (Radice, 2004). Such educational traditions fostered a culture where certainty and rigidity were considered integral to individual success and societal stability, embedding these traits as core expectations within teaching and learning processes. This historical backdrop has had profound implications for leadership and organizational behavior in the CEE region. The preference for rigid structures and the expectation of certainty often create challenges for leaders operating in these environments. The fast-paced, continuously evolving global business landscape introduces complexities that clash with the deeply ingrained need for stability, making adaptability and resilience critical leadership traits. Studies on leadership in transitional economies have highlighted how leaders in these contexts struggle to reconcile historical expectations of control with the demands for flexibility and innovation (House et al., 2004; Javidan et al., 2006). Thus, leadership in CEE countries requires balancing maintaining order and embracing change.

Agility in leadership has gained traction as a vital capability for managing change effectively. Agility refers to the ability to anticipate, adapt to, and thrive amid rapid changes and growing complexities. Agile leaders excel in uncertain environments, using adaptability to drive innovation, foster resilience, and maintain organizational performance (Joiner & Josephs, 2007). This capability is particularly relevant in CEE countries, where the entrenched cultural preference for certainty often exacerbates the stress of operating in volatile conditions. For example, research suggests that agility helps leaders manage external changes but also enables them to mitigate the psychological pressures associated with leading in unpredictable contexts (Heifetz et al., 2009; Denning, 2021).

Leaders must develop a paradox mindset to effectively lead in the CEE region, which involves embracing and managing contradictions rather than attempting to eliminate them. A paradox mindset encourages leaders to adopt both/and thinking, balancing opposing demands and viewing tensions as opportunities for creativity and innovation (Miron-Spektor et al., 2011). This approach fosters a dynamic leadership style that integrates stability with adaptability, enabling leaders to align organizational goals with evolving external conditions. Research in organizational behavior highlights that leaders who adopt paradoxical frames are better equipped to handle complex challenges, as they can integrate diverse perspectives and leverage conflicting demands to enhance decision-making and performance (Smith & Lewis, 2011).

Moreover, the role of communication in managing paradoxes cannot be overstated. Effective communication allows leaders to create a culture of openly discussing conflicting tensions, enabling teams to collaboratively explore solutions and align around shared objectives (Fairhurst, 2001). By fostering an environment of trust and transparency, leaders can mitigate the adverse effects of uncertainty while encouraging innovative thinking. For instance, studies have shown that teams operating under leaders with strong communication skills are likelier to experience higher levels of engagement, collaboration, and problem-solving capacity (Tjosvold, 2008; Carmeli et al., 2013).

The integration of agility and paradoxical leadership further enhances organizational performance. Agile leaders who employ paradox thinking can harness the tensions between conflicting demands, such as innovation vs. efficiency or flexibility vs. control, to drive sustainable change. This capability is critical in CEE countries, where historical legacies often impose additional challenges on leaders striving to foster transformation within rigid structures. Research has demonstrated that organizations led by paradoxical leaders are better positioned to navigate periods of change, as these leaders facilitate continuous learning and adaptation (Lüscher & Lewis, 2008; Waldman & Bowen, 2016).

Recent studies from 2023 and 2024 further underscore the importance of agile and paradoxical leadership in CEE countries. Research indicates that leaders who effectively balance conflicting demands and embrace paradox thinking are better equipped to foster innovation and adaptability within their organizations (Danneels & Viaene, 2022). This approach is particularly vital in the CEE region, where historical preferences for certainty and rigid structures impede responsiveness to change. Additionally, integrating digital transformation strategies has been identified as a critical factor in enhancing organizational agility, enabling leaders to manage complex and rapidly evolving business environments more effectively (Danneels & Viaene, 2022). These findings highlight the necessity for CEE leaders to cultivate a paradox mindset and leverage digital tools to drive sustainable growth and resilience in the face of ongoing challenges (Ahsan & Khawaja, 2024).

The interplay of historical and educational legacies with modern leadership demands in CEE countries reveals a significant research gap in understanding how leaders balance agility and paradoxical thinking in this unique context. While the need for embracing both/and thinking, fostering open communication, and balancing competing demands is acknowledged, limited empirical studies explore how these approaches are practically implemented in CEE nations. This lack of research underscores the necessity of investigating how leaders navigate the tension between adaptability and stability, providing insights for the region and enhancing global leadership practices.

## 5.3 Research Methodology

### *5.3.1 Research Problem, Method, and Analytical Procedure*

The study's central research question was: Are there different expectations of leaders, non-leaders, and non-working students, leading to leadership paradoxes? By addressing this question, the study aimed to uncover variations in how leadership behaviors and attitudes are perceived across different roles, providing insight into the potential leadership paradoxes that emerge in various organizational roles and stages of professional development.

The research sample comprised three distinct groups: Leaders from various organizations (L), non-leader employees (N), and non-working students (S), representing future employees and leaders. These groups were chosen to capture a broad spectrum of perspectives on leadership across different stages of professional development.

The study used the Leadership Practices Inventory (LPI) as the primary assessment tool. Developed by James Kouzes and Barry Posner, the LPI is a well-established leadership competency evaluation instrument designed around five core styles of effective leadership (within the tool used – LPI – referred to as dimensions): Enabling Others to Act, Encouraging the Heart, Inspiring a Shared Vision, Modeling the Way, and Challenging the Process. The LPI facilitates self-assessment and 360° feedback, enabling leaders to enhance their skills, improve team relationships, and achieve organizational goals more effectively. It is widely recognized for its application in assessing leadership styles and behaviors across various contexts (Kang et al., 2021; Posner, 2016; Husin et al., 2014). This tool's comprehensive approach to evaluating leadership behaviors provides a solid foundation for understanding how leadership preferences and expectations vary across different professional and generational groups.

The study modified the scale from a nominal (categorical) system, which classified leadership dimensions into five distinct categories, to an ordinal scale, enabling a more precise analysis of preferences related to leadership styles. This adjustment was made by identifying a common factor across the five leadership dimensions – the degree to which they build and strengthen interpersonal relationships. This dimension emphasizes interpersonal interactions, trust, and shared values. The nominal scale allowed only the classification of leadership dimensions without considering their relative hierarchy. By shifting to an ordinal scale, it became possible to rank the leadership styles based on how much they foster interpersonal relationships. This change enabled the identification of the most preferred dimensions (e.g., Enabling Others to Act as the most relationship-oriented style) and the application of more advanced statistical analyses, such as non-parametric tests and Principal Component Analysis (PCA).

The five leadership dimensions in the LPI are systematically ranked according to the strength with which they build and enhance interpersonal relationships. This ranking is based on the emphasis each style places on interpersonal interactions, trust, and shared values, where 1 represents the strongest relationship-building style and 5 the weakest:

- *Enable Others to Act* is ranked highest in relationship-building strength because it focuses primarily on trust, cooperation, and empowering others, which are foundational elements for healthy and effective interpersonal relationships.
- *Encourage the Heart* by acknowledging individual contributions, this style directly strengthens relationships, enhancing morale and fostering a sense of community, which reinforces interpersonal bonds.
- *Inspires a Shared Vision* builds relationships by aligning team members around a shared purpose, fostering a sense of belonging and collective effort, which supports the development of stronger relational ties.

- *Models the Way* focuses more on setting clear values than directly fostering interpersonal interactions, but it nonetheless strengthens relationships through reliability and respect.
- *Challenge the Process* is ranked lowest in relationship-building because it introduces uncertainty and risk, which may undermine stability and trust.

Table 5.4 attempts to relate LPI dimensions to Elmore's (2021) paradoxes.

*Table 5.4* Relation between LPI Dimensions (Kouzes & Posner, 2003) and Elmore's (2021) Leadership Paradoxes

| *No.* | *LPI Dimension* | *LPI Dimension Description* | *Linked Elmor's Paradox* |
|---|---|---|---|
| 1. | Enable Others to Act | Effective leaders empower their employees by fostering trust, collaboration, and active participation. They encourage individuals to take responsibility, contributing to developing competencies and autonomy among team members. | Confidence and Humility<br>Visibility and Invisibility<br>Teaching and Learning |
| 2. | Encourage the Heart | Leaders employing this style recognize and reward individual achievements, creating an environment where employees feel appreciated and motivated. Emotional support and celebration of successes are key components. | High Standards and Generosity |
| 3, | Inspire a Shared Vision | Visionary leaders can craft and communicate a compelling vision of the future, motivating and engaging their teams to work together toward common goals. | Stubbornness and Open-Mindedness<br>Visionary Thinking and Detail Orientation |
| 4. | Model the Way | Leaders who "model the way" act as role models, demonstrating their values and beliefs through their actions. Authenticity, consistency, and reliability are essential for this leadership dimension. | Confidence and Humility<br>Leading and Serving |
| 5. | Challenge the Process | Leaders using this style are unafraid to introduce innovation, take risks, and promote experimentation in pursuit of better outcomes. They constantly seek new opportunities and encourage their teams to embrace change. | Stubbornness and Open-Mindedness<br>Visionary Thinking and Detail Orientation |

The following is a rationale for the assignment of the individual LPI dimensions presented in Table 5.4 to the specific Elmore's leadership paradoxes:

- *Enable Others to Act ↔ Confidence and Humility, Visibility and Invisibility, Teaching and Learning* – empowering employees involves balancing active support with the ability to step back, fostering trust and collaboration. Confidence to lead and humility to empower others align well with this dimension. Leaders who are confident in their decision-making also recognize the value of collaboration, fostering an environment where team members feel empowered to contribute. While leaders guide and teach, they remain open to learning from others. This mindset demonstrates humility and a commitment to growth.
- *Encourage the Heart ↔ High Standards and Generosity* – recognizing achievements aligns with driving excellence while showing empathy. Leaders who celebrate success provide the support and motivation that encourages improvement without undue pressure.
- *Inspire a Shared Vision ↔ Stubbornness and Open-Mindedness, Visionary Thinking and Detail Orientation* – visionary leadership requires holding a strong commitment to a clear vision while staying receptive to new ideas and adjusting as necessary. This combination of big-picture vision and detail orientation supports the effective pursuit of shared goals.
- *Model the Way ↔ Confidence and Humility, Leading and Serving* – leaders who "model the way" rely on consistency, authenticity, and humility, striking a balance between guiding others through example and serving their needs.
- *Challenge the Process ↔ Stubbornness and Open-Mindedness, Visionary Thinking and Detail Orientation* – encouraging innovation requires a balance between a firm commitment to long-term goals and flexibility to experiment with new ideas, adjusting as necessary while keeping an eye on practical details.

Frequency analysis served as the initial analytical tool to assess the prevalence of specific leadership dimensions selected by different groups. This provided an overview of preferred dimensions based on professional roles (leaders, non-leaders, students), gender, and generational affiliation. Next, descriptive statistical analyses were conducted to provide a more detailed understanding of the distribution of preferences within each group. These analyses offered insights into typical response patterns and facilitated comparisons of mean scores for specific leadership styles across different groups. To assess whether the differences between the groups were statistically significant, significance tests were employed, with the Kruskal-Wallis rank test used due to the nature of the dependent variable. This non-parametric test enabled the determination of whether preferences for leadership styles varied significantly based on professional role, gender, and generational affiliation. Finally, PCA was conducted to facilitate a deeper investigation, provide a broader context for the phenomenon under study, and enable the identification of key factors influencing preferences for leadership dimensions. PCA allowed presenting data in the form of a smaller number of uncorrelated variables called principal components (Everitt et al., 2011). Input data for PCA were prepared using correlation matrices. Mathematical modeling was done using SPSS Statistics software ver. 29.0.0.0 (241) by IBM.

By employing these analytical methods, the study identified the differences and similarities in leadership style preferences. This approach considered both demographic and professional factors, leading to a more accurate interpretation of leadership paradoxes across various professional roles, genders, and generations.

### *5.3.2 Sample Selection and Data Collection*

The study, conducted from February to April 2024, involved 240 Poles, 80 from each of three groups distinguished by role: Leaders of various business organizations (referred to as "leaders"), employees in non-leadership positions, and working students. In the study, participants were divided into four generational groups – baby boomers (BB) (born in 1946–1964), Generation X (born in 1965–1980), Generation Y (Millennials) (born in 1981–1996), and Generation Z (born after 1996) (Twenge & Campbell, 2008).

Information regarding the demographic data of the respondents is presented in Table 5.5. Due to the large scope of data, the table presents only the subjectively largest groups in terms of size and was distinguished according to demographic variables.

The generational distribution reveals that a majority of respondents belong to the younger generations, specifically Generation Y (Millennials) and Generation Z, with 80 individuals (33%) from Generation Y and 96 individuals (40%) from Generation Z. This demographic composition may influence preferences regarding leadership dimensions, particularly in the context of contemporary leadership practices and interpersonal relationships at work. Generation X was represented by 58 individuals (24%), forming a medium-sized group. The smallest demographic group consisted of 5 individuals (2%) from the Baby Boomer generation, which aligns with the observed trend of a declining presence of this generation in the active workforce.

In the study examining leadership style preferences by gender, the participant groups comprised 143 women (W), representing 60% of the total respondents, making it the largest demographic segment. The study also included 95 men (M), accounting for 40%, constituting another significant group. Additionally, one participant identified as a different gender, while one declined to specify their gender.

*Table 5.5* Study Population According to Demographic Variables

| *Demographic Variable* | *Category* | *Frequency (n)* | *Percentage (%)* |
|---|---|---|---|
| Role | Manager | 143 | 59.6 |
| | Non-manager | 95 | 39.6 |
| | Student | 80 | 33.3 |
| | Not specified | 1 | 0.4 |
| Generation | BB | 60 | 25.0 |
| | X | 58 | 24.2 |
| | Y | 80 | 33.3 |
| | Z | 96 | 40.0 |
| Gender | Female | 143 | 59.6 |
| | Male | 95 | 39.6 |
| | Other | 80 | 33.3 |
| | Not specified | 1 | 0.4 |

The regional distribution of respondents reveals that the majority were from the Pomeranian Voivodeship, with 119 participants registered, accounting for 49.58% of the total. The Lesser Poland Voivodeship followed, albeit with a much smaller representation, comprising 29 respondents (12.08%). The Masovian Voivodeship had 17 participants (7.08%), while the Greater Poland Voivodeship included 16 respondents (6.67%). The remaining voivodeships were represented by numbers ranging from 14 to 2 participants.

Regarding sector representation, the largest group of respondents was employed in the production sector, with 60 individuals (25%), underscoring the sector's significance within the study. Business services ranked second, comprising 59 respondents (24.58%). The higher education sector was represented by 46 participants (19.17%), while the logistics and transport sector had the smallest representation, with 14 respondents (5.83%). Other industries were represented by varying numbers of participants, ranging from 9 to 1.

## 5.4 Empirical Findings

### *5.4.1 Leadership Style Preferences*

The first comprehensive analysis focused on comparing leadership style preferences among three groups of respondents: Leaders, non-leaders, and students. To achieve this, the Kruskal-Wallis test was employed, which assesses differences in median leadership dimension preferences among the groups. The test results indicated statistically significant differences ($H (2, N = 240) = 9.670851$, $p = 0.0079$), suggesting that the preferences for leadership dimensions vary among these groups. Subsequent analyses utilizing multiple comparisons of mean ranks across all samples provided a more precise identification of the specific differences between the groups.

The analysis revealed significant differences in leadership style preferences between non-leaders and students ($p = 0.035609$). In contrast, no statistically significant differences were found between leaders and non-leaders ($p = 0.137559$) or between leaders and students ($p = 0.898754$). The z-value for the multiple comparisons indicated $z = 2.515999$ for the non-leaders compared to students. These findings highlight the necessity for further investigation into the factors influencing leadership style preferences based on professional role and level of experience. The Kruskal-Wallis test results indicate no statistically significant differences in leadership style preferences among groups distinguished by generation ($H(4, N = 240) = 3.156007$, $p = 0.5321$). Although there are variations in the medians of leadership style preferences across the individual groups ($Me_X = 124.40$; $Me_Y = 112.06$; $Me_Z = 125.00$; $Me_{BB} = 132.50$), these differences are insufficient to indicate varying preferences based on generational affiliation. The results of the Kruskal-Wallis test also revealed no statistically significant differences in leadership dimension preferences between groups based on gender ($H(3, N = 240) = 2.941038$, $p = 0.4008$). Similar to the generational analysis, the differences in the medians of leadership style preferences between the gender groups were insufficiently significant to confirm any notable disparities ($Me_W = 119.73$; $Me_M = 121.15$).

Then, the potential dominance of the preferred leadership style was assessed according to the role played in the organization (leaders, employees in non-leader positions, students). The answers concern preferences in the context of five leadership dimensions, referring to the LPI model (Figure 5.1).

As illustrated in Figure 5.1, the Enable Others to Act dimension is the most preferred leadership dimension among all three groups. Non-leaders preferred this style, with 62 responses, followed by leaders with 47 responses, and students with 45 votes. This trend suggests that this style, which emphasizes building trust and cooperation, is vital for all respondents, particularly for leaders.

Although receiving significantly fewer votes, the second most preferred dimension was Encourage the Heart. Preferences in this category are more evenly distributed, with leaders leading the count at 18 votes, non-leaders expressing 9 preferences, and students casting 14 votes for this dimension. Although this dimension, which focuses on appreciating and motivating team members, is less dominant, it remains popular among respondents. Both dimensions are instrumental in fostering and strengthening relationships, emphasizing interpersonal interactions, trust, and shared values. The next three styles received markedly fewer votes. Consequently, it can be concluded that there is a dominant preferred leadership style among groups distinguished by role.

To further enhance the analysis, data regarding preferred leadership styles based on professional role were evaluated using descriptive statistics. To present

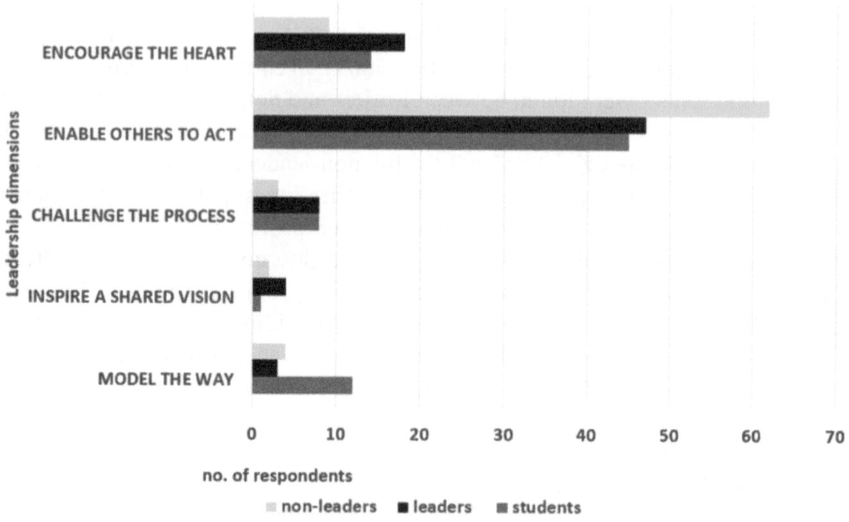


*Figure 5.1* Leadership Dimensions According to Role in the Organization.

*Source:* Own elaboration based on research findings.

this information more succinctly, it has been displayed in box plots rather than in a tabular format (Figure 5.2).

In addition to the box plots, descriptive statistics were also examined. Due to editorial constraints, only the key conclusions from the analyses are presented below.

Groups L1, N1, N3, N4, S1, and S3 exhibit distinct characteristics compared to the other groups under analysis. L1 and N1 are notable for their pronounced left-skewness and sharp distribution peaks (high kurtosis), along with the presence of outliers. These features make them particularly unusual relative to the other groups. This suggests that, while many in these groups rate this leadership dimension highly, a few outliers could indicate potential challenges in how this style is applied. In contrast, N3, N4, S1, and S3 are characterized by high data dispersion, reflected in their elevated standard deviation and coefficient of variation. This suggests greater variability within these groups. Additionally, these groups show left-skewed distributions, indicating a tendency toward higher values, with the left-sided asymmetry being especially pronounced in N1 and L1.

These findings suggest that these groups exhibit unique distributional properties, potentially warranting a different analytical or interpretive approach compared to more normally distributed groups.

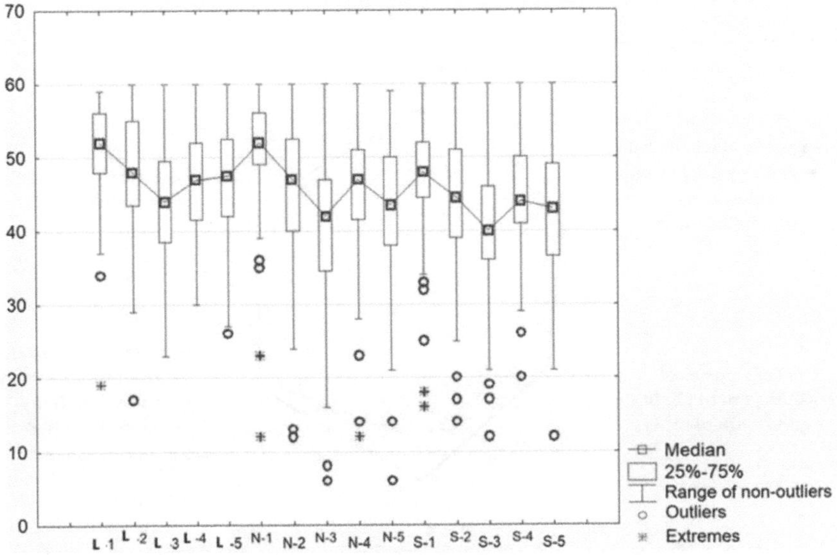


*Figure 5.2* Box-and-Whisker Charts of Preferred Management Styles According to Role in the Organization.

*Note:* The numbers (L1…, N1…, S1…) associated with the three analyzed groups represent specific management dimensions, as outlined in the methodology.

*Source:* Own elaboration based on research findings.

### *5.4.2 Leadership Paradoxes in the Studied Groups: Leaders, Non-Leaders, and Students within Five Tested LPI Dimensions*

The following section analyzes the collected results in detail to identify leadership paradoxes and explore differences and similarities between the tested groups of respondents.

#### *5.4.2.1 Encourage the Heart*

The findings prove that leaders, non-leaders, and students appreciate leaders who balance high standards with generosity, particularly valuing praise and personal involvement in recognizing achievements. Leaders and non-leaders prioritize expressing confidence in others and creative recognition methods, seeing these as motivating excellence while offering meaningful support. Students, however, slightly prefer direct, straightforward recognition over abstract encouragement, indicating a need for clarity and consistency. All groups agree that leaders' involvement in celebrating accomplishments boosts motivation and team cohesion. Overall, this analysis highlights that effective leadership should combine

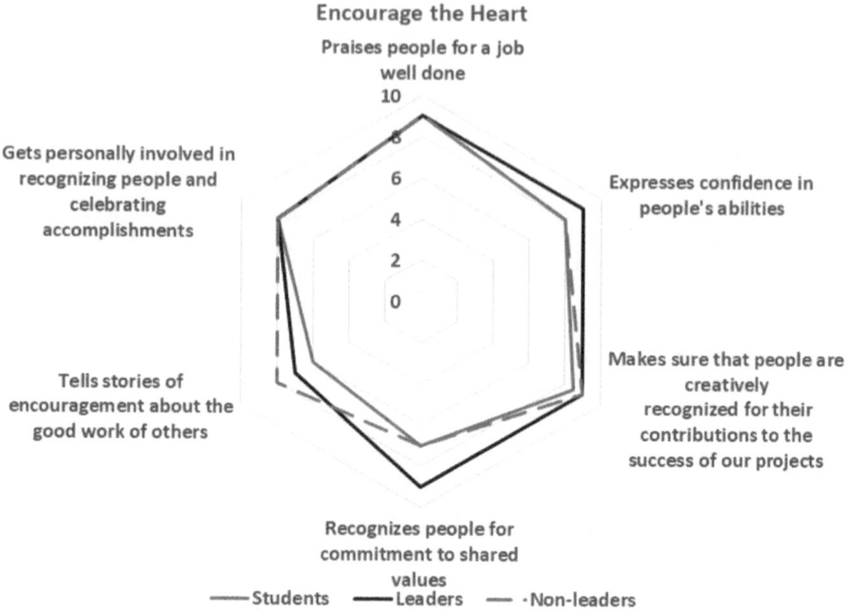


*Figure 5.3* Summary of Median Values for Each of the LPI Questions by Study Group – Encourage the Heart Dimension.

Scores 1–10: 1 – almost never, 2 – rarely, 3 – seldom, 4 – once in a while, 5 – occasionally, 6 – sometimes, 7 – fairly often, 8 – usually, 9 – very frequently, 10 – almost always.

*Source:* Own elaboration based on research findings.

high expectations with empathetic, visible support, though each group values these elements differently based on experience (Figure 5.3).

#### *5.4.2.2 Enable Others to Act*

The study showed that leaders, non-leaders, and students all value leadership qualities that reflect Confidence and Humility, Visibility and Invisibility, and Teaching and Learning paradoxes, though with nuanced preferences. Leaders and non-leaders prioritize cooperative relationships, shared decision-making, and autonomy, reflecting a blend of confident guidance with humility and openness to others' input. This balance is seen as essential for fostering trust and empowerment within teams. Students also appreciate these qualities but rate visible actions, like direct involvement in decision-making and guidance, slightly higher, likely reflecting their need for clear support as they grow professionally. The strong emphasis on respect and cooperative relationships across all groups underscores the universal importance of a respectful, growth-oriented environment. Leaders

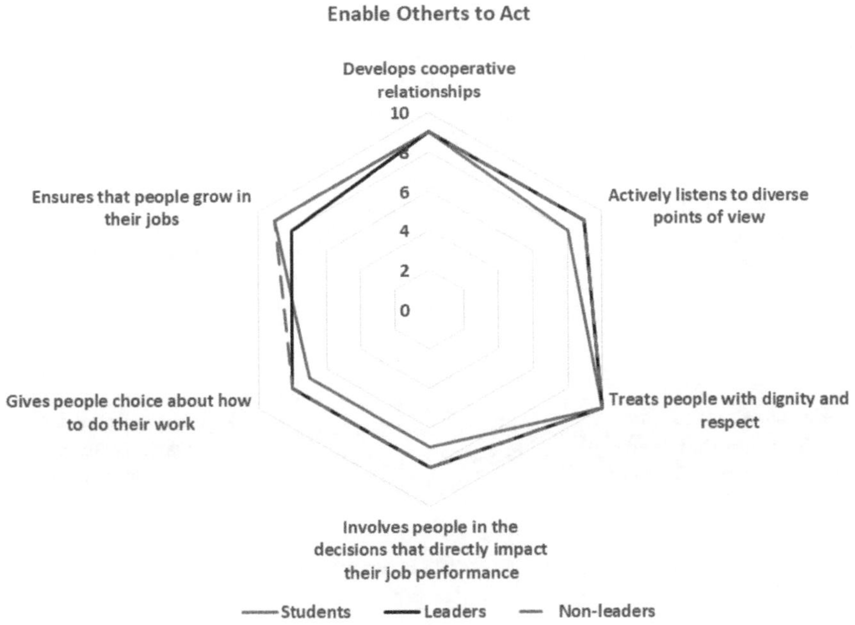


*Figure 5.4* Summary of Median Values for Each of the LPI Questions by Study Group – Enable Others to Act Dimension.

Scores 1–10: 1 – almost never, 2 – rarely, 3 – seldom, 4 – once in a while, 5 – occasionally, 6 – sometimes, 7 – fairly often, 8 – usually, 9 – very frequently, 10 – almost always.

*Source:* Own elaboration based on research findings.

slightly prefer allowing self-directed growth, while non-leaders and students place a high value on visible support for development. Overall, each group's responses highlight the value of leaders who can balance presence with empowerment, confidence with humility, and guidance with ongoing learning (Figure 5.4).

### *5.4.2.3 Challenge the Process*

All three groups recognize the value of balancing vision with actionable steps, though their preferences reveal some differences. Leaders and non-leaders emphasize challenging themselves and others to try new approaches and seek innovation, aligning with the Stubbornness and Open-Mindedness paradox by blending commitment with openness. Students, however, rate stability and clear guidance slightly higher, showing a preference for consistency over frequent changes. All groups agree on the importance of setting measurable milestones and proactively responding to change, supporting the Visionary Thinking and

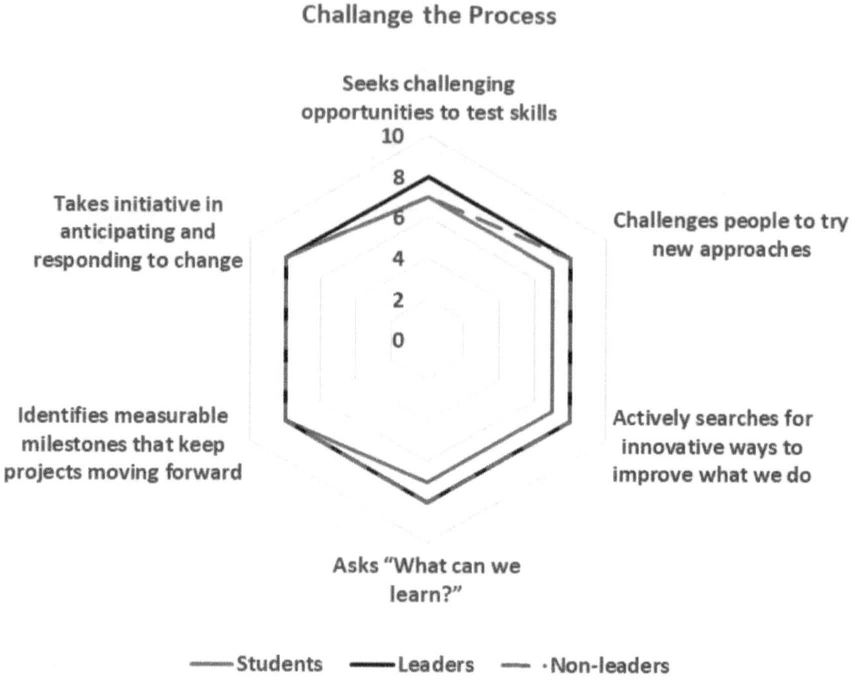


*Figure 5.5* Summary of Median Values for Each of the LPI Questions by Study Group – Challenge the Process Dimension.

Scores 1–10: 1 – almost never, 2 – rarely, 3 – seldom, 4 – once in a while, 5 – occasionally, 6 – sometimes, 7 – fairly often, 8 – usually, 9 – very frequently, 10 – almost always.

*Source:* Own elaboration based on research findings.

Detail Orientation paradox as essential for achieving realistic and adaptable goals. This alignment highlights a universal appreciation for leaders who combine strategic vision with detail, even as each group values different aspects of innovation and stability (Figure 5.5).

#### *5.4.2.4 Inspire a Shared Vision*

Although they emphasize different aspects, leaders, non-leaders, and students all recognize the importance of balancing vision with practical relevance. Leaders strongly emphasize articulating a compelling future and speaking with conviction about the meaning of work, aligning with both the Stubbornness and Open-Mindedness and Visionary Thinking and Detail Orientation paradoxes. Non-leaders and students prioritize seeing how the vision connects to their roles

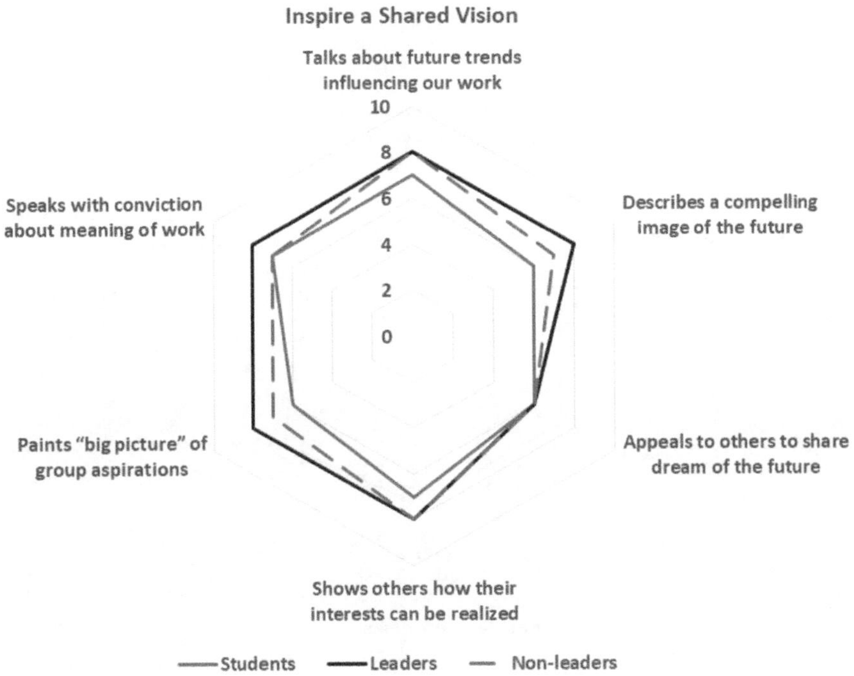


*Figure 5.6* Summary of Median Values for Each of the LPI questions by Study Group – Inspire a Shared Vision Dimension.

Scores 1–10: 1 – almost never, 2 – rarely, 3 – seldom, 4 – once in a while, 5 – occasionally, 6 – sometimes, 7 – fairly often, 8 – usually, 9 – very frequently, 10 – almost always.

*Source:* Own elaboration based on research findings.

and appreciate actions that directly impact them. Leaders balance commitment to long-term goals with flexibility and detail, while students and non-leaders lean toward actionable, immediate relevance. This analysis suggests that successful leadership combines strategic foresight with attention to practical needs, though each group values these elements differently (Figure 5.6).

#### *5.4.2.5 Model the Way*

Leaders, non-leaders, and students all appreciate leadership behaviors that reflect the Serving-Leading and Confidence and Humility paradoxes, though each group emphasizes different aspects. Setting a clear example of what is expected is essential for all three groups. Non-leaders and students value leaders who consistently follow through on promises and commitments, underscoring a desire for consistency and support. Leaders and non-leaders align in prioritizing

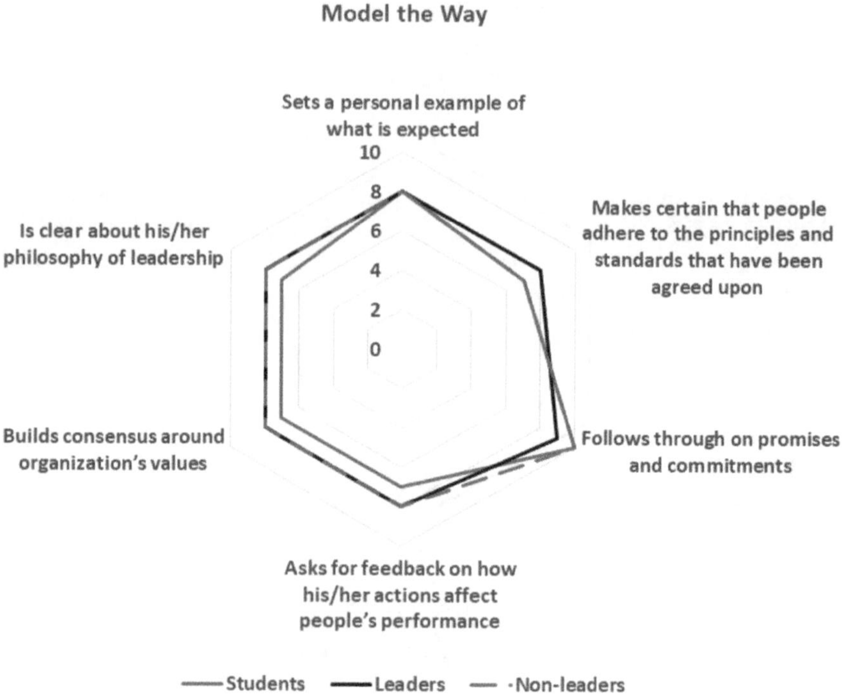


*Figure 5.7* Summary of Median Values for Each of the LPI Questions by Study Group – Model the Way Dimension.

Scores 1–10: 1 – almost never, 2 – rarely, 3 – seldom, 4 – once in a while, 5 – occasionally, 6 – sometimes, 7 – fairly often, 8 – usually, 9 – very frequently, 10 – almost always.

*Source:* Own elaboration based on research findings.

consensus-building and openness to feedback, reflecting a blend of authority with approachability. Students with less direct leadership experience may focus more on visible actions than strategic alignment with values. In sum, serving the team while showing confidence balanced by humility is widely respected but perceived uniquely across these groups (Figure 5.7).

Figure 5.8 presents the most important information as a mind map to clarify the data discussed in Figures 5.3–5.7.

### *5.4.3 In-Depth Analysis of the Differences between the Studied Groups in the Context of Leadership Paradoxes*

Further in-depth analysis of the discrepancies in leadership style preferences among the study groups was conducted using PCA analysis. Figure 5.9 presents

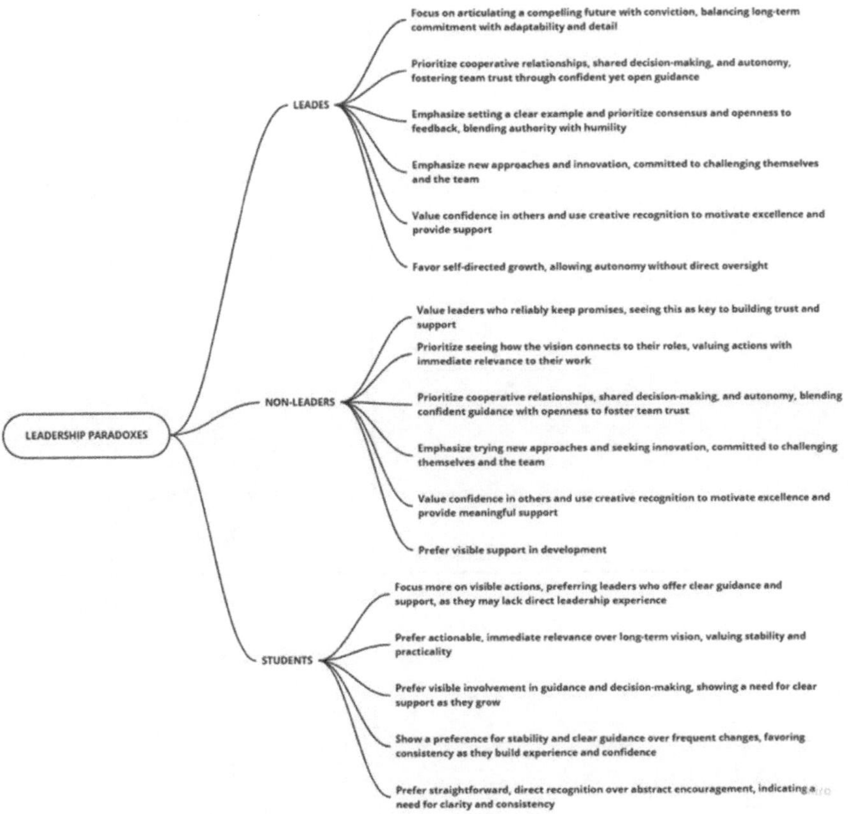


*Figure 5.8* The Most Significant Leadership Paradoxes within Groups Tested – Mind Map.

*Source:* Own elaboration based on research findings.

PCA charts for each respondent group, showing how the surveyed groups perceived the analyzed leadership dimensions. In addition, Table 5.6 presents the first two principal components (PC1 and PC2) and the percentage of total variance explained.

The total variance explained indicates how much of the original data can be captured by these components – students: 83.6% variance explained by PC1, 7.1% by PC2; leaders: 75.9% variance explained by PC1, 10.9% by PC2; and non-leaders: 77.8% variance explained by PC1, 9.3% by PC2. The higher total variance explained by PC1 in students (83.61%) suggests a more rigid, unified view of leadership traits, whereas leaders (75.92%) and non-leaders

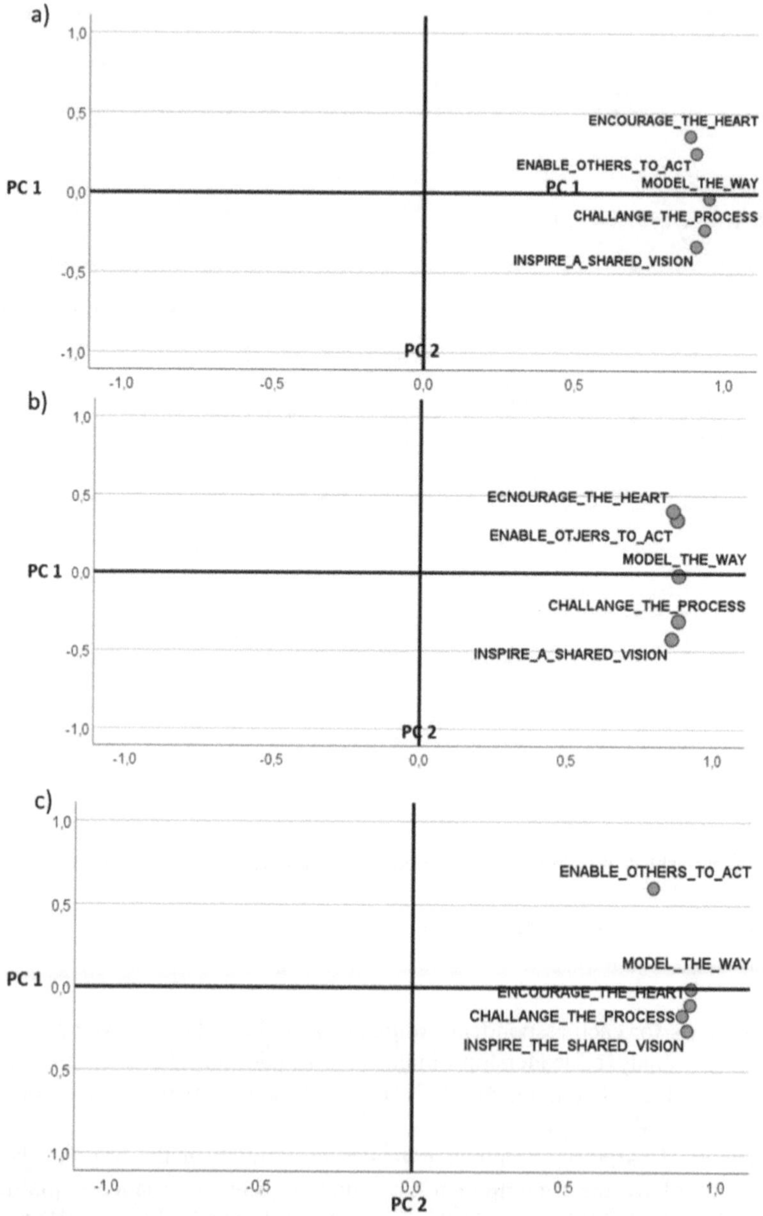


*Figure 5.9* PCA Component charts: a) Students, b) Leaders, c) Non-leaders.

*Source:* Own elaboration based on research findings.

*Table 5.6* Principal Components (PC1 and PC 2) and % of Total Variance Explained for Three Respondent Groups

| *Dimension* | *PC 1* | *PC 2* |
|---|---|---|
| **Students** | | |
| Model the Way | 0.947 | −0.310 |
| Inspire a Shared Vision | 0.904 | −0.333 |
| Challenge the Process | 0.932 | −0.228 |
| Enable Others to Act | 0.904 | 0.250 |
| Encourage the Heart | 0.883 | 0.358 |
| Total variance explained (%) | 83.606 | 7.097 |
| **Leaders** | | |
| Model the Way | 0.881 | −0.015 |
| Inspire a Shared Vision | 0.859 | −0.421 |
| Challenge the Process | 0.881 | −0.304 |
| Enable Others to Act | 0.875 | −0.341 |
| Encourage the Heart | 0.861 | −0.399 |
| Total variance explained (%) | 75.924 | 10.912 |
| **Non-leaders** | | |
| Model the Way | 0.915 | −0.007 |
| Inspire a Shared Vision | 0.902 | −0.255 |
| Challenge the Process | 0.886 | −0.166 |
| Enable Others to Act | 0.790 | −0.603 |
| Encourage the Heart | 0.912 | −0.102 |
| Total variance explained (%) | 77.844 | 9.327 |

*Source:* Own elaboration based on research findings.

(77.84%) have a more nuanced understanding, reflected in slightly greater PC2 contributions.

In the case of leaders on the dominant dimension (PC1), the high loadings across all dimensions (*Model the Way*: 0.881, *Challenge the Process*: 0.881, *Enable Others to Act*: 0.875) were obtained, with 75.92% of variance explained. This reflects a balanced approach to leadership, focusing on Confidence and Humility (reliability, modeling values), Stubbornness and Open-Mindedness (embracing change and risk-taking), and Teaching and Learning (empowering and fostering autonomy). On the PC2, which represents a subtle dimension, negative correlations between *Inspire a Shared Vision* (−0.421) and *Encourage the Heart* (−0.399) were obtained. These are linked to Visionary Thinking and Detail Orientation (balancing strategic vision and details) and High Standards and Generosity (emotional support, recognizing success). It might indicate that leaders will likely see these elements as more situational or dependent on team context, not central to their primary leadership approach.

In the case of non-leaders, the PC1 represents high loadings for *Model the Way* (0.915), *Encourage the Heart* (0.912), and *Inspire a Shared Vision* (0.902).

These are in strong alignment with Confidence and Humility (trustworthiness, modeling), High Standards and Generosity (emotional engagement), and Stubbornness and Open-Mindedness (articulating a vision). This might indicate that non-leaders view leadership as a combination of reliability, emotional connection, and vision. Strong negative loadings for *Enable Others to Act* (−0.603), linked to Teaching and Learning and Visibility and Invisibility (fostering autonomy, stepping back to let others shine), are observed on subtle PC2. Conversely, this might indicate that non-leaders may struggle to associate leadership with empowerment, emphasizing direct guidance instead.

In the case of students on the dominant dimension (PC1), high loadings for the following dimensions were observed: *Model the Way* (0.947), *Challenge the Process* (0.932), and *Inspire a Shared Vision* (0.904). These align with the paradoxes: Confidence and Humility (e.g., modeling values, showing reliability), Stubbornness and Open-Mindedness (embracing innovation and a compelling vision), Visionary Thinking, and Detail Orientation (balancing broad goals with actionable plans). This indicates that students strongly associate leadership with role modeling, innovation, and visionary thinking. On PC2, positive loadings for *Enable Others to Act* (0.250) and *Encourage the Heart* (0.358) were obtained. These are linked to the following paradoxes: Teaching and Learning, Visibility and Invisibility (empowering teams with trust and collaboration), and High Standards and Generosity (recognizing individual contributions). Students view these aspects as secondary to innovation and role modeling but still crucial for fostering trust and emotional engagement.

## 5.5 Conclusions and Discussion

### *5.5.1 Conclusions of the Study*

These findings contribute to the growing body of knowledge on paradoxical leadership, particularly in the underexplored context of CEE countries. They underscore the need for further empirical studies examining how historical and cultural influences shape leadership behaviors and leaders' practical strategies to balance competing demands in transitional economies.

Our study observed that Role Modeling and Vision are closely linked to Confidence and Humility, highlighting the interplay between personal conviction and openness in leadership. Interestingly, students and non-leaders predominantly associate leadership with paradoxes of Stubbornness and Open-Mindedness, viewing these as dominant traits. In contrast, leaders demonstrate a more balanced integration of these traits with other leadership dimensions. We found that the practice of Challenging the Process and Driving Innovation is intricately tied to paradoxes such as Stubbornness, Open-Mindedness, Visionary Thinking, and Detail Orientation. Leaders highly value these qualities, seeing them as central to effective leadership. Students also regard innovation and challenge as critical, whereas non-leaders place less emphasis on these aspects, perceiving them as less integral to their understanding of leadership. The paradox of Empowerment vs. Emotional Connection is reflected in two critical dimensions of leadership: Enable Others to Act and Encourage the Heart. Leaders in our study appeared to balance these dimensions, demonstrating the ability to empower others while maintaining emotional engagement. Students, however, prioritize emotional connection over empowerment, focusing more on relational aspects of leadership. Non-leaders, by contrast, emphasize emotional support while de-emphasizing autonomy, favoring direct guidance over empowering practices.

For students, leadership is primarily about visible role modeling and inspiring innovation, with emotional connection and empowerment valued but viewed as secondary. This reflects their preference for leaders who actively demonstrate their advocacy behaviors and encourage creative problem-solving. Leaders, in contrast, define leadership as integrating multiple dimensions, balancing vision, innovation, empowerment, and emotional connection. They prioritize flexibility and adaptability while maintaining a strong strategic focus, underscoring the importance of agility in navigating complex challenges. Non-leaders associate leadership with reliability, vision, and emotional connection, favoring visible support and direct guidance. They place less emphasis on empowerment and autonomy, indicating a preference for structured and directive leadership styles.

These findings align with the broader context of leadership in CEE countries, where historical and educational legacies have shaped a preference for certainty, structure, and hierarchical control (Bakacsi, 2002; Purg & Derganc, 2015). The detailed differences between leaders, students, and non-leaders in their approach to paradox thinking reflect the ongoing tension between traditional leadership expectations and the demands of modern, agile practices in the region (Szabo et al., 2002). By understanding these group-specific perspectives, we gain valuable insights into how leaders in CEE countries can navigate the complexities of balancing stability with adaptability while addressing cultural and historical influences on leadership behaviors (House et al., 2004; Chhokar et al., 2013). This highlights the critical need for leaders in CEE countries to develop a paradox mindset, embracing both/and thinking to reconcile opposing demands such as innovation and control or flexibility and structure. Agility and effective communication emerge as essential capabilities, enabling leaders to foster trust, collaboration, and resilience in navigating these complexities. Further research is needed to explore how these approaches can be practically implemented to transform profoundly ingrained leadership traditions into more adaptive and innovative practices.

Our research, therefore, has great practical potential. Leadership development programs in CEE countries should emphasize building paradoxical thinking skills and agility, enabling leaders to navigate historical rigidity while fostering innovation and collaboration. Organizations can adopt effective communication and trust-building training to empower teams and drive sustainable change.

### *5.5.2 Research Limitations, Further Studies, and Practical Implications*

This study was conducted exclusively in Poland, which may limit the applicability of its findings to the broader CEE region. While Poland shares historical and cultural similarities with other CEE countries, significant differences exist within the region, necessitating future research across a broader range of CEE nations. Such studies could help identify common leadership challenges and country-specific nuances, offering a more representative understanding of regional leadership features.

Secondly, the study focused on the perceptions of leaders, students, and non-leaders, which, while insightful, might not fully capture the complexities of leadership in diverse organizational contexts. Future research could include other stakeholder perspectives, such as employees or external collaborators, to provide a more holistic view of leadership preferences and paradoxes.

Thirdly, the reliance on a survey-based methodology may introduce subjective biases. Employing mixed-method approaches, including longitudinal studies or experimental designs, could strengthen the robustness of findings and track changes over time. Lastly, while this research highlights essential leadership paradoxes, future studies could delve deeper into how specific organizational contexts, such as industry type or organizational size, mediate the impact of these paradoxes on leadership effectiveness. Addressing these limitations would provide a more comprehensive understanding of leadership in CEE countries and its implications for handling paradoxes.

The findings of this study suggest several directions for future research on leadership in CEE contexts. Investigating how historical and educational legacies influence leadership behaviors across generations could provide valuable insights, particularly as younger leaders adopt global leadership paradigms. Future research could also examine the impact of digital transformation on leadership paradoxes in the region, especially in navigating rigid organizational structures.

Exploring the effects of paradoxical leadership traits, such as balancing empowerment with emotional connection, on team performance and innovation would further enrich understanding. Comparative studies between CEE countries and regions with different historical legacies could highlight unique leadership challenges and opportunities. Additionally, research into culturally tailored leadership training programs could identify effective strategies for fostering agility and paradoxical thinking in leaders.

## References


Ahsan, M. J., & Khawaja, S. (2024). Sustainable leadership impact on environmental performance: Exploring employee well-being, innovation, and organizational resilience. *Discover Sustainability, 5*, 317. https://doi.org/10.1007/s43621-024-00422-z

Axon, L., Friedman, E., & Molloy, J. (2019). Leading for today and tomorrow: Capabilities for a changing world. *Harvard Business Publishing.*

Bakacsi, G. (2002). Central Eastern Europe cluster: Tradition and transition. *Journal of World Business, 37*(1), 69–80. https://doi.org/10.1016/S1090-9516(01)00073-9

Bertsch, A., Saeed, M., Ondracek, J., Abdullah, A., Pizzo, J., Dahl, J., Scheschuk, S., Moore, W., & Youngren, D. (2022). Variation in preferred leadership styles across generations. *Journal of Leadership in Organizations, 4*(1), 1–16. https://doi.org/10.22146/jlo.70057

Carmeli, A., Gelbard, R., & Reiter-Palmon, R. (2013). Leadership, creative problem-solving capacity, and creative performance: The importance of knowledge sharing. *Human Resource Management, 52*(1), 95–121. https://doi.org/10.1002/hrm.21514

Chhokar, J. S., Brodbeck, F. C., & House, R. J. (2013). *Culture and Leadership across the World: The GLOBE Book of In-depth Studies of 25 Societies.* New York: Routledge.

Dakin, E. (1991). Education and authority in Eastern Europe: Historical perspectives and modern implications. *The Journal of Modern European Studies, 5*(2), 132–146.

Danneels, L., & Viaene, S. (2022). Identifying digital transformation paradoxes: A design perspective. *Business & Information Systems Engineering, 64*(5), 483–500. https://doi.org/10.1007/s12599-021-00735-7

Dat, L., & Nam, V. (2023). How generational differences influence leadership styles: The case study of SMEs in Vietnam. *VNU University of Economics and Business, 3*(2), 50. https://doi.org/10.57110/vnujeb.v3i2.154

Denning, S. (2021). Why business agility requires a shift from a hierarchy to a network. Forbes. https://www.forbes.com/sites/stevedenning/2021/08/29/why-business-agility-requires-a-shift-from-a-hierarchy-to-a-network/

Elmore, T. (2021). *The Eight Paradoxes of Great Leadership: Embracing the Conflicting Demands of Today's Workplace*. Nashville, TN: Harper Collins Leadership.

Everitt B. S., Landau S., Leese M. & Sathl D. (2011). Cluster Analysis, 5th ed (pp. 71–110). New York: Wiley.

Fairhurst, G. T. (2001). Dualisms in leadership research. In F. M. Jablin & L. L. Putnam (Eds.), *The New Handbook of Organizational Communication: Advances in Theory, Research, and Methods* (pp. 379–439). Los Angeles, CA: Sage Publications.

Feynman, R. P. (1965). *The Character of Physical Law*. Cambridge, MA: The MIT Press.

Gabriel, Y. (2015). The caring leader – What followers expect of their leaders and why? *Leadership, 11*, 316–334. https://doi.org/10.1177/1742715014532482

Gabrielova, K., & Buchko, A. (2021). Here comes Generation Z: Millennials as leaders. *Business Horizons, 64*(4), 489–499. https://doi.org/10.1016/J.BUSHOR.2021.02.013

Heifetz, R., Grashow, A., & Linsky, M. (2009). *The Practice of Adaptive Leadership: Tools and Tactics for Changing Your Organization and the World.* Boston, MA: Harvard Business Press.

Hill, L. A., & Lineback, K. (2011). *Being the Boss: The 3 Imperatives for Becoming a Great Leader*. Boston, MA: Harvard Business Review Press.

House, R. J., Hanges, P. J., Javidan, M., Dorfman, P. W., & Gupta, V. (2004). *Culture, Leadership, and Organizations: The GLOBE Study of 62 Societies*. Thousand Oaks, CA: Sage Publications.

Husin, W., Ibrahim, M., Jaafar, J., & Abuhasan, S. (2014). The dimensional structure of the Student Leadership Practices Inventory. *Journal of Education and Practice, 5*, 109–117

Javidan, M., Dorfman, P. W., Sully de Luque, M., & House, R. J. (2006). In the eye of the beholder: Cross-cultural lessons in leadership from Project GLOBE. *Academy of Management Perspectives, 20*(1), 67–90. https://doi.org/10.5465/amp.2006.19873410

Joiner, B., & Josephs, S. (2007). *Leadership Agility: Five Levels of Mastery for Anticipating and Initiating Change*. San Francisco, CA: Jossey-Bass.

Kang, K., Noor, M., Mansor, M., & Awang, Z. (2021). Exploring and Developing Item Measuring Leadership Practices Inventory (LPI): An Exploratory Factor Analysis Procedure. *International Journal of Academic Research in Business and Social Sciences, 11*(7), 222–231. https://doi.org/10.6007/ijarbss/v11-i7/10157

Kouzes, J. M., & Posner, B. Z. (2003). *The Leadership Practices Inventory (LPI): Self Instrument*. San Francisco, CA: John Wiley & Sons.

Lüscher, L. S., & Lewis, M. W. (2008). Organizational change and managerial sensemaking: Working through paradox. *Academy of Management Journal, 51*(2), 221–240. https://doi.org/10.5465/amj.2008.31767217

Miron-Spektor, E., Gino, F., & Argote, L. (2011). Paradoxical frames and creative sparks: Enhancing individual creativity through conflict and integration. *Organizational Behavior and Human Decision Processes, 116*(2), 229–240. https://doi.org/10.1016/j.obhdp.2011.03.006

Posner, B. (2016). Investigating the reliability and validity of the leadership practices inventory. *Administrative Sciences, 6*, 17. https://doi.org/10.3390/ADMSCI6040017

Purg, D., & Derganc, D. (2015). Leadership development in the Central and East European context. In T. A. Scandura & E. M. Werner (Eds.), *Handbook of Leadership Research Methods* (pp. 383–401). Edward Elgar Publishing.

Radice, H. (2004). Teaching obedience: Education in Central and Eastern Europe under state socialism. *Comparative Education Review, 48*(4), 497–516. https://doi.org/10.1086/424829

Sauer S. (2011). Taking the reins: The effects of new leader status and leadership style on team performance. *The Journal of Applied Psychology, 96*(3), 574–87. https://doi.org/10.1037/a0022741

Schad, J., Lewis, M. W., Raisch, S., & Smith, W. K. (2016). Paradox research in management science: Looking back to move forward. *Academy of Management Annals, 10*(1), 5–64. https://doi.org/10.5465/19416520.2016.1162422

Smith, W. K., & Lewis, M. W. (2011). Toward a theory of paradox: A dynamic equilibrium model of organizing. *Academy of Management Review, 36*(2), 381–403. https://doi.org/10.5465/amr.2009.0223

Szabo, E., Brodbeck, F., Den Hartog, D., Reber, G., Weibler, J., & Wunderer, R. (2002). The Germanic Europe cluster: Where employees have a voice. *Journal of World Business, 37*(1), 55–68. https://doi.org/10.1016/S1090-9516(01)00072-7

Tjosvold, D. (2008). The conflict-positive organization: It depends upon us. *Journal of Organizational Behavior, 29*(1), 19–28. https://doi.org/10.1002/job.473

Twenge, J. M., & Campbell, S. M. (2008). Generational differences in psychological traits and their impact on the workplace. *Journal of Managerial Psychology, 23*(8), 862–877. https://doi.org/10.1108/02683940810904367

Waldman, D. A., & Bowen, D. E. (2016). Learning to navigate complexity: Leadership for the 21st century. *Academy of Management Perspectives, 30*(3), 243–254. https://doi.org/10.5465/amp.2014.0133

# 6 Diversity, Equity, and Inclusion Policy Paradoxes

## Insights from the Central and East European Hospitality Sector

*Marcin Panek*

### 6.1 Introduction

Across Europe, nations have proven to be highly diverse, with a continuous tendency to become even more varied. On May 1, 2004, when seven countries in Central and Eastern Europe (CEE) (the Czech Republic, Estonia, Hungary, Latvia, Lithuania, Poland, and Slovakia) acceded to the European Union (EU), these newly admitted countries opened their borders to expand the market for their goods, stabilize their economic and legal systems, obtain the foreign capital needed to modernize their economies, create new jobs (Ambroziak, 2024), and implement new standards regarding demographic diversity dimensions such as race, ethnicity, and religion, especially related to international and transnational backgrounds (Kaldewey et al., 2024).

In 2010, the European Commission recognized the need to address discrimination and promote equal opportunities in the workplace (Andrejczuk & Strzelczak, 2017). The EU Platform of Diversity Charters was established to invite organizations with expertise in diversity to participate in developing the document and to encourage businesses in CEE countries to commit to diversity and inclusion by joining their National Diversity Charters as signatories. Although companies and other organizations from Poland and other CEE countries are signatories of the Diversity Charters and strive to implement the best practices outlined in diversity, equity, and inclusion (DEI) policies, it is important to acknowledge that these countries carry historical legacies and have undergone political and economic transformations, including a democratic transition and entry into the free market with open borders since the early 1990s. Years of isolation in CEE countries have resulted in a homogeneous population regarding nationality and religion. In 2014, Poland had an ethnic cohesion index of nearly 95%, placing it among the most ethnically homogeneous countries in Europe and worldwide (Rykała, 2014). Unlike many other nations, Poland is also characterized by a clear dominance of one religious denomination – Roman Catholicism – which accounted for over 81% of the population in 2021 (Szałtys, 2023). All these aspects, and others, present Poland as a country with limited openness to DEI policy. As reported by the Responsible Business Forum, which coordinates the Diversity Charter in Poland for the European Commission, only

DOI: 10.4324/9781003541394-9

3% of large and medium-sized firms in Poland have a formal document dedicated to their corporate diversity management strategy (Ptak, 2023; Bierca & Strzelczak, 2023). These facts highlight the contradictions between mutually exclusive elements that often exist in the hospitality sector, where employees' personal beliefs, traditional upbringing, strong religious influence, and homogeneous ethnic backgrounds can conflict with company-imposed values. When these conflicting elements persist over time, creating tension between inherent values and corporate values, a paradox occurs (Lewis, 2000). Typically, when a team is open to new ideas, concepts, perspectives, approaches, or initiatives and understands the rationale behind them, such paradoxes can serve as powerful motivators for personal and organizational development. This can lead to improved outcomes, achievement of desired goals, enhanced customer service, a better environment for diverse employees, greater workplace satisfaction, and increased creativity (Ely & Thomas, 2020).

While much of the existing literature on DEI focuses on Western Europe and North America, there is a distinct lack of research examining the unique challenges and paradoxes that arise in CEE, particularly in sectors like hospitality. Most DEI research has been based on the assumption that diversity strategies and inclusion models developed in Western contexts are universally applicable. However, there is a gap in understanding how DEI initiatives are implemented in traditionally homogeneous societies, where cultural norms, historical legacies, and sociopolitical contexts differ markedly from those in the West. Central and Eastern Europe countries offer an important context for this research due to their gradually expanding hospitality industry and evolving approach to DEI. The hospitality sector, which relies heavily on cultural adaptability and customer service, presents a particularly interesting case for such an investigation. However, very few studies have examined the implementation of DEI policies in this sector in the CEE region. This research aims to contribute to the growing literature on DEI by offering new insights into the paradoxes and challenges of implementing global DEI standards in local CEE cultural contexts. It will enhance understanding of how historical legacies of communism, religious homogeneity, and sociopolitical isolation shape the reception and execution of DEI initiatives in this region. Additionally, this research may provide practical insights for managers and organizations operating in CEE, outlining strategies to reconcile global DEI principles with local cultural norms.

The chapter introduces DEI concepts and examines the paradoxes arising when global standards meet local CEE cultural norms. It explores how the region's communist past and religious homogeneity influence resistance to DEI. A theoretical framework highlights tensions between personal beliefs and organizational values at individual, team, and organizational levels. The *findings* illustrate key DEI paradoxes in the hospitality sector and offer practical strategies for managers and Human Resource (HR) to reconcile global standards with local norms. The chapter concludes by summarizing contributions and suggesting future research directions.

## 6.2 Literature Review

### *6.2.1 Introduction to DEI Paradoxes*

Diversity, equity, and inclusion are often used interchangeably, but each has distinct meanings. *Diversity* pertains to the array of identities and characteristics within a group, encompassing gender, race, age, religion, sexual orientation, ethnicity, national culture, socioeconomic status, weight, height, attractiveness, language, (dis)abilities, parental status, education, values, beliefs, and other social identities. Diversity ensures that the variety of approaches, ideas, and experiences brought by diverse employees, and the knowledge shared among them help create a community or organization that is more competent, stronger, and better equipped to succeed (Friedman & Vlady, 2024). In contrast, *equity* revolves around the principle of affording individuals fair access, opportunities, resources, and empowerment to thrive. Finally, *inclusion* embodies the proactive efforts undertaken to comprehend, embrace, and leverage the unique strengths and facets of individual identities, fostering a sense of welcome, value, and support for all (Espinoza & Horne, 2022). When a company applies DEI principles, its performance in terms of efficiency, effectiveness, and competitiveness increases, helping to achieve organizational goals (Dang et al., 2021). The synergistic combination of these practices can directly influence employees' performance and overall company outcomes (Esch et al., 2016). A McKinsey & Company report indicates that the link between diversity on executive teams and the chances of financial outperformance has become even stronger over time while the business case for diversity continues to be solid (Dixon-Fyle, et al., 2020).

*Paradoxes* are often defined as situations where two opposing elements or ideas coexist, creating a contradiction that challenges conventional thinking or action (Lüscher & Lewis, 2008; Smith & Lewis, 2011). One can imagine the paradox as a lens that embraces contradictions as inevitable, persistent, and unresolvable (Lewis, 2000); they are conflicting but inseparable (Schad & Miron-Spektor, 2021). Paradox can be perceived as a "persistent contradiction between interdependent elements" (Schad et al., 2016, p. 10). When individual elements are discussed, they may seem logical and naturally acceptable, appearing reasonable and realistic. However, when these elements are considered together, without isolation, their coexistence may seem impossible, absurd, or irrational (Lewis, 2000).

Paradoxes related to companies implementing DEI policies can be divided into three levels (Boroş & Gorbatai, 2024). At *the personal level*, managers or team leaders may experience both the positive and negative effects of DEI policies firsthand. In this case, middle managers are particularly influential in implementing DEI principles. These managers are highly familiar with the daily operations and often the personal lives of their team members. As they implement DEI principles, managers may encounter tensions, especially when balancing DEI policies that are strictly controlled versus those that are more self-managed. In the latter scenario, managers may wish to exert personal influence on the organization's development by contributing their expert perspectives and competencies. However, DEI principles may sometimes conflict with employees' personal beliefs, upbringing, religion, or other contrasting factors. Acting by DEI may be manageable on its own, as might an individual's contradictory approach. However, when these elements coexist simultaneously and persistently, they create tension. Addressing such paradoxes requires a special approach. One way to resolve this issue is to limit the manager's direct involvement by providing clear procedures, criteria, and structured guidelines that specify how, when, and to whom the DEI policies should be applied, regardless of the employee's attitude (Gorbatai et al., 2022).

At *the team level*, managers need to navigate the dynamics that arise within groups of employees. The processes stemming from the introduction of DEI policies can be of two types: They may foster a positive, welcoming environment, or, conversely, they may create negative impressions or even reinforce biases (Van Knippenberg et al., 2004). A team may find benefits in completing tasks according to DEI policies while simultaneously having concerns and reservations or perceiving these policies as harmful. This duality creates paradoxes as teams struggle with balancing these conflicting approaches while trying to achieve their goals or targets. Teams might recognize situations where marginalized groups feel uncomfortable, demotivated, or fearful of expressing themselves at work. However, at the same time, these teams might feel threatened by the very same individuals facing injustice, perceiving them as a challenge to their dominant positions, opportunities, or even job security. This sense of uncertainty and fear of losing status may prevent team members from fully embracing DEI initiatives, even though they understand the moral and ethical correctness of doing so. When managers identify such paradoxical behavior patterns, they should promptly issue an official statement to reassure the team members, emphasizing the importance of DEI initiatives and ensuring that these policies are implemented without any restrictions or negative consequences for the team (Boroş & Gorbatai, 2024).

Finally, managers face *organizational-level* paradoxes, particularly when balancing the need for short-term results with the long-term goals of innovation, competence, and staying ahead of competitors. This challenge often makes it difficult to accommodate DEI policies, such as hiring the best employees from minority groups, educating the current team about the importance of creating a fair and inclusive environment, and managing the paradox between the immediate need for results and the long-term process of acquiring a diverse workforce

(Boroş & Gorbatai, 2024). For this reason, middle managers dealing with DEI issues must adopt a paradox mindset to effectively navigate and resolve these tensions (Miron-Spektor et al., 2017).

### *6.2.2 Origin of Diversity, Equity, and Inclusion Initiatives*

Diversity, equity, and inclusion sets the guidelines, educates, opens minds, and encourages groups within organizations and institutions to adhere to its values efficiently. This is why the most successful organizations have already recognized the great potential of DEI initiatives and the benefits they bring. Organizations that incorporate these concepts strengthen their cultural values at the organizational level, improve their reputation, and have greater chances of attracting and retaining talented employees. They also enhance the motivation and efficiency of existing staff, provide better services, and increase client/citizen satisfaction (Cugler, 2015), which is highly needed and required throughout the hospitality sector.

It is assumed that DEI initiatives originated from numerous social movements and changes in legal regulations that took place in the United States of America in the mid-1960s. These were driven by activists fighting for equal rights, primarily in employment, particularly for Black individuals and women (Wasserman, 2015). Such activities had a direct impact on the corporate world, changing perceptions in areas of equal treatment, equal employment conditions, and equal pay for work performed (Jackson, 2007).

The indisputable merit in the fight for gender equality should be attributed to women and the suffrage activist movements. The greatest changes in the perception of women and their treatment as equals to men occurred during the Second World War. Due to the general mobilization of men, who were sent largely to the war front, women began to fill numerous vacated jobs, occupying positions previously identified mainly with men (Sandua, 2023). However, it was mass migration that contributed to changes in modern societies, particularly in terms of race and ethnicity, leading to the emergence of *super-diversity* (Kothari et al., 2022). The so-called super-diversity among migrants is an important factor in understanding equality and social inclusion. Kothari et al. emphasize (2022) that when migrants move from one country to another, they bring a range of skills and perspectives, becoming an extremely diverse human resource that supports innovation and stimulates economic growth.

The application of DEI policies has become widespread across the globe, addressing gender identity, race, ethnicity, sexual orientation, Indigenous identity and origin, religion, (dis)ability, neurological conditions, native language, immigration status, and a range of other categories that distinguish individuals from one another (Newburry, 2022). Although DEI initiatives and policy implementations have existed in the corporate world for decades, they have mainly been limited to human resource management and guided either by the logic of discrimination and justice or the logic of access and legitimization (Ely & Thomas, 2020). Few organizations have managed to implement DEI holistically at an advanced level, fully exploiting its educational and strategic potential (Ely et al., 2020; Georgiadou et al., 2019).

As mentioned, DEI principles have been implemented and utilized for a significant time. However, some countries, particularly those in CEE under the influence of the Soviet Union, did not have the opportunity to recognize, implement, and manage the values aligned with DEI policies, which is the cause of the paradoxes present within certain organizations. Additionally, countries with strong Catholic roots and traditional upbringings did not see the necessity of considering DEI as elements of everyday life.

### *6.2.3 Central and Eastern Europe Cultural Norms*

After the transition and abandonment of socialism in the 1990s, CEE countries, members of the former so-called socialist bloc, still faced significant social and economic inefficiencies. Moreover, these countries were generally characterized as homogeneous in terms of ethnicity, origin, and language spoken (Fuller, 2000), with exceptions made for various nationalities visiting, studying, working, or living in certain areas. People of foreign origin were mainly concentrated in large cities and universities. These individuals, often recognizable by external biological features such as skin color, were sometimes directly affected by prejudicial behavior. Although some acts of discrimination did occur within these countries, prejudice and discrimination in the CEE region were relatively low (Zick et al., 2008).

Compared to Canada and the United States, CEE countries do not consider themselves as countries of immigration. Countries with significant immigrant communities, like Great Britain or France, accepted many people from other countries due to their former colonies. Despite this, even third-generation immigrants are often still considered foreigners despite their citizenship. In some nations, such as Germany, most immigrants and their descendants have never received citizenship, even if they were born and raised in the country (Zick et al., 2008). Some countries, like Belgium, exhibit greater prejudice, racism, and right-wing opinions than most EU countries, demonstrating the most anti-immigrant attitudes. In contrast, neighboring Holland is considered one of the most tolerant European countries, with a long history of liberal immigration and integration policies (Billet & de Witte, 2008).

Central and Eastern Europe countries do not have the same experience with large groups of immigrants of different origins. As countries separated from Western Europe, their interactions were mostly limited to nations within the region. These countries were primarily of Slavic origin, similar in terms of culture, broadly understood values, and language. Most importantly, they shared a common oppressor – the Soviet Union – which united them to a large extent.

From an early age, children were educated about neighboring countries, and books from the region were distributed within the socialist bloc. The Russian language was mandatory to learn in primary and secondary schools, and Russian children's and teen magazines were circulated in schools' libraries. The so-called "friendship" among these countries existed in people's minds. Literature, movie production, opera, and ballet from CEE countries were shown only within the bloc. Participation in the Eurovision Competition was strictly forbidden (Yugoslavia was the only country to be an exception), with an alternative provided in the form of the InterVision Festival or Festival of Soviet Songs. Student exchanges could only occur within the socialist bloc. Studies on Eastern Europe were dominated by political scientists interested in Cold War geopolitics (Fleron & Hoffmann, 1993). The borders were closed, and the only countries available to visit were, again, CEE countries. Lithuania, Estonia, and Latvia were part of the Soviet Union and only claimed independence after perestroika (McNair, 2006). CEE countries were severely isolated, and people could not freely visit countries beyond the Iron Curtain. These countries were closed off from trends, initiatives, diverse lifestyles, and different concepts and approaches to living, working, or socializing. At that time, all these countries appeared to be on an isolated island, where no one could watch movies from Western Europe or America, and access to foreign books, newspapers, or magazines was either illegal or censored (Sik & Wellman, 2018; Burks, 2015). People were limited to their ways of living and they created, or practiced concepts within their homogeneous and similar environments. Ideas could not be exchanged with Western countries; everything had to be created and originated within the bloc. The socialist governments, instructed and supervised by Moscow, tended to limit creativity, innovation, openness, and broad-mindedness. The everyday life of ordinary citizens involved countless struggles to obtain basic consumer goods, manage the material environment, and improve living conditions. At the same time, people tried to define their values, fears, and hopes. There was no space for considering social inequality or injustice as a higher value, let alone different forms of diversity. People tried not to get lost in the crowd of ordinariness, fighting for their individualism (Zakharova, 2013). Later reforms focused on improving people's living standards and competing with the West, leading to new forms of consumption and leisure (Gorsuch, 2011). In the early 1990s, after four decades of communism, the idea of shaping social, political, and economic attitudes with values promoted by the West began to dominate in postcommunist countries (Schöpflin, 1993).

In the late 1980s, the Catholic Church had a significant influence on social culture and everyday life. Across all CEE countries, there was a strong demand for change. During that time in Poland, the most Catholic country in the region, the Church began to play a crucial role in liberating the nation from communism. This situation was not replicated in other socialist bloc countries like Czechoslovakia, where the Catholic Church was persecuted and marginalized.

Such a situation could not be accepted in a country with strong religious traditions like Poland. The situation changed dramatically when the Polish priest Karol Wojtyla became Pope John Paul II (Buczynski, 2016). The Catholic Church began to resist communist rules, maintaining broader contact with the Western world (Stanley, 2010), and became a natural opposition to communism in Poland, influencing Polish life. During these times, the Church was a source of hope, a place where people could find refuge from government oppression, and a space where they could gather freely and hear priests proclaim that the end of communism was near. The Church earned the full trust of the nation and, along with the Solidarity movement, led to the victory over communism. However, this trust was later used to promote values that were not aligned with DEI, standing in opposition to the values promoted by progressive Western countries (Alvis, 2016).

Poland has been aptly characterized by: "One Nation, One Religion – Tradition and Change." The authors highlight the paradox of Polish society, which is homogeneous in terms of ethnicity and religion, with a high degree of distance and a lack of tolerance for diversity. Yet, at the same time, a typical Pole is perceived as proud, generous, hospitable, stubborn, religiously tolerant, a great patriot, always ready to make sacrifices for the fatherland, and strongly averse to compromise (Pilch & Turska, 2015). Recently, cultural diversity has been portrayed by the right-wing government as a threat to the cohesive Polish identity. Multicultural ideas were viewed as alien concepts, unnecessary, and inapplicable locally, just as tolerance for sexual minorities and nonbelievers has been framed as a threat to traditional Polish families. Nevertheless, through the efforts of liberal, anarchist, feminist, and nongovernmental organizations, new elements and forces are emerging that promise ongoing improvements in the situation of minority groups in Poland, despite the slow pace of progress (Cutts et al., 2023).

### *6.2.4 Paradox of Diversity, Equity, and Inclusion Standards and Prejudice*

The concept of symbolic threat refers to the perceived challenges or attacks on one's way of life, including values, beliefs, practices, and norms (Rios et al., 2018). After the transition from communism in the 1990s, the traditional values cultivated in CEE countries for decades remained deeply embedded in their citizens. An influence in these countries has been the Catholic Church, whose values often stand in stark contrast to those promoted by DEI initiatives. These values may influence, change, or replace existing organizational policies and practices, leading to perceptions of potential or actual harm. Despite the positive intentions behind DEI initiatives, some individuals may view these policies as conflicting with traditional beliefs, or they may be influenced by national or local organizations that question or oppose DEI values, perceiving them as controversial or as threats to core values and ideals (Iyer, 2022).

Organizations that openly communicate their commitment to DEI values on their websites may either attract or deter potential employees. While the majority might value workplace equality, some individuals may perceive an emphasis on diversity as a potential source of discrimination against their own racial or ethnic group, or as favoring other groups (Dover et al., 2016). Certain groups may see DEI policies as a threat, fearing that these initiatives could diminish their opportunities for employment, decent wages, or promotion. Ideally, a fair system would ensure that all individuals, regardless of group background, receive the outcomes they have earned (Shteynberg et al., 2011). Implementing a transparent DEI policy within an organization can help reduce barriers and alleviate the anxieties faced by disadvantaged groups. However, recent studies have shown that advantaged groups also perceive diversity initiatives as potentially harmful to themselves, even when these initiatives are presented as benefiting all groups (Brown & Jacoby-Senghor, 2021).

Poland, which is largely homogeneous in terms of ethnicity and has a strong traditional approach to family life, is heavily influenced by the Catholic Church, which often opposes DEI values. These values are perceived as threats, particularly when familiar customs, views, or expectations are challenged or replaced by external DEI influences (Renfro et al., 2006). Poland is one of only five countries within the EU where same-sex marriage or other alternative family arrangements are not legally recognized. The traditional view of the heterosexual family is the only acceptable model according to the Catholic Church and the previously ruling right-wing party, which view any other forms of same-sex arrangements as a threat to the traditional heterosexual nuclear family. During a recent presidential campaign, the President of Poland referred to LGBT+ movements as merely an ideology, not as representing people. Similar views are held in other CEE countries, including Bulgaria, Slovakia, Lithuania, and Romania. Despite these conservative views, there are paradoxes within Polish society. For instance, while the government opposes LGBT+ rights, a majority of Poles support same-sex civil partnerships. According to a survey, over half of Poles (52%) support the legalization of civil partnerships for same-sex couples, and 90% support them for heterosexual couples (CBOS, 2024).

Additionally, after the outbreak of the war in Ukraine, Poland accepted over one million Ukrainian refugees, primarily women and children, who now benefit from temporary protection in Poland. The borders were widely opened, and Polish citizens provided extensive support, offering shelter, food, assistance, and more. This response to the refugee crisis shows that when immigrants arrive from different cultural backgrounds, they are not always perceived as threats to traditional values. The successful integration of Ukrainian refugees demonstrates that effective DEI policies can increase the representation and power of historically disadvantaged groups (Iyer, 2009). Currently, cultural assimilation of Ukrainian citizens in Poland is high, and there are few negative attitudes, even among those who were initially opposed. The brutal aggression by the Russian Federation and the mass arrival of displaced people have provided a strong justification for DEI policies, increasing support for these initiatives.

The paradoxes that arise in CEE countries may differ in nature from those in Western countries due to historical backgrounds, periods of isolation, and the imposition of conflicting values, beliefs, standards, and ethics by communist authorities, as well as the dominance of orthodox Catholic doctrines. This complex environment affects all groups in society, both majority and minority, and efforts to create change must ensure that the values and interests of advantaged groups are not overlooked. This approach is expected to lessen the perceived threat to mainstream culture and identity (Yogeeswaran & Dasgupta, 2014) while increasing support for DEI policies. It is important to focus not just on one group of interest but to show that DEI values are applied universally to reduce fears of exclusion and enhance feelings of belonging within the organization (Ballinger & Crocker, 2021). Even though the citizens of CEE countries have been shaped by different ideals, values, and beliefs, they are still influenced by a sense of morality. Despite prejudices and biases against DEI values, a moral imperative can arise that often shifts group attitudes (Leach et al., 2007).

## 6.3 Research Method and Sample

The emerging paradoxes within organizations that value and implement DEI policies were assessed by evaluating the organization's environment and identifying potential barriers that may hinder the development of the desired employees' attitudes. The study adopted a qualitative research approach to comprehensively explore the complex interrelationships between employee practices and DEI policies in the hospitality sector. This approach provided valuable insights into everyday tasks and activities within the hospitality industry, allowing for a holistic investigation of the experiences of regular employees and managers. The qualitative research paradigm explored individuals' experiences, perceptions, and attitudes through in-depth interviews (Cresswell, 2014). Based on interviewees' accounts, this method provided deeper insights into how employee practices and DEI policies influence employee attitudes in the hospitality sector, particularly in the presence of barriers. The approach yielded rich, contextualized data to uncover the underlying mechanisms and personal perspectives on DEI paradoxes and their relationship with everyday work.

The study addresses the following research questions:

1. How do interviewees perceive their workplace regarding DEI values?
2. According to interviewees, what barriers hinder the provision of expected services regarding DEI in their organizations?
3. According to interviewees, what practices support employees' attitudes in applying required DEI policies?

4. What contradictions arise from the necessity of complying with norms and standards imposed by organizational values?

The study involved in-depth interviews with a carefully selected group of regular hotel employees and managers. The research group covered eleven hotels from the following cities: Poznan, Krakow, Warsaw, Gdansk, Wroclaw, Szczecin, Lublin, Bialystok, and Rzeszow, and included eighteen employees (12 managers and 6 regular employees). Open-ended questions, structured around a predefined scenario, were utilized to elicit comprehensive insights (McCracken, 1988). These interviews were conducted between June and August 2024, both in person and remotely via telephone conversations. In most cases, the snowball sampling method was employed, which helped earn the trust of additional participants. Each interview lasted around an hour and was recorded. Some interviewees hesitated to answer certain questions or share their thoughts and experiences. They sought assurance that their names would not be published and that their cases would not be associated with the organizations they worked for. Questions regarding the contradictions between personal beliefs and the organization's expectations to align with DEI policies led to discomfort and difficulty providing candid responses. No pressure was placed on respondents, no suggestive questions were asked, and no specific answers were expected (Riessman, 1993).

A positive aspect of the study was that neither gender dominated the participant pool. The participants included employees, middle managers, senior managers, and executives. It is important to note that Poland, like other CEE countries, presents a compelling context for this research due to its growing hospitality sector and evolving approach to DEI. The research featured a nonrandomly selected sample of hotel employees and managers from five- and four-star hotels affiliated with prominent international brand chains in Poland. The hotels represented different regions across Poland, acknowledging that values related to DEI vary regionally. Some regions are more open to DEI values, while others are more closed-minded, which presents a significant context for interpreting the results. Maps illustrating societal attitudes were considered (Figures 6.1–6.4), including (a) right-wing party support during the 2015, 2019, and 2023 national parliamentary elections and (b) the "Atlas of Hate," which highlights municipalities, counties, and voivodeships whose local authorities have adopted, rejected, or are working on adopting anti-LGBT declarations.

In addition to interviews, hotel websites were subjected to thorough analysis, along with documents and presentations provided by the organizations. The documents were analyzed with consideration of the meanings and concepts emerging from the specific issues addressed. The companies' values and ideas shared a common background and were presented as a collection of similar attitudes toward DEI. The combination of the information provided and the interview outcomes offered deep insight into the clashes between traditional worldviews and workplace actions, attitudes, and engagement in line with DEI values.

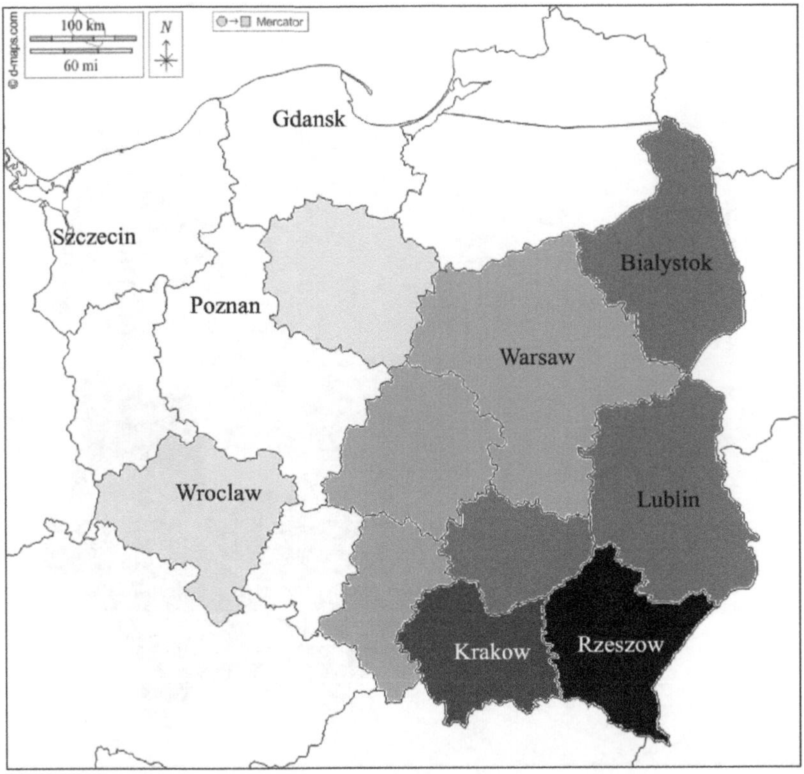


*Figure 6.1* Parliamentary Elections 2015.

*Note:* The more intensive the gray color, the greater the majority of right-wing supporters.

*Source:* Adapted from Free Maps, maps d-maps.com, State Electoral Commission (2024).

## 6.4 Findings

The hotels covered in this study begin their talent sourcing processes by identifying diverse channels, focusing on finding employees with a natural attitude for hospitality, either through human resources departments or carefully selected hiring agencies.

### *6.4.1 The Scope of Prejudice*

The Hotel Department Director of one of the most prestigious, luxurious, and intimate cruise lines shared the challenges of finding individuals who can deliver service excellence without prejudice: *One of our ongoing challenges*

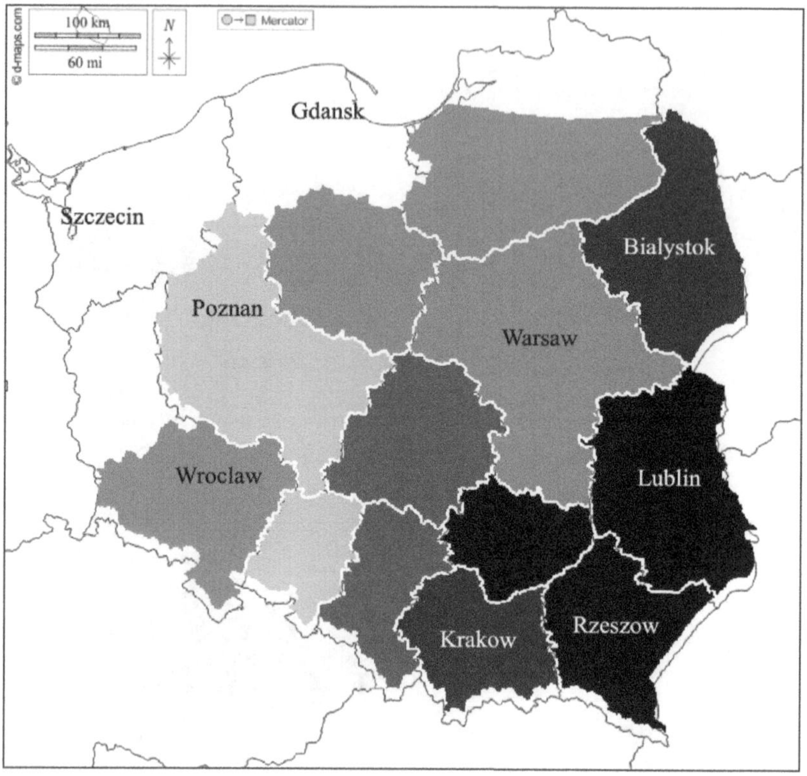


*Figure 6.2* Parliamentary Elections 2019.

*Note:* The more intensive the gray color, the greater the majority of right-wing supporters.

*Source:* Adapted from Free Maps, maps d-maps.com, State Electoral Commission (2024).

*is explaining that DEI is not just about compliance or corporate image, but about creating a fair and welcoming environment for everyone*. This cruise line proudly emphasizes its commitment to DEI as core values, promoting an environment where every individual feels seen, heard, and empowered. The cruise line is also a strong supporter of the LGBTQ+ community, recognizing that its strength lies in its diversity. The company is now exploring Poland and other CEE countries as potential sources of workforce talent but has expressed slight concerns regarding the cultural backgrounds of individuals from these regions. "*Hiring people with different backgrounds is one thing but ensuring that they work harmoniously with long-standing staff can be a real challenge*, the director said.

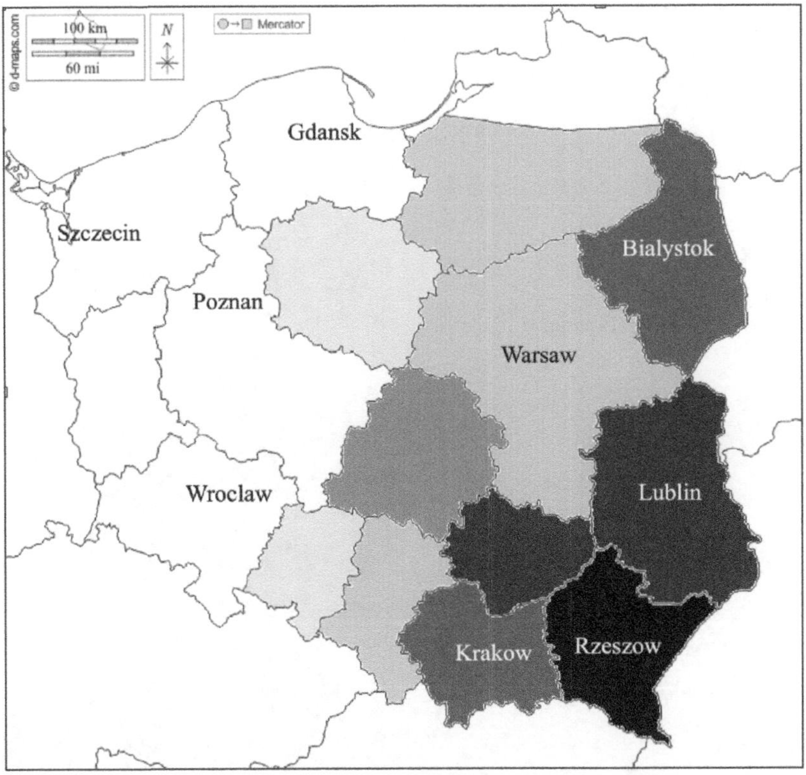


*Figure 6.3* Parliamentary Elections 2023.

*Note:* The more intensive the gray color, the greater the majority of right-wing supporters.

*Source:* Adapted from Free Maps, maps d-maps.com, State Electoral Commission (2024).

### *6.4.2 The Role of Human Resource Department*

All interviewed hotel department managers agreed that the human resources department plays a transformative role in shaping organizational culture and values. The implementation of DEI values creates a welcoming environment where employees and guests feel safe and authentic. The research reveals that all studied hotels have developed their DEI policies and have dedicated websites to promote these values. However, as the hotel manager from Warsaw explained: *While we are trying to implement DEI values, we find that some employees are still holding onto traditional views, making it challenging to create a truly inclusive environment.* The HR specialist from Poznan emphasized that prospective and current employees have immediate access to information about the

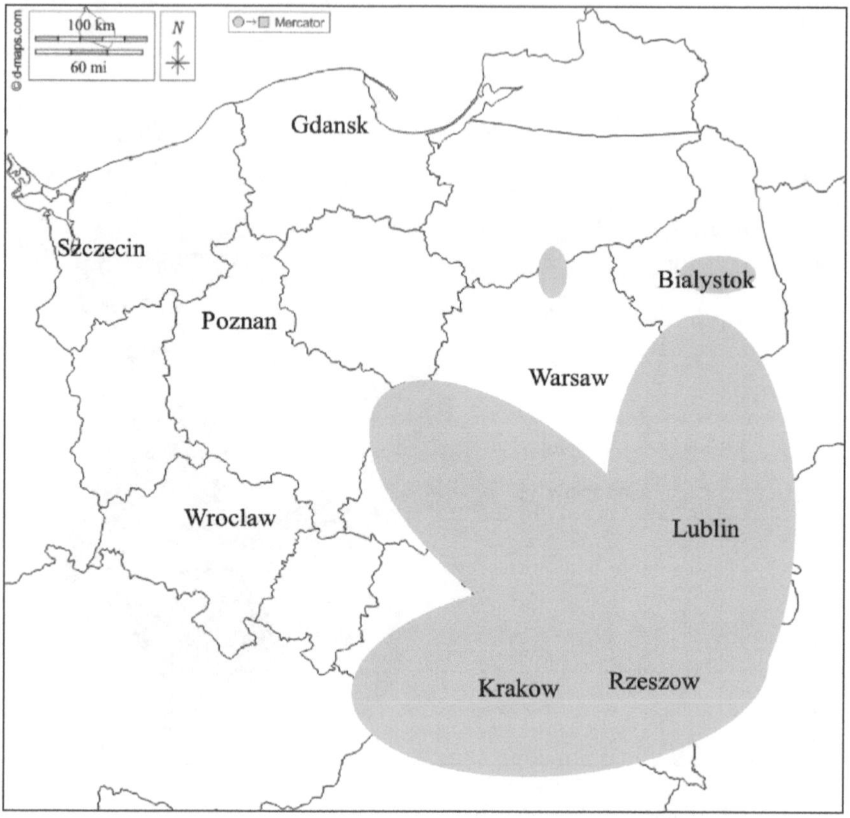


*Figure 6.4* Atlas of Hate.

*Note:* Gray color represents municipalities, counties, and voivodeships whose local authorities have adopted, rejected, or are working on adopting anti-LGBT+ declarations.

*Source:* Adapted from Free Maps, d-maps.com. Atlas of Hate (2024).

company's expectations. If their principles differ from the company's values, they are made aware of the need to adjust to the standards and follow the policy. The specialist informed: *Diversity training is comprehensive, but the real test comes when employees face situations where their values clash with company policies.* Once employed, new hires undergo training programs and recurring sessions to develop and refresh their skills in line with DEI values.

### 6.4.3 Self-awareness of Diversity, Equity, and Inclusion Values

According to the Room Division Manager from Krakow, the onboarding process can be a significant turning point for new hires, offering a deeper understanding of DEI principles. She stated: *The DEI policies have improved their work environment, but it's clear that not everyone shares the same enthusiasm. Some colleagues still hold on to old stereotypes*. Thorough training sessions are provided, covering essential topics such as the use of inclusive language. Some hotel chains even publish a list of words and phrases to be used during guest interactions. For example, a trainee waitress once asked two women if they needed two receipts, only to be informed that they were married and one receipt would suffice. The waitress's reaction was inappropriate, showing disbelief or astonishment, and the training aimed to prevent such awkwardness. Similarly, a night receptionist witnessed a trainee's discomfort when serving two men with a double bed reservation, hastily offering twin beds instead. The Room Division Manager explained: *The hardest part, is not introducing diversity policies, but changing the deep-rooted mindset that some employees carry with them, especially regarding gender and LGBTQ+ issues*. Such instances highlight the need for proper DEI training to ensure employees handle these situations professionally.

### *6.4.4 Personal Beliefs versus Diversity, Equity, and Inclusion Standards*

The General Manager from Bialystok explained: *A lot of employees don't openly resist DEI policies, but you can tell from their body language and the way they avoid certain topics that they're not fully on board.* Managers from various departments noted that, while some employees might still privately disagree with DEI values, however, they tend to follow the company's principles at work, with many showing a gradual shift toward embracing these values. Contradictions between DEI principles and personal beliefs were more frequently mentioned by managers from hotels in southeastern Poland, whereas managers in cities like Warsaw, Gdansk, Poznan, Wroclaw, and Krakow reported fewer such instances. For example, the HR Director from a hotel in Gdansk explained that open-ended questions are used during the hiring process to assess candidates' attitudes toward people of different backgrounds, such as race, religion, or sexual orientation. The HR Director from Wroclaw noted that some candidates ask whether they will have colleagues of different religious backgrounds, expressing concerns about working with Muslims or Jews. The HR Director from Lublin admitted: *They had instances where new hires were hesitant about working with colleagues from different religious backgrounds. Overcoming this bias requires ongoing education.* Thus, employees gradually shift their perspectives with continuous training, even if it goes against their personal beliefs.

### *6.4.5 Significance of Supervision*

The Director of Sales and Marketing from Szczecin explained that new employees must be open-minded and willing to accept norms and standards they may not have encountered before. This often leads to clashes requiring constant supervision and quick corrective actions. The Front Office Manager of a five-star hotel in Krakow mentioned: *They found that pairing new employees with experienced staff helps in breaking down initial resistance to DEI values, especially in more conservative areas*. Often, new team members need to unlearn attitudes formed by their upbringing or societal influences, which requires constant reinforcement. One of the employees from Bialystok shared: *At first, she didn't understand why the company was pushing DEI policies so hard. But after interacting with colleagues from different backgrounds, she started to see the value.*

### *6.4.6 Training Consistency*

The General Manager of a hotel in Warsaw emphasized that instilling values begins with orientation and onboarding meetings and continues through training programs that promote open communication and embed inclusive practices into policies, procedures, and anti-discrimination laws. These training programs start with basic cases and gradually evolve into more complex scenarios. Alas, the situation may evolve differently, as the Manager from Rzeszow raised, *Even though we conduct regular DEI training, I still encounter resistance from employees who feel that diversity policies are 'Western ideals' that don't align with our local culture*. HR professionals focus on raising awareness about unconscious biases, not just among employees but also in their interactions with guests. The Front Office Manager from Lublin highlighted an incident where a receptionist repeatedly asked a brunette woman with dark skin about her origin, despite her insistence that she was from Poland. This caused an uncomfortable situation and likely resulted in the guest deciding not to return.

The hospitality industry, where competition is fierce, relies on creating exceptional guest experiences and delivering top-tier service. For instance, the Ritz-Carlton credo states that genuine care and comfort for guests are their highest mission. They pledge to provide the finest personal service and facilities in a warm, relaxed, yet refined ambience, fulfilling even unexpressed wishes and needs. Delivering this level of service must include embracing DEI values, with no room for prejudice. A regular employee from Gdansk explained: *When I started, I didn't fully buy into the DEI training, but over time, I came to appreciate how it fosters a more respectful workplace.*

### *6.4.7 The Power of Practice*

HR managers in smaller cities in southeastern Poland mentioned sending newly hired receptionists and waitstaff to larger cities like Warsaw for two-week training programs to immerse them in a more diverse environment and foster DEI values. The regular employees from Lublin and Bialystok openly shared that they *understand the company's commitment to diversity, but sometimes they feel uncomfortable working alongside people with very different beliefs from theirs. It's a difficult adjustment*. Another employee mentioned that he supports diversity, but he admits that sometimes he finds it difficult to work with colleagues whose views on family and religion are so different.

### *6.4.8 Equity Concerns*

One important topic raised during the interviews was the issue of equitable career advancement and ensuring everyone has a voice within the organization. The case was raised by the HR manager from Szczecin: *They had some push-back from employees who felt threatened by the focus on diversity, especially when it comes to leadership positions being opened up to women and minorities.* Many HR managers noted concerns about salary equity, with female applicants often doubting they could reach high managerial positions or earn the same as their male counterparts. HR professionals address this challenge by fostering open dialogue and promoting the benefits of equity. Marriott International, for example, aims to significantly increase the representation of women and people of color at the vice president level and higher. Similarly, the Radisson Hotel Group, during its inaugural "Diversity Week," reaffirmed its commitment to achieving balanced leadership, setting a goal of having 50% of leadership positions filled by women by 2030. In 2023, the Radisson Hotel Group made significant progress by creating dedicated talent pools to identify and nurture female leadership potential, resulting in a 30% increase in female hires for general manager positions, marking an 11% rise from the previous year (Radisson Hotel Group, 2024).

All hotel managers agreed on the importance of building awareness around DEI as a crucial step to overcoming resistance and challenges. However, as the sales manager from Gdansk pointed out: *One of the biggest challenges is convincing long-term employees that diversity initiatives aren't just about compliance, but about genuinely improving the workplace environment.*

Managers and supervisors play a critical role in consistently communicating the benefits of DEI policies and their tangible impact on guest experiences. HR professionals, in collaboration with department heads, must organize awareness campaigns, training sessions, and workshops to educate employees on the value of diverse perspectives. The Front Office Manager from Lublin shared best practices, where teams meet weekly to discuss DEI-related challenges they have encountered. These meetings allow employees to share their experiences, offer solutions, and ensure alignment with DEI standards. For all hotel managers interviewed, the key priority was to create a safe and inclusive environment where every team member felt valued and heard. One cruise line director stated that employees who refuse to adhere to DEI values have no place in the organization.

## 6.5 Discussion and Conclusion

### *6.5.1 Research Implications*

Implementing DEI policies has become an increasingly significant focus within global organizations, with companies recognizing the potential benefits of fostering a diverse and inclusive workforce. However, as this study has explored, the application of DEI initiatives within the hospitality sector of CEE countries presents a unique set of challenges, contradictions, and paradoxes. These challenges highlight the deep clash between progressive ideals promoted by multinational organizations and CEE's established cultural and societal frameworks, exposing a fundamental question: Can a global DEI framework truly coexist with local traditions? The findings suggest that while DEI policies promote inclusivity, they often encounter resistance rooted in deep-seated cultural norms, historical legacies, and personal beliefs, particularly in societies like Poland, where homogeneity and traditional values dominate. This resistance, far from being simply an operational issue, reflects broader societal discomfort with globalization's push to standardize values across cultures.

One of the most prominent paradoxes observed in this study is the tension between global DEI standards and local cultural norms. As organizations, particularly international hotel chains, attempt to implement DEI policies, they must navigate the complexities of local cultural values that may not align with the principles of diversity and inclusion. In some cases, this has led to accusations that DEI initiatives represent a form of cultural neo-colonialism, where the "progressive West" imposes its values on regions with distinct historical and cultural legacies. This clash is particularly evident in countries like Poland, where strong religious influences and a history of ethnic homogeneity create a cultural environment resistant to change. The findings indicate that in southeastern Poland, where traditional values are more deeply ingrained, employees and managers often struggle to reconcile their personal beliefs with the DEI values promoted by their organizations. This struggle raises the uncomfortable possibility that DEI policies, as currently framed, might not always be universally applicable or even appropriate in certain contexts.

This paradox raises questions about the feasibility of universal DEI policies in regions with distinct cultural backgrounds. While DEI initiatives are often framed as globally beneficial, they can be perceived as disruptive or threatening in societies that have long maintained a homogenous social structure. The insistence on implementing these policies without regard for local context risks alienating employees and broader communities, potentially leading to backlash that undermines the very inclusivity these policies aim to achieve. For example, the study highlighted instances where employees in Poland expressed discomfort with DEI policies, particularly those related to LGBTQ+ inclusion. In such cases, the policies are resisted and actively questioned, with some employees perceiving them as a direct attack on their cultural and religious identity. Despite the growing support for same-sex civil partnerships in Poland, there remains a significant divide between public opinion and governmental policies, as well as between personal beliefs and workplace expectations. This divide is a stark reminder that societal progress is not always linear and that policies perceived as forward-thinking in one context may appear intrusive or even regressive in another.

Another paradox observed in this study is the duality in employee behavior. On the one hand, employees may outwardly comply with DEI policies while privately holding conflicting views. This phenomenon, often referred to as "surface acting" (Deng et al., 2017), reflects the tension between conforming to organizational standards and maintaining personal values. This duality is not just a symptom of resistance but a coping mechanism. It is a way for employees to navigate a workplace environment they perceive as increasingly at odds with their personal identity. In regions where cultural homogeneity is the norm, such as southeastern Poland, employees may struggle to fully embrace DEI initiatives, leading to a superficial application of these policies. The prevalence of "surface acting" raises ethical questions about whether organizations are genuinely fostering inclusivity or merely enforcing compliance. Is a policy truly inclusive if it silences dissent rather than engages? This creates a disconnect between the organization's stated values and the everyday experiences of its employees, ultimately undermining the effectiveness of DEI efforts.

At the organizational level, the paradox between short-term results and long-term DEI goals is another critical area of tension. Hospitality organizations, especially those in highly competitive markets, are often under pressure to deliver immediate financial results. However, the long-term benefits of DEI policies, such as fostering innovation, enhancing employee satisfaction, and improving customer service, may not be immediately apparent. This tension is broadened by the lack of tangible metrics to measure the success of DEI initiatives in the short term, leaving managers in a precarious position where their commitment to inclusivity might be viewed as a liability rather than an asset. This creates a paradox for managers, who must prioritize short-term performance metrics while also working to create a diverse and inclusive workforce. The findings suggest that many managers in the hospitality sector struggle with this tension, as they are expected to achieve quick results while also adhering to DEI standards that require time and effort to implement effectively. The critical question is whether organizations are willing to invest the resources and time necessary to reconcile these conflicting demands, or whether DEI initiatives are doomed to remain symbolic gestures in the face of financial pressures.

### *6.5.2 Practical Implications*

The research highlights the critical role of managers in mediating DEI paradoxes, particularly middle managers, who often balance organizational expectations with local cultural realities. Managers must navigate the fine line between enforcing DEI policies and accommodating personal employee beliefs, emphasizing the need for adequate training and support to address these complexities effectively.

HR departments are critical in promoting DEI initiatives tailored to local cultural contexts. While HR teams in Poland's hospitality sector have integrated

DEI values into hiring, training, and policies, resistance from employees unfamiliar with or opposed to these principles underscores the importance of continuous education and awareness campaigns.

Organizations must adapt global DEI standards to local cultural norms to ensure effectiveness. Region-specific DEI strategies that are sensitive to the unique cultural, historical, and social dynamics of areas like Poland are crucial. For instance, DEI initiatives should be carefully framed in culturally conservative contexts to avoid alienating employees and reducing resistance.

Managers require tools and training in cultural sensitivity, conflict resolution, and inclusive leadership to bridge gaps between global DEI standards and local cultural values. Their ability to mediate tensions is essential to the success of DEI efforts, fostering an inclusive and productive workplace environment.

### *6.5.3 Study Limitations and Future Research*

While this study provides valuable insights into the paradoxes of DEI in the CEE hospitality sector, several limitations must be acknowledged. The study focuses primarily on hotels in Poland, which, while offering a solid case study, may limit the generalizability of the findings to other CEE countries or industries. Future research should expand to other nations in the region, such as Hungary, the Czech Republic, and Romania, to assess whether similar DEI paradoxes emerge and identify any regional differences in the reception and implementation of DEI policies. The qualitative nature of the research, based on in-depth interviews, provides a rich contextual understanding of employee experiences and perceptions but may also limit the broader application of findings. A more quantitative approach, including surveys across a larger sample of hotels or other hospitality sectors, could provide additional data to support or challenge the current findings and uncover further trends in DEI policy implementation. The study mainly captures the perspectives of middle managers and employees, while future research could benefit from including the views of senior executives and policymakers who shape DEI strategies at a higher organizational level. Understanding their decision-making processes and the barriers they face could offer a more comprehensive view of how DEI policies are formulated and how cultural and historical factors influence top-down directives. Another limitation involves the temporal scope of the study, which was conducted within a specific timeframe. Given the rapidly evolving sociopolitical landscapes in CEE countries, particularly with events such as the war in Ukraine and shifting political climates, future research should adopt a longitudinal approach to track how these external factors continue to influence attitudes toward DEI over time. Finally, this research touches on a gap in DEI literature related to traditionally homogeneous societies, but future studies could further investigate how religious and cultural legacies, particularly the role of the Catholic Church, continue to shape or hinder DEI initiatives. Comparative studies between secular and more religiously influenced regions could offer deeper insights into how DEI values are either embraced or resisted.

## References

Alvis, R. E. (2016). *White Eagle, Black Madonna: One Thousand Years of the Polish Catholic Tradition.* New York: Fordham University Press.

Ambroziak, A. (2024). Poland in the European Union. 20 years of membership: Experiences and forecasts. Report 2024. *SGH Magazine*.

Andrejczuk, M. & Strzelczak, M. (2017). *Diversity Management in Central and Eastern Europe Lesson Learned and Potential for Growth*. Publications Office of the European Union.

Atlas of Hate (2024). https://atlasnienawisci.pl. Accessed on September 15, 2024.

Ballinger, T. & Crocker, J. (2021). Understanding Whites' perceptions of multicultural policies: A (non)zero-sum framework? *Journal of Personality and Social Psychology*, *120*, 1231–1260. https://doi.org/10.1037/pspi0000315

Bierca, M. & Strzelczak, M. (2023). *Zarządzanie różnorodnością w Polsce. Gdzie jesteśmy, dokąd zmierzamy.* Forum Odpowiedzialnego Biznesu. https://odpowiedzialnybiznes.pl/wp-content/uploads/2023/01/FOB_Zarzadzanie_roznorodnoscia_raport_10lecieKR.pdf. Accessed on August 1, 2024.

Billet, J. & De Witte, H. (2008). 'Everyday racism' as predictor of 'political racism' in Flemish Belgium. *Journal of Social Issues*, *64*(2), 253–267.

Boroş, S. & Gorbatai, A. (2024). Walking the tight rope of DEI implementation: Paradox mindset and emotional capabilities as preconditions for middle managers' success. *Frontiers in Psychology*, *15*, 1396512. https://doi.org/10.3389/fpsyg.2024.1396512

Brown, N. D. & Jacoby-Senghor, D. S. (2021). Majority members misperceive even "win-win" diversity policies as unbeneficial to them. *Journal of Personality and Social Psychology*, *122*(6), 1075–1097. Advance online publication. https://doi.org/10.1037/pspi0000372

Buczynski, B. (2016). *Role of the Catholic Church in Resisting Communist Rule in Poland.* Guided History.

Burks, R. V. (2015). *Dynamics of Communism in Eastern Europe.* Princeton, NJ: Princeton University Press.

CBOS - Public Opinion Research Center (2024). *Civil partnerships – yes or no?* https://www.cbos.pl/PL/publikacje/news_tekst.php?nr=15/2024. Accessed on August 24, 2024.

Cresswell, J. W. (2014). *Research Design: Qualitative, Quantitative, and Mixed Methods Approaches.* Thousand Oaks, CA: Sage Publications.

Cugler, N. (2015). Diversity Management. Training course for implementing Diversity Charter. *Assistance and Programs for Sustainable Development – Agenda 21*.

Cutts, S., DeBoard, E., Filardi, M., Fuoco, C., Graves, A., Hall, J., Kaim, E., Meng, P., Kaiser, J., Sanders, H., Schrantz, S., Ogaki, J., Ozawa, R. & Zeng, A. (2023). *Countering the Illiberal Drift in Europe: Mobilizing Civil Society and Governments to Defend Liberal Democracy.* The Donald C. Hellman Task Force Program, Jackson School of International Studies.

Dang, T. M. H., Tran, T. T. H., Tran, A. H. (2021). High-performance human resource management practices and creative organizational climate effects on manufacturing industry performance. *Polish Journal of Management Studies*, 23(2), 72–89. https://doi.org/10.17512/pjms.2021.23.2.05

Deng, H., Walter, F., Lam, C. K., & Zhao, H. H. (2017). Spillover effects of emotional labor in customer service encounters toward coworker harming: A resource depletion perspective. *Personnel Psychology*, *70*(2), 469–502. https://doi.org/10.1111/peps.12156

Dixon-Fyle, S., Dolan, K., Hunt, V. & Prince, S. (2020). *Diversity Wins: How Inclusion Matters.* McKinsey & Company, https://www.mckinsey.com/featured-insights/diversity-and-inclusion/diversity-wins-how-inclusion-matters. Accessed August 10, 2024.

Dover, T. L., Major, B. & Kaiser, C. R. (2016). Members of high-status groups are threatened by pro-diversity organizational messages. *Journal of Experimental Social Psychology*, *62*, 58–67. https://doi.org/10.1016/j.jesp.2015.10.006

Ely, R. J., & Thomas, D. A. (2020). Getting serious about diversity: Enough already with the business case. *Harvard Business Review*, *98*(6).

Esch, E., Wei, L., Chiang, F. (2016). High-performance human resource practices and firm performance: the mediating role of employees' competencies and the moderating role of climate for creativity. *The International Journal of Human Resource Management*, *29*(10), 1–26. https://doi.org/10.1080/09585192.2016.1206031

Espinoza, E., & Horne, Ch. (2022). *Diversity, Equity & Inclusion: Key Action Areas for Investors.* Principles for Responsible Investment, https://www.unpri.org/download?ac=15712. Accessed August 10, 2024.

Fleron, F. J. & Hoffmann, E. P. (1993). *Post-Communist Studies and Political Science: Methodology and Empirical Theory in Sovietology.* Boulder, Colorado, US: Westview Press.

Friedman, H., H., & Vlady, S. (2024). The paradox of DEI: How lofty ideals became hated. *SSRN Electronic Journal 44*(4), 78–105. https://doi.org/10.2139/ssrn.4744783

Fuller, L. (2000). Socialism and the Transition in East and Central Europe: The Homogeneity Paradigm, Class, and Economic Inefficiency. *Annual Review of Sociology*, *26*, 585–609. https://doi.org/10.1146/annurev.soc.26.1.585

Georgiadou, A., Gonzalez-Perez, M. A., & Olivas-Luján, M. R. (2019). *Diversity with Diversity Management: Types of Diversity in Organizations.* Emerald Group Publishing Limited.

Gorbatai, A., Boroş, S. & Ullman, K. (2022). Why Middle Managers Struggle to Implement DEI Strategies. *Harvard Business Review*.

Gorsuch, A. E. (2011). *All This Is Your World: Soviet Tourism at Home and Abroad after Stalin.* Oxford: Oxford University Press.

Iyer, A. (2009). *Increasing the Representation and Status of Women in Employment: The Effectiveness of Affirmative Action*, pp. 257–280 Washington, DC: American Psychological Association.

Iyer, A. (2022). Understanding advantaged groups' opposition to diversity, equity, and inclusion (DEI) policies: The role of perceived threat. *Social and Personality Psychology*, *16*(5), e12666. https://doi.org/10.1111/spc3.12666

Jackson, T. F. (2007). *From Civil Rights to Human Rights: Martin Luther King, Jr., and the Struggle for Economic Justice.* Philadelphia, PA: University of Pennsylvania Press.

Kaldewey, D., Rymarzak, M., Stoppa, B., Schmitt, K., & Riedmiller, L. (2024). Managing internationalization versus managing diversity? Global imperatives and national trajectories in German and Polish universities. *European Journal of Higher Education*, 1–19. https://doi.org/10.1080/21568235.2024.2348680.

Kothari, T., Elo, M. & Wiese, N. (2022). Born as a citizen and reborn as an alien: migrant superdiversity in global business. *AIB Insights*, *22*(3). https://doi.org/10.46697/001c.35243.

Leach, C. W., Ellemers, N., Barreto, M. (2007). Group Virtue: The Importance of Morality (vs. Competence and Sociability) in the Positive Evaluation of In-Groups. *Journal of Personality and Social Psychology*, *93*(2), 234–249. https://doi.org/10.1037/0022-3514.93.2.234

Lewis, M. W. (2000). Exploring paradox: Toward a more comprehensive guide. *Academy of Management Review*, *25*(4), 760–776. https://doi.org/10.5465/amr.2000.3707712

Lüscher, L. S., & Lewis, M. W. (2008). Organizational change and managerial sensemaking: Working through paradox. *Academy of Management Journal*, *51*(2), 221–240. https://doi.org/10.5465/amj.2008.31767217

McCracken, G. D. (1988). *The Long Interview*. Thousand Oaks, CA: Sage Publications.

McNair, B. (2006). *Glasnost, Perestroika and the Soviet Media*. Routledge. https://doi.org/10.4324/9780203192191

Miron-Spektor, E., Ingram, A., Keller, J., Smith, W. K. & Lewis, M. W. (2017). Microfoundations of organizational paradox: The problem is how we think about the problem. *Academy of Management Journal*, *61*(1), 26–45. https://doi.org/10.5465/amj.2016.0594.

Myers, V. (2015). *Diversity Is Being Invited to the Party: Inclusion Is Being Asked to Dance*. AppNexus' inaugural Women's Leadership Forum. https://www.youtube.com/watch?v=9gS2VPUkB3M

Newburry, W., Rašković, M., Colakoglu, S. S., Gonzalez-Perez, M. A. & Minbaeva, D. (2022). Diversity, Equity and Inclusion in International Business: Dimensions and Challenges. *AIB Insights*, *22*(3). https://doi.org/10.46697/001c.36582

Pilch, I. & Turska, E. (2015). *Workplace Abuse, Incivility and Bullying*. Imprint London, UK: Routledge.

Ptak, A. (2023). Only 3% of medium and large firms in Poland have diversity management document. *Notes from Poland Foundation*.

Radisson Hotel Group (2024). *Radisson Hotel Group celebrates Diversity, Equity, and Inclusion at inaugural 'Diversity Week'*. https://www.radissonhotels.com/en-us/corporate/media/press-releases/RHG-celebrates-DEI-at-inaugural-diversity-week. Accessed on August 30, 2024.

Riessman, C. K. (1993). *Narrative Analysis*. New Park, California, US: Sage Publications.

Renfro, C. L., Duran, A., Stephan, W. G. & Clason, D. L. (2006). The role of threat in attitudes toward affirmative action and its beneficiaries. *Journal of Applied Social Psychology*, *36*, 41–74. https://doi.org/10.1111/j.0021-9029.2006.00003

Rios, K., Sosa, N., & Osborn, H. (2018). An experimental approach to Intergroup Threat Theory: Manipulations, moderators, and consequences of realistic vs. symbolic threat. *European Review of Social Psychology*, *29*, 212–255.

Rykała, A. (2014). National and ethnic minorities in Poland from the perspective of political geography. *Acta Universitatis Lodziensis Folia Geographica Socio-Oeconomica*.

Sandua, D. (2023). *The Evolution of Feminism and the Struggle for Gender Equality*. Amazon Digital Services LLC.

Schad, J., Lewis, M. W., Raisch, S., & Smith, W. K. (2016). Paradox research in management science: Looking back to move forward. *Academy of Management Annals*, *10*(1), 5–64. https://doi.org/10.5465/19416520.2016.1162422

Schad, J., Miron-Spektor, E. (2021). Lewis, Marianne W.: Paradoxes of change and changing through paradox. In Szabla, D. B. (Ed.), *Palgrave Handbook of Organizational Change Thinkers* (pp. 951–965). Cham: Springer.

Schöpflin, G. (1993). Culture and identity in Post-Communist Europe. In S. White, J. Batt, P. G. Lewis (Eds.), *Developments in East European Politics* (pp. 16–34). Palgrave Macmillan. https://doi.org/10.1007/978-1-349-22898-0_2

Shteynberg, G., Leslie, L. M., Knight, A. P. & Mayer, D. M. (2011). But affirmative action hurts us! Race-related beliefs shape perceptions of White disadvantage and policy unfairness. *Organizational Behavior and Human Decision Processes, 115*, 1–12. https://doi.org/10.1016/j.obhdp.2010.11.011

Sik, E. & Wellman, B (2018). *Network Capital in Capitalist, Communist, and Postcommunist Countries.* Milton: Imprint Routledge.

Smith, W. K. & Lewis, M. W. (2011). Toward a Theory of Paradox: A Dynamic Equilibrium Model of Organizing. *Academy of Management Review*, *36*(2): 381–403.

Stanley, J. (2010). *Sex and Solidarity, 1980–1990. Canadian Slavonic Papers*, *52*(1/2), 131–51.

State Electoral Commission (2024). https://pkw.gov.pl. Accessed on September 15th, 2024.

Szałtys, D., Cierniak-Piotrowska, M., Chmielewska, A., Kaczorowski, P., Kuchta, A., Gudaszewski, G., Potocka, M., Stelmach, K., Szymczuk-Kupryś, M. & Wysocka, A. (2023). National Population and Housing Census 2021 Population. Size and demographic-social structure in the light of the 2021 Census results. Statistics Poland, Warsaw.

Van Knippenberg, D., De Dreu, D. & Homan, C. K. W. (2004). Work group diversity and group performance: An integrative model and research agenda. *Journal of Applied Psychology*, *89*(6), 1008–1022. https://doi.org/10.1037/0021-9010.89.6.1008

Wasserman, I. C. (2015). *Dialogic OD, Diversity, and Inclusion: Aligning Mindsets, Values, and Practices.* Emerald Group Publishing Limited, *23*, 329–356. https://doi.org/10.1108/S0897-301620150000023008

Yogeeswaran, K. & Dasgupta, N. (2014). The devil is in the details: Abstract versus concrete construals of multiculturalism differentially impact intergroup relations. *Journal of Personality and Social Psychology*, *106*, 772–789. https://doi. org/10.1037/a0035830

Zakharova L. (2013). Everyday life under communism: Practices and objects. *Histoire, Sciences Sociales, 2*, 305–314.

Zick, A., Pettigrew, T. F., & Wagner, U. (2008). Ethnic prejudice and discrimination in Europe. *Journal of Social Issues*, *64*(2), 233–251. https://doi.org/10.1111/j.1540-4560.2008.00559.x

# Part III

# Managing Learning Paradoxes

# 7 Paradoxes in Innovation

## Navigating the Duality of Closed versus Open Innovation and Business versus Non-profit Innovations

*Elżbieta Wojnicka-Sycz, Piotr Sycz, and Candace TenBrink*

### 7.1 Introduction

The chapter presents the evolution of the science and practice of innovation towards its current holistic perspective. Innovation theory has evolved from closed to open innovation and now includes business and nonprofit innovation. These paradoxes reflect the change in the epistemology of innovation science from a reductionist to a holistic perspective. This is related to the evolution of paradigms in general science from the mechanistic paradigm to the systemic and postmaterialistic paradigm.

The mechanistic paradigm was built at the beginning of the 18th century. The research perspective at that time included the reductionist approach. Reductionism in science assumes that knowing a phenomenon at a lower level can explain the phenomenon at a higher level and that qualitative properties can be explained quantitatively (Skytnerr, 2001). Einstein's theory of relativity has challenged determinism, characterizing the mechanistic paradigm. In addition, the paradigm shift in science was caused by the development of particle physics. Quantum mechanical systems are not deterministic – the results of the experiments may be random, but as repeated many times, the average results correspond to the expectations of classical physics. The new scientific paradigm, the systemic paradigm, implies a holistic research approach. A systemic paradigm is a way of thinking, solving a problem, or proceeding in which phenomena are treated holistically in their internal and external dependencies. The systems approach to research is characterized by a comprehensive view of biological, technical, and social objects, as well as phenomena inside these objects (Bokulich, 2008).

The emerging postmaterialistic paradigm is related to the spiritual dimension of research, dating back to the turn of the 20th and 21st centuries. In social terms, postmaterialism establishes altruism aimed at the higher goals of evolution. It posits the preservation of values as an alternative to selfishness in serving personal goals and satisfying material and physiological needs. It aims to shape the rules of existence based on the search for society's common goal. It also assumes that material well-being is not a condition for a person's happiness. An

DOI: 10.4324/9781003541394-11

element of the postmaterialist paradigm is synergetic, derived from the ancient concept of synergy or cooperation. The basis of self-organization is collaborative processes that include both material and nonmaterial structures (Shabanova, 2019). According to Maslow's Hierarchy of Needs, people attend to their most urgent needs first, and only when these are satisfied, they attend to other needs. Basic needs are physiological and related to physical and economic security. Once these are met, people seek to satisfy other less materialistic needs, such as social relationships, quality of life, or self-actualization (Tormos, 2012). Postmaterialism as a scientific paradigm refers to Ronald Inglehart's (1977) concept. People with high levels of postmaterialist attitudes are concerned with a sense of community, self-expression, environmental values, and quality of life (Jeroense et al., 2021).[1]

The development of the science of innovation has led to the paradox of the coexistence of closed and open innovation, as well as business and nonprofit (environmental, public, and social) innovation. Closed innovation is at the core of the mechanistic paradigm, while open innovation requires a holistic approach. Business innovation, which creates purely economic value, is related to mechanistic and systemic paradigms, while nonprofit innovation is related to the postmaterialist paradigm. However, in the systemic paradigm, business innovation is perceived in broader terms than just technological, as in the case of the mechanistic paradigm. Criticism of purely profit-driven innovation has led to a change in European Union (EU) law, making companies responsible for sustainable development goals.[2] The complexity of today's products and services and hyper-competition inspire closer collaboration with partners in the innovation ecosystem, namely open innovation. The objectives of this chapter are:

1. To present the evolution of the paradigm in the science, policy, and practice of innovation from a reductionist to a holistic one that has led to paradoxes in innovation. That is from closed, business, and technology-driven innovation to those that are also open, green, and inclusive of nonprofit and social development.
2. To examine changes in the intensity of open and green innovation over time in the EU countries.
3. To examine the impact of open and closed innovation on the development of enterprises in Poland and the importance of open and green innovation for the level of social development as measured by the Human Development Index in the EU.

In this chapter, we present a literature review and bibliometric analysis on the evolution of paradigms in innovation science from reductionist and mechanistic to holistic, systemic, and postmaterialist paradigms. The literature review is followed by an analysis of data from the European Innovation Scoreboard and Human Development Reports on the popularity of open and green innovation and its correlation with the Human Development Index (HDI) in the EU27 countries. We also look for differences between the former communist Central and Eastern European (CEE) countries within the EU and the Western European (WE) countries. We also run panel regressions to determine whether open and green innovations stimulate well-being. Moreover, we compare the effects of open and closed innovations on the perspectives of the development of enterprises, as well as the differences in their goals, including sustainable development goals.

## 7.2 Literature Review

Paradoxes in innovation are caused by the evolution of the paradigms in innovation theory and practice. According to Kuhn (1962), the research paradigm reflects the beliefs of a given scientific group regarding the cause-effect relationships and standards in each scientific discipline. Crises in science, such as increasing cognitive gaps and paradoxes, often lead to the emergence of new paradigms. Science could not exist without paradigms; they allow scientists and entrepreneurs to pursue disciplined, progressive research that leads to technological development (Giannopoulos & Munro, 2019). Entrepreneurs, creators, and pioneers who introduce innovative products and processes often modify current paradigms in socioeconomic development based on technological discoveries (Winslow & Solomon, 1993).

### *7.2.1 Mechanistic Paradigm and Closed Innovation*

From a reductionist perspective, scientific-technological changes could only inspire product and process innovations. This view underlined varied initiatives to support technology transfer from the science sector to firms in the form of technology parks and technology transfer centers. This was reflected in the first model of innovation policy, which focused on stimulating economic growth through science and technology. This innovation policy model also focused on the development of new industries and an increase in the efficiency of production factors (Schot & Steinmueller, 2018). Reductionism through a rigid path direction is reflected in the linear innovation and demand-driven models. The first model positions innovation from idea to invention to innovation. The innovation process also has a linear function: Research, development, design and tooling, production, and marketing (Neely & Hii, 1998). The demand-driven model recognizes that innovation and technological progress respond to market demand and that greater expenditures are directed toward inventions that can generate greater profits (Schmookler, 1966).

The mechanistic paradigm in science, based on a reductionist approach, also implies closed innovation: In the closed model, innovation is based on a company's human resources, in-house R&D, and self-financing by companies that aim to be first to market with new products for which they secure intellectual property rights (Chesbrough, 2003; Lopes & de Carvalho, 2018). In this traditional mode, producers view their research and development (R&D) as covering all required market facets, from design to technology. Thus, in-house R&D substitutes for potential contributions from users as innovators (Gambardella et al., 2016).

Both reductionism and the linear innovation model are reflected in the first generations of innovation management models (Miller, 2015). The first generation of innovation management models added R&D units to the traditional hierarchical organizational structure. In this first generation, incremental innovation was dominant, with radical innovation coming from a random process or event. The second generation, which began during World War II, brought a collaborative cost-sharing R&D model between companies and universities (Miller, 2015).

### *7.2.2 Systemic Paradigm and Open Innovation*

The change towards a holistic approach in science is reflected in the ontology of innovation studies. The Manual on Definitions and Statistics in Innovation of the OECD and the European Commission – the Oslo Manual 3rd edition of 2005 – departed from the emphasis on technological and non-technological innovations. It created new divisions into product, process, marketing, and organizational innovations, thus paying attention to innovations that have no source in technology. Innovation management from 1975 to 2000 introduced modern strategic planning, venture capital, new digital information tools, and the Internet, portfolio management of R&D to mitigate risk, technology roadmaps for R&D, knowledge management, globalization, and new hybrid business models.

The holistic systemic paradigm is reflected in the concepts of national and regional innovation systems. The innovation system consists of institutions and entities that generate knowledge and innovation with supporting institutions and links between them (Nelson, 1993). Learning processes and knowledge spillovers resulting from interactions are fundamental to the innovation system (IS). However, the basic IS concept is limited to interactions between firms and academia. These are supported by public authorities. Interactions between firms, academia, and government form the "triple helix" phenomenon (Leydesdorff & Zawdie, 2010). The crucial change from the mechanistic paradigm to the systemic paradigm is the inclusion of open innovation at the micro level. Open innovation relies on extensive collaboration between external entities and the firm, thus integrating external and internal knowledge (Chesbrough, 2003).

Hobcraft (2011) proposes a distributed innovation model involving an organization based on open innovation. Organizations using this approach must be able to absorb, anchor, and distribute external knowledge. Trust, behavior, and relationships are critical to the success of open innovation. If individuals are able to collaborate with others, organizations should benefit from this exploration and knowledge sharing.

Current innovation management sees the modern innovation process as iterative and nonlinear, emphasizing different actors and partners, as well as knowledge sharing with customers facilitated by the Internet, open innovation labs near universities, and innovation hubs. Radical innovation is a team effort that also spans multiple industries (Miller, 2016).

### *7.2.3 The Postmaterialistic Paradigm and Nonprofit Innovation*

The latest holistic paradigm in science, postmaterialism, is visible in innovation studies incorporating nonprofit goals, such as green, social, and public innovations. Green technology innovation, also called eco-innovation, aims to reduce the negative impact on the environment. Eco-innovations, among others, lead to a circular economy that uses and recycles natural resources (Thomas & Mishra et al., 2022). Green innovations can be both for-profit and not-for-profit. They are like the postmaterialistic ecological values based on Inglehart's (1977) concept.

Nonprofit innovations, also referred to as public sector innovations, include a deliberate initiative process, practical adoption, and dissemination of creative ideas. It aims to bring about qualitative change in a specific context (Hagen & Higdem, 2019). Thus, the range of sectors involved in innovative systems is expanding to include users and public organizations previously perceived as external to these systems. The latest Oslo Manual (2018) provides new recommendations for measuring innovation and adapting definitions to include a broader vision of innovation-generating entities. This now includes social and public organizations, emphasizing the systemic nature of innovation.

From a social development perspective, innovation refers to social phenomena and ventures that often result from interpersonal interactions that promote transformation and the development of social capabilities. Social innovations are the processes of reconfiguring social relations to respond to social problems. They create opportunities for positive social change through initiatives promoting social inclusion, well-being, and citizen empowerment (Silva-Flores, 2019).

The original definition of open innovation focused on revenue generation and did not consider the value created by grassroots communities focused on sharing knowledge for nonprofit purposes. Chesbrough (2007) further developed the concept of open innovation as a distributed innovation process based on knowledge flows between organizations managed through monetary and non-monetary tools. He also explained how this concept overlaps with and differs from user-driven innovation. He also explained how this concept overlaps with and differs from user-driven innovation. Both open and user-driven innovation pay attention to the role of users in the distributed innovation process. Incorporating user-based knowledge into the innovation process requires companies to collaborate across borders. In the open innovation model, companies remain the site of innovation production, while the user innovation model favors the decentralization of innovation, which shifts the place of innovation from companies to users and leads to the "democratization of innovation" (Gambardella et al., 2016).

Tidd and Bessant (2009) believe that today's innovation process models are nonlinear, network-based, and rely on the ability to process information and learn faster. Each organization may use its own innovation model; there is no single optimal solution. For example, innovations can be the outcome of internal or externally derived R&D. Innovations can also be user-driven or the result of inter-firm collaboration. Innovation can also result from rediscovering markets and business models or coordinating activities within the firm.

Today, borderless ecosystems are being analyzed instead of national or regional innovation systems. This approach considers that innovation often involves global interdependencies facilitated by information and communication technologies and better transport. In fact, we can speak of different innovation ecosystems, often with global dimensions. The triple helix model has been developed to quadruple and quintuple helixes as important subsystems of innovative systems such as users (society, nongovernmental organizations – NGOs, activists) and the natural environment are added to business, science, and administration components (Carayannis et al., 2012). In fact, the six-armed helix should consider the role of intermediary institutions, which have been omitted in previous models. Intermediaries facilitate the diffusion of knowledge and independently generate innovations (Wojnicka-Sycz & Sycz, 2023). The networks in the IS are created with various types of intermediaries and pro-innovation infrastructure that facilitate the contact between science and business, such as technology transfer centers, technology parks, clusters, and knowledge-based services, such as private consulting companies.

At the policy level, the holistic postmaterialist paradigm in innovation studies is best reflected in the smart specialization policy. This is the EU policy of innovative development, which consists of identifying strategic, internationally competitive sectors that are distinguished in terms of R&D and innovation activities. At the same time, smart specializations are innovative ecosystems based on the cooperation of strategic sectors with science and social organizations in the sector's value chain and among competitors. A new model of innovation policy is emerging, reflecting a shift towards nonmarket innovation: Social or green. There are growing objections to the superficial treatment of innovation as focused on firms that generate profit and economic growth, but which are largely internalized in the income of a narrow group of individuals – the founders, owners, and managers of innovation firms or innovative enterprises. These firms benefit in the innovation process from the available public knowledge base and often from substantial public support for innovation. Still, the gains from innovation contribute too little to sustainable development (Mazzucanto, 2021). Table 7.1 shows the characteristics of the paradigms discussed above in innovation theory.

*Table 7.1* Topics Characterizing Paradigms in Innovation Theory

| *Reductionism – Partial Studies and Details Analyzed Without Context* | *Holism – Whole, Complex Concepts Considering Context* | |
|---|---|---|
| *Mechanistic Paradigm* | *Systemic Paradigm* | *Postmaterialist Paradigm* |
| • Technological innovation<br>• Closed innovation<br>• Not connected actors with technology transfer of R&D from academia to enterprises commercializing innovations based on scientific research | • Business innovation, not only technological<br>• Open innovation<br>• Interactions in geographical or technological systems based on triple helix<br>• Economic growth as the main goal of innovations | • Not only business but also not-for-profit innovations: Social and public innovation<br>• Green innovations<br>• Interactions in complex sextuple helix<br>• Open and user innovation<br>• Dynamic innovation ecosystems<br>• Sustainable development, not only economic growth |

The aspirations for transformative change are embodied in the United Nations Sustainable Development Goals for 2030. These include eradicating poverty and inequality in all its forms worldwide, promoting inclusive and sustainable consumption and production systems, and the fight against climate change. The aim is to use science and technology policy to meet societal needs, and in sustainable development and social integration of policies (Schot & Steinmueller, 2018). It is also reflected in the transformation of smart specialization strategies into "smart specialization strategies for sustainability" – S4. Sustainable objectives are already visible in the updated strategy of many European regions (Nakicenovic et al., 2021). In the United States, innovation policy is often linked to specific policy missions. In mission-oriented ISs, the primary role of the state is to direct innovation to meet state needs, such as security and citizen needs, such as health or education, and to help create socially desirable markets (Edler et al., 2016). The shift in innovation policy is also exemplified by the change in the name of the European Commission's Joint Research Center (JRC) directorate from Growth and Innovation to A Fair and Sustainable Economy (Wojnicka-Sycz & Sycz, 2023). Table 7.1 summarizes the topics that reflect different paradigms and approaches in science from the perspective of innovation.

### *7.2.4 Bibliometric Analysis*

We performed a bibliometric analysis of all publications registered in the WoS database on September 17, 2024, in the categories of economics, business, or management. We searched for topics that characterize different paradigms in innovation theory. Table 7.2 shows the publication count and the percentage of publications in the selected categories by keywords from 1986 to 2021 and 2022 to September 1, 2024. We analyzed 6-year periods since the topics first appeared in the WoS.

The analysis shows that topics connected with the mechanistic paradigm started to become popular in the 1980s, with the highest popularity in 2004–2009 and again in the last two years. Topics connected with systemic and postmaterialist paradigms have become increasingly popular, with the highest popularity among scholars since 2016. This illustrates the evolution of innovation science.

As of September 17, 2024, we did not find any articles containing the keywords "closed innovation," "open innovation," and "green innovation" together in the WoS. However, we found 45 publications containing these three terms; 18 were published since 2022, 17 in 2016–2021, and 10 in 2009–2015. They mainly refer to open, green innovation. We found 1,955 articles containing open and closed innovation as the topic of interest. Of these, 257 were published in 2023–2024, over 100 publications per year from 2013 to 2022. Between 2004 and 2012, more than 10 publications per year were published on closed and open innovation. This is indeed a paradigm shift and an important paradox in innovation management.

However, searching only the keywords, we found 44 articles combining open and closed innovation and 1 article combining "business innovation" and "nonprofit innovation." Six of them compared different aspects of open and closed innovation, similar to the aims of our chapter (Table 7.3). Nevertheless, the topic of our chapter, which tries to analyze both paradoxes in innovation management, that is open versus closed innovation, as well as business versus not-for-profit (green, social, public) from the perspective of the evolution of innovation science, remains uninvestigated in the literature so far. Table 7.3 lists the WoS articles that present conclusions on the paradoxes of open and closed innovation.

The paradox of business and nonprofit, which today also refers to innovation, has been analyzed by Austin et al. (2007). They show that business and nonprofit organizations are converging. Traditionally, nonprofits were perceived as creating social value, while businesses created economic value. In the 1970s, under pressure from environmentalists, corporations began to listen to nonprofits. In the 1980s, cutbacks in government social services forced nonprofits to become more entrepreneurial and look for business management models. At the same time, corporations increased their social contributions (Austin et al., 2007). Eventually, social enterprises and social and nonprofit innovations emerged, governed to some extent by the same management rules

*Table 7.2* Bibliometric Analysis of Topics Related to the Paradigms in Innovation Science

| *Approach* | *Reductionistic* | | *Holistic* | | | |
|---|---|---|---|---|---|---|
| *Paradigms* | *Mechanistic* | | *Systemic* | | *Postmaterialistic* | |
| *Keywords* | *"Technology Transfer" or "Technological Innovation" or "Closed Innovation"* | | *"National Innovation System" or "Regional Innovation System" or "Triple Helix" or "Open Innovation"* | | *"Innovation Ecosystem" or "Quadruple Helix" or "Quintuple Helix" or "Green Innovation" or "Social Innovation" or "Public Innovation"* | |
| | *Count* | *%* | *Count* | *%* | *Count* | *%* |
| 2022–2024 | 1354 | 0.49 | 791 | 0.29 | 2828 | 1.0232 |
| 2016–2021 | 2142 | 0.32 | 1751 | 0.26 | 3027 | 0.4469 |
| 2015–2010 | 1196 | 0.21 | 1139 | 0.20 | 1314 | 0.2352 |
| 2009–2004 | 1178 | 0.36 | 380 | 0.12 | 352 | 0.1077 |
| 2003–1998 | 332 | 0.18 | 71 | 0.04 | 54 | 0.0297 |
| 1997–1992 | 167 | 0.10 | 6 | 0.004 | 11 | 0.0067 |
| 1991–1986 | 27 | 0.02 | 0 | | 2 | 0.0015 |

*Note:* Number of publications registered in WoS connected with given keywords and as a percentage of all publications of the WoS categories Economics, Business, and Management.

*Table 7.3* Open and Closed Innovation Paradox in the Literature

| *Publication* | *Conclusions on Open versus Closed Innovations* |
|---|---|
| Hungund & Mani (2019) | Small and Medium Sized Enterprises (SMEs) in the Indian software industry use both open and closed innovation. Factors favoring:<br>• Open innovation: a) Internal factors: Young age and smaller size of the firm, lower level of education, such as being a graduate, of the decision maker, and higher experience of the decision maker, research and development (R&D) focus, and pro-open organizational culture with features such as sourcing external ideas and rewarding employees for new ideas, and free expression culture and not penalizing employees for unsuccessful ideas; b) External factors: Higher competition and technological advances<br>• Both closed and open innovation – larger companies, postgraduate or doctoral education of a decision maker, influence of customers, influence of Bangalore ecosystem<br>• Closed innovation: Company culture of innovation, customer demands |
| Lee, Park, & Song (2009) | 215 Korean SMEs: Closed innovation strategy, such as family control, is associated with better financial performance |
| Hungund, Gaur, and Narayan (2023) | 200 biotechnology firms in India; open innovation, in the form of interaction with large R&D firms or customers, positively affects performance parameters. Similarly, both closed and open innovation have a positive impact on a firm's innovation and economic performance |
| Biswas and Akroyd (2022) | Innovative company undergoing a transition from closed to open innovation<br>The introduction of management control systems enabled improvements in the practice of closed innovation but did not drive open innovation. They did, however, help reduce new product development time and increase customer satisfaction |
| Alawamleh at al. (2018) | Open innovation had a greater impact on employee performance than closed innovation. Open innovation was used by the studied company in the investment department to attract more customers, investments, and to increase profits |
| Nawroth, Brem & Rymarczyk (2023) | Open innovation leads to the success of SMEs by using more human resources, while closed innovation is better in the case of a higher market share but requires more financial resources |

as business innovation. But differences remain. The main role of nonprofits is to ensure that businesses and governments do not harm social welfare. Businesses, on the other hand, should carry out their economic functions in a way that stimulates development but considers its sustainability (Austin et al., 2007).

## 7.3 Research Methodology

We present the results of five surveys conducted between 2014 and 2024, which include 2,388 entities, most of which are businesses. The 2022 survey also includes 31 representatives of institutions and NGOs. The characteristics of the studies are shown in Table 7.4. The statistical method used was the analysis of the significance of the differences in proportions. The two-sample test for large samples was used, which depends on the proportion and size of the population (Szymczak, 2010). This method makes it possible to compare the specificity of open and closed innovators, the main paradox analyzed.

In addition, we used data from the European Innovation Scoreboard (EIS) for the years 2017–2024 and data from the Human Development Reports (HDR). The Human Development Index (HDI) is a summary measure of countries' scores based on the variables: Life expectancy at birth, expected and average years of schooling, and gross national income per capita in purchasing power parity. The index is standardized to values ranging from a minimum of 0 to a maximum of 1. The latest available HDI for 2024 is based on data available in 2023 and refers to data from 2022. The HDI is calculated for the whole world, while the EIS is calculated for the EU, neighboring countries, and other major global players. The EIS variables are also standardized to range from 0 to 1, and synthetic indicators are created for the dimensions. The EIS data are presented in Table 7.4. We used these data, as well as HDI scores, in panel regressions for 27 and 26 EU countries for seven periods.

We calculated fixed and random effects models according to the indications of panel regression tests (test of overall significance of inequality of group means, Breusch-Pagan test, Hausman test). The general formula of the panel model is (1):

$$Y_{it} = \beta_0 + \mathbf{X}_{it}\boldsymbol{\beta} + \alpha_i + v_t + \varepsilon_{it} \qquad i = 1,\dots,N;\ t = 1,\ \dots,T. \qquad (1)$$

where:

$\beta_0$ – constant term, $\mathbf{X}_{it}$ – matrix of explaining variables covering especially those referring to open and green innovation, $\boldsymbol{\beta}$ – vector of structural parameters of the model, $\alpha_i$ – individual effects, that is, the part of the variability of the explained variable, in the chapter HDI or sales of innovations, characteristic of the $i$ -th territorial unit ($N$ effects), $v_t$ – time effects, the portion of the variability of the variable $y$ characteristic of the period $t$ ($T$ effects), $\varepsilon_{it}$ – error term. Table 7.5 describes the variables of the EIS used in this chapter.

In the fixed effects (FE) models, individual and/or time effects are constant over time or for a certain entity and do not depend on random factors. This model can be estimated by eliminating individual effects and replacing the values of the levels of the variables with their deviations from the means for each country (transformation within). Random effect models (RE) assume that individual and time effects are parts of the error term (Kufel, 2015; Ciołek et al., 2020).

*Table 7.4* Survey Research Carried Out in the Years 2014–2024

| *Number of Respondents and Their Location* | *Method of Research* |
|---|---|
| **University of Gdansk, 2024** | |
| 142 Computer Programming companies from Europe; answers received from Poland (40), Portugal (20), Finland (20), Germany (17), Estonia (8), Hungary (7), Lithuania (6), UK (6), Norway (5), Bulgaria (4), Slovenia (3), Slovakia (3), Romania (2), and Czech Republic (1). Micro – 45, small – 58, medium and large – 38.[3] 115 respondents CEO/directors or owners. | Computer Assisted Web Interviews (CAWI), e-mails from Orbis database,[4] invitations sent to 18858 firms. |
| **University of Gdansk, 2024** | |
| Service companies apart from Computer Programming from Poland, provided answers from 73 firms: 6 large, 34 medium, and 33 small companies. Of the respondents, 36 respondents were CEO/directors or owners. | CAWI, questionnaires sent to all large (1.3 ths.) and medium firms (6.2 ths.) from service industries and approximately 17.3 ths. out of circa 50 ths. small service firms from Poland registered in the Orbis database. |
| **For Marshall Office of Podkarpackie Voivodeship, Rzeszow, 2022[5]** | |
| Answers from 114 enterprises, 31 NGOs, scientific organizations, and administration; 42 micro entities, 94 small, 51 medium and large. | CAWI, non-probabilistic sample. Representatives of Podkarpackie businesses, science and education, local government units, and NGOs. |

(*Continued*)

*Table 7.4* (*Continued*)

| *Number of Respondents and Their Location* | *Method of Research* |
|---|---|
| **For Marshall Office of Podkarpackie Voivodeship, Rzeszow, 2020**[6] | |
| Answers from 673 enterprises: 455 micro, 61 small, 72 medium, and 85 large. 12 – agriculture, 113 – industry, 77 – construction, 234 – market services, 63 – high-tech services, 134 – other knowledge-based services, 40 – other services. | Computer Assisted Telephone Interviews (CATI), sample representative in relation to the following characteristics: Localization (subregions), employment class, and categories of economic sections. |
| **For Ministry of Infrastructure and Development, 2014**[7] | |
| Answers from 1,355 enterprises that applied for innovation grants: 716 from those who received a grant and 639 from a control sample of those who unsuccessfully applied. | CATI, enterprises applying for support for innovation from the Innovative Economy Operational Program 2007–2013 according to the type of innovation grant. |

Because the composite indices of the EIS are composed of different variables, we used lags of the variables or lags of the composite indices when they served as explanatory variables whenever at least one variable was based on data from 2023.

## 7.4 Results

### *7.4.1 The Paradox of Open and Closed Innovation at Companies' Level*

The 2014 research showed that 747 out of 1,355 surveyed companies in Poland that applied for innovation grants did not cooperate with scientific or pro-innovation institutions such as technology transfer centers, technology parks, or clusters. Of those that cooperated, 90% reported some type of innovation activity such as R&D or product, process, organizational, or marketing innovation, and about 75% conducted R&D activity. These proportions were much higher than in the case of noncooperating firms, of which only 60% reported any innovation activity and only 29% conducted R&D. Cooperation with science seems to be particularly important for R&D. The development prospects in

*Table 7.5* Description of Variables of the EIS

| *Dimension (Abbreviation)* | *Variables (Abbreviation and/or Units) with the Year of the Newest Available Data* |
|---|---|
| Employment impacts (lag: empl_1) | Employment in knowledge-intensive activities (percentage of total employment) 2023, Employment in innovative enterprises 2020 (percentage of total employment for firms with over 10 employees) |
| Intellectual assets (intellect) | PCT patent applications per billion GDP (in Purchasing Power Standard (PPS)) 2020 (patents), Trademark applications per billion GDP (in PPS) 2022 (trademarks), Design applications per billion GDP (in PPS) 2022 |
| Sales impacts (sales) | Medium and high technology product exports (share in total service exports) 2023, Knowledge-intensive service exports (share in total service exports) 2022, Sales of new-to-market and new-to-enterprise innovations 2020 |
| Environmental sustainability (Environment) | Resource productivity 2022 (resource), Air emissions by fine particulates (PM2.5) in Industry 2021, Development of environment-related technologies (envir_tech) |
| Innovators (innovators) | SMEs introducing product innovations (percentage of SMEs) 2022, SMEs introducing business process innovations (percentage of SMEs) 2022 |
| Firm investments (Firminvestments) | Non-R&D innovation expenditures (percentage of turnover) 2020, R&D expenditure in the business sector (percentage of GDP) 2022, Innovation expenditures per person employed 2020 |
| Linkages (lag: Linkeages_1) | Innovative SMEs collaborating with others (percentage of SMEs) 2022, Public-private co-publications per million population 2023 (lag: pppubl_1), Job-to-job mobility of Human Resources in Science & Technology 2020 |
| Attractive research systems | Scientific publications among the top 10% most cited publications worldwide as a percentage of total scientific publications of the country in 2021 (lag: toppubl_1) |

*Source:* EIS (2024) and authors.

all dimensions analyzed (turnover, profit, employment, innovation expenditure, and sales) were more frequently reported by enterprises with open innovation models (Table 7.6).

The research conducted in 2020 on a sample of 673 companies' representatives from the Podkarpackie voivodeship in Poland concerned the adoption of digital innovations. 26% (177) of the surveyed companies reported any innovation activity, and 90% (160) of them introduced digital innovations. Cooperation

*Table 7.6* The Effects of Open and Closed Innovations According to the Research from 2014 (Percentage of Respondents)

| *Prospects of the Increase of* | *Any Business Innovation (R&D, Product, Process, Organizational, and Marketing)* | | *R&D Activity* | |
|---|---|---|---|---|
| | *Open*[1] | *Closed* | *Open* | *Closed* |
| Revenues | 81.0% | 74.4%*** | 82.0% | 73.8%*** |
| Profits | 76.4% | 71.5%** | 76.7% | 71.0%* |
| Employment | 58.2% | 47.8%*** | 59.1% | 49.5%*** |
| Innovation outlays | 67.8% | 50.0%*** | 68.6% | 54.7%*** |
| Sales of innovations | 77.0% | 65.7%*** | 79.8% | 72.9%** |
| n | 543 | 446 | 455 | 214 |

*Note:* [1] Open refers to cooperation with science, innovation support organizations, or in clusters, *** statistically significant on 0.01 level, ** statistically significant on 0.05 level, * statistically significant on 0.1 level, the statistically significant difference of values in the subgroups of a given variable to the value/s of the subgroup in italics.

during the implementation of digital innovations with any external parties such as other companies, science, business support institutions, administration, suppliers, or customers was reported by 73% (93) of these companies. However, in only two areas, the positive effects of digital innovation implementation were more frequently noticed by companies that used open instead of closed digital innovation. 54% of open innovators noted increased job safety, while only 29% of closed innovators did. In addition, 59% of open innovators reported an increase in revenue because of digital innovation, compared to 43% of closed innovators. Due to the paradox of open and closed innovation, a certain duality also arises in the case of digital innovation.

The analysis of the data from the CAWI survey of firms and institutions in the Podkarpackie voivodeship in Poland in 2022 showed that 112 respondents had some cooperation in their IS, and 88 of them carried out research, development, and innovation (R&D&I) projects. Among 33 noncooperating units, only 12 were innovative. Cooperation seems crucial, especially for R&D and innovation, as 79% of cooperating agents were innovative. The analysis of the differences in the proportions of open and closed innovators in terms of their organization's objectives showed a significantly higher share – 70% of open innovators had the strategic objective of engaging in R&D projects as opposed to 33% of closed innovators. Similarly, 42% of open innovators considered the organizational goal of supporting innovative start-ups to be important, compared to 25% of closed innovators. An organization's social responsibility as a commitment to social action and social innovation was more important to open innovators, as reported by 70% of respondents, compared to 50% of closed innovators. Thus, the duality of innovation practice, even from the perspective of the postmaterialist innovation paradigm, becomes visible through the lens of the open and closed innovation paradox. However, the strategic goal of environmental protection and eco-innovation showed similar importance in both groups, as reported by nearly 70% of respondents. Similarly important for open and closed innovators was activity aimed at improving the quality of life. About 90% of both types of innovators indicated the goal of long-term sustainable development of the organization, and nearly 80% wanted to achieve a quick profit.

According to the surveys carried out in 2024 in the computer programming industry in Europe and other service firms in Poland, open innovation is characteristic of more innovative companies. However, in the case of IT being a high-tech service industry, high innovativeness refers to having more than 50% of projects associated with innovation. On the contrary, in more traditional service industries, the threshold for high innovativeness is having 11–30% of innovative products in the portfolio, with very few exceeding 30% (Table 7.7). Among other service companies in Poland, those that cooperate with external partners have a strong competitive position three times more often than those that do not, and a much smaller proportion of them have a weak competitive position. However, in the case of IT companies, closed innovators report a strong competitive position more often than open innovators. It seems that the paradox of open and closed innovation is not uniform, but varies across industries, depending on

*Table 7.7* Open and Closed Modes in European IT firms and Other Service Firms from Poland Surveyed in 2024 (Percentage of Respondents)

| *Categories* | *IT Europe (n = 142)* | | *Service Firms Other than IT Poland (n = 73)* | |
|---|---|---|---|---|
| | *Open*[1] | *Closed* | *Open* | *Closed* |
| **Share of Innovative Services:** | | | | |
| Over 50% | 44.3%** | 18.2% | 3.6% | 5.6% |
| 31–50% | 23.7% | 36.4% | 9.1% | 5.6% |
| 11–30% | 20.6% | 36.4% | 40.0%** | 11.1% |
| Less than 10% | 11.5% | 9.1% | 47.3%** | 77.8% |
| **Competitive Position:** | | | | |
| Strong | 34.4%** | 63.6% | 49.1%*** | 16.7% |
| Average | 48.1%*** | 9.1% | 40.0% | 44.4% |
| Weak | 16.0% | 18.2% | 10.9%*** | 38.9% |
| **Development Prospects:** | | | | |
| Very good and good | 53.4% | 72.7% | 65.5%** | 38.6% |
| n | 131 | 11 | 55 | 18 |

*Note:* [1] Open – any cooperation with other firms, competitors, science, business support institutions, administration, suppliers, or customers.

*** statistically significant on 0.01 level, ** statistically significant on 0.05 level, * statistically significant on 0.1 level, the statistically significant difference of values in the subgroups of a given variable to the value/s of the subgroup in italics.

their overall innovativeness. Some strong, incumbent innovators may capitalize on their past innovations by restricting the practice of open innovation to protect their profits. This is also probably because they are able to innovate internally, although a very small fraction of the European IT companies surveyed reported no cooperation (8%). As a result, there were no significant differences in the proportions of open and closed innovators in IT among those reporting very good and good development prospects. In other services, significantly more open innovators reported such an optimistic outlook (Table 7.7).

The paradox of open and closed innovation is also not uniform through the lens of being closed or open to certain innovation partners. We observed differences in cooperation patterns between CEE and WE countries. Almost 56% of the 72 computer programming firms surveyed from the CEE cooperate with multinational companies as customers, while only 29% of the 70 IT firms surveyed from the WE do so. The firms from CEE countries cooperate much more frequently with firms from other industries than their customers (24% in CEE and 6% in WE). They also cooperate more often with consulting firms (17% in CEE and 7% in WE) and public administration (13% in CEE and 4% in WE). It seems that the cooperation of enterprises in CEE is mainly based on their subcontracting relations. This differs for WE companies, which are more likely to collaborate with a variety of partners in their innovation ecosystem.

The popularity of most of the partners, however, is similar in the CEE and the WE. The most important of them for enterprises in the whole of Europe are other IT companies (40% of respondents), technology suppliers (34% of enterprises), universities (27% of enterprises), and individual experts from science (21% of IT enterprises). Cooperation with NGOs, innovation support organizations, and customers other than multinationals ranges from 7% to 11% of respondents' companies (Figures 7.1 and 7.2).

### *7.4.2 Open and Green Innovation and Social Welfare*

European countries, both CEE and WE, stand out in terms of human development compared to the rest of the world, but there are differences between these groups. Since 2017, the average HDI for CEE increased relative to the best country in each edition of the HDR, but only by 0.01 to 0.87. At the same time, the HDI for WE increased from 0.91 to 0.93 (Figures 7.1 and 7.2).

The innovativeness of CEE compared to the rest of the EU-27 is still much lower on average than that of WE. In 2024, the average Synthetic Innovation Index (SII) for CEE was 70.4% of the EU average, up from 67.5% in 2017. At the same time, the average SII for WE decreased slightly from 109.7% of the EU average in 2017 to 108.6% in 2024.

Although open innovation, as reflected by the linkages dimension of the EIS, improved in the CEE during this period, it remains much lower in the CEE than in the WE. In 2024, open innovation indicators, on average, reflected 172% of

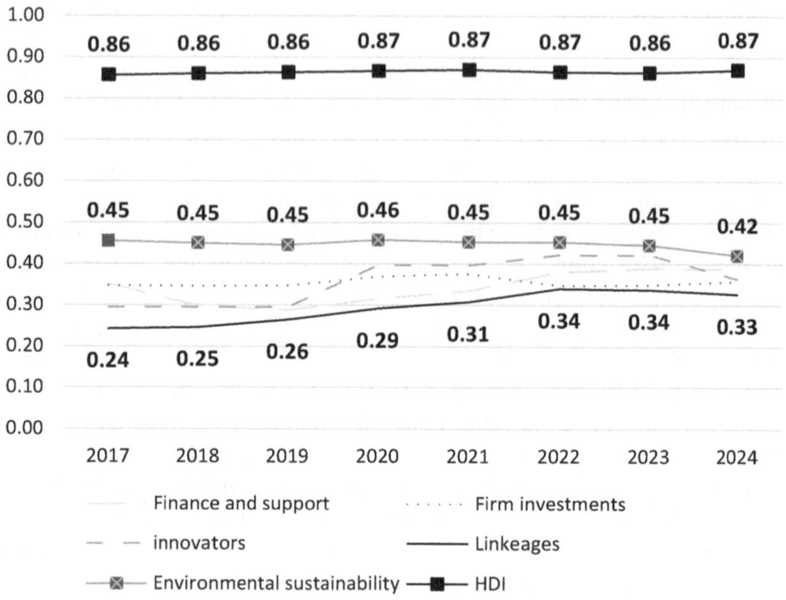


*Figure 7.1* CEE Countries: Average Indices for EIS Dimensions.
*Source:* EIS 2024 and Human Development Report 2024.

the EU average in the WE in 2024, 4 percentage points lower than in 2017. In the CEE, they reflected 97.4% of the EU mean in 2024, an increase of 8 percentage points since 2017 (Table 7.8).

The differences in green innovations between CEE and WE are not so large. Environmental sustainability indicators are also higher on average in WE, increasing from 0.51 to 0.61 since 2017 in terms of distance to the best country. In CEE, the average for the environmental sustainability dimension decreased from 0.45 of the benchmarks to 0.42. It seems that the CEE countries face obstacles in implementing eco-innovations, probably due to fewer available resources. Financing and support for innovation increased in both groups, but it remains lower in CEE than in WE (0.31 and 0.51 values of the average indices). The values of the indices for innovators and firm investment increased in both groups but remained much lower in CEE (Figures 7.1 and 7.2).

The panel regressions confirmed the role of open innovation in the well-being of societies (Table 7.8). In all models, innovation-related variables were correlated with higher HDI in EU countries in 2017–2024. In the first model, the increase of public-private publications (PPP) in the previous period in relation to inhabitants increased the HDI: 1 additional public-private publication per million inhabitants increased the HDI indicator by 0.00007. At the same

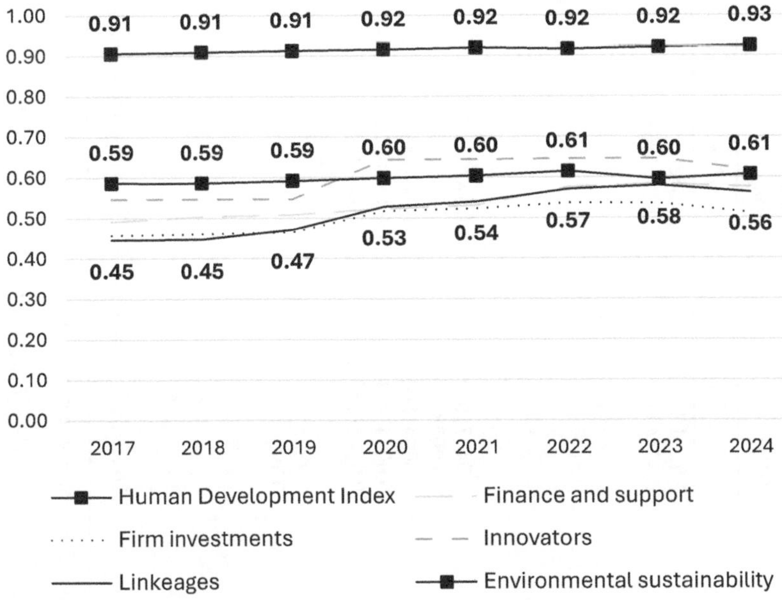


*Figure 7.2* WE Countries: Average Indices for EIS Dimensions

*Source:* EIS 2024 and Human Development Report 2024.

time, increasing resource productivity (Gross Domestic Product in relation to domestic material consumption) by 1 percentage point increased the HDI index by 0.006. This indicates that both green and open innovation are important for social welfare. As measured by PPP, open science is significant for the increase in HDI, while the increase in patent or trademark applications is not significant. Thus, it appears that open science is better for welfare than closed science.

Increasing the value of the synthetic indicator of linkages by 1 correlates with an HDI increase of 0.048 points. However, dimensions of EIS, such as intellectual assets, employment effects, innovators, firm investment, and the overall environmental sustainability index, were not significant. Thus, open innovation and knowledge diffusion improve social welfare as measured by HDI.

The fourth model showed that sales of innovations in the EU (excluding Romania due to lack of data) increased due to firm investment in R&D&I, increased employment in knowledge-based industries, and an increase in the strength of linkages in the IS. Among these, the impact of linkages and firm investment was the strongest for the increase in the share of sales from innovation.

In particular, the estimates show the crucial role of open innovation and its importance for social welfare compared to protecting intellectual property

*Table 7.8* Results of Estimations of Panel Regressions

| *Explained Variables* | *HDI* | | *HDI* | *Sales* |
|---|---|---|---|---|
| *Type of Estimation* | *Fixed Effects Robust SE* | | | *Random Errors Robust SE* |
| Explaining Variables | Model 1 | Model 2 | Model 3 | Model 4 |
| const | 0.871254*** | 0.888513*** | 0.874637*** | 0.297686*** |
| Envir_tech[a] | −0.000236684 | −0.000289972 | | |
| Resource[b] | 0.00624776** | | | |
| Patents | −0.000828109 | | | |
| Pppubl_1 | 7.38236e-05*** | 8.21780e-05*** | | |
| Toppubl_1 | | −0.000775916 | | |
| Trademarks | | 0.000156745 | | |
| Linkeages_1 | | | 0.0477100*** | 0.183052** |
| Intelect | | | −0.00283767 | −0.0521452 |
| Empl_1 | | | 0.000518646 | 0.109183* |
| Innovators | | | 0.00443431 | 0.0820679 |
| Environment | | | 0.00413753 | 0.0492397 |
| Firminvestments | | | | 0.158234* |
| LSDV R-kwadrat | 0.988171 | 0.987844 | 0.986354 | |
| Within R-kwadrat | 0.411958 | 0.395726 | 0.390698 | |
| Correlation coefficient of empirical and theoretical values – pseudo $R^2$ | | | | 0.31 |
| n | 189 | 189 | 182 | 182 |
| Time periods | 7 | 7 | 7 | 7 |
| Numer of countries | 27 | 27 | 26 (without Romania) | 26 (without Romania) |

*Source:* Authors based on EIS 2024 data and HDR 2024 data (https://research-and-innovation.ec.europa.eu/statistics/performance-indicators/european-innovation-scoreboard en; https://hdr.undp.org/data-center/documentation-and-downloads).

*Note:* models 3 and 4 on standardized variables. *** statistically significant on 0.01 level, ** statistically significant on 0.05 level, * statistically significant on 0.1 level, the statistically significant difference of values in the subgroups of a given variable to the value/s of the subgroup in italics.

[a] Percentage of patents for environmental technologies in all.

[b] Resource – Gross Domestic Product (GDP) to Domestic Material Consumption, resource productivity measures the total amount of materials used by an economy in relation to GDP.

rights. However, green investments, particularly higher resource productivity in the form of lower material consumption relative to GDP, also increase social welfare as measured by the HDI.

## 7.5 Discussion and Conclusions

### *7.5.1 Theoretical and Policy Level Conclusions and Implications*

Our literature review showed that the paradigm shift in general science from a reductionist, mechanistic paradigm to holistic systemic and postmaterialistic paradigms has influenced innovation science, policy, and practice. It triggered an emergence of paradoxes in innovation, such as the rise of open innovations as a new mode of innovation management compared to closed innovations. In the closed mode, firms implemented innovations based on their own resources, commercializing knowledge created in the science sector. As a result, innovations were mostly incremental, with breakthroughs coming from science. In the time of the mechanistic paradigm in innovation, technology transfer policy was the dominant type of innovation policy, and innovation was perceived as technology-based.

The systemic paradigm introduced not only technological but also other business innovations, as organizational and marketing innovations emphasized cooperation in the IS, as opposed to the earlier unidirectional technology transfer. However, agents of an IS were perceived only as firms, science, and administration, as well as bridging institutions (although omitted in the "triple helix" model). Open innovation, which resulted from stronger firms' investment in R&D activities, showed that firms no longer had to depend solely on internal R&D efforts. In fact, the complexity of today's technology requires cooperation with external agents for success in developing innovations. Better linkages in the IS became an important goal of innovation policy. However, in the systemic paradigm, innovation was still focused on economic value, which could also be achieved by cooperation with competitors and the joint increase of value added based on alliances.

Among the paradigms in science, we distinguish another one in comparison with Skyttner (2001), the postmaterialist paradigm. It led to the emergence of nonprofit and green innovations, which created a paradox – a tension with business innovation. The increase in the wealth of nations, largely caused by business innovation, led to a greater understanding of the damage triggered by rapid economic growth without regard for the natural environment or those members of society who were outside the innovative industries or developed countries. At the same time, people whose basic needs were satisfied began to seek higher-order needs such as esteem, self-actualization, and transcendence. Therefore, various nonprofit institutions forced governments to focus on the rights of deprived social groups and nature. This has led to the emergence of social and eco-innovation policies, forcing companies to consider economic and social value. Thus, the paradox of business and nonprofit (social, green, and public) innovations appeared. This led to society, users, and environmentalists being perceived as change agents, driving innovation alongside science, companies, public administration, and intermediaries.

These types of innovations, as well as economic and social value, are interdependent. Without a well-functioning economic system based on business innovation, society would not have enough slack resources to invest in social welfare, such as education, health, and environmental protection. Without public education or health care, businesses would not have a skilled workforce, and customers would not be able to understand their products. Without businesses and wages, workers would not be able to buy the products and services offered in markets, and businesses would not have customers and income. Therefore, promoting balance in the socioeconomic system by facilitating economic and social value creation should be the central goal of innovation policy. This means that the paradoxes of business and nonprofit innovation are not opposites and substitutes but rather complements, and therefore, the tensions between them should be minimized by innovation policy. This can be done by promoting open science and further linkages in the IS, namely open innovation. Our analysis shows that open innovation in the EU positively impacts the HDI level, while securing intellectual property is not important. Increasing resource productivity is important for the growth of social welfare, which shows that the circular economy concept is beneficial for HDI.

It also seems that postmaterialistic attitudes in developed societies make business innovation more open and nonprofit. Thus, societies force companies to acknowledge that the basis of their new solutions is the previously accumulated public knowledge. Therefore, antitrust authorities could propose new regulatory solutions, such as setting price limits for innovative products that acquire intellectual protection, thus creating a temporary monopoly. Such a solution is used in the case of natural monopolies. This would reduce the tension between the paradoxes of business and nonprofit innovation and increase the impact of even closed innovations on HDI while ensuring that innovators receive a fair return for their R&D&I efforts that can be easily imitated.

Theoretically, we believe that different paradigms and paradoxes can coexist and complement each other. Like Bokulich (2008), who proposes the concept of interstructuralism, we trust that previous theories continue to play an important theoretical role in scientific research and economic life. We do not contend that new theories explain the world well enough without the old ones. Regarding innovation, the previous reductionist approach and closed innovation can be applied to noncomplex service or product innovation activities, such as incremental innovation. They may be based on technology transfer. However, a holistic approach and open innovation considering using different knowledge sources will be needed to create breakthrough innovations. Innovation support policies will also be needed. Social or public sector innovation that addresses social and environmental challenges will require collaboration in a complex innovation helix.

Our theoretical analysis classifies the evolution of innovation science according to paradigms and scientific research approaches and shows the genesis of paradoxes in innovation. Such an analysis is not available in the literature we reviewed. We also applied the concept of postmaterialism to innovation science. This theoretical framework allowed us to use green and social innovations as a proxy for nonprofit innovations. We collected data from direct research and the European Innovation Scoreboard and Human Development Reports. Our bibliometric analysis showed that topics related to systemic and postmaterialist paradigms have become increasingly popular among scholars, especially since 2016. This implies the growing importance of open, green, and social innovation.

### *7.5.2 Practical Conclusions and Implications*

As our research showed at the firm level, both open and closed innovation models still exist, but the paradox is not uniform across industries and in terms of the presence or absence of specific innovation partners. Open innovation is particularly intense in high-tech industries such as computer programming in Europe, especially in companies with the highest share of innovative projects. In the case of this sector, both closed and open innovation translates into good development prospects. However, the open innovation mode is associated with better development prospects among more traditional service companies, where innovation activity is rarer. Open innovators focus more on strategic goals related to R&D and scientific activity than closed innovators. Moreover, commitment to social responsibility was more important for open innovators than closed ones.

In our research, somewhat stronger cooperation with a variety of partners forming ISs was more important for IT companies from WE countries than for companies located in CEE countries. However, the CEE companies cooperate very strongly with their multinational customers, which suggests subcontracting contracts.

At the country level, both open and green innovation modes are more advanced in WE than in CEE. Moreover, although the open innovation indicators have increased in CEE since 2017, the intensity of green innovation has decreased in the CEE countries. This is probably due to the lack of resources for this type of innovation and technologies, as the level of support for innovation remains low in CEE compared to WE. It also means that environmental protection requirements should be varied so as not to hinder the development prospects of countries that are lagging behind the most developed countries, which are also the most advanced in green technologies. As Maslow's pyramid shows, postmaterialistic values can only be the goal of human beings if their basic needs are met. Without external support for green innovation, poorer countries and their businesses will not be able to finance it.

### *7.5.3 Research Limitations and Further Studies*

The limitation of our study is the low response rate of companies in CAWI research in Europe and the fact that, from an international perspective, we only included IT companies. Further research in other industries and the analysis of direct research results in light of the HDI level would be required. In addition, a deeper understanding of the paradoxes of closed and open and business and non-profit innovation based on qualitative research would be needed. Future research could also answer how companies deal with imposed environmental, social, and governance requirements from the perspective of their business innovation and efficiency objectives.

Further research could find solutions to make closed innovators more responsible for social and environmental issues, as the increase in open and green innovation leads to an increase in HDI. Moreover, since intellectual property protection was insignificant for the increase in HDI, other ways of supporting firms' innovation activities, such as public subsidies, should be proposed to make R&D results more open.

## Notes

1. https://www.worldvaluessurvey.org, accessed on September 18, 2024.
2. For example, the Sustainable Finance Disclosure Regulation – the European Union regulation of 2021, which came into force in January 2023.
3. Micro: up to 9 employees, small: 10–49 employees, medium firms: 50–249 employees, large: over 249 employees.
4. https://login.bvdinfo.com/R0/Orbis, accessed on September 18, 2024.
5. Good practices in strengthening stakeholder involvement in regional innovation systems, Marshal's Office of the Podkarpackie Province, Rzeszów, 2022 (in Polish).
6. The economy of the Podkarpackie Voivodeship facing the challenges of Industry 4.0, 2020, Marshal's Office of the Podkarpackie Voivodeship, Rzeszów (in Polish).
7. Impact assessment of the Innovative Economy Operational Program on increasing the innovativeness of enterprises, 2014, Ministry of Infrastructure and Development, Warsaw (in Polish).

## References

Alawamleh, M., Ismail, L. B., Aladwan, K., & Saleh, A. (2018). The influence of open/closed innovation on employees' performance. *International Journal of Organizational Analysis*, *26*(1), 75–90. https://doi.org/10.1108/ijoa-08-2017-1207

Austin, J. E., Gutiérrez, R., Ogliastri, E. & Reficco, E. (2007). Capitalizing on Convergence. *Stanford Social Innovation Review*, *5*(1), 24–31. https://doi.org/10.48558/AW6E-CF05

Bernard, H., Markianidou, P., Pétré, H., & Rosenfeld, D. (Eds.). (2024). European Innovation Scoreboard 2024. Methodology report. Brusseles: EIS.

Biswas, S. S. N., & Akroyd, C. (2022). Management control systems and the strategic management of innovation. *Qualitative Research in Accounting & Management, 19*(5), 513–539. https://doi.org/10.1108/qram-04-2021-0083

Bokulich, A. (2008). *Reexamining the Quantum-Classical Relation*. Cambridge: Cambridge University Press.

Carayannis, E. G., Barth, T. D., & Campbell, D. F. (2012). The Quintuple Helix innovation model: Global warming as a challenge and driver for innovation. *Journal of Innovation and Entrepreneurship, 1*(1), 2. https://doi.org/10.1186/2192-5372-1-2

Chesbrough, H. (2007). Business model innovation: It's not just about technology anymore. *Strategy & Leadership, 35*(6), 12–17, 2007.

Chesbrough, H. W. (2003). The Era of Open Innovation. *MIT Sloan Management Review, 44*(3), 35–41.

Ciołek D., Wojnicka-Sycz E., Sycz P., Klimczak T., & Miller A. (2020). *Measuring the impact of smart specialization on the economic development of Małopolska-edition* 2020. Cracow.

Edler, J., Cunningham, P., Gok, A., & Shapira, P. (Eds.). (2016). *Handbook of Innovation Policy Impact*. Eu-SPRI Forum on Science, Technology and Innovation Policy series. Cheltenham: Edward Elgar Publishing Ltd.

Gambardella, A., Raasch, C., & Von Hippel, E. (2016). The User Innovation Paradigm: Impacts on markets and welfare. *Management Science, 63*(5), 1450–1468. https://doi.org/10.1287/mnsc.2015.2393

Giannopoulos, G. & Munro, J. (2019). *The Accelerating Transport Innovation Revolution*. Amsterdam: Elsevier. https://doi.org/10.1016/B978-0-12-813804-5.00003-6

Hagen, A., & Higdem, U. (2019). Calculate, communicate, and innovate: Do we need "Innovate" as a third position? *Journal of Planning Literature, 34*(4), 421–433. https://doi.org/10.1177/0885412219851876

Hobcraft, P. (2011). *Moving Towards a Distributed Innovation Model*. https://www.disruptorleague.com/blog/2011/01/18/moving-towards-a-distributed-innovation-model/. Accessed on October 31, 2024.

Hungund, S., Gaur, J., & Narayan, A. (2023). The influence of open and closed innovation practices on economic performance: Empirical evidence from Indian biotechnology industry. *Management Decision*. https://doi.org/10.1108/md-10-2022-1440

Hungund, S., & Mani, V. (2019). Benchmarking of factors influencing adoption of innovation in software product SMEs. *Benchmarking an International Journal, 26*(5), 1451–1468. https://doi.org/10.1108/bij-05-2018-0127

Inglehart, R. (1977). *The Silent Revolution: Changing Values and Political Styles among Western Publics*. Princeton: Princeton University Press.

Jeroense, T., Luimers, J., Jacobs, K., & Spierings, N. (2021). Political social media use and its linkage to populist and postmaterialist attitudes and vote intention in the Netherlands. *European Political Science, 21*(2), 193–215. https://doi.org/10.1057/s41304-020-00306-6

Kufel, T. (2015). *Econometrics Problem Solving Using GRETL Program*. PWN: Warsaw (in Polish).

Kuhn, T. S. (1962). *The Structure of Scientific Revolutions*. Chicago, IL: University of Chicago Press.

Lee, Y., Park, S., & Song, Y. (2009). Which is better for a firm's financial performance: An externally oriented or inwardly oriented innovation strategy? An empirical study on Korean SMEs. *Asian Journal of Technology Innovation, 17*(1), 57–73. https://doi.org/10.1080/19761597.2009.9668666

Leydesdorff, L., & Zawdie, G. (2010). The triple helix perspective of innovation systems. *Technology Analysis and Strategic Management, 22*(7), 789–804. https://doi.org/10.1080/09537325.2010.511142

Lopes, A. P. V. B. V., & De Carvalho, M. M. (n.d.). Evolution of the open innovation paradigm: Towards a contingent conceptual model. *Technological Forecasting and Social Change, 132*, 284–298. https://doi.org/10.1016/j.techfore.2018.02.014

Mazzucato, M. (2021). *Mission Economy. A Moonshot Guide to Changing Capitalism.* London: Allen Lane.

Miller, W. L. (2015). Innovation Management Theory and Practice: Part 1. *Journal of Creating Value, 1*(2), 235–255.

Miller, W. L. (2016). New fourth generation of innovation management theory & practice: Part 2. *Journal of Creating Value, 2*(1), 124–149. https://doi.org/10.1177/2394964315627259

Nakicenovic, N., Zimm, C., Matusiak, M., & Ciampi Stancova, K. (2021). *Smart Specialisation, Sustainable Development Goals and environmental com- mons. Conceptual framework in the context of EU policy.* Luxembourg: EUR 30882 EN, Publications Office of the European Union.

Nawroth, G., Brem, A., & Rymarczyk, C. (2023). Open innovation and closed innovation: A simulation study on market conditions and innovation strategies. *International Journal of Technology Management, 92*(1/2), 63. https://doi.org/10.1504/ijtm.2023.128796

Neely, A., Hii, J. (1998). *Innovation and Business Performance: A Literature Review.* Cambridge: University of Cambridge.

Nelson, R. R. (ed.) (1993). National innovation systems: a comparative analysis, Oxford University Press.

Oslo Manual. (2005, 2018). OECD & Eurostat, Paris.

Schmookler, J. (1966). *Invention and Economic Growth.* Cambridge, MA: Harvard University Press.

Schot, J., & Steinmueller, W. E. (2018). Three frames for innovation policy: R&D, systems of innovation and transformative change. *Research Policy, 47*(9), 1554–1567. https://doi.org/10.1016/j.respol.2018.08.011

Shabanova, Y. (2019). Conceptual foundations of the Postmaterialist paradigm of science. *Philosophy and Cosmology, 22*, 162–173.

Silva-Flores, M. L. (2019). Social Innovation Policies: A Way Through Consolidating Emerging Innovation Infrastructures, *The Innovation Journal: The Public Sector Innovation Journal, 24*(3), 1–19.

Skyttner, L. (2001). *General Systems Theory, Ideas and Applications.* World Scientific.

Szymczak, W. (2010). *Fundamentals of Statistics for Psychologists* (in Polish). Difin.

Thomas, A., & Mishra, U. (2022). A sustainable circular economic supply chain system with waste minimization using 3D printing and emissions reduction in plastic reforming industry. *Journal of Cleaner Production, 345*, 131128. https://doi.org/10.1016/j.jclepro.2022.131128

Tidd, J., & Bessant, J. (2009). *Managing innovation. Integrating Technological, Market and Organizational Change.* Hoboken, NJ: Wiley and Sons.

Tormos, R. (2012). Postmaterialist values and adult political learning. Changing Intracohort Values in Western Europe. *Revista Española de Investigaciones Sociológicas (REIS)*, *140*(1), 201–228.
Winslow, E. K., & Solomon, G. T. (1993). Entrepreneurs: Architects of innovation, paradigm pioneers and change. *Journal Creative of Behaviour*, 27(2), 75–88.
Wojnicka-Sycz, E., & Sycz, P. (2023). Innovative ecosystem based on a sixtuple helix on the example of the Podkarpackie Voivodeship. *Journal of Modern Science*, *52*(3), 172–189. https://doi.org/10.13166/jms/173122

# 8 Workplace Learning through Organizational and Leadership Paradoxes

## Insights from Multinational Enterprises in Central and Eastern Europe

*Agnieszka Miarecka*

### 8.1 Introduction

Workplace learning (WL) has become increasingly crucial for organizational success facing difficulties in attracting and retaining well-qualified employees, the aging society in Europe, rapid technological advancements, and various turbulations. Consequently, research on WL has gained significant traction, aiming to understand factors that facilitate and hinder effective learning within organizations. This is particularly relevant in Central and Eastern Europe (CEE), a region experiencing continuous economic development, economic and political transition, and integration into the global economy. As multinational enterprises (MNEs) establish subsidiaries in CEE, and CEE-based companies expand their operations internationally, understanding WL and the balance between formal and informal learning in this vibrant environment becomes even more critical. Furthermore, applying paradox theory to organizational and leadership dynamics sheds light on learning from managing the conflicting yet interconnected elements prevalent in modern organizations (Rajan & Aiswarya, 2022). This study develops a conceptual framework linking organizational and leadership paradoxes (OLP) within MNEs in CEE and WL, offering a novel perspective on how these factors interact.

The literature on WL from paradoxes within the specific context of CEE is underdeveloped. Thus, this chapter fills a critical gap by offering empirical insights into how WL from paradoxes manifests in MNEs in CEE. Paradoxes are contradictory but parallel demands that leaders must navigate in managing organizations effectively, such as stability vs. change or global standardization vs. local adaptation. Leaders in MNEs in the region face context-specific paradoxes. Embracing these tensions can lead to growth and innovation. The region's historical, political, and economic transitions have created local flexibility needed while implementing global strategies. MNEs must adapt to diverse local markets and regulatory frameworks, balancing consistency with adaptability. The transitional nature of CEE's economies requires companies to rely on informal learning and adaptive leadership to manage rapid market changes effectively. The historical context of centralized

DOI: 10.4324/9781003541394-12

control in CEE's countries contrasts with the decentralized approaches in Western business environments, adding complexity to managing WL and OLP. As CEE organizations integrate into global markets, they must balance historical influences with modern demands for innovation and flexibility. Understanding and managing paradoxes in OLP is crucial for MNEs operating in CEE to succeed amid these complexities. Therefore, this chapter explores how MNEs in CEE manage tensions between global and local demands, formal and informal learning, and stability vs. change. Furthermore, this chapter presents the often-overlooked aspect of undesirable consequences that can arise from mismanaged paradoxes, a dimension rarely explored in existing literature. By examining both the positive and negative outcomes of learning from paradoxes, this study provides a more comprehensive and nuanced understanding of the phenomenon in the CEE context.

By examining how WL processes link with organizing and leadership, this research contributes valuable insights into organizational behavior, leadership, and human resource development, providing practical implications for MNEs operating in complex environments. The findings have practical implications for managers seeking to foster learning environments that embrace paradoxes and leverage them for organizational effectiveness. Furthermore, the study contributes to paradox theory by examining the role of specific contextual factors in CEE in the manifestation and management of paradoxes in MNEs, and how these paradoxes shape WL processes.

Choosing participants from various CEE nations for the study intends to encompass the vast array of viewpoints influenced by the distinct backgrounds that emerged during CEE's post-communist growth. Every country in CEE has taken a unique route in moving towards market economies, joining the European Union (when relevant), and handling globalization. By involving individuals from different countries in CEE, the study can achieve a deeper and more detailed comprehension of how contextual factors interact with the complexities of WL through paradoxes in organizations.

The first part introduces the foundational concepts of WL and learning paradoxes and analyzes their interaction across multiple levels: Individual, leadership, team, and organizational. The next part details the qualitative methodological approach employed in the study. Next, the author presents the empirical findings, highlighting paradoxes as presage, processes, and products of WL. The final part discusses the results, managerial implications, study limitations, and potential areas for further research.

## 8.2 Workplace Learning and Paradox Theory

### *8.2.1 Introduction to Workplace Learning*

Learning is a multifaceted and complex concept encompassing organizational knowledge, organizational learning, and WL, which are key components that shape how employees acquire, share, and use knowledge. Organizational knowledge provides the basis for organizational learning and WL. A solid organizational knowledge foundation helps with the learning process, while efficient learning methods ensure that the organizational knowledge stays up-to-date and is applicable. For the organization to succeed, it must incorporate these components, ensuring that information is regularly refreshed and shared efficiently throughout all its levels. Organizational learning involves the collective learning of the organization as a whole, leading to improved practices, processes, and overall performance. Organizational learning is the process by which an organization improves itself over time through better knowledge gathering and understanding. It focuses on creating, retaining, and transferring knowledge within an organization (Alerasoul et al., 2022; Basten & Haamann, 2018; Xie, 2019). It is also the process through which organizations adjust or update their mental models, rules, processes, or knowledge to sustain or enhance their performance (Chiva et al., 2014). The link between organizational knowledge, organizational learning, and WL is fundamental. Organizational learning involves organizations improving their knowledge base with experience and new information. It is an ongoing process that enables organizations to adjust to changes in their environment. In contrast, WL concentrates on employees gaining skills and knowledge in their organizational environment. It serves as both a driver and a result of organizational learning, as individuals' acquired knowledge adds to the overall knowledge of the organization. WL is an indispensable component of organizational learning.

Scholars have defined WL in various ways. Marsick and Watkins's 1990 book is frequently regarded as the foundational text in WL research. The authors characterize WL as an unintended activity, often a by-product of work. Such learning frequently occurs in non-routine situations, especially when regular procedures break down, leading individuals to recognize previously unexamined assumptions. Through these experiences, individuals often gain new perspectives on problems, resulting in learning (Marsick & Watkins, 2015). WL focuses on individual employees and their professional development within the work environment. It is more about how individuals learn and develop skills that apply to their job roles. According to Jacobs and Park, WL refers to "[...] the process used by individuals when engaged in training programs, education and development courses, or some type of experiential learning activity to acquire the competence necessary to meet current and future work requirements" (2009, p. 134).

Workplace learning occurs in various forms, typically categorized into formal and informal learning (Park & Lee, 2018). *Formal learning* involves training programs, workshops, and educational courses designed to address specific skills or competencies. It is structured and often institutionalized. This type of learning is typically quantifiable and aligned with organizational goals, emphasizing hard skills development and measurable outcomes (Gronseth & Hutchins,

2020; Manuti et al., 2015; Muzam et al., 2023). *Informal learning* is experiential, often incidental, and integrated into daily work activities through job experiences, mentoring, coaching, and employee collaboration. This form of learning, while less tangible, is crucial for fostering adaptability, problem-solving abilities, and tacit knowledge acquisition. It occurs outside structured programs (Marsick and Watkins, 2015). A vital aspect of both formal and informal learning is *self-directed learning*. In the context of WL, self-directed learning refers to a practice where individuals and teams take primary responsibility for their learning and development, often within the flow of their daily work tasks (Lemmetty & Collin, 2020). This approach is particularly relevant in rapidly changing and competitive industries like information and communication technology, where continuous learning and adaptation are essential for success. It empowers employees to take ownership of their development, adapt to changing demands, and contribute to organizational success (Ulrich & Mengiste, 2014). Moreover, some scholars like Billett (2014) distinguish additionally *non-formal learning* as bridging the gap between formal and informal learning. Non-formal learning, while not strictly structured, is purposefully designed to facilitate learning through guided experiences and interactions.

To summarize, WL is an ongoing process of individuals acquiring knowledge, competencies, and skills through activities and experiences that occur within a work environment. For over 20 years, WL has been seen as a significant contributor to the organization's learning culture, adaptability, and strategic coherence (Matthews, 1999; Patky, 2020). Workplace learning is vital for personal development. Individuals engaged in WL are better equipped to embrace new challenges and manage career transitions. The effective implementation of WL strategies enhances organizational adaptability, knowledge, and overall performance. Promoting continuous learning in the workplace enables the creation of coherent and comprehensive learning ecosystems. This integration supports individual career development and enhances the organizational capacity for innovation and competitiveness (Billett & Choy, 2013). Workplace learning is a strategic imperative. By fostering a culture of continuous learning, organizations can cultivate a workforce that is agile, skilled, and capable to grow sustainably (Khandakar & Pangil, 2019).

### *8.2.2 Learning Paradoxes*

Over the last 30 years, the study of paradox and related concepts, such as contradictions, tensions, duality, dilemma, and dialectics, in organizational studies has grown rapidly (Schad et al., 2016). Paradoxes are not simply dilemmas or problems to be solved; they represent inherent tensions that must be continuously balanced. The most cited authors regarding paradox theory define *paradox* as "contradictory yet interrelated elements that exist simultaneously and persist over time." (Smith and Lewis, 2011, p. 382). Paradoxes are elements that appear logical on their own but become absurd and irrational when combined (Lewis, 2000). A paradox can likewise be understood as a "persistent contradiction between interdependent elements" (Schad et al., 2016, p.10). Management scholars like Ospina and Saz-Carranza (2010) describe how leaders face inherent tensions when focusing on internal and external tasks due to network collaboration's contradictory but essential demands. These tensions are correspondingly paradoxes. Actors' perspectives on these tensions as dilemmas or paradoxes depend on their mindset. Those with a *paradox mindset*, value the creative friction and recognize opportunities for learning and agility. They accept and feel comfortable with the discomfort of those tensions (Miron-Spektor et al., 2018).

Smith and Lewis provided scholars in 2011 with a novel framework by mapping paradoxes into four main categories: Learning (knowledge), belonging (identity/interpersonal relationships), organizing (processes), and performing (goals). Those paradox categories represent core activities and elements of organizations. *Learning paradoxes* reflect the tensions that arise from changes in knowledge, such as the conflict between fostering radical and incremental innovation. These paradoxes arise from the inherent tension between stability and change, especially regarding knowledge acquisition, development, and innovation. They represent corresponding tensions of the time: Today vs. tomorrow, tradition vs. modern. They revolve around the integral tension between acquiring new knowledge and unlearning the old one, exploring new possibilities while exploiting existing ones, and managing the balance between stability and change. Learning paradoxes may overlap with other paradoxes, e.g.:

- *Learning and performing*: This paradox highlights the tension between investing in long-term learning and development while simultaneously delivering strong current performance.
- *Learning and belonging*: It means balancing the need for adaptation and change with the desire to retain an ordered sense of self and purpose.
- *Learning and organizing*: It reflects organizational routines and capabilities, seeking stability and efficiency while also enabling dynamic and flexible outcomes.

Smith and Lewis' concept offers a framework for understanding organizations' complexities and innate contradictions and linking them with organizational learning. However, their idea does not directly refer to WL.

### *8.2.3 Relationship between Workplace Learning and Paradoxes on Different Levels*

#### *8.2.3.1 Personal Level*

Paradox scholars emphasize the importance of learning to navigate paradoxical demands (Lewis & Smith, 2022; Smith & Lewis, 2011). This ability involves developing a paradox mindset, which requires a "learning journey" (Jay, 2013) and support from various paradox actors, e.g., peers (Pamphile, 2022; Pradies et al., 2021). This learning process also involves collaboration (Lüscher & Lewis, 2008; Pradies et al., 2021), emotional engagement (Pradies, 2022), and understanding different types of tensions. Individuals' approaches to paradox are also influenced by societal culture (Li, 2020; Nisbett et al., 2001). Culture plays a vital role in shaping how individuals experience and manage the tension inherent in paradoxical situations (Keller et al., 2018). Through an implicit learning process within their cultural environment, individuals develop distinct strategies for coping with these tensions. This means that cultural norms, values, beliefs, and practices significantly influence how people perceive, interpret, and respond to paradoxical demands, going beyond individual cognitive processes. Culture, therefore, provides a framework for understanding and navigating the complexities of paradoxes (Keller et al., 2018). It suggests that different cultures may foster different approaches to managing paradoxes, leading to a diverse range of coping mechanisms and solutions. Keller (2018) underlined the importance of considering cultural context when examining individual responses to paradoxes and the need for cross-cultural research to better understand the interaction between culture and paradox management and learning paradoxes. Thus, studying paradoxes in the unique context of CEE is necessary.

#### *8.2.3.2 Leadership Paradoxes, Paradoxical Leadership, and Paradox Mindset*

Paradoxes create tension that requires careful management and paradoxical leadership rather than outright resolution. Leadership paradoxes are inherent and unavoidable; they are a natural part of organizational life and leadership. They cannot be resolved like other paradoxes but they can be managed. This is crucial, not to eliminate tensions, but to find ways to manage them effectively. This requires a "both/and" mindset, known as a paradox mindset (Liu et al., 2020). Leaders should embrace the complexity of paradoxes and find creative solutions and ways to approach both sides of the tension. Leadership paradoxes may refer to the following (Waldman & Bowen, 2016):

- *Confidence vs. Humility*: Having a confident self-image vs. staying humble.
- *Continuity vs. Change*: Emphasizing consistency and evolution/adaptation.
- *Direction vs. Autonomy*: Providing clear vision and guidance vs. empowering subordinates to decide and take ownership.
- *Profitability vs. Social responsibility*: Balancing financial goals with ethical considerations and social impact.

Leadership paradoxes are opportunities for learning and growth because navigating paradoxes can help leaders, their employees, and organizations develop greater adaptability, resilience, and innovation (Liu et al., 2020; Rubin et al.,

2023; Yin, 2022). This connects leadership paradoxes directly to WL, as these very paradoxes can become valuable learning opportunities for individuals and teams. By encouraging a paradox mindset, leaders and whole organizations can create a continuous learning culture, where individuals are comfortable with ambiguity and embrace the tensions inherent in growth and change. This requires facilitating learning experiences that help individuals and teams understand, manage, and leverage paradoxical situations.

Leaders may employ a variety of methods to foster WL, with the most frequent being those that capitalize on learning opportunities embedded within daily work tasks. These activities spanned a spectrum from planned initiatives to more spontaneous occurrences. Leaders adapt their behaviors based on the situation and learning activity, providing support, education, and constructive confrontation, while also acting as role models for employees. However, according to prior research, certain factors hindered the implementation of learning-oriented leadership, including resource constraints and insufficient commitment from top management, employees, or the managers themselves (Wallo et al., 2022). Managers' beliefs and assumptions about learning and development are crucial for effectively enacting learning-oriented leadership. Therefore, providing managers with training on how to promote WL is essential (Wallo et al., 2022).

#### *8.2.3.3 Team and Organizational Levels*

Organizations and teams also face paradoxes (Clauss et al., 2021; Edwards, 2021; Hahn et al., 2018). Organizations might grapple with the paradox of exploration vs. exploitation, needing to balance pursuing new opportunities with leveraging existing resources and knowledge. On the other hand, teams might face the paradox of autonomy vs. interdependence, seeking individual agency while also needing to collaborate effectively for collective success. Other common organizational paradoxes include managing short-term performance vs. long-term vision, balancing efficiency and innovation, and reconciling profitability with social responsibility. Similarly, teams often handle tensions between competition and cooperation, structure and flexibility, and task focus vs. relationship building. Effectively managing these paradoxes may increase agility and innovation (Smith & Lewis, 2011), enhance organizational growth (Miron-Spektor et al., 2018), and improve collaboration and communication (Lüscher & Lewis, 2008). Organizations face a growing challenge in managing hybridity – the combination of seemingly incompatible elements like identities, forms, or logic. Leaders play a crucial role by holding "paradoxical frames," recognizing the contradictory yet interdependent nature of the hybrid elements while establishing structures, expertise, and relationships that support both sides. This interaction of stability and adaptability enables ongoing adjustments in the meanings and practices associated with the hybrid elements, ensuring their persistence (Smith & Besharov, 2019).

Paradoxes act as catalysts for learning by stimulating critical reflection and adaptation. They force employees and leaders to manage complex, conflicting demands, fostering resilience and innovative thinking. Recognizing paradoxes as learning opportunities allows organizations to harness the inherent tensions as drivers of growth and development. Moreover, it allows individuals and organizations to move beyond either/or thinking, embrace innovative solutions (Smith, 2016), and foster agility, performance, and innovation (Miron-Spektor et al., 2018). Organizations can support this by creating structures and processes that encourage a paradox mindset, such as flexible organizational designs, cross-functional teams, and open communication channels. Leaders can also play a crucial role by modeling a paradox mindset, encouraging experimentation and risk-taking, and creating space for dialogue and dissent. By leveraging paradoxes, organizations can address grand challenges related to sustainability and social responsibility, for example, by integrating competing logic (Berti, 2021) and balancing business demands with societal needs (Carmine & De Marchi, 2023; Carmine & Smith, 2021; Smith & Besharov, 2019).

## 8.3 Methodology

This research follows a qualitative methodology rooted in Grounded Theory (Charmaz & Thornberg, 2021; Chun Tie et al., 2019) to investigate how employees perceive, manage, and learn from OLP within MNEs operating in CEE. The study is based on semi-structured interviews conducted between July and September 2024, with purposefully selected 26 participants (14 men and 12 women), aged between 28 and 55. To recruit participants, 134 individuals from various MNEs operating in the region were identified and contacted through LinkedIn. Initially, 34 individuals expressed interest and confirmed their participation. While data saturation was achieved after conducting 21 semi-structured interviews, 5 additional interviews were carried out to ensure the robustness of the findings, each lasting between 60 and 90 minutes, with the duration varying based on the participants' professional and leadership experience.

Participants were selected based on their diverse experiences with MNEs in CEE, specifically targeting individuals who were either born during the communist era in CEE, have experience working within MNEs in the region during the transition era, entered the modern labor market in CEE, or worked for companies outside the region that had headquarters or subsidiaries in CEE. They also provide geographic variety, representing Poland, Czech Republic, Slovakia, Hungary, Bulgaria, Romania, Lithuania, Latvia, and Estonia. Furthermore, they contribute diverse international experiences from other regions and countries like Ukraine, the U.S., Germany, France, Spain, Italy, Belgium, the U.K., Scandinavia, Russia, Kazakhstan, Mexico, China, Japan, Korea, and India, enabling potential comparisons of WL through paradoxes in a diverse global context. These participants hold a range of roles within their organizations, drawn from over 90 enterprises spanning various sectors, including automotive, IT, energy, protection systems, FMCG, cosmetics, education, maritime clusters, hospitality, agriculture, logistics, insurance, and banking. The participants held positions in different organizational departments (Human Resource (HR), production, development, quality, sales, marketing, business development, project management, and logistics). Every interviewee shared their perspectives from employee and leadership roles within their organizations, if relevant. These leaders represented various experiences, from emerging leaders at the start of their careers to experienced executives at the top of their organizations. Some participants who held high-ranking positions, like Chief Executive Officer, Head of HR, Head of Sales and Marketing, and Head of Quality, naturally described their career progression and leadership development journeys, outlining their previous roles and experiences that contributed to their current expertise.

The primary aim of the research was to explore how employees perceive and respond to paradoxes in leadership and organizational contexts, the strategies to manage these paradoxes, and the role of such experiences in their learning and professional development. Additionally, it seeks to understand how organizational culture, leadership styles, and learning practices are visible in the workplace, particularly within CEE.

Data gathering enabled participants to provide in-depth descriptions of their experiences, which were transcribed for detailed analysis. The mainly open-ended questions were designed to investigate four major themes:

1. Types of paradoxes encountered in organizations.
2. Role of paradoxes in WL.
3. Approaches to paradoxes vs. individual and organizational performance.
4. Future directions on approaching paradoxes and WL.

At the beginning of the interviews, participants were asked to describe paradoxes they had encountered. The questions explored how these paradoxes manifested in daily operations and leadership dynamics within the team or organization. In the second section, the focus shifted to WL and how paradoxes contribute to learning. The participants were asked to reflect on the uniqueness of CEE-specific paradoxes and whether they noticed differences between how these paradoxes are managed in CEE vs. other regions worldwide. They were also asked to share examples from their own experiences in dealing with these paradoxes, and how they manage paradoxes in different cultural contexts as both leaders and employees. The third section of the interviews examined the relationship between approaches to paradoxes and individual and organizational performance. Participants were asked to consider whether they view paradoxes as challenges or opportunities, and how re-framing paradoxes as opportunities could enhance both personal leadership styles and broader organizational outcomes. The final section of the interviews examined possible future strategies for dealing with paradoxes in the workplace. Participants were questioned about how leaders in CEE can use paradoxes as opportunities for development, innovation, and enhancing cultural sensitivity. They were asked to consider future challenges, resources or training to manage paradoxes more effectively, what types of support or training could help them handle contradictions better, and how their companies could improve in helping employees leverage paradoxes as learning opportunities.

The data analysis process followed a Grounded Theory approach (Charmaz & Thornberg, 2021), using open coding, axial coding, and selective coding (Chun Tie et al., 2019). In the first phase of open coding, the interview data was broken down into separate parts, and recurring themes were identified, e.g., possible/not possible, trans, conflict, context, cultural differences, generation gap, and paradox mindset. These codes were then organized during the axial coding phase, where relationships between the identified categories were established with key categories followed. Seven key categories emerged (Table 8.1).

Selective coding centered on the core category: "Workplace learning through navigating paradoxes in multinational enterprises in CEE," integrating the various themes into a cohesive theoretical framework.

The analysis of the research was further refined using Tynjälä's 3P Model (Tynjälä, 2013). Applying Grounded Theory (Charmaz & Thornberg, 2021) in conjunction with Tynjälä's 3P Model, particularly during the selective coding stage, offers a comprehensive framework for investigating how managing OLP shapes WL. This approach allowed the researcher to examine comprehensively the origins, process, and outcomes of learning, providing valuable insights into how employees and organizations in the CEE's context can leverage paradoxes for innovation, creativity, expansion, and development within a dynamic environment. The theoretical framework is structured around *Tynjälä's 3P Model* (Table 8.2), which consists of *Presage* (factors influencing WL such as organizational structures and leadership), *Process* (the strategies employees use to manage paradoxes), and *Product* (the outcomes of paradoxical learning, including individual and organizational growth).

## 8.4 Results

This study provides evidence that paradoxes exist at various levels of organizational life in CEE. Leaders who recognize and address these paradoxes strategically can generate learning opportunities for themselves, their teams, and the organizations they lead. The examples correspondingly highlight the importance of the cultural context in CEE and individual factors in shaping how paradoxes are perceived and managed, enriching the understanding of WL in this specific region.

*Table 8.1* Axial Coding on Workplace Learning through Paradoxes in MNEs in CEE

| *Axial Coding* | *Sample Statements from Interviews* |
|---|---|
| Leadership paradoxes | *So, either the leader must be authoritarian, decisive, leading by the hand, imposing his will, or he must be coaching-oriented, understanding, inquisitive. But what if we combined both? I want this, and I want that too. And at this moment* [...] *a leader, a person in general, a leader could be both, like this and like that.* P1 |
| | *Leaders have to develop and implement strategies, while they have a lot of operational work.* P21 |
| Organizational paradoxes | *A little we want to the West, a little we want to stay ourselves.* P21 |
| | *This organizational change (globally, nationally, regionally) perfectly exemplifies the paradox between focusing on results, costs, and finances versus prioritizing the human aspect and its potential impact on the organization and the future of employees.* P13 |
| Learning experiences | *Learning in CEE is more informal.* P23 |
| | *There is a constant state of firefighting there is not enough time to develop different competencies through organized learning.* P21 |
| Paradoxical leadership | *Leaders acknowledge sometimes complex and contradictory demands and foster a culture of flexibility and openness and enable employees to find creative solutions.* P26 |
| | *Everything writes into this openness to these changes or empathy, because if we make the assumption that 'both: this and that' can appear, and a great many more things will appear that we don't know that exist.* P15 |
| Paradox managing strategies | *Building resilience and adaptability in a changing environment.* P12 |
| | *The agile approach, whether applied to process management, organizational management, or even what I refer to as 'personal agility' – managing oneself – is a crucial competency for the future.* [...] *This personal agility is the ability to adapt quickly.* P14 |
| Individual growth | *Through paradoxes, you can develop valuable skills and experience. This can lead to personal and professional development and enhance even your employability.* P26*Paradoxes are opportunities for a person with a growth mindset.* P21 |
| Organizational innovation and growth | *Openness to new solutions arises when individuals or organizations feel they've exhausted traditional approaches and sense a need for growth, prompting them to seek innovative alternatives.* P1 |
| | *There is a complex process of organizational change which includes the development of skills and competencies, to adapt to a changing market's requirements.* P21 |

*Table 8.2* Key Findings on Workplace Learning from Paradoxes in MNEs in CEE: Tynjälä's 3P Model

| *Presage* | *Process* | *Product* |
|---|---|---|
| CEE's contextual factors (historical, political, and economic influences) | Acknowledging and defining paradoxes, e.g., corporate culture vs. CEE mentality,<br>Diversity vs. inclusion,<br>National pride vs. global mindset,<br>Short-term gain vs. long-term goals,<br>Managing global needs vs. local,<br>Private life of leader vs. company interests,<br>Building personal relationships vs. performance | Desired outcomes like development or improvement of a paradox mindset, effective teamwork on a multinational level, organizational development |
| Individual characteristics of CEE's employees (e.g., experience with paradoxes, CEE's background, a paradox mindset) | Reflecting on cultural differences | Undesirable outcomes like shallow learning methods, participation in activities lacking authentic significance, and tolerance for questionable practices |
| Leadership approach to paradoxes | Negotiating conflicting expectations | |
| Support systems for learning and development | Building cross-cultural networks | |
| Networks outside the organization | Seeking clarification and providing feedback<br>Experimenting with different approaches to problem-solving | |

### *8.4.1 Paradoxes as Preconditions for Workplace Learning*

Several factors contributed to the emergence of WL from paradoxes. The unique historical, political, and economic scenery of the region, referred to as CEE's contextual factors, influenced learning opportunities and challenges.

Many participants underlined the general perceptions of people from CEE including being hardworking and resilient, with a strong sense of belonging to a group, and prioritizing family and social ties over individualism, due to their history of overcoming hardships. Interviewees see CEE employees as creative and inventive, with *a Slavic soul* P1. They are also seen as well-educated and skilled, with strong expertise in technical fields. CEE's societies, known for their hospitality and generosity, are viewed as family-oriented and traditional, which can be positive and negative and lead to tensions between workplace and family life. People from CEE may be perceived as reserved and less expressive than Westerners leading to potential misunderstandings. Additionally, nations in CEE have a strong national identity, rooted in their history of historical upheavals, foreign influences, and a sense of pride in their culture and traditions, especially in Poland, and Hungary. Dynamic, vibrant, and rapidly developing environments characteristic of the region necessitate adaptability and creative problem-solving. The shadow of communism still influences work practices, with some older employees preferring traditional methods over digital innovations. P22 described it as: *I think Lithuania is a little bit more Scandinavian now. Aligned with Scandinavia, of course, the social values are still different. We cannot delete the 70 years of communism, but I think this is where our, so to say, target is, from a cultural perspective.*

The organizational culture of MNEs operating in CEE, encompassing the organizational structure, work organization, and a culture that encourages learning from mistakes, is also crucial: *Pressure from Western companies to achieve results while neglecting employee well-being, leads to burnout and high turnover. This illustrates how an overemphasis on performance metrics can create a paradoxical culture that ultimately harms both employees and the organization, hindering sustainable learning.* P14 Furthermore, the leadership approach to paradoxes, particularly leadership styles of local managers that support autonomy and experimentation and foster partnerships and networks within the organization, was essential. Support systems for learning and development, including mentorship programs, cross-cultural training, opportunities for knowledge sharing (knowledge-sharing platforms), and access to knowledge resources, were also instrumental. Finally, networks outside the organization could further contribute to the learning process.

Individual characteristics of CEE's employees (the individual factors) also play a significant role in WL from paradoxes, including prior knowledge and experience with paradoxes, CEE's background, experience in MNEs, cognitive flexibility, tolerance for ambiguity, life situation, self-confidence, and a paradox mindset, which can be both a pre-existing condition and a learning outcome. The interviewees highlighted how growing up in the post-communist era has shaped their perspectives and approaches to work. As P18 explains, *The experience of transitioning from a controlled economy to a market-driven one has fostered a sense of resourcefulness and adaptability in many CEE professionals.* Exposure to diverse perspectives and experiences further enriched the learning process. P8 described his learning through paradoxes world journey: *Initially viewing paradoxes as conflicts, now sees the potential for synergy and intends to apply this learning in future roles.* His shift in perspective from "either/or" to seeking a "both/and" solution highlights how individual reflection and experience can facilitate learning from paradoxes. P12 viewed paradoxes as a source of frustration and an opportunity for growth and innovation. He believes that navigating paradoxes effectively requires strong leadership, a willingness to challenge assumptions, and a commitment to adapting to the local context. P14 described the personal shift from *a black-and-white, all-or-nothing youthful mindset* to embracing nuances and "shades of gray" as he matured. This highlights the role of personal growth and experience in developing the capacity to recognize and navigate paradoxes, a crucial precondition for WL.

### *8.4.2 Activities of Workplace Learning through Paradoxes*

Learning occurs through a variety of formal, informal, non-formal, self-directed, unintentional, and intentional activities and experiences (Choy & Le, 2023; Lemmetty & Collin, 2020; Manuti et al., 2015). The research indicated acknowledging and defining paradoxes and recognizing and comprehending conflicting demands and perspectives. Reflecting on cultural differences between CEE and other countries or regions, their impact on work is also crucial, allowing employees to develop new perspectives through participation in cross-cultural training, development programs, or mentoring initiatives. An example from an interview: *Observations on the "tribal" mentality in Southern Poland, where familial ties influence professional relationships, creating a paradox of loyalty vs. professional objectivity. Reflecting on such cultural differences is crucial for leaders to understand how paradoxes manifest in specific contexts and develop culturally sensitive management approaches.* P14

Furthermore, the study revealed WL as negotiating conflicting expectations involves developing skills in mediating between diverse stakeholders and finding common ground. Another activity of WL was building cross-cultural networks, a social process that involved collaborating and interacting with others through dialogue, debate, feedback seeking, collaborative problem-solving, and participation in networks within MNEs. WL also encompassed seeking clarification and providing constructive feedback across cultures. Learning from mistakes and failures was another vital aspect, encouraging employees in CEE to embrace a growth mindset and utilize setbacks as learning opportunities. Finally, experimenting with different approaches to problem-solving, a behavioral process, involved adapting global best practices to the local context, reflecting on experiences, adapting behaviors, and tackling new challenges and tasks. For example, P15 stated: *Experiencing a paradox encourages a more agile and adaptable approach to problem-solving, recognizing that one-size-fits-all solutions rarely work in the complex and dynamic CEE's environment.*

### *8.4.3 Paradoxes and Products of Workplace Learning*

Based on the study, gaining insights from paradoxes led to various results at personal, team, and corporate scales.

Personal benefits included a more profound comprehension of the CEE's business climate, improved cross-cultural communication and cooperation skills, better problem-solving and decision-making capabilities, heightened adaptability and resilience, improved career prospects and self-development, and the development or improvement of a paradox mindset. P26 said: *I have seen my paradox mindset as very useful. I see paradoxes as opportunities in our team challenges. As a leader, I need to nuance and work on paradoxes to guide people to success. Very quickly, I saw the effectiveness of this tool, its usefulness, and as an opportunity to growth for me and my teams.* This leadership style demonstrates the benefit of embracing a paradox-driven mindset: Seeing challenges and paradoxes as opportunities, leading to business success and personal growth. This serves as a model for how individual leaders can leverage paradoxes to drive personal and organizational achievements. P14 underlined the positive aspects of paradoxes: *I don't have to choose between embracing the new or remaining in my comfort zone; I can nuance my approach with a bit of both. I can maintain as much comfort as I need while embracing as much novelty as satisfies my curiosity. I have the power to adjust the balance.'*

Team and organizational outcomes encompassed innovation, improved performance in terms of productivity and quality, enhanced team/organizational learning, effective teamwork on a multinational level, organizational development, and a better work climate. For example, P8 suggested that acknowledging and managing paradoxes, rather than ignoring or forcing one side, can lead to better outcomes for both individuals and the organization, e.g., the potential for improved performance and employee retention if paradoxes like overtime vs. productivity are addressed through open dialogue and collaborative problem-solving. P14 said: *The growing awareness in Western companies that focusing solely on results can be detrimental, leading to investments in employee well-being programs and soft skills training.* This demonstrates a positive outcome: organizations learn from the negative consequences of neglecting the "human" side of paradoxes and take steps to create a more sustainable and inclusive workplace culture. P22's emphasis on cross-generational team composition reflects the belief that diverse perspectives enhance problem-solving and organizational adaptability. This suggests that effectively managing the paradox of experience vs. new ideas can lead to more robust teams and a culture of continuous learning. P22 stated: *It should be a problem-solving environment, so the people mind how you solve it. So, when you establish the dynamics of taking problems as an opportunity or establishing a common ground for solving it, then the rest of the team or the new team members, they will circulate a center.*

One interviewee also indicated *societal outcomes*, i.e., P8 observed the evolving expectations of younger generations, challenging traditional hierarchies and demanding greater inclusivity in the workplace, which contributed to a broader understanding of generational shifts and their impact on organizational practices.

### *8.4.4 Undesirable Consequences of Workplace Learning from Paradoxes in CEE*

While WL from paradoxes can yield positive outcomes, it is crucial to acknowledge the potential for undesirable consequences, particularly in MNEs with headquarters in CEE and in Post-communist Privatized Multinationals (PPMs). These companies, now privately owned, are acquiring businesses in Western Europe and other parts of the world. However, a significant number of employees across various departments may still retain a mentality shaped by the previous era. This can be demotivating and hinder the learning process of new hires, potentially leading them to adopt outdated and ineffective practices. These undesirable consequences manifested in six primary ways:

1. **Embracing shallow learning methods:** The pressure to resolve paradoxes quickly and demonstrate progress to Western headquarters, or within a company still grappling with its legacy past, can lead to superficial solutions rather than deep learning. This can involve:
   - **"Tick-box" training:** Sending employees to training sessions as a symbolic gesture to appease Western headquarters or showcase a commitment to modernization, without a genuine commitment from leadership (often still influenced by old mentalities) to implement the learnings or participate themselves. This creates a facade of learning without actual behavioral change.
   - **"Painting the grass green":** Engaging in superficial activities to create a positive impression for Western headquarters or mask lingering inefficiencies from the past, especially during evaluations or visits, without addressing underlying issues. This fosters a culture of short-term fixes and hides systemic problems.

The author gleaned this from several comments. For example, P25 described the prevailing approach in some companies as *putting lipstick on a corpse*, where efforts are focused on masking problems rather than addressing them.

2. **Participation in activities lacking authentic significance:** The paradoxical nature of organizational life, amplified by the clash between Western expectations and legacy practices, can push employees towards activities that lack genuine value, driven by:

- **KPI-driven work:** Focusing solely on meeting short-term, quantifiable targets (quarterly or half-yearly) imposed by Western headquarters or demonstrating rapid progress in a transitional context, rather than engaging in continuous, meaningful work aligned with long-term goals. This can lead to a disconnect between individual efforts and overall organizational success.
- **Meaningless work under micromanagement:** Performing tasks dictated by excessive owner or managerial control, often stemming from a distrustful, top-down management style inherited from the past, even when those tasks lack a clear purpose or contribute little to overall objectives. This fosters a sense of powerlessness and reduces intrinsic motivation, hindering the adoption of new practices and potentially reinforcing outdated, inefficient habits. P26: *The CEO decides everything. Everything. It's a lot of micromanagement. You have to do as they are telling you. It doesn't matter, if they know or not the subject. It's unbelievable.*

3. **Divergent goals between HR departments and employees from less-developed countries:** Additional undesirable consequences arose from the influx of employees from less-developed countries seeking economic opportunities in CEE. These individuals often prioritize earning potential over professional development, creating a paradox where the HR department's efforts to promote learning and upskilling might be met with disinterest. This mismatch in priorities can render even the most well-intentioned initiatives ineffective, highlighting a fundamental disconnect between organizational goals and the immediate needs of a significant portion of the workforce. P25: *Those workers primarily learn what they are required to, and while HR departments may try and develop programs, their efforts are often in vain, as this type of employee doesn't prioritize learning and development.*
4. **Ethical compromises and tolerance for questionable practices:** In some instances, particularly in countries like the Czech Republic, Slovakia, and Romania, the legacy of opaque practices and relaxed ethical standards from the past can linger, influencing workplace behavior. P12 described it as a dangerous path: *This is the core issue that needs to be addressed within this group's mentality: demonstrating that it's our company, not the competition, that pays our salaries. This distinction highlights what our responsibilities and obligations truly are. The current market dynamic, with its emphasis on building pseudo-relationships, is incredibly demoralizing for these individuals. It unfortunately erodes company identity in favor of a "be everyone's buddy" approach. This mentality suggests that being agreeable and friendly is the path to success, but it's an incredibly dangerous path to tread.*

Tolerance for unethical conduct challenged efforts to promote transparency, accountability, and ethical behavior, hindering the establishment of best corporate governance practices. If *bending the rules* (P12's comment) or engaging in ethically questionable behavior is tolerated or even rewarded, it can inadvertently reinforce these practices as acceptable norms. This can negatively influence the learning and development of new employees, who might adopt these behaviors as a means to succeed.

5. **Ethnocentrism and "colonial" management style:** The P11 and P8 interviewees observed that the parent company's potentially "colonial" management style resonated with historical power dynamics between Western and Eastern Europe. The perceived top-down approach, resistance to local input, and lack of cultural sensitivity could be interpreted as a form of ethnocentrism, where the parent company imposes its values and practices without fully understanding or appreciating the local context. This dynamic could exacerbate the paradox of belonging and create a sense of alienation among local employees. These quotations portray the observation: *Based on my experience with French companies, I'd say Poland is sometimes treated like their colony.* P8; P11 described the reaction of the Belgian owner to the local initiative: *He listened to me, he listened patiently till the end, nodded his head, and then he said, You know, but this is probably not your role.*
6. **Generational divides and the digital gap:** A new generation of globally-minded, digitally savvy employees is entering the workforce in CEE, who learn and network through online channels and social media. However, this creates a potential clash with older employees who remember the pre-transition era or the initial period of change. While some of these senior employees might struggle to adapt to the modern, digital world, they often possess valuable experience and deep organizational knowledge. Imposing Westernized, "modern" methods without considering this generational divide can be counterproductive. P19 described it: *In Poland and the Czech Republic, new approaches to training are okay, because there's this trend that everything new is great, and maybe the younger generation already understands this better, but I've also seen training delivered on paper. Where I am in the West (the U.K., Germany), paper-based training is viewed negatively, everything is digital. In Poland, employees, especially the older generation, prefer standard paper-based methods.* [...] *I think those who are still in the workforce would find it extremely difficult to change now and try all these new things. I think it wouldn't be positive, but very stressful for them. So, we have to respect these cultural differences.* [...] *There is no single best method for learning, there are different ones to help everyone succeed.*

These undesirable consequences represent a significant finding in understanding the outcomes of WL from paradoxes in CEE, particularly within organizations navigating the complexities of internationalization, legacy systems, workforce diversification, and generational shifts. They highlight the potential for paradoxical tensions to be mismanaged, leading to superficial learning, wasted resources, employee demotivation, ethical compromises, cultural clashes, and a widening generational gap.

## 8.5 Discussion and Conclusion

This chapter highlights the multifaceted nature of WL derived from navigating paradoxes in CEE. By understanding the antecedents, processes, and outcomes of this learning, individuals and organizations can harness the power of paradoxes to drive innovation, growth, and development. The findings offer a thorough perspective on how employees in MNEs in CEE learn by confronting OLP. By examining the presage, process, and product of learning in this particular setting, we can obtain valuable knowledge for enhancing personal and company development in a dynamic and demanding environment and conditions. This information can shape leadership development programs, organizational strategies, and human resource practices that cater to the region's specific requirements and the individuals employed there.

The findings of this study resonate with existing literature on WL and paradox theory, confirming that paradoxes are inherent in organizational life and can be powerful triggers for learning. This aligns with prior research (Schad et al., 2016; Schad & Miron-Spektor, 2021; Smith & Lewis, 2011) which shows that the need to navigate conflicting demands forces individuals and teams to reflect critically, adapt, and develop innovative solutions. The study also echoes the importance of a paradox mindset (Miron-Spektor et al., 2018) for effectively managing tensions and leveraging them for learning. Individuals who embrace complexity, tolerate ambiguity, and seek "both/and" solutions are better equipped to learn from these situations. Furthermore, the results of the study align with existing research on the role of formal, informal, and self-directed learning in WL (Lemmetty & Collin, 2020; Manuti et al., 2015; Marsick & Watkins, 2015), as participants engaged in various learning activities, including reflection, dialogue, knowledge sharing, and experimentation, to navigate paradoxes and develop new understandings. Similar to previous research (Smith & Lewis, 2011; Miron-Spektor et al., 2018), the study highlights the positive outcomes of effectively managing paradoxes, such as enhanced adaptability, resilience, innovation, and improved organizational performance. However, this study also offers insights specific to the CEE's context. It provides a novel contribution by focusing on the region's unique historical, political, and economic transitions. The findings underscore how the legacy of communism, the transition to market economies, and the integration into the globalized world have shaped organizational cultures, leadership styles, and individual approaches to navigating paradoxes. Furthermore, the study highlights the significant role of culture in shaping how individuals experience and manage paradoxes (Keller et al., 2017, 2018), emphasizing the need for culturally sensitive approaches to leadership and learning. Unlike most paradox research, this study explicitly addresses the potential for undesirable consequences arising from mismanaged paradoxes in CEE, revealing how the pressure to adapt to Western practices, legacy systems, and generational divides can lead to superficial learning, ethical compromises, and cultural clashes. Finally, the study introduces the concept of PPMs and their unique challenges in navigating paradoxes and fostering WL. The lingering influence of past practices and mentalities within these organizations adds another layer of complexity to the studied context.

### *8.5.1 Managerial Implications*

This study has important implications for practical managerial strategies regarding WL through paradoxes. Its findings are relevant to managing employee development in MNEs in CEE. Specifically, managers should recognize the importance of understanding and managing paradoxes to enhance WL. Paradoxes, such as balancing global integration with local adaptation, can be harnessed to create a dynamic and innovative learning culture. Organizations need to encourage formal and informal learning opportunities that focus on managing paradoxes at both global and regional (CEE) levels. This might involve workshops, mentorship programs, and platforms for peer learning that promote the exchange of effective strategies for managing conflicting tensions.

In terms of leadership development, it is crucial to develop customized training programs that provide leaders with the necessary skills to effectively handle paradoxes. These programs should prioritize adaptive leadership, cultural competency, and the skills to identify and navigate contradictions in both local and global settings. Managers must prioritize developing leaders who can handle uncertainty and balance conflicting priorities, such as ensuring stability while welcoming change, to promote the organization's expansion.

Regarding the execution of policies and organizational tactics, MNEs in CEE must cultivate a culture that prioritizes continuous learning, acknowledges the tension between stability and change, and balances global and local demands to foster innovation. In the analyzed region, it is particularly important for MNEs to effectively manage paradoxes to enhance global coordination and local flexibility through a careful balance of global integration and local responsiveness. Integrating WL into their organizational strategies can give CEE-based MNEs a competitive edge, enabling them to succeed in fast-changing business environments.

### *8.5.2 Limitations and Further Research Directions*

Research exploring the relationship between paradoxes and WL in MNEs in CEE provides valuable preliminary insights while revealing limitations that highlight the need for further investigation. The qualitative nature of the study, based on interviews with 26 participants, limits the generalizability of findings to the broader population of MNEs in the region and beyond. The small sample size raises concerns about its representativeness and suggests the need to include larger and more diverse samples from all CEE's countries in future research. The lack of quantitative research hinders the statistical validation of connections between variables, such as OLP and WL processes. Furthermore, the subjective experiences of participants, upon which the study relies, may influence data objectivity.

Future research should focus on validating preliminary insights, enhancing generalizability, and exploring specific areas within the scope of WL. This includes conducting cross-industry and cross-company size comparisons within MNEs in CEE to identify differences in paradox management and learning strategies. Investigating how paradoxes are utilized for learning, growth, and innovation in specific CEE countries could provide insights into the influence of national culture on these practices. Conducting quantitative research on paradox management strategies within the CEE context would support the development of effective practices for enhancing WL. Furthermore, examining the role of headquarters in shaping learning practices and outcomes in CEE subsidiaries is crucial. This involves understanding how headquarters influence knowledge transfer, training programs, and the overall learning environment within subsidiaries. Investigating the extent to which headquarters promote a unified learning culture across different subsidiaries and how they address the unique contextual factors influencing learning in each location would be valuable.

## References

Alerasoul, S. A., Afeltra, G., Hakala, H., Minelli, E., & Strozzi, F. (2022). Organisational learning, learning organisation, and learning orientation: An integrative review and framework. *Human Resource Management Review, 32*(3), 100854. https://doi.org/10.1016/j.hrmr.2021.100854

Basten, D., & Haamann, T. (2018). Approaches for organizational learning: A literature review. *SAGE Open, 8*(3), 215824401879422. https://doi.org/10.1177/2158244018794224

Berti, M. (2021). Logic(S) and paradox. In Bednarek, R., Cunha, M.P., Schad, J. and Smith, W.K. (Eds.), Interdisciplinary *Dialogues on Organizational Paradox: Investigating Social Structures and Human Expression*, Part B (Research in the Sociology of Organizations, Vol. 73b, pp. 27–47). https://doi.org/10.1108/S0733-558X2021000073b003

Billett, S. (2014). Mimesis: Learning through everyday activities and interactions at work. *Human Resource Development Review, 13*(4), 462–482. https://doi.org/10.1177/1534484314548275

Billett, S., & Choy, S. (2013). Learning through work: Emerging perspectives and new challenges. *Journal of Workplace Learning, 25*(4), 264–276. https://doi.org/10.1108/13665621311316447

Carmine, S., & De Marchi, V. (2023). Reviewing paradox theory in corporate sustainability toward a systems perspective. *Journal of Business Ethics*, *184*(1), 139–158. https://doi.org/10.1007/s10551-022-05112-2

Carmine, S., & Smith, W. K. (2021). Organizational paradox. Oxford University Press. https://doi.org/10.1093/obo/9780199846740-0201

Charmaz, K., & Thornberg, R. (2021). The pursuit of quality in grounded theory. *Qualitative Research in Psychology*, *18*(3), 305–327. https://doi.org/10.1080/14780887.2020.1780357

Chiva, R., Ghauri, P., & Alegre, J. (2014). Organizational learning, innovation and internationalization: a complex system model. *British Journal of Management*, *25*(4), 687–705. https://doi.org/10.1111/1467-8551.12026

Choy, S., & Le, A. H. (2023). Workplace practices that support learning across working life. *Australian Journal of Adult Learning*, *63*(3), 320–342.

Chun Tie, Y., Birks, M., & Francis, K. (2019). Grounded theory research: A design framework for novice researchers. *SAGE Open Medicine*, *7*, 1–8. https://doi.org/10.1177/2050312118822927

Clauss, T., Kraus, S., Kallinger, F. L., Bican, P. M., Brem, A., & Kailer, N. (2021). Organizational ambidexterity and competitive advantage: The role of strategic agility in the exploration-exploitation paradox. *Journal of Innovation and Knowledge*, *6*(4), 203–213. https://doi.org/10.1016/j.jik.2020.07.003

Edwards, M. G. (2021). The growth paradox, sustainable development, and business strategy. *Business Strategy and the Environment*, *30*(7), 3079–3094. https://doi.org/10.1002/bse.2790

Gronseth, S. L., & Hutchins, H. M. (2020). Flexibility in formal workplace learning: Technology applications for engagement through the lens of universal design for learning. *TechTrends*, *64*(2), 211–218. https://doi.org/10.1007/s11528-019-00455-6

Hahn, T., Figge, F., Pinkse, J., & Preuss, L. (2018). A Paradox perspective on corporate sustainability: Descriptive, instrumental, and normative aspects. *Journal of Business Ethics*, *148*(2), 235–248 . https://doi.org/10.1007/s10551-017-3587-2

Jacobs, R. L., & Park, Y. (2009). A proposed conceptual framework of workplace learning: Implications for theory development and research in human resource development. *Human Resource Development Review*, *8*(2), 133–150. https://doi.org/10.1177/1534484309334269

Jay, J. (2013). Navigating paradox as a mechanism of change and innovation in hybrid organizations. *Academy of Management Journal*, *56*(1), 1–53. https://doi.org/10.5465/amj.2010.0772

Keller, J., Loewenstein, J., & Yan, J. (2017). Culture, conditions and paradoxical frames. *Organization Studies*, *38*(3–4), 539–560. https://doi.org/10.1177/0170840616685590

Keller, J., Wen Chen, E., & Leung, A. K. Y. (2018). How national culture influences individuals' subjective experience with paradoxical tensions. *Cross Cultural and Strategic Management*, *25*(3), 443–467. https://doi.org/10.1108/CCSM-02-2017-0013

Khandakar, M. S. A., & Pangil, F. (2019). Relationship between human resource management practices and informal workplace learning: An empirical study. *Journal of Workplace Learning*, *31*(8), 551–576. https://doi.org/10.1108/JWL-04-2019-0049

Lemmetty, S., & Collin, K. (2020). Self-directed learning as a practice of workplace learning: interpretative repertoires of self-directed learning in ICT Work. *Vocations and Learning*, *13*(1), 47–70. https://doi.org/10.1007/s12186-019-09228-x

Lewis, M. W. (2000). Exploring paradox: toward a more comprehensive guide. *The Academy of Management Review*, *25*(4), 760. https://doi.org/10.2307/259204

Lewis, M. W., & Smith, W. K. (2022). Reflections on the 2021 AMR decade award: Navigating paradox is paradoxical. *Academy of Management Review*, *47*(4), 528–548. https://doi.org/10.5465/amr.2022.0251

Li, P. P. (2020). Organizational resilience for a new normal: balancing the paradox of global interdependence. *Management and Organization Review*, *16*(3), 503–509. https://doi.org/10.1017/mor.2020.30

Liu, Y., Xu, S., & Zhang, B. (2020). Thriving at work: How a paradox mindset influences innovative work behavior. *Journal of Applied Behavioral Science*, *56*(3), 347–366. https://doi.org/10.1177/0021886319888267

Lüscher, L. S., & Lewis, M. W. (2008). Organizational change and managerial sensemaking: Working through paradox. *The Academy of Management Journal*, *51*(2), 221–240. https://about.jstor.org/terms

Manuti, A., Pastore, S., Scardigno, A. F., Giancaspro, M. L., & Morciano, D. (2015). Formal and informal learning in the workplace: A research review. *International Journal of Training and Development*, *19*(1), 1–17. https://doi.org/10.1111/ijtd.12044

Marsick, V. J., & Watkins, K. (2015). Informal and incidental learning in the workplace (Routledge Revivals) (1st ed.). London and New York: Routledge. https://doi.org/10.4324/9781315715926

Matthews, P. (1999). Workplace learning: Developing a holistic model. *The Learning Organization*, *6*(1), 18–29. https://doi.org/10.1108/09696479910255684

Miron-Spektor, E., Ingram, A., Keller, J., Smith, W. K., & Lewis, M. W. (2018). Microfoundations of organizational paradox. *The Academy of Management Journal*, *61*(1), 26–45. https://doi.org/10.2307/26528843

Muzam, J., Bendkowski, J., Mah, P. M., & Mudoh, P. (2023). The state-of-the-art of modern workplace learning: an applied assessment method of a pre-train deep learning on modern learning tools. *Learning Organization*, *30*(5), 607–629. https://doi.org/10.1108/TLO-01-2023-0019

Nisbett, R. E., Peng, K., Choi, I., & Norenzayan, A. (2001). Culture and systems of thought: Holistic versus analytic cognition. *Psychological Review*, *108*(2), 291–310. https://doi.org/10.1037//0033-295x.108.2.291

Ospina, S. M., & Saz-Carranza, A. (2010). Paradox and collaboration in network management. *Administration and Society*, *42*(4), 404–440. https://doi.org/10.1177/0095399710362723

Pamphile, V. D. (2022). Paradox peers: A relational approach to navigating a business–society paradox. *Academy of Management Journal*, *65*(4), 1274–1302. https://doi.org/10.5465/amj.2019.0616

Park, S., & Lee, J. Y. (2018). Workplace learning measures for human resource development: Review and summary. *Industrial and Commercial Training*, *50*(7/8), 420–431. https://doi.org/10.1108/ICT-08-2018-0068

Patky, J. (2020). The influence of organizational learning on performance and innovation: A literature review. In *Journal of Workplace Learning* *32*(3), 229–242. https://doi.org/10.1108/JWL-04-2019-0054

Pradies, C. (2022). With head and heart: how emotions shape paradox navigation in veterinary work. *Academy of Management Journal, 66* (2), 521–552. https://doi.org/10.5465/amj.2019.0633

Pradies, C., Tunarosa, A., Lewis, M. W., & Courtois, J. (2021). From vicious to virtuous paradox dynamics: The social-symbolic work of supporting actors. *Organization Studies*, *42*(8), 1241–1263. https://doi.org/10.1177/0170840620907200

Rajan, P., & Aiswarya, B. (2022). The influence of paradoxical leadership behaviour towards organizational creativity: the mediating role of resilience. *Business, Management and Economics Engineering*, *20*(2), 1–11.

Rubin, M., Miron-Spektor, E., & Keller, J. (2023). Unlocking creative tensions with a paradox approach. In Roni Reiter-Palmon and Sam Hunter (Eds.), *Handbook of Organizational Creativity: Individual and Group Level Influences* (pp. 125-145), *Second Edition*. https://doi.org/10.1016/B978-0-323-91840-4.00006-2

Schad, J., Lewis, M. W., Raisch, S., & Smith, W. K. (2016). Paradox research in management science: Looking back to move forward. *The Academy of Management Annals*, *10*(1), 5–64. https://doi.org/10.1080/19416520.2016.1162422

Schad, J., & Miron-Spektor, E. (2021). Lewis, Marianne W.: Paradoxes of Change and Changing Through Paradox. In Szabla, D.B. (Ed.), *The Palgrave Handbook of Organizational Change Thinkers: volume 1–2, Second Edition* (pp. 951–966). Springer International Publishing. https://doi.org/10.1007/978-3-030-38324-4_114

Smith, W. K. (2016). Navigating paradoxes in organizations: Embracing, meaning-making and managing tensions. *Academy of Management Proceedings*, *2016*(1), 12493. https://doi.org/10.5465/ambpp.2016.12493symposium

Smith, W. K., & Besharov, M. L. (2019). Bowing before dual gods: How structured flexibility sustains organizational hybridity. *Administrative Science Quarterly*, *64*(1), 1–44. https://doi.org/10.1177/0001839217750826

Smith, W. K., & Lewis, M. W. (2011). Toward a theory of paradox: A dynamic equilibrium model of organizing. *Academy of Management Review*, *36*(2), 381–403. https://doi.org/10.5465/amr.2011.59330958

Tynjälä, P. (2013). Toward a 3-P model of workplace learning: A literature review. *Vocations and Learning*, *6*(1), 11–36. https://doi.org/10.1007/s12186-012-9091-z

Ulrich, F., & Mengiste, S. A. (2014). The challenges of creativity in software organizations. *IFIP Advances in Information and Communication Technology*, *429*, 16–34. https://doi.org/10.1007/978-3-662-43459-8_2

Waldman, D. A., & Bowen, D. E. (2016). Learning to be a paradox-savvy leader. *Academy of Management Perspectives*, *30*(3), 316–327. https://doi.org/10.5465/amp.2015.0070

Wallo, A., Kock, H., Reineholm, C., & Ellström, P. E. (2022). How do managers promote workplace learning? Learning-oriented leadership in daily work. *Journal of Workplace Learning*, *34*(1), 58–73. https://doi.org/10.1108/JWL-11-2020-0176

Xie, L. (2019). Leadership and organizational learning culture: A systematic literature review. *European Journal of Training and Development* 43(1–2), 76–104. https://doi.org/10.1108/EJTD-06-2018-0056

Yin, J. (2022). Living with tensions in the workplace: A grounded theory of paradoxical leadership in cultivating subordinates' paradox mindset. *Leadership and Organization Development Journal*, *43*(6), 862–873. https://doi.org/10.1108/LODJ-04-2021-0151

# Part IV

# Sustainability Paradoxes

# 9 Conflicting Demands of Sustainable Digital Transformation

*Damian Ciachorowski and Elem Miranda*

## 9.1 Introduction

Sustainable digital transformation is a combination of two contemporary strong trends in management: Sustainability and digital transformation, creating an approach that is based on a paradigm shift in the creation of contemporary organizational management strategies, generating considerable interest among the academic community and practitioners (Kupilas et al., 2022). However, so far, the term sustainable digital transformation is not only not yet adequately grounded in the literature, but there is even no consensus on what is hidden beneath the term (Shang & Zhang, 2022). The last decade has witnessed a growing discussion concerning the replacement of humans by digital technologies (Constantiou et al., 2023). There is no shortage of voices that digital transformation if unintended, uncontrolled, or underestimated, can become a destructive force (Carnerud et al., 2020; Flyverbom et al., 2019; Ghobakhloo, 2020).

Implementing digital transformation does not only refer to technological aspects. It is a process that primarily affects people, both those involved in this process and those influenced by it (both inside and outside companies). The process is primarily people-focused and strategy-driven (Dash et al., 2023) leading to several paradoxical tensions. Consequently, it requires a new approach or even, looking more broadly, a new paradigm relating to sustainable digital transformation (Pacolli, 2022). Although this approach is interesting, it suffers from the choice of an ideal theoretical framework that may not align perfectly with the internal challenges that businesses will face during the transformation process (Ruiz-Real et al., 2020). Therefore, it becomes an initial challenge to adequately investigate the relations between different areas of companies in the frame of sustainable digital transformation. This is troublesome because, as the very concept of "sustainability" is often difficult to understand – it is multidisciplinary and transdisciplinary, affecting the organization at all levels through actions, decisions, and behaviors (Caputo et al., 2021).

Over the past decades, researchers have sought various ways to optimize an organization's strategic management processes in an era of disruptive technology. The paradox theory emphasizes that paradoxes reflect the simultaneous presence of coexistence, interconnectedness, and contradictions within and

DOI: 10.4324/9781003541394-14

between organizations. Paradoxes involve opposing but interdependent forces (W. K. Smith & Lewis, 2011) highlighting the intertwined nature of contradictory elements (Lewis, 2000). These contradictions emerge and persist over time, revealing an ongoing interplay of contradictory but interrelated factors (Huq et al., 2017).

Therefore, the purpose of the empirical studies in this chapter is to clarify the complexity and contradictory nature of sustainable digital transformation by identifying the relationships between different areas of the process, which, when combined, can create paradoxical tensions. The research questions addressed by this study are as follows:

RQ1: How are paradoxes of sustainable digital transformation identified and understood?

RQ2: What are the relationships between factors that can create paradoxical tensions?

As a response to these investigations, this chapter explores the paradoxical impacts of a sustainable approach to strategizing regarding digital transformation processes. The current perspective on sustainability was developed at a time when access to advanced digital technologies was limited, and the development of artificial intelligence applications was at a very early stage. Today's management environment in no way resembles previous times, and the disruptive nature of technology takes place in a dynamic context of uncertainty and constant change (Baiyere et al., 2020). The novelty of undertaking this article relates to determining the paradoxical nature of sustainable digital transformation, its understanding, and what areas are included in it, based on expert interviews.

The chapter consists of four sections. First, it presents the literature review; then it outlines the sampling methodology as well as data collection and analysis. Next, it describes the research results, which are accompanied by expert statements from Central and Eastern Europe. Finally, there is a discussion and conclusions.

## 9.2 Literature Review

Digital transformation has significantly impacted modern businesses and organizations, as the rapidly evolving business landscape creates dynamic environments for value creation across various industries. As businesses become more globalized and fast-paced, digital transformation is increasingly recognized as a strategic necessity across industries, particularly in traditional sectors where disruptive technologies can revolutionize existing business models and structures (Liu et al., 2022; Warner & Wäger, 2019). Digital transformation not only enables competitive advantage but also demands a new way of thinking, balancing the intricacies of technology, culture, and business objectives (P. Smith &

Beretta, 2021). As such, emerging technologies like artificial intelligence (AI) are reshaping organizational activities, providing companies with opportunities (Fitzgerald et al., 2014; A. Singh & Hess, 2020) to build a competitive advantage (Sun et al., 2021; Warner & Wäger, 2019) through knowledge and innovation. However, the complexity and uncertainty associated with digital transformation present paradoxes that organizations must navigate. Implementing digital transformation innovatively and sustainably presents considerable complexities, particularly regarding digital ethics and privacy. These challenges arise from the need to integrate emerging technologies that enhance business performance while simultaneously ensuring alignment with ethical standards and sustainability objectives.

The sustainable adoption of innovative technologies requires a thoughtful approach to resource allocation, stakeholder engagement, and risk management. Organizations must ensure that their digital transformation initiatives align with environmental and social objectives, such as minimizing carbon emissions and fostering inclusivity while prioritizing privacy and data security. The inherent tension between innovation and sustainability arises from the ongoing need to integrate emerging technologies – such as AI and big data analytics – without compromising ethical standards, particularly in areas of surveillance, data privacy, and security (Pappas et al., 2023). Moreover, digital transformation provides AI with extensive data resources, advancing its rapid developments across diverse fields. AI is already reshaping work in our daily lives and how businesses are conducted since it holds substantial potential to drive economic growth, contributing to the pursuit of global sustainability goals (Benbya & McKelvey, 2006; O'Halloran & Winston, 2019; Pappas et al., 2023).

Managing paradoxical strategies – where contradictory yet interconnected approaches are required – has become essential for organizations' long-term success (Danneels & Viaene, 2022; P. Smith & Beretta, 2021). Addressing these challenges involves leveraging digital technologies, applying flexible strategies, and integrating both internal and external skills to successfully navigate the conflicting demands of the transformation process, especially when it comes to emerging technologies.

There is a diverse distribution of paradoxes in the literature, which often replicates the same areas of companies' activities. Regarding research on sustainable digital transformation, the authors chose to present selected paradoxes due to the paradoxes' focus on specific areas. N. Singh et al. (2024) describe a set of eight paradoxes in the digital transformation process communalized from the literature review, such as automation (relates to productivity, employment, skill gaps, and human-machine relations), cost, information (access to data vs. information overload), transparency (relates privacy issues), innovation (relates to the system integration, competitiveness, risks, and uncertainties), security (relates to cybersecurity threats and a user-friendly interface), complexity (relates to a simplified user experience and complex backend systems), and sustainability (relates to efficiency and environmental impact). Chaudhary et al. (2022) focus on three paradoxes, including the paradox of organizing, where they address the areas of autonomy, efficiency, formalization, and the needs of different stakeholders; the paradox of learning concerning the relationship of acquired knowledge with new knowledge; and the paradox of performing, where they place the essence on long- and short-term tasks (Chaudhary et al., 2022).

Organizations that embrace digital transformation leverage new technologies to restructure operations and create new opportunities for growth and innovation. However, this transition often presents a range of challenges, many paradoxical challenges (N. Singh et al., 2024). Organizations must navigate these contradictory challenges in the rapidly evolving digital environment, leading to complex paradoxes that can impact their success. Understanding the paradoxes of AI is crucial for harnessing its full potential to maximize its benefits. N. Singh et al. (2024) described paradoxical situations as involving conflicting elements. Nevertheless, nothing will be as important in the digital transformation process as the organization's employees' attitude and acceptance of the process. Neglecting the role of employees, although employee support is vital (Klein et al., 2024) leads to the most important of paradoxes – the Mindset Paradox.

The swift progress of emerging technologies like AI outpaces the establishment of appropriate ethical guidelines and frameworks. In their pursuit to leverage these technologies, organizations may prioritize efficiency at the expense of ethical considerations, leading to potential ethical paradoxes in their implementation. Such paradoxes arise because, although technology offers the promise of enhanced efficiency and innovation, it frequently presents new challenges that contradict the original objectives (N. Singh et al., 2024).

Data is essential to the functioning of AI since AI utilizes large amounts of data to make more accurate predictions and decisions. Nonetheless, relying on data creates a paradox between innovation and privacy (G. Smith, 2019). While digital transformation creates new opportunities for innovation and economic growth, it raises ethical concerns about data privacy and security. This raises significant concerns about how organizations collect, store, and utilize data, prompting reactions that range from perceiving data as a threat to viewing it as an opportunity (Dick, 2019).

According to Bailey and Barley (2020), understanding the challenges posed by the technologies is essential to engage in reflective, critical discussions on responsible AI. In return, it can foster research that addresses issues of power dynamics, ideological influences, and institutional transformation (Bailey & Barley, 2020). Especially because of the reliance on AI's training dataset and capacity for real-time execution raises critical questions regarding ethics, accountability, and responsibility, particularly concerning unintended harmful consequences associated with the adoption of AI (Ågerfalk et al., 2022). Yet, they also introduce complex challenges, including issues related to bias, accountability, and context-dependent transparency; whether these benefits can be achieved sustainably remains uncertain.

The complexities surrounding transparency make it particularly challenging to detect and address instances of reproduced or even reinforced social biases within AI systems. Therefore, balancing innovation with sustainability presents both distinct challenges and opportunities. Innovation has the potential to advance sustainability by optimizing processes, minimizing waste, and enhancing energy efficiency. At the same time, the accelerated pace of digitalization can also lead to environmental drawbacks, such as increased energy consumption and electronic waste, alongside social issues like digital divides and job displacement. To address these complexities, organizations must develop frameworks that embed sustainability at the core of their transformation strategies, ensuring that emerging technologies, including AI and machine learning, are implemented with a focus on ethical standards and long-term sustainability. Organizations must strategically balance the application of AI for business growth with its associated social and environmental impacts.

In conclusion, achieving a harmonious equilibrium among innovation, digital ethics, and sustainability necessitates a multifaceted approach. This approach should encompass adopting frameworks that integrate sustainable objectives with digital transformation efforts while effectively managing the complexities that AI and other technologies pose to privacy, labor markets, and environmental consequences.

## 9.3 Methodology

### *9.3.1 Sample Composition*

The study included 10 experts who were selected for their extensive experience in the field of digital transformation processes in both academia and business. The experts were selected so that their knowledge and experience covered the broadest possible area affected by the transformation process; this includes not only their academic degrees but also their industry and specialization, as well as the size of the company they work for.

### *9.3.2 Data Collection and Analysis*

Data from this chapter is part of a more extensive mixed-methods study investigating a sustainable digital transformation approach in management science. Part of this study involved interviews with experts from academia and businesses previously involved in digital transformation processes. This qualitative research consists of 10 semi-structured interviews with experts with over 10 years of experience in the field.

Data analysis consisted of three steps: (1) Preparation of transcription of interviews, (2) coding phase, and (3) extraction of data and analysis of the

*Table 9.1* Detailed Breakdown of Sampling

| *Interviewee* | *Symbol* | *Field* | *Industry/Field* | *Title* | *Country* | *Size of Organization* |
|---|---|---|---|---|---|---|
| Expert 1 | A | Business | Production | Head of Digital Transformation | Poland | Middle |
| Expert 2 | B | Business | Production | Head of Digital Transformation | Poland | Big |
| Expert 3 | C | Business | Technology | CEO | Poland | Middle |
| Expert 4 | D | Science | AI | Professor | Poland | Big |
| Expert 5 | E | Science | Psychology | Associate Professor | Poland | Big |
| Expert 6 | F | Business and Science | Creative industry | PhD/CEO | Austria | Small |
| Expert 7 | G | Business | Creative industry | CEO | Germany | Small |
| Expert 8 | H | Business | Futurology | Expert | Romania | Small |
| Expert 9 | I | Business | Technology/AI | PhD/CEO | Poland | Small |
| Expert 10 | J | Business/Public | Law/AI | Expert | Poland | Big |

results. In the first step, the interviews were transcribed using an external software system. The transcriptions were subsequently reviewed and corrected by the authors before being downloaded for further analysis. In the second step, the coding phase started using a deductive approach, the coding phase started by developing a codebook with an initial set of 24 codes. The set of pre-defined codes and definitions of the codes were based on a previous systematic literature review, depicted in Table 9.2.

The authors consider the classification of these paradoxes based on selected subdivisions that best suit the purpose of the study. The definitions of codes used

*Table 9.2* Set of Codes and Definitions

| *Author(s)* | *Paradoxes* | *Code* | *Definition Used in the Context of the Study* |
|---|---|---|---|
| (N. Singh et al., 2024) | Automation | Social | Building responsible digital practices for society |
| (N. Singh et al., 2024) | Automation | Human | Improving working conditions through technology |
| (N. Singh et al., 2024) | Automation | Process | Digitization and automation of business processes |
| (N. Singh et al., 2024) | Automation | Organizational ecosystem | Creating collaboration between all parts of the organization |
| (N. Singh et al., 2024) | Cost | Economic | Increasing efficiency and generating economic value |
| (N. Singh et al., 2024) | Sustainability | Environmental | Minimizing the environmental impact of technology |
| (N. Singh et al., 2024) | Innovation | Operational | Optimizing operational processes with digital tools |
| (N. Singh et al., 2024) | Innovation | Technological | Implementing new technologies |
| (N. Singh et al., 2024) | Innovation | Business sophistication | Implementing digital strategies for business development |
| (N. Singh et al., 2024) | Complexity | Infrastructural | Building appropriate infrastructure to support technology |
| (N. Singh et al., 2024) | Complexity | Market sophistication | Adapting to rapidly changing market conditions |
| (N. Singh et al., 2024) | Transparency | Legal | Alignment with technology regulations |
| (N. Singh et al., 2024) | Security | Customer experience | Improving customer interaction through technology |

(*Continued*)

*Table 9.2* (*Continued*)

| *Author(s)* | *Paradoxes* | *Code* | *Definition Used in the Context of the Study* |
|---|---|---|---|
| (Chaudhary et al., 2022) | Paradox of Organizing | Individual | Personalization of technology for individual user needs |
| (Chaudhary et al., 2022) | Paradox of Organizing | Creative outcomes | Stimulating innovation and creativity in the organization |
| (Chaudhary et al., 2022) | Paradox of Organizing | Cultural | Shaping a technology-friendly organizational culture |
| (Chaudhary et al., 2022) | Paradox of Performing | Governance | Implementing effective digital management strategies |
| (Chaudhary et al., 2022) | Paradox of Performing | Organizational agility | Increasing the company's flexibility to respond to change |
| (Chaudhary et al., 2022) | Paradox of Performing | Structural | Modifying organizational structures in response to technology |
| (Chaudhary et al., 2022) | Paradox of Learning | Knowledge and support | Development of competence and availability of technical support |
| (Klein et al., 2024) | Mindset Paradox | Psychological | Nurturing the impact of technology on psychological well-being |
| (N. Singh et al., 2024) | Ethical Paradox | Ethical | Ensuring ethical standards in digital operations |
| Not applicable | Not applicable | Political | Establishing relationships with political and regulatory stakeholders |
| Not applicable | Not applicable | External | Integrating with the external environment in a digital context |

are the authors' understanding of these factors, which have emerged through the literature research conducted prior to this study. To ensure precision and objectivity, the authors extracted data from transcribed interviews and assigned excerpts to codes using an In Vivo coding approach.

## 9.4 Results

A total of nearly 200 interactions and influences between areas were identified across all interviews. From these, 99 pairs of areas with interactions were identified, 20 of which were characterized as paradoxes. Based on the analysis of the collected data, nine areas were identified that, when interacting with other areas, potentially led to a paradox. The area of business sophistication had the highest number of interactions (8), followed by the economic area (5). The technological, operational, social, knowledge and support, psychological, and external areas had three interactions; the environmental and organization ecosystem had two; and the remaining areas had only one interaction, i.e., human, organization agility, ethical, governance, and legal.

### *9.4.1 Characteristics of Business Sophistication Area*

In this study, Business Sophistication is defined as implementing digital business development strategies. It refers to the skillful use of available resources to execute a process within the company, which may involve the creation of new products and processes. Table 9.3 presents the survey results, showing the paradoxical tensions of the area of business sophistication in other areas.

*Table 9.3* Paradoxical Tensions between Areas – Business Sophistication

| *Paradoxical Areas of Sustainable Digital Transformation* | | *Citation* |
|---|---|---|
| Business sophistication | Economic | • *Digitization is a big cost, but it has paid for itself in future revenues.* (Expert 2)<br>• *Digital transformation is a certain process that can contribute to greater efficiency, lower costs, and, ultimately, to improved economic performance.* (Expert 3)<br>• *So, there is a huge productivity boost. Definitely.* (Expert 6)<br>• *You can digitize businesses and optimize costs. I, however, would like to put the accent on increasing my growth opportunities and revenues. It's very important to put it that way because usually digital transformation has been advertised as "optimize, you'll know everything, you'll be able to fire people, you'll have cheaper, and so on."* (Expert 10) |
| Business sophistication | Environmental | • *These are changes carried out in the care of the environment.* (Expert 5)<br>• *Bottom-up objective – minimizing costs (...) energy transformation, thermo-modernization, reducing environmental impact.* (Expert 2)<br>• *To transform the energy is required. Digital technologies use various kinds of toxic rare earth materials, and the devices are often made in ways that don't work forever and also are obsolete very quickly. And the challenges associated are quite big. So, digital commuting can save fossil fuels and reduce greenhouse gas emissions.* (Expert 9) |

(*Continued*)

*Table 9.3* (*Continued*)

| *Paradoxical Areas of Sustainable Digital Transformation* | | *Citation* |
|---|---|---|
| Business sophistication | Knowledge and support | • *I think this knowledge of these people getting pushed off the plate right now is missing.* (Expert 7)<br>• *(...) influences personal development and, above all, in the context of the employee's competence in a given job, hence challenges such as the "Future of Work" have now emerged; it is one thing or, for example, a typology of the use of artificial intelligence technology in the workplace, how does this affect the individual? Does he thrive by going into a digital environment, or conversely, is there a reduction in his capabilities, which can also happen?* (Expert 10)<br>• *(...) There is much easier access to documents.* (Expert 5) |
| Business sophistication | Organization ecosystem | • *Communication is not created well because it's economically driven. So that means there's a lot about, like trying to find a safe space in your little bubble. There's a lot of misinformation going on.* (Expert 7)<br>• *The use of the robots as telepresence devices allows human beings remotely teleport through the robots to have face-to-face conversations through this three-dimensional animated physical embodiment. So, the robot moves away from the person, makes eye contact, and is almost like a holographic projection of the remote person.* (Expert 9) |
| Business sophistication | Psychological | • *However, I think there is a gap between the comprehension of the people and the speed of digital transformation. So, I don't think that everybody is actually on the boat. There is a gap between how fast things go and how fast people can actually comprehend what's happening. (Expert 6)*<br>• *Actions that aim to digitize some processes sometimes cause concern if process owners miscommunicate changes within the company to employees.* (Expert 3)<br>• *When people get overwhelmed and get basically sick from being too digital, they go on a digital diet or digital detox, and the funny thing is, everybody comes back.* (Expert 7) |

(*Continued*)

*Table 9.3 (Continued)*

| *Paradoxical Areas of Sustainable Digital Transformation* | | *Citation* |
|---|---|---|
| Business sophistication | Social | • *Employees feel better after the digital transformation changes. They don't do the manual tasks they complained about, i.e., paperwork, boring work, tedious.* (Expert 1)<br>• *Digital transformation is affecting human capital both globally and locally. There is a need to slow down or for robots to replace humans in workplaces.* (Expert 10)<br>• *There is a gap between how fast things go and how fast people can actually comprehend what's happening. I don't think that everybody is actually on the boat. Those who couldn't adapt lost their jobs.* (Expert 6)<br>• *I am concerned about newer positions that need people with a higher skill set. Unfortunately, not everyone is able to train up to those skill levels.* (Expert 8)<br>• *More specialized employees, especially in IT areas, thanks to transformation.* (Expert 2) |
| Business sophistication | Ethics | • *When you now look into the music world, artists are becoming more and more creative and they find new ways of expression in the digital world.* (Expert 6)<br>• *And then you had the piracy, and you had the streaming and downloads. I definitely lived in the environment* [music industry] *where you had a huge digital transformation.* (Expert 6)<br>• *Within the OECD, an expert group was set up in 2018 to develop recommendations on artificial intelligence, "Stewardship for Trustworthy Artificial Intelligence," to ensure that abuses do not occur not only in the areas of the environment, sustainability or local economies but also at the human level and at the level of fair competition opportunities.* (Expert 10) |

The economic area is among the most important areas related to a sustainable digital transformation process. The costs of running a business, its efficiency, revenue, and profitability are at the heart of any process that is initiated. Nevertheless, the process itself is a costly endeavor (Expert 2). The prospect of higher earnings in the future is an insufficient argument for entrepreneurs who are looking for measurable solutions in the short term. Higher revenues in the future can be hard to quantify and are linked to several factors that are not necessarily the result of the transformation process. It is far more predictable to influence the costs incurred by a company (Expert 3). The theme of economic efficiency is particularly dominant among entrepreneurs, who collectively emphasize the advantages of the implemented process (Expert 6). However, reducing a company's costs, despite yielding tangible benefits, will not drive economic growth for the company, region, or country (Expert 10).

Studies indicate that the process of sustainable digital transformation, in contrast, imposes additional elements related to the well-being of people as well as silent stakeholders, such as future generations and the planet (Expert 5). When addressing environmental sustainability, while implementing a strategy based on reducing the carbon footprint (Expert 2), entrepreneurs face the challenge that, in striving for greater environmental sustainability, they may end up using more energy, harmful materials, and generating additional waste (Expert 9).

These are not the only challenges they encounter. In the context of digital transformation, human beings are also affected in the process, particularly when redundancy occurs. In such cases, the organization faces an opportunity cost. However, this presents a major loss from a sustainable digital transformation approach (Expert 10). The speed at which change is implemented plays a major role, especially when it comes to lower-level employees (Expert 6). Redundancies are one of the most frequently addressed issues in the digital transformation process (Expert 8). Paradoxically, a loss for some workers can be a gain for others, and this is true in this case as well. By automating processes, we eliminate monotonous work and replace it with work with higher demands (Expert 2). New jobs are being created, and new, previously non-existent professions and occupations are being created, as discussed by Expert 6, who works in the creative industries at a scientific and business level, combining AI and music.

Empirical evidence highlights that the gain in knowledge due to digital change is undeniable. Still, the concept of sustainable digital transformation also draws attention to the loss in the knowledge area of an organization due to redundancies (Expert 7). Expert 10 goes even further in his reflections, not only addressing the loss of knowledge within the organization but also raising concerns about the diminishing capacity of those excluded from the digital transformation process. In the flow and preservation of information and knowledge in an organization, a good practice related to digitization is creating knowledge repositories and databases (Expert 5). This is one of the elements that also supports the interaction between the areas of business sophistication and the organization ecosystem, which specifically addresses the issue of communication during a sustainable digital transformation process. The experts address the paradox of communication in the transformation process, which can simultaneously be inclusive and exclusionary (Expert 7). The development of remote communication between team members, which played an important role during the COVID-19 pandemic, has also had unexpected positive consequences for individuals with disabilities. Thanks to increased digitalization, they are now, for the first time, able to compete on a level playing field in the labor market (Expert 9).

Sustainable digital transformation differs from digital transformation in that it prioritizes people and their needs alongside economic outcomes, an aspect that businesses may overlook or fail to consider. Research findings point to the paradox of this situation, that despite the many positive effects of the transformation process, it raises much anxiety, which in turn can cause further incidents, creating a snowball effect out of fear of transformation (Expert 6). The reasons for this phenomenon were also sought by Expert 3, pointing to the important role of team leaders in the change process. In some cases, the new situation faced by employees requires non-standard solutions. This is particularly true for employees who have not had previous significant exposure to digital technologies (Expert 7). Overcoming initial fears and difficulties leads to more engaged employees with better attitudes and motivations to continue their education (Expert 1).

In addition to organizational leaders, the global digital transformation situation has also been a concern for government representatives and global policymakers. Due to the rapid, uncontrolled development of technology and emerging breaches and crimes (Expert 6), the international community has responded by making a concerted effort to address this situation and establish a common set of ethical guidelines related to the implementation of new technologies, particularly those related to AI, fairly rapidly (Expert 10).

### *9.4.2 Characteristics of External Area*

The external area in the survey appears to be the integration of the business with the external environment in a digital context. Table 9.4 presents three links identified through the empirical research.

Public institutions and state governments began to work on producing legislation to stop bad practices in the area of technology development and business (Expert 10). A sustainable digital transformation forces all stakeholders to comply with the law and take an ethical approach to the transformation, which would not be possible without the participation of the administration sector (Expert 8). Data confirms that the influence of governments on legislation has both positive and negative characteristics. A lack of regulation leads to market anomalies and abuses, while excessive regulation can block business growth and, in the case of digital transformation, may even result in its failure. In addition to mandates and prohibitions, public administrations can implement measures that are more favorably received by the business community, such as promoting and rewarding positive behaviors that contribute to the success of transformational

*Table 9.4* Paradoxical Tensions between External Areas

| *Paradoxical Areas of Sustainable Digital Transformation* | | *Citation* |
|---|---|---|
| External | Business sophistication | • *There is a philosophical question because it is clear that some people say government should stay out, like government regulation should stay out. But if you make something purely good, we know it is the right thing to do. There is, I think, a pretty long history of that not working for everyone.* (Expert 8)<br>• *If we do not play with incentives and government regulations, we will not achieve anything more.* (Expert 8)<br>• *One is catastrophes. I give an example in the nuclear industry, there were the catastrophes of Chornobyl and Fukushima, and so if you have something that goes horribly wrong, not just one car somehow malfunctioning and crashing.* (Expert 8)<br>• *Another example is COVID-19. You have to do a very large test before something is released. We didn't have such a thing. We had to act quickly with the help of technology.* (Expert 8) |
| External | Economic | • *The government put more regulations on (...) they would cost.* (Expert 8)<br>• *So, saying we're going to take tax money, so we're essentially taking money that's been given from the whole society, and we're going to redistribute it.* (Expert 8) |
| External | Legal | • *International organizations have recognized that a certain breakthrough in digital technologies, especially when it comes to artificial intelligence, is so extraordinary that it not only threatens the global south but even the status quo of existing economies and economic advantages, and this has just awakened the world of international organizations to take this issue seriously, to try to politically impose frameworks and different kinds of recommendations towards the implementation for the purposes of artificial intelligence, which finally ended up in the creation of, first, the Ethical Guideline for Trustworthy AI and then the AI Act.* (Expert 10)<br>• *There's not a good track record of companies in the past doing this without either regulations or incentives.* (Expert 8) |

efforts (Expert 8). This also has implications for the company's economic area. Government regulations related to digitalization may lead to a decrease in economic profit due to the mandatory implementation of measures such as security features or specific technologies. Still, these regulations may also be linked to tax or other financial benefits.

Another type of paradoxical impact between the external area and the area of business sophistication is what we classify as extreme events, such as disasters, pandemics, and catastrophes. These events can be both negative and positive (Expert 8).

### 9.4.3 Characteristics of Technological Area

The technological area appears in the study in many configurations and interpretations, but its importance has been limited to the implementation of new technologies. Table 9.5 presents three paradoxical tensions arising from the technological area in the process of sustainable digital transformation.

Technological developments require employees to acquire new skills and adapt to a new way of working in an increasingly high-tech environment (Expert 1). However, findings reveal that this is not a situation where the outcome is binary. Staff development is likely to be influenced by various factors, and the result does not necessarily always lead to knowledge gains. In some cases, both staff and team leaders reported a reduction in skills (Expert 8). The development of employees, companies, and society in general can also be driven by isolated technological developments and complex technological developments linked to breakthrough projects (Expert 4). From the operational point of view, implementing new technology in the workplace and training employees to use it may not be enough of an effort by corporate transformation leaders to succeed (Expert 3). New technologies in sustainable digital transformation must be correlated with changes in the company's operational processes so that the benefits of technological functionalities are fully exploited (Expert 5). The human in the workplace is a key element on which the entire change process depends. Sustainable digital transformation places particular emphasis on driving through a human-centered approach. According to Expert 7, based on experience as a consultant and trainer of C-level staff, this is not a standard or easy aspect of the transformational process. However, if successful, it can lead to an unexpected surge in employee engagement, with employees not only taking on new tasks but also assuming responsibility for the company's development (Expert 1).

### 9.4.4 Characteristics of Other Areas

In the following section of the results, areas that make fewer connections between other areas are presented (Tables 9.6–9.11). Still, their impacts are highlighted in Table 9.6 because of their importance to sustainable digital transformation.

*Table 9.5* Paradoxical Tensions between Areas – Technological

| *Paradoxical Areas of Sustainable Digital Transformation* | | *Citation* |
|---|---|---|
| Technological | Operational | • *We once had an example in one of the accounting departments where a lady accountant had been doing everything in tables on paper for 20 years, and despite the introduction of spreadsheet software, she continued to do it as she had for many years. I think sometimes such strong resistance can be more due to ignorance and inadequate implementation of processes.* (Expert 3)<br>• *The implementation of the new tool in the institution has automated the process and eliminated physical contact in administrative matters, which has had a number of other positive consequences, including more time for substantive work.* (Expert 5) |
| Technological | Knowledge and support | • *The introduction of the mobile warehouse system has enhanced the digital skills of employees who previously performed the same tasks on cards, which they now handle via radio terminals and smartphones.* (Expert 1)<br>• *A long time ago, calculators became common. And so, most of us don't do math in our heads unless it's really simple, and we're in the past, probably what people have spent more time doing long math. And so, our ability may be somewhat diminished, but most of us can still do the math. We need to go to the grocery store and figure out basic things. But if you extrapolate that to a lot of other areas of learning, do we continue to push our own minds? Is it needed to be a broadly educated person, a broadly educated populace? These things concern me, but I also think that they're not necessarily going to be all bad.* (Expert 8)<br>• *When the Americans flew to the moon, 400,000 people were working on this project; they spent billions of dollars at the time. It was a really huge amount, but it spread all over the country and raised the country's profile because a lot of different engineering competencies had to be developed by different companies to make the program happen.* (Expert 4) |

(*Continued*)

*Table 9.5 (Continued)*

| *Paradoxical Areas of Sustainable Digital Transformation* | | *Citation* |
|---|---|---|
| Technological | Human | • *It is important to adjust the tools to the humans, not the humans to the tools. A good digital transition leaves room for people within the company who do not have to turn transit.* (Expert 7)<br>• *They prefer to work on new solutions. Learning new systems and acquiring new skills makes them happy to be key employees familiar with the system. We have implemented a system where the employee can implement his ideas. The employee is not alone in the process.* (Expert 1) |

*Table 9.6* Paradoxical Tensions between Areas – Operational

| *Paradoxical Areas of Sustainable Digital Transformation* | | *Citation* |
|---|---|---|
| Operational | Economic | • *The lack of integration of technologies and processes entails greater financial and time investment in their completion.* (Expert 3)<br>• *Better control of the company's processes results in efficient and cost-effective management because we are able to consciously draw logical conclusions about how individual processes are taking place, moreover how we are able to control these processes, and on the basis of these conclusions, we are able to make appropriate adjustments in real-time and eliminate these negative impacts.* (Expert 2) |
| Operational | Organizational agility | • *An example of a government social security platform to which we are able to create a user account based on electronic proof, but the authorization of this account is done by printing a document from this platform, physically signing it, and taking this confirmation to the institution's premises.* (Expert 3)<br>• *Proper automation and control of the process means fewer products of inappropriate quality and faster execution; consequently, the same production line can make more products in the same amount of time.* (Expert 2) |

*Table 9.7* Paradoxical Tensions between Areas – Environmental

| *Paradoxical Areas of Sustainable Digital Transformation* | | *Citation* |
|---|---|---|
| Environmental | Economic | *Digital transformation is a kind of investment that requires quite a lot of money, which will only pay back to the company in the form of generated savings after some time.* (Expert 3) |

*Table 9.8* Paradoxical Tensions between Areas – Governance

| *Paradoxical Areas of Sustainable Digital Transformation* | | *Citation* |
|---|---|---|
| Governance | Psychological | • *Digital transformation starts first and foremost in the heads of leaders.* (Expert 3)<br>• *Thanks to the success of the transformation and good management decisions, resistance has decreased as employees have seen the positive effects.* (Expert 1)<br>• *At some point, the obligation for digital documentation came in (…) I remember that I delayed using it for a long time, and then I had to (…) the resistance is a bit human as always.* (Expert 5) |

*Table 9.9* Paradoxical Tensions between Areas – Knowledge and Support

| *Paradoxical Areas of Sustainable Digital Transformation* | | *Citation* |
|---|---|---|
| Knowledge and support | Social | • *And those who are able, like super competent people, but sometimes even they fall off the wheel, (...) when people are welcome and invited, they are able to learn.* (Expert 7)<br>• *Thanks to an internal training and recruitment system, our company's digital transformation process is characterized by low employee turnover within the company.* (Expert 2) |

The planning of processes and the purchase of technology must meet certain criteria for the transformation to be implemented; the tools could be fully utilized through integration with the company's existing solutions without unnecessary and redundant costs (Expert 3). The proper integration of technology

*Table 9.10* Paradoxical Tensions between Social and Economic Areas

| *Paradoxical Areas of Sustainable Digital Transformation* | | *Citation* |
|---|---|---|
| Social | Economic | • *The problem with good specialists is the high financial and non-financial outlay that a company has to meet in order to be able to compete in the market.* (Expert 1)<br>• *The introduction of a performance-based bonus system on production lines has resulted in increased efficiency of individual teams, faster production, and less waste.* (Expert 2) |

*Table 9.11* Paradoxical Tensions between Organization Ecosystem and Psychological Areas

| *Paradoxical Areas of Sustainable Digital Transformation* | | *Citation* |
|---|---|---|
| Organization ecosystem | Psychological | • *Measures that aim to digitize some processes sometimes raise concerns among employees that their jobs will be eliminated, and these are some of the fears that accompany digitization, which perhaps needs to be properly balanced and properly communicated.* (Expert 3)<br>• *The remote communication system for employees and customers during the pandemic helped to make contacts and create better relationships with them, resulting in increased sales during such difficult times.* (Expert 2) |

and processes will, in turn, have long-term results and further benefits in other areas of the company, especially those related to economic efficiency (Expert 2). Failure to integrate technology and processes means a loss not only economically but also in organizational agility, which in this case was caused by wasted time (Expert 3). The paradox between the operational area and the area of organizational agility lies in the appropriate creation of processes for the changing situation in the company. Mapping processes appropriately brings value to the organization in the form of greater capacity (Expert 2).

A paradox related to the environmental and economic areas is investment in environmentally positive solutions, which can be a barrier to entry for small and medium-sized enterprises. It may be considered an investment that will only pay back to the company in the form of generated savings (Expert 3).

Governance decisions in sustainable digital transformation are undoubtedly challenging, yet they are key to the success of the process in the long term (Expert 3). Human-centered management, in this case of an employee of a particular company, is important for all those thinking about the long-term results of a company and contributes to the leveling of resistance to change (Expert 1). It will depend on the decisions of those in management positions whether we have a paradoxical situation that manifests as a reduction or an increase in employee resistance (Expert 5).

According to previous expert statements, resistance to change is related to a lack of or low awareness and understanding of the processes. This situation can have various consequences, the initial stage being knowledge gaps that can end in redundancy or even social exclusion (Expert 7). Through a training and support system, companies can reverse this negative trend and avoid a paradoxical situation (Expert 2). This situation can cause interactions between further areas, in this case, the social and economic areas.

Staff shortages may affect the continuity of processes and, above all, bridging these gaps may incur much higher costs than internal training systems (Expert 1). Hence, the company's incentive systems play a key role in building the company's human capital and strengthening the company's resilience, which has a far-reaching impact on other areas of sustainability in the organization (Expert 2).

The relationship between the organizational ecosystem area and the psychological area, which focuses on appropriate communication within the organization, pays special attention to balancing fears of the process with digitalization goals (Expert 3). Poor communication will create unrest between employees and teams. Among those who work with each other remotely, keeping in touch is a key element for creating relationships between employees, which is of considerable importance for the functioning of the entire organization (Expert 2).

### *9.4.5 Discussion*

Sustainable digital transformation is a paradigm shift in how businesses undertake digital transformation. The literature review presents different approaches to defining paradoxes in the digital transformation process. The multiplicity of paradoxes and overlapping definitions can make it difficult to respond to the challenges they bring. Additionally, interviews with digital transformation experts in science and business revealed the simultaneous strengthening and weakening of transformation processes, revealing the paradoxical nature of sustainable digital transformation.

Figure 9.1 shows the intensity of the paradoxical tensions and the interactions between the different areas that create these tensions. The work goes beyond the divisions proposed by other authors; it shows that it is important to connect these areas with each other, which can be inspiring in science, but especially in business practice.

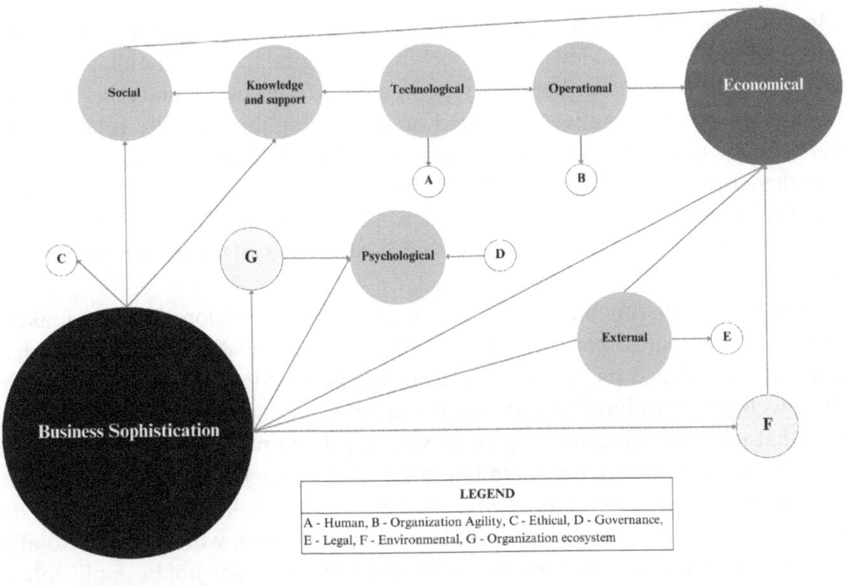


*Figure 9.1* The Flow of Paradoxical Tensions.

Figure 9.1 shows the most significant areas, i.e., those with the highest number of outgoing and incoming connections, by increasing the size of the area circle and showing the tension flow illustrated by the arrowhead. The process of sustainable digital transformation is very complex and multidimensional in nature. Using existing models to create strategies based on the sustainable characteristics of the digital transformation process may not be applicable and may not lead to the intended results. The diagram shows the flow of paradoxical tensions between areas. The distribution of tensions is uneven, as is the intensity of interactions between areas, as illustrated by the size of the circles. Out of the 15 defined areas, the most frequently involved areas are Business Sophistication and Economic, which form 8 and 5 connections to other areas, respectively. The flows originate from several areas and do not form a closed loop, which involves all areas classified in the survey.

Digital transformation has gone too far without any attempt to consciously direct or understand where it will take us. Further development of the use of digital methods in the digital transformation process should be researched to make the process more efficient. Digital transformation, in many ways, can confuse issues of sustainability, and the creation of strategies for the benefit of both people and the planet is most often overlooked. Nonetheless, it is leaders who shape the nature of the changes a company undertakes during the digital transformation process. The resilience of the changes made will depend on them.

## 9.5 Conclusion

The study outlines how the paradoxes of digital transformation are understood and identified. With a view to approaching the digital transformation process in a sustainable way, the authors propose an approach based on analyzing the flow of paradox tensions between defined areas and highlighting the relationships between areas as key to responding to the challenges posed by these paradoxes. The development of digital transformation processes in companies based on sustainable principles will overwhelmingly be based on the willingness and calculation of the profits and losses that the boards of the organizations are prepared to bear.

The results of this study can help organizations develop decision-making models or strategies that consider the long-term implications of technological innovation. Defined paradoxes and identified paradoxical tensions can support the development of internal and external technology and data management policies that integrate sustainability goals with legal and market requirements. The results demonstrate that the pursuit of innovation through implementing sustainable digital transformation processes is related to the multifaceted impact of the solutions implemented. Existing implementation models, which use an isolated approach of carrying out changes only in selected areas, may not be applicable to companies that want to implement AI systems due to their disruptive nature. The study's results indicate that implementations based on sustainable digital transformation are more resilient to change and have far greater long-term benefits. The digital transformation brings paradoxes that appear universal to the studied Central and Eastern European and Western European countries.

The results of this study justify the need for empirical research to verify the relevance of the various areas of sustainability occurring in the digital transformation process. Nevertheless, to do that, there is a need to diagnose the relations between sustainability areas when implementing the sustainable digital transformation process. These results are an excellent initial step towards developing an enterprise digital transformation strategy based on sustainable factors. Our research suggests that a sustainable digital transformation approach could be used to implement digital changes in an organization in a way that benefits the organization and all the stakeholders involved.

The main limitation of this study is the small research sample, which may imperfectly represent the problem. Nevertheless, the high experience and diversity of the research sample in business and science provide a basis for further empirical research. It should focus on identifying and perceiving paradoxes in the process of sustainable digital transformation by investigating a larger sample that consists directly of employees and company executives. An additional advantage would be the investigation of individual paradoxical tensions in relation to interactions between areas and the implications for the overall process of sustainable digital transformation.

## References


Ågerfalk, P. J., Conboy, K., Crowston, K., Eriksson Lundström, J. S. Z., Jarvenpaa, S., Ram, S., & Mikalef, P. (2022). Artificial intelligence in information systems: State of the art and research roadmap. *Communications of the Association for Information Systems, 50*(1), 420–438. https://doi.org/10.17705/1CAIS.05017

Bailey, D. E., & Barley, S. R. (2020). Beyond design and use: How scholars should study intelligent technologies. *Information and Organization, 30*(2), 100286. https://doi.org/10.1016/j.infoandorg.2019.100286

Baiyere, A., Salmela, H., & Tapanainen, T. (2020). Digital transformation and the new logics of business process management. *European Journal of Information Systems, 29*(3), 238–259. https://doi.org/10.1080/0960085X.2020.1718007

Benbya, H., & McKelvey, B. (2006). Using coevolutionary and complexity theories to improve IS alignment: A multi–level approach. *Journal of Information Technology, 21*(4), 284–298. https://doi.org/10.1057/palgrave.jit.2000080

Caputo, A., Pizzi, S., Pellegrini, M. M., & Dabić, M. (2021). Digitalization and business models: Where are we going? A science map of the field. *Journal of Business Research, 123*, 489–501. https://doi.org/10.1016/j.jbusres.2020.09.053

Carnerud, D., Mårtensson, A., Ahlin, K., & Slumpi, T. P. (2020). On the inclusion of sustainability and digitalisation in quality management – An overview from past to present. *Total Quality Management & Business Excellence, 148*, 1–23. https://doi.org/10.1080/14783363.2020.1848422

Chaudhary, S., Dhir, A., Gligor, D., Khan, S. J., & Ferraris, A. (2022). Paradoxes and coping mechanisms in the servitisation journey. *Industrial Marketing Management, 106*, 323–337. https://doi.org/10.1016/j.indmarman.2022.09.005

Constantiou, I., Joshi, M., & Stelmaszak, M. (2023). Organizations as digital enactment systems: A theory of replacement of humans by digital technologies in organizational scanning, interpretation, and learning. *Journal of the Association for Information Systems, 24*(6), 1770–1798. https://doi.org/10.17705/1jais.00833

Danneels, L., & Viaene, S. (2022). Identifying digital transformation paradoxes: A design perspective. *Business & Information Systems Engineering, 64*(4), 483–500. https://doi.org/10.1007/s12599-021-00735-7

Dash, B., Sharma, P., & Swayamsiddha, S. (2023). Organizational digital transformations and the importance of assessing theoretical frameworks such as TAM, TTF, and UTAUT: A review. *International Journal of Advanced Computer Science and Applications, 14*(2), 1–6. https://doi.org/10.14569/IJACSA.2023.0140201

Dick, S. (2019). Artificial intelligence. *Harvard Data Science Review*. https://doi.org/10.1162/99608f92.92fe150c

Fitzgerald, M., Kruschwitz, N., Bonnet, D., & Welch, M. (2014). Embracing digital technology: A new strategic imperative. *MIT Sloan Management Review, 55*(2), 1–12.

Flyverbom, M., Deibert, R., & Matten, D. (2019). The governance of digital technology, big data, and the internet: New roles and responsibilities for business. *Business & Society, 58*(1), 3–19. https://doi.org/10.1177/0007650317727540

Ghobakhloo, M. (2020). Industry 4.0, digitization, and opportunities for sustainability. *Journal of Cleaner Production, 252*, 119869. https://doi.org/10.1016/j.jclepro.2019.119869

Huq, J.-L., Reay, T., & Chreim, S. (2017). Protecting the paradox of interprofessional collaboration. *Organization Studies*, *38*(3–4), 513–538. https://doi.org/10.1177/0170840616640847

Klein, S. P., Spieth, P., & Söllner, M. (2024). Employee acceptance of digital transformation strategies: A paradox perspective. *Journal of Product Innovation Management*, *41*(5), 999–1021. https://doi.org/10.1111/jpim.12722

Kupilas, K. J., Rodriguez Montequin, V., Diaz Piloneta, M., & Alonso Alvarez, C. (2022). Sustainability and digitalisation: Using Means-End Chain Theory to determine the key elements of the digital maturity model for research and development organisations with the aspect of sustainability. *Advances in Production Engineering & Management*, *17*(2), 152–168. https://doi.org/10.14743/apem2022.2.427

Lewis, M. W. (2000). Exploring paradox: Toward a more comprehensive guide. *The Academy of Management Review*, *25*(4), 760. https://doi.org/10.2307/259204

Liu, Y., Wang, W., & Zhang, Z. (Justin). (2022). The dual drivetrain model of digital transformation: Role of industrial big-data-based affordance. *Management Decision*, *60*(2), 344–367. https://doi.org/10.1108/MD-12-2019-1664

O'Halloran, D., & Winston, G. (2019). Our shared digital future—Responsible digital transformation. World Economic Forum.

Pacolli, M. (2022). Importance of change management in digital transformation sustainability. *IFAC-PapersOnLine*, *55*(39), 276–280. https://doi.org/10.1016/j.ifacol.2022.12.034

Pappas, I. O., Mikalef, P., Dwivedi, Y. K., Jaccheri, L., & Krogstie, J. (2023). Responsible digital transformation for a sustainable society. *Information Systems Frontiers*, *25*(3), 945–953. https://doi.org/10.1007/s10796-023-10406-5

Ruiz-Real, J. L., Uribe-Toril, J., Torres, J. A., & De Pablo, J. (2020). Artificial intelligence in business and economics research: Trends and future. *Journal of Business Economics and Management*, *22*(1), 98–117. https://doi.org/10.3846/jbem.2020.13641

Shang, Z., & Zhang, L. (2022). The sustainable digitalization in the manufacturing industry: A bibliometric analysis and research trend. *Mobile Information Systems*, *2022*, 1–11. https://doi.org/10.1155/2022/1451705

Singh, A., & Hess, T. (2020). How chief digital officers promote the digital transformation of their companies. In *Strategic information management* (pp. 202–220). Routledge.

Singh, N., Vishnani, S., Khandelwal, V., Sahoo, S., & Kumar, S. (2024). A systematic review of paradoxes linked with digital transformation of business. *Journal of Enterprise Information Management*, *37*(4), 1348–1373. https://doi.org/10.1108/JEIM-07-2023-0397

Smith, G. (2019). Artificial intelligence and the privacy paradox of opportunity, big data and the digital universe. *2019 International Conference on Computational Intelligence and Knowledge Economy (ICCIKE)*, 150–153. https://doi.org/10.1109/ICCIKE47802.2019.9004264

Smith, P., & Beretta, M. (2021). The Gordian knot of practicing digital transformation: Coping with emergent paradoxes in ambidextrous organizing structures*. *Journal of Product Innovation Management*, *38*(1), 166–191. https://doi.org/10.1111/jpim.12548

Smith, W. K., & Lewis, M. W. (2011). Toward a theory of paradox: A dynamic equilibrium model of organizing. *Academy of Management Review*, *36*(2), 381–403. https://doi.org/10.5465/AMR.2011.59330958

Sun, Y., Fang, S., & Zhang, Z. (Justin). (2021). Impression management strategies on enterprise social media platforms: An affordance perspective. *International Journal of Information Management*, *60*, 102359. https://doi.org/10.1016/j.ijinfomgt.2021.102359

Warner, K. S. R., & Wäger, M. (2019). Building dynamic capabilities for digital transformation: An ongoing process of strategic renewal. *Long Range Planning*, *52*(3), 326–349. https://doi.org/10.1016/j.lrp.2018.12.001

# 10 Energy Clusters in Reconciling Paradoxes in Corporate Sustainability

*Anna Maria Lis and Malgorzata Rozkwitalska-Welenc*

## 10.1 Introduction

As environmental concerns are growing around the world and the discourse regarding the green economy draws attention to the capabilities of business communities for generating shared value, there is an increasing need among countries for activities focused on reducing waste and non-renewable resource usage to be organized within industrial, so-called cleantech clusters (Altenburg & Vrolijk, 2020; Hessevik, 2022; Kamath et al., 2022; Tvedt, 2019). Green energy clusters, as an example of cleantech clusters, "are increasingly promoted throughout the world as a strategy to advocate economic vitality while stimulating a sustainable energy transition" (McCauley & Stephens, 2012, p. 213). The green energy clusters' goal is to create a conducive environment for the attraction and development of innovative firms focused on sustainable, renewables-based energy. Such clusters consist of an amalgam of industries representing various links in a value-added chain and the technologies directed toward increasing energy efficiency both on the supply and demand sides (McCauley & Stephens, 2012). Their members should strive toward sustainability, which is a constraint imposed on achieving their goals and has social, economic, environmental, and technological facets (Kajikawa et al., 2014). Consequently, aiming for sustainability, companies attempt to balance economic, environmental, and social objectives and interests formulated by their diverse group of stakeholders, which may run counter to one another, producing intrinsic and intertemporal tensions. These sustainability tensions are considered paradoxical yet manageable (Daddi et al., 2019).

Empirical studies on paradoxical tensions in corporate sustainability are scarce (Carmine & De Marchi, 2023; Daddi et al., 2019), and there is a lack of research that would scrutinize the phenomena in energy clusters or from an interorganizational perspective (Brix-Asala et al., 2018; Koliousis et al., 2018). Even the very energy clusters have barely been studied from the management angle.[1] Given that sustainability issues are context-dependent (Maher et al., 2018), this chapter adopts the interorganizational perspective of the management discipline in research on sustainability in the context of energy clusters. We intend to discover whether there is awareness and acknowledgment of paradoxical tensions

DOI: 10.4324/9781003541394-15

in the sustainability pillars of their member companies and whether and how energy clusters help their member companies reconcile paradoxes in the sustainability pillars. Acknowledging paradoxes is a prerequisite for successful management (Daddi et al., 2019). We are also curious about the role of clusters in supporting sustainable value chain creation and solving sustainability tensions in energy clusters and whether the sustainable value chain responds to identified concerns generated by these sustainability paradoxes. We apply a responsive use of the paradox concept (Carmine & De Marchi, 2023) as we identify practices that clusters implement to address tensions.

In our research grounded in paradox theory, we relate to three case studies of renewables-oriented energy clusters from Romania, Hungary, and Germany. The study explains the nature of intrinsic and intertemporal tensions in companies involved in energy clusters and how the clusters may solve these paradoxes. By addressing them, the clusters would efficiently respond to the sustainability challenges of the present times. Therefore, scholarly attention to energy clusters is needed because they may support green growth and the transition toward sustainable economies. Hence, the study offers vital implications in this matter.

To reach our aim, we first present the contribution of the paradox theory to the explanation of managing tensions in the sustainability pillars. Afterward, the chapter comments on the peculiarities of green energy clusters as a specific type of energy cluster. We also discuss prior research on sustainable value chain adoption practices. To illustrate the phenomenon, after introducing the description of methods and analytical procedures, the chapter refers to three examples of energy clusters. In the subsequent section, we discuss our findings and how the study contributes to the existing knowledge, and we delineate its limitations and directions for further investigation.

## 10.2 Literature Overview and Theoretical Framework

### *10.2.1 Paradox Theory and Sustainability*

Corporate sustainability has gained importance in business. For example, the Business Roundtable, which associates chief executive officers of America's leading enterprises, recognizes that corporate purpose goes beyond maximizing shareholder value; it also requires delivering value to all stakeholders (Walker et al., 2020). Corporate sustainability reflects a company's effort to simultaneously reach its operations' social, economic, and ecological objectives. They are known as the triple-bottom-line objectives, and accordingly, there are three frequently competing pillars of sustainability that can produce paradoxical tensions in company management (Daddi et al., 2019; Mousavi et al., 2018). Therefore, paradox theory can shed light on our study of the role of green energy clusters in helping their member companies reconcile tensions in the sustainability pillars.

Paradox theory has gained scholarly interest in the sustainability literature (Brix-Asala et al., 2018; Carmine & De Marchi, 2023; Daddi et al., 2019; De

Angelis, 2021; Ivory & Brooks, 2018; Rey-Garcia et al., 2020; Walker et al., 2020). Nevertheless, more empirical work applying methodological rigor concerning the paradox concept is needed (Daddi et al., 2019). Moreover, only Daddi et al. (2019) scrutinized firms from paper and tannery industrial clusters, not clusters themselves. Thus, there is a vacuum in research on paradoxical tensions in energy clusters, although there have been several studies concerning sustainability in clusters (e.g., Battaglia et al., 2010; Casarotto Filho et al., 2020; Czaplicka-Kotas et al., 2020; McCauley & Stephens, 2012; Tvedt, 2019). In addition, Stephens and Mccauley (2013) claim that the green energy sector challenges the traditional assumptions of the cluster strategy, which is focused on a growth-based economic paradigm, while a sustainable energy transition requires a broader long-term approach that goes beyond economic objectives. On the other hand, coordinating efforts of cluster initiatives may facilitate socio-technical change and link various groups of stakeholders. Sustainability problems are frequently combined. Consequently, they need to be governed in more complex structures that enable joining resources and capabilities beyond the boundaries of enterprises (Niesten et al., 2017), and clusters provide such governance (Berkowitz, 2018). Therefore, studies that address sustainability (paradoxical) tensions may enrich both the clustering and the sustainability literature.

Paradox theory holds that due to the complexity of their environments, currently existing companies are challenged with paradoxical demands stemming from the divergent needs of multiple stakeholders. Internal and external stakeholders generate performing paradoxes (Brix-Asala et al., 2018; De Angelis, 2021) and are of particular significance concerning sustainability. Moreover, Walker et al. (2020) and Ivory and Brooks (2018) affirm that paradox theory recommends concurrently managing all three competing sustainability goals. *Paradoxes* are interrelated, contradictory tensions that coexist and persist over time. As such, they have to be approached simultaneously (Carmine & De Marchi, 2023). They are perceived as a lens through which managers should view organizations and work through them.

The paradox literature lists four groups of tensions (Daddi et al., 2019; Rey-Garcia et al., 2020) that can also be referred to as green energy clusters. First, cluster members may face *performing tensions* since collaborating partners simultaneously pursue certain common interests and their objectives, which may clash with one another and with the goal of the cluster as a whole. Second, since cluster members strive toward sustainable, renewables-based energy, this creates *learning tensions*, i.e., between incremental solutions that accumulate past knowledge and experience and disruptive, breakthrough innovations. Third, cluster enterprises may witness identity tensions due to their differing values, missions, roles, or motivations at the individual, organizational, and cluster levels. Finally, functioning within a complex (cluster) structure may expose its stakeholders to *organizing tensions,* "the divergent demands of empowerment and direction, control and flexibility, and competition and collaboration (...)

both across value aspects and across stakeholder groups" (Rey-Garcia et al., 2020, p. 10).

The theory defies trade-offs among tensions and advises managers to accept paradoxes as natural working conditions that must be handled. Therefore, there are two specific pathways to deal with paradoxes: The organization-wide acknowledgment of their occurrence and their resolution, which involves novelty and creativity. The former implies "a recognition of inconsistencies, conflict, and ambiguity" (Ivory & Brooks, 2018, p. 354) as inherent in today's business reality. Such an attitude benefits from tensions since managers demonstrate a more open, active, and mindful approach while seeking to resolve paradoxes. The latter involves various options, e.g., splitting tensions, their integration, or combining both, as well as usage of organizational meta-capabilities such as collective commitment (language and dialogue, safe experimentation space, reward, and incentive structures) and resource fluidity (supply chain management, organizational design, organizational slack) (Ivory & Brooks, 2018). The paradox lens applied to sustainability management goes beyond a mere integrative view that assumes balancing the environmental, social, and economic goals without prioritizing any of them. In the paradox approach, an attempt is made "to understand the tensions, their nature, and how actors deal with them" (Brix-Asala et al., 2018, p. 424). It requires continuous, cyclical, and iterative responses to satisfy contradictory pressures and to create long-term sustainability performance.

To recap, industrial clusters are mainly concerned with economic growth, which compels favoring economic objectives over social or environmental ones. Nevertheless, they also provide linking and coordination of the activities of cluster companies as well as a complex governance system, which may help mobilize resources and take action to meet compound and contradicting sustainability pressures (Berkowitz, 2018). In particular, such a bridging role is embedded in the idea of cleantech clusters. Hence, we intend to address the following research questions:

RQ1. Are energy clusters aware, and do they acknowledge paradoxical tensions in the sustainability pillars of their member companies?
RQ2. If so, how do energy clusters reconcile paradoxical tensions in the sustainability pillars of their member companies?

### *10.2.2 Green Energy Clusters and Sustainable Value Chain*

Recent years have brought the emergence of cleantech clusters worldwide, with green energy clusters as one of their manifestations (Hessevik, 2022; Kamath et al., 2022; McCauley & Stephens, 2012; Tvedt, 2019). *Cleantech clusters* include enterprises and other entities related to such sectors as "recycling, renewable energy (wind power, solar power, biomass, hydropower, biofuels), information technology, green transportation, green buildings, electric motors, green chemistry, lighting, gray-water, and many other energy-efficient appliances" (Marra et al., 2020, p. 2). These clusters are perceived as a trigger in the socio-technical transition toward a greener economy that promises regional economic growth that is not harmful to the natural environment (McCauley & Stephens, 2012; Tvedt, 2019). They reflect "the techno-optimistic discourse of ecological modernization" of the economy and "a win-win scenario for the economy and the environment" (Tvedt, 2019, p. 54). Tvedt (2019) claims that cleantech clusters, such as knowledge, innovation, and collaboration networks, differ from traditional business clusters, which are more oriented toward production systems and value chains. Moreover, actors involved in cleantech clusters have a clear environmental focus.

*Green energy clusters* are also distinctive from traditional cluster initiatives. McCauley and Stephens (2012) delineate the following features of the former, namely diffuseness in terms of industries that the cluster involves, lack of defining technologies, slower innovation cycle, a complex regulatory system that does not enforce regional competition and the standard setting, dependence on the existing energy regime, and a necessity to induce the demand for sustainable energy products. On the other hand, like other knowledge-based cluster initiatives, they can rely on broad institutional support. Green energy clusters can include entities representing various nodes in different external value chains, and clusters should join partners and enable cooperation along the chain. These clusters' chains consist of companies producing energy resources, offering supply systems, conversion technologies, and energy services (Von Geibler, 2013). Cluster coordinators may mitigate the conflicting interests of members, look for complementary activities among them, and help them establish a sustainable value chain that reconciles the tensions mentioned above.

*Sustainable value chains* efficiently and effectively coordinate the flow of materials, values, and information by all entities and activities along the product life cycle, simultaneously considering various stakeholders' economic, ecological, and social goals (Von Geibler, 2013). Such a chain contains the full range of activities in different sectors that bring products from their formation to their end use and final disposal. It involves removing waste and effectively managing the flow of materials, and it requires inter-sector collaboration (Jnr, 2019).

Several practices identified in the literature facilitate building, maintaining, and operating sustainable value chains (Brix-Asala et al., 2018), which can be applied to energy clusters. They include orientation, continuity, collaboration, risk management, and proactivity. *Orientation* about green energy clusters would assume every entity involved to be directed toward sustainability goals in its value chain. *Continuity* practices predict that the cluster would help to forge a proper structure of partners in value chains, guided by the same value system, through a conscious selection and development of their members. *Collaboration* practices require the cluster to become a platform for enhanced communication, joint development of products, and logistical and technological integration of chain partners. *Risk management* aims to gain legitimacy for the cluster members by establishing standards (e.g., codes of conduct) and adopting certifications or cooperation with pressure groups. Finally, *proactivity* practices look for sustainability performance improvements of the cluster entities, which may further foster sustainable innovations. It also involves the implementation of recycling and reusing within value chains. *Stakeholder management* is another proactivity practice that can be approached from the cluster level. Moreover, the clustering literature stresses the role of clusters in fostering a *learning* process (Brosnan et al., 2016; Rozkwitalska & Lis, 2020) that can later contribute to improvements in sustainable value chains.

To sum up, green energy clusters are a peculiar form of cluster initiatives that have the potential to support sustainable growth and solve paradoxical sustainability tensions. They likely alleviate the clashing interests of cluster companies and bridge complementary activities to form a sustainable value chain that may resolve the paradoxes. By analyzing three cases of renewables-oriented energy clusters, we plan to identify whether our predictions are noticeable in practice. Therefore, we address the following research questions:

RQ3. What is the role of clusters in supporting sustainable value chain creation to solve sustainability tensions in energy clusters?
RQ4. Does a sustainable value chain respond to identified concerns generated by sustainability paradoxes in energy clusters?
RQ5. Do clusters from CEE and WE address paradoxes differently?

## 10.3 Research Methodology and Empirical Findings

### *10.3.1 Sample Selection*

The authors conducted an exploratory qualitative study in selected industrial clusters in the energy sector to identify the central paradoxical tensions in clusters and their consequences for sustainable development cooperation. The activities of the energy clusters are closely related to sustainable development and are aimed at promoting renewable energy sources and raising energy awareness. The energy clusters provide a platform for cooperation, bringing together stakeholders from various sectors, including businesses, the R&D sector, and public administration, to implement joint projects, stimulate innovation, develop environmentally sustainable solutions, and improve business models. In this way, they contribute to forming a sustainable economy and society.

Three renewables-oriented energy clusters operating within the EU have been purposively selected for the research sample. Two clusters are operating in CEE, in Romania (C1) and Hungary (C2), and third in the WE, in Germany (C3). The choice of European countries is associated with well-developed cluster-based policies, both at the EU and national and regional levels. It enables, on the one hand, the observation of the differences between clusters with very similar profiles and, on the other hand, the partial leveling out of the cultural context. The studied clusters have many characteristics in common – they were founded at a similar time (they have been operating in the market for more than 10 years), have a similar number of members (between 70 and 90), also have a quality certificate awarded to clusters by the European Cluster Excellence Initiative ECEI (C1 – Silver Label, C2 – Gold Label, C3 – Bronze Label). However, some differences became apparent in how clusters were launched and their territorial scope of activity (C1 and C2 are bottom-up clusters with national scope, while C3 is a top-down one with intraregional reach).

### *10.3.2 Data Collection Methods*

The survey was carried out in three stages: 2017, 2020, and 2022. At each stage, the authors adopted the perspective of cluster coordinators since they should have had the most complete knowledge of cluster operations (Figure 10.1).

Stages 1 and 2 aimed to learn the studied clusters' specifics. They were based on the same close-ended questionnaire interview. Both stages were conducted with three cluster coordinators (one from each cluster). The thematic blocks included in the interview concerned general information on clusters, the development of cooperation, the role of the cluster and the goals it achieved, and the activities of cluster members. In addition, Stage 1 included a group interview with representatives of clusters C1 and C3, represented by one coordinator, while two other coordinators were from C2. Interview subjects focused on the collaboration within these clusters, primarily in the context of their involvement in building value chains, with the participation of internal and external stakeholders. In Stage 3, in-depth interviews were conducted with three cluster coordinators. The questions in the interview scenario focused on cluster cooperation and activity, mainly regarding sustainable development and green transformation. A document analysis was also done in each stage to complement the interviews. The authors analyzed available publications on the studied clusters and online resources (e.g., private websites and social media).

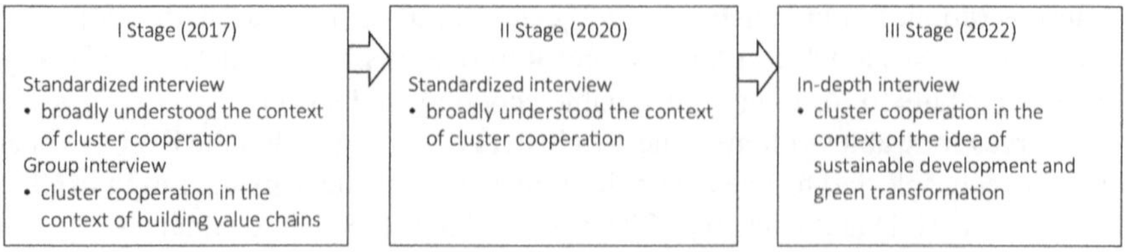


*Figure 10.1* Stages of the Research Process.

The applied methodology enabled us to compare the dynamics of the changes made in the time segments adopted between the clusters and within a given cluster.

### *10.3.3 Analytical Procedure*

The study adopted a qualitative content analysis (Saldana, 2021). The data was grouped according to the similarities and dissimilarities noted. Comparisons were made within each cluster by considering the three measurement moments and between the three cases analyzed. This approach enabled the identification of different types of paradoxical tensions in the clusters (Table 10.1).

Two paradoxical tensions, performing and organizing tensions, were revealed around two identified categories that described the specifics of the cluster structure regarding goals and links between cluster members. The authors did not observe identity and learning tensions directly but only as a derivative of the previously mentioned tensions. Nevertheless, they were found to co-occur in the clusters. They focus on members' identification with the cluster and access to knowledge in the cluster. Opposing subcategories were identified within the four categories to illustrate the emerging tensions.

All paradoxical tensions require special care by cluster coordinators, so it is important to identify and manage them appropriately. Practices were highlighted for all paradoxical tensions, reflecting how the clusters dealt with them. In addition, the study focuses on the sustainability pillars, indicating which of the paradoxical tensions and practices are related to each pillar. The applied practices can strengthen cooperation toward achieving various sustainability goals related to the economic, social, and environmental pillars.

## 10.4 Paradoxical Tensions

The first revealed *performing tensions* focused on the nature of the goals uniting the entities associated with the clusters. They grouped entities that consciously and voluntarily joined them to achieve individual goals of their parent companies or collective goals usually aimed at improving external and internal conditions for business. The research showed that *identity tension* occurred for members pursuing common goals, i.e., identification with the cluster was more robust than for members focused on achieving individual goals. Performing and identity tensions were seen in every analyzed cluster. Coordinators admitted that companies' primary motivation to join clusters was to achieve particularistic goals, expressed most often economically. Nevertheless, gradually, in each cluster, a group of members emerged committed to goals common to the cluster and the entire sector or region.

The commonality of goals and the high identification of members within the cluster were most evident in C1, whose coordinator emphasized the common motivation linking cluster companies to develop innovative solutions. At the

*Table 10.1* Paradoxical Tensions Identified in the Studied Clusters

| *Paradoxical Tensions* | *Main Category* | *Subcategories* | *Practices* | *Sustainability Pillars* |
|---|---|---|---|---|
| Performing tensions | The character of the goals of the cluster members | Individual goals<br>Common goals | Orientation<br>Continuity<br>Collaboration<br>Risk management<br>Proactivity<br>Stakeholder management<br>Learning support | Economic<br>Environmental<br>Social |
| Organizing tensions | The character of links between cluster members | Competition<br>Cooperation | | |
| Identity tensions | Identification with the cluster | Poor<br>Medium or strong | | |
| Learning tensions | Access to knowledge | Poor<br>Medium or high | | |

opposite extreme was C2, in which companies were mainly oriented towards pursuing their own goals, thus revealing less of their identification with the entire cluster. C3, on the other hand, represented an intermediate position. The coordinator was aware of the innate, individual orientation of the cluster companies, but at the same time, noted the common motivations and willingness of the companies to combine their interests (and thus their goals) by engaging in joint cluster activities, which strengthened their cluster identification (Table 10.2).

Further identified paradoxical tensions emerged in the *organizing dimension* and resulted from the nature of links between cluster members. Indeed, companies in the studied clusters acted as cooperators and competitors. There were vertical relationships between cluster companies along the value chain, which were conducive to the development of cooperation, and horizontal relationships between companies located at the same stage of the chain, which were more difficult due to the conflict of interest occurring between competing companies.

The study did not reveal tensions between incremental and breakthrough innovations. It noted, however, that collaborative relationships established between cluster members facilitated access to knowledge and information, which was associated with *learning tensions*. Collaborative active members were more able to participate in knowledge and information flows within the cluster, which enhanced their cognitive potential.

The authors observed interesting differences between the clusters concerning cooperative relationships. C1 manifested the highest cooperative approach toward developing joint solutions based on members' complementary resources,

*Table 10.2* Performing and Identity Tensions – Selected Quotes

| *Paradoxical Tensions* | *Selected Quotes* |
|---|---|
| Common goals/strong identification with the cluster | "They are similar in their motivations – they want to work out common solutions." (C1) |
| In between/medium identification with the cluster | "Of course, most firms or even everybody has first individual goals. I think from my perspective, it is also clear. Then, we have a few firms thinking outside the box and relating more to the regional context." (C3) |
| | "When you have a common goal, and it comes to the details – how to implement this one, of course, there will be conflicts because everybody wants a piece of the cake. Funds and projects gather people; it's a nice issue. Everybody wants to be a part of it." (C3) |
| Individual goals/poor identification with the cluster | "Cluster members are not very open to cooperating, so they would like to achieve their goals, just alone – individual goals. They have their own goals and don't want to share them. They don't want to support each other." (C2) |

*Table 10.3* Organizing and Learning Tensions – Selected Quotes

| *Paradoxical Tensions* | *Selected Quotes* |
|---|---|
| Cooperation/great access to knowledge | "I cannot see any conflict regarding cooperation. They are willing to work together to provide this whole solution. It's common for them to cooperate and give a solution to a customer." (C1)<br>"I don't see any competitors, so I see them complementing each other. They are not competing because the market is very open, very large, everyone has their share of the market." (C1) |
| Coopetition/medium access to knowledge | "Within vertical relationships, at the moment, we are in the process of building up our bioeconomy cluster or a subdivision." (C3)<br>"In our cluster, there is a mix of competitors and collaborators. We have a cluster, so we have vertical and horizontal structures. Within the vertical structure, we have firms from suppliers to end producers or consumers. Moreover, within the horizontal structure, we also have competitors." (C3)<br>"For example, we have three IT companies related to the energy management field. So they compete with each other and will hardly cooperate. We have an energy supply company. Then, we have engineering service providers. We have the universities, other research institutions, and our network. If they have one project, nobody is competing with each other because everybody is the right stakeholder for this project, and therefore, they come together." (C3) |
| Competition/poor access to knowledge | "They are very unwilling to cooperate. It's because of a lack of trust. It's started from our history." (C2)<br>"If the government wants to support and push them to cooperate, they have their solution because they must put them in the consortium. They need to cooperate because they can achieve and win the funds together. I think that that could be one solution for it." (C2) |

including shared knowledge. Members of C2 appeared to be the least open to cooperation, which the coordinator explained by cultural context and low levels of trust that inhibited knowledge flows. The middle position was occupied by C3, where coopetition relationships developed, allowing cooperating entities to access information and knowledge reserved for trusted partners (Table 10.3).

## 10.5 Practices Relieving Paradoxical Tensions

The coordinators were partially aware of the paradoxical tensions and chose a path to alleviating them through specific practices. At the forefront was the *collaboration* practice related to creating conditions for joint efforts to achieve sustainability goals, which allowed the mitigation of tensions in all the highlighted dimensions. Two other practices were closely related to it: *Orientation* and *continuity*. The orientation practice reinforced the commitment of the clusters and their members to activities embedded in various areas of sustainable development, especially in the context of developing integrated value chains. It mitigated performing and identity tensions by redefining goals and values and promoting the commonality of interests among cluster companies. Orientation practices associated with value chain cooperation offset organizing and learning tensions, prompting cluster companies to adopt a cooperative (rather than competitive) approach, which also translated favorably into knowledge-sharing processes. In turn, continuity practices were related to the appropriate selection of actors in the value chain and other identified forms of cluster cooperation (e.g., projects, cooperation for developing favorable conditions for industry development). Different types of paradoxical tensions were addressed with criteria for grouping companies for cooperation. To counter performing tension, companies were grouped based on the revealed goals and interests, identity tensions were handled with a clear division of roles in the group, organizing tensions required grouping companies based on the complementarity of resources, and learning tensions were overcome by creating groups based on cognitive potential – similarity and level of competence.

The following two practices – *risk* and *stakeholder management* – refer to unification processes between cooperating cluster companies and activities aimed at creating favorable conditions for the industry and the region where the clusters and their affiliated companies operate. This mainly offset the paradoxical tensions in the performing and identity dimensions. Unification was linked to establishing common standards and jointly implementing selected processes. In contrast, industry development activities strengthened integration more broadly, bringing together cooperating entities around goals common to the entire industry. At the same time, it compensated for paradoxical tensions in the organizing and learning dimensions, creating new incentives for greater cooperation and mutual learning.

Finally, interrelated *proactivity* and *learning support* practices became apparent in the clusters through their drive to develop innovative solutions. This relieved organizing tensions, forcing companies to work more collaboratively within the value chain and in project activities. At the same time, it translated into a reduction in learning tensions due to the effects of demonstrations, group learning, and joint knowledge creation.

The following section discusses specific activities that fit into the abovementioned practices, applied by each cluster (paradoxical tensions – practices used).

### *10.5.1 Collaboration, Orientation, and Continuity Practices*

The clusters supported the creation and development of value chains composed of the diverse competencies of their members based on local resources. They also built environmental awareness among the public by promoting and creating demand for green products. The composition of value chains was assisted by appropriately selected sets of competencies of cluster companies, which enabled the development of cooperation based on complementarity. This is because the inclusion in the cluster structure of a wide range of entities with different development potentials gives excellent flexibility in shaping the specifics of cooperative ties within the cluster. The clusters established appropriate barriers to entry for new members. They analyzed the level of resources and competencies of members so that, on this basis, they could accurately combine them according to a certain similarity to increase the effectiveness of role-playing activities and the creation of value chains. All three clusters had smaller subgroups of companies involved in value chain cooperation.

The activities of C1 are closely related to the potential for biomass development in the region, which includes all the significant links necessary for biomass production, including trees and woody plants, energy crop plantations, industrial and urban wood waste, and boiler producers, including end users (farmers, industrial plants). One of the most important goals of C1 is fostering cooperation in the value chain, which puts a premium on developing innovative solid biomass solutions and developing links along the biomass value chain, including initiating business-to-business and R&D cooperation, consulting, attracting new businesses in the cluster, and generating new start-ups. The value chain created in C1 includes energy willow crops, green waste management, industrial waste management, and developing the market for the sustainable use of biomass for energy purposes. This involves developing logistics, gathering best practices, building successful public-private partnerships, and raising awareness among communities and decision-makers about the socioeconomic impact of biomass. Thanks to the cooperation of various groups of actors, the solid biomass value chain operating in C1 is a complex but well-integrated system. The primary input in this value chain is energy willow, green waste, wood waste (feedstock), a biomass-based heating system, and a boiler.

In contrast, the final product of the chain is biomass-based thermal energy. The main functions in the value chain that lead to the final product are energy willow cultivation, harvesting, and processing, green waste collection and wood residue collection, machinery component production, integration, and entering the market. The last links are marketing and sales and after-sales service. The chain also includes organizations providing business and technical consulting and training. Moreover, C1 leads projects linked to the energy willow cultivators' value chain concept, which are aimed at creating and developing business models for the use of biomass for sustainable local economic development and encouraging the development of local eco-businesses along the biomass value chain. C1 is also involved in fostering the concept of Bioenergy Villages, as part of the BioVill project, which promotes and supports regional/communal bioenergy concepts.

The goal of C2 was to develop cooperation between related parties in building value chains and developing common product paths. Two key value chains are being developed in C2. The first chain relates to developing renewable energy and energy efficiency services for the construction industry. The manufacturers of solar thermal, solar panels, inverters, heat pumps, and energy-efficient lighting equipment, as well as commercial consulting companies (building energy consultants, energy auditing, etc.), are at the beginning of the chain. The last link in the chain is offering final products and services related to the implementation of solar systems and heat pumps, as well as companies offering energy consulting and building energy performance measurement services. The chain also includes entities offering support services involving logistics and sales, finance, and promotion. The second value chain processes organic hemp products for the construction industry. Hemp used in the construction industry allows buildings to achieve higher energy efficiency and reduce costs. The beginning of the value chain includes industrial hemp producers, agricultural machinery and equipment manufacturers, and hemp processors. Processed hemp as an intermediate product is sent to manufacturing companies producing final products (such as hemp bricks and fiber). Packaging and distribution companies play an essential role in supplying final products. Companies and stores that sell construction materials market the final products. Moreover, the chain distinguishes the entities implementing support activities, including lobbyists, institutions creating legislation, suppliers, traders, exporters, and construction companies.

In turn, two value chains were developed in C3: Smart mobility and smart infrastructure. C3 promoted intersectoral cooperation, unleashing great innovative potential. R&D institutions contributed significantly to developing these chains, which are part of designed network systems and within which they implemented joint innovation projects. In each cluster, the design of chains and the development of cooperation between their various links required regular meetings of key stakeholders, through which students had opportunities to get to know each other and identify complementary competencies. Training sessions and events on energy transition issues were also implemented, during which knowledge, experiences, and good practices were transferred.

### *10.5.2 Risk and Stakeholder Management Practices*

Risk and stakeholder management practices were applied to the interaction of the clusters with public authorities to create favorable solutions for the development of the energy industry. This was done by engaging companies in legislative work, lobbying, and promoting green solutions and initiatives. Since the problems and challenges member companies face are common to the entire industry, the clusters acted as exponents of the interests of the energy sector. Given the cluster and cluster companies, the development of the energy sector can bring many positive effects in terms of environmental protection and regional and socioeconomic development. This involved better use of the region's natural resources, the development of the local economy, and higher energy efficiency and savings. Thus, the effects of the activities developed by the clusters were not limited to committed members but also spread to passive members and, even more broadly – to society and the economy.

This was particularly evident in C1, which supported public authorities in co-shaping policies and strategies for regional development and smart specialization strategy. C1 members were involved in promoting regional economic development and raising environmental awareness, especially in the field of renewable energy, including preparing promotional campaigns on renewable energy sources. C1 member companies jointly launched a research center for renewable energy sources and created the Consortium of Clusters Transylvania. C1 members also participated in numerous projects dedicated to promoting the use of biomass (promotion of energy willow cultivation technology as an alternative source of clean energy project in Romania), through which they acquired new knowledge, experience, and business contacts.

C3 similarly pursued its strategic goals related to the development of the industry and the region. The coordinator and the most committed members supported the public authorities in shaping industrial and innovation policies while representing the interests of the entire energy industry in various political and economic bodies. As C3 is embedded in the city's structures, it has actively participated in activities to improve the public sector's capacity to plan territorial low-carbon strategies by EU and national legislation. It also supported activities related to the development of e-mobility, raising awareness among residents about sustainable and environmentally friendly means of transportation. C3 members engaged in the promotion and development of the smart infrastructure ecosystem.

The second area was to improve the quality of education in the region and strengthen the development of the regional skills resource base for the energy industry. The coordinators and the most active members were involved in improving curricula, organizing extracurricular activities (training, vocational courses, apprenticeships), and promoting learning through the development of various forms of extracurricular education for children and young people, working with schools at different levels of education from vocational to post-doctoral education. As in the first area, benefits from the developed results went beyond the most active members because the actions were aimed at aligning the educational process with the needs of the entire regional economy and energy sector. In this way, the clusters represented the interests of employers in the region, who expect graduates to have competencies that closely matches their current needs.

C1 was very active in this area. The goal of improving the quality of education for the energy industry is enshrined in the cluster's strategy, and one of the working groups operating within the cluster focused on education, training, and human resource development. With the support of its members, C1 offered numerous training courses, study courses, and curricula on biomass application. Cluster companies were involved in improving curricula for vocational training and organizing training for students and university teachers. The cluster participated as a partner in projects aimed at developing education systems. One of these was a project supporting European cooperation to ensure a highly skilled and innovative workforce across the bioenergy value chain. The project's goal was to create new curricula at the postgraduate level in key bioenergy disciplines. The cluster was also a consortium partner in an international, interdisciplinary, cross-sector project focused on enhancing collective research excellence and creating new postgraduate training in key disciplines supporting bioenergy. C2, an important partner for public authorities in developing the labor market, was also very active in the discussed area. The cluster was involved in raising the quality of education through the development of the continuing education system, vocational training, and the higher education level. The cluster's activities included developing training programs and organizing internships, lectures, vocational training, and courses. Together with regional universities, the cluster's companies engaged in energy education projects to develop education in cooperation with businesses. In addition, in partnership with other regional clusters, the cluster initiated the development of a special training system including energy consulting and design, and an internship program for students.

### *10.5.3 Other Proactivity Practices*

To develop cluster cooperation, the coordinators used various means of proactivity and exchange of information and knowledge: They organized meetings and various business events (including conferences, trade missions, and study tours), to which members, as well as entities from outside the cluster, were invited. The clusters created records of members' resources as competency maps to identify potential collaborators and entities with matching needs. Moreover, to connect members around common activity areas, the clusters built smaller subsets (e.g., task forces), facilitating integration at the process level. In the clusters, some processes were carried out jointly, including market activities related to market research and analysis, marketing activities, and logistical processes (e.g., a joint supplier program, group purchasing, or joint distribution channels).

In addition, cluster members participated in joint research, innovation, and business projects. They were supported by coordinators involved at all stages of the project life cycle (from sourcing funding to forming project teams to project management). Some of these projects were carried out within clusters based on the competencies of cluster members. In contrast, some other projects were run in cooperation with external entities, such as other clusters from home and abroad. All clusters participated in international projects to develop transnational networks and share knowledge and best practices. The coordinators also supported them in sourcing and executing external contracts and developing and marketing joint offerings (seeking project financing, tracking tender opportunities, monitoring public procurement, preparing bids, energy efficiency, and renewable energy services).

## 10.6 Pillars of Sustainable Development

Clusters are economic structures that primarily seek to satisfy their members' economic goals, and the study confirmed this. The coordinators of all three clusters unanimously agreed that the economic pillar had primacy for their companies. Therefore, the objectives of the clusters were primarily focused on supporting the economic potential of cluster enterprises, increasing their production capacity, and project activity. Ultimately, this was to lead to an increase in employment, domestic sales, and exports, and consequently strengthen the competitiveness of the regional economy. Two other pillars – environmental and social – which were particularly emphasized in C1 and C3, were much lower on the priority list, and, as the coordinators noted, the activity of companies in these areas was still economically motivated (Table 10.4).

Nevertheless, the clusters demonstrated proactivity in the environmental area due to their business profiles and that of their affiliated companies, as the energy industry is closely linked to the environment, climate, and green economy efforts. The direction of the development of the clusters is in line with the EU's energy strategy, which seeks to ensure energy security and sustainable development by providing the necessary energy resources, increasing energy efficiency, and promoting energy production based on renewable sources.

The development of cooperation within the environmental pillar was associated with all identified practices. The coordinators and members of the clusters developed a system of partnerships around common problems in the renewable energy industry, as well as cooperation with various stakeholder groups, including R&D institutions and universities, public authorities, and other clusters. This was closely related to collaboration, risk, and stakeholder management practices. An example is the COSMENERG project promoting the international development of energy cluster cooperation, in which all the surveyed clusters participated, indicating high proactivity and related learning support practices.

C1's activities aim to support the formation of a sustainable economy and society (sustainability, social justice, local economic development) based on the use of clean energy. The research showed that C1 members worked together to innovate the use of solid biomass by developing the biomass value chain (strong orientation and collaboration). A clear link to continuity practices can also be seen here; many of these projects were carried out by carefully selected teams, in co-partnership with R&D institutions, universities, and public authorities. As part of its internationalization strategy, C1 also collaborated with other clusters on biomass issues, sharing ideas, experiences, and good practices (link to learning support practices).

*Table 10.4* Sustainable Development Pillars – Selected Quotes

| *Sustainable Development Pillars* | *Selected Quotes* |
|---|---|
| Economic pillar | "I believe that the economic aspect is the most important aspect for companies. I'm skeptical about SMEs because they are not sufficiently aware of environmental issues. Moreover, I see they are focused on the economic part, economic goals." (C1)<br>"Our main focus is the economic dimension, of course. So the main focus is to bring economic impulses for our companies here." (C3)<br>"All three pillars are important. For our companies, the first is economic reasons; then we have environmental reasons, and then social reasons. Because all companies are doing their business or managing their business just for the profit." (C2) |
| Environmental pillar | "From the perspective of our cluster, the most relevant is the environmental pillar. I think the companies should be more environmentally conscious and more ecological. Probably they don't have enough information or interest." (C1)<br>"We are covering a lot of environmental topics in our cluster. We have four subdivisions. One is like new energy systems focusing on energy or new energy technology. The other ones are focusing on smart mobility. The third one is more [related] to urban bioeconomy that's more about regional value chains of bio-based products, and the fourth one would be the topic of natural resources." (C3)<br>"The environmental pillar became more important because electricity and gas became more expensive. So, it just became important for economic reasons. The companies want to save more profits. Therefore, they want to develop their factories and business parks following the green transition. This should not be such a motivation, but this is the reality." (C2) |
| Social pillar | "The social aspect is equally important as the environmental topic – how to involve local communities, how to involve local companies, how to find local solutions to local problems." (C1)<br>"The social dimension in our cluster is important. We were isolated 11 years ago from the Department for Economic Development in the city. In Germany, all clusters started as a federal initiative. They introduced this cluster concept and started creating a city cluster strategy." (C3) |

The main areas of activity of C2 concern energy, environmental protection, and the building industry. The cluster was established to support the renewable energy sector economically and socially, promote better use of green energy, improve business processes, and implement innovative projects (based on collaborative practices). C2's activities are developing in two areas: Renewable energy carriers and the development of energy-efficient and sustainable solutions. Within the first area, activities and projects are being undertaken to support the industrial cultivation, use, and processing of hemp. Among other things, the launch of a green incubator and the start of a training center to promote and develop innovative green energy (learning support practices) are being planned. The second area of cluster activity focuses on developing and introducing energy-efficient technological solutions to reduce carbon emissions in construction and the amount of energy used to produce raw materials based on cooperation between members (proactivity practices).

C3's activities are part of the city's cluster and innovation strategy, which focuses on selected economic sectors related to energy and environmental technologies, among others. How the cluster operates reflects the nature of continuity practices well. This is because the cluster acts as a catalyzing institution, creating networks of connected entities with specific competencies in energy transformation along value chains. The study found that solid teams of cluster members were formed in C3, each with a different area of focus. Seven thematic lines were developed within C3 and were linked to environmental issues: Bioeconomy (development of a platform for monitoring the smart use of bioenergy), smart mobility, environment (with emphasis on water and waste management), dealers and service providers (energy trading), new energy systems, educational qualifications, and wastewater.

## 10.7 Discussion and Conclusion

### *10.7.1 Discussion of Findings*

Our study has revealed that the energy clusters are partially aware of and acknowledge the sustainability paradoxes of their member companies. They bridge the economic interests of various partners, enabling the building of a sustainable value chain that facilitates managing tensions. Moreover, the energy clusters are a platform to influence the social environment and cultivate the end-user market for green energy. Consequently, they can solve the performing paradoxes of their participants.

The study indicated that the energy clusters alleviate paradoxical tensions through specific practices in four highlighted areas (performing, identity, organizing, and learning). This positively affects the commonality of goals and interests, increases identification with the cluster, the development of various forms of cooperation (especially building shared value chains), and access to knowledge and information. Consequently, this supports achieving sustainability goals in the economic pillar and other dimensions, especially the environmental ones (Figure 10.2).

The identified interconnection between paradoxical tensions, practices, and sustainable development pillars is common to the energy clusters and universal to this sector. We found no significant differences in clusters from CEE (C1 and C2) versus WE (C3). This is especially true for prioritizing the various dimensions of sustainability. For all the clusters surveyed, the economic pillar was the most important, followed by the environmental and social pillars.

The differences between the clusters that emerged in the study are due to the peculiarities of the clusters themselves rather than their geographic location or cultural background. For example, regarding performing and identity tensions, commonality of goals and high identification of members with the cluster were most evident in C1 and least in C2, and both clusters operate in CEE. We observed a similar situation regarding organizing and learning tensions. C1 members showed the most incredible commitment to developing cooperation based on shared knowledge, while C2 members showed the lowest. In either case, C3, representing WE, occupied the middle position.

Even more minor differences between clusters (regardless of their location in CEE or WE) were noted regarding practices. The three clusters, regardless of location, undertook very similar collaboration, orientation, and continuity practices. All three supported the creation and development of value chains, woven from the complementary resources of member companies, properly selected based on established barriers to entry into the cluster. The same was true for risk and

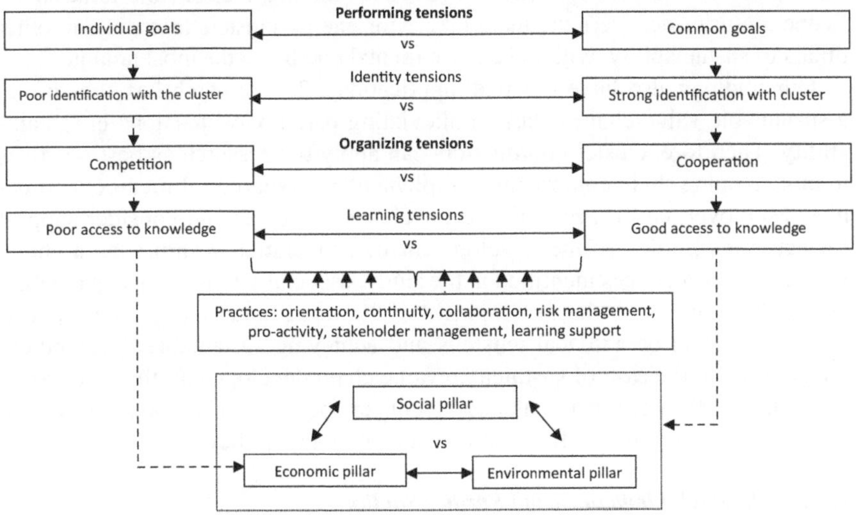


*Figure 10.2* The Interconnection of Paradoxical Tensions, Practices, and Sustainable Development Pillars.

stakeholder management practices. The above practices were reflected through the interactions of the clusters and their members with public authorities to create favorable solutions for the development of the energy sector (which was especially observed in C1 from CEE and C3 from WE) and the commitment to improve the quality of education in the region and strengthen the development of the regional skills resource base for the energy sector (most evident in C1 and C2 from CEE).

### *10.7.2 Research Contributions and Implications*

There is a rich literature describing some of the problems of cluster functioning, such as cooperation-competition, identity-identification, commonality of goals and interests, knowledge sharing, and learning (e.g., Lis & Lis, 2021). However, they are treated separately and studied in different contexts. In this research, these issues have been examined in parallel to sustainable development. In this way, the study enriches the underdeveloped literature on energy clusters and paradoxical tensions in corporate sustainability. The authors have applied the interorganizational perspective of the management discipline to the study of sustainability in the context of energy clusters. They have documented the sources of tensions identified in the literature and the various practices used by clusters to resolve them. The research has shown that awareness and recognition of paradoxes in energy clusters can help manage them, while a sustainable value chain is an effective way to resolve paradoxes, and clusters support it mainly through the complementarity of their members. The study has found two central paradoxes in energy cluster operations: Performing and organizing tensions (manifested as cooperation versus competition) and all five practices aimed at building a sustainable value chain. Economic priorities were the main driver for energy clusters to engage in other pillars of sustainability, with the environmental one being the most notable.

Our findings also have practical applications. The research has shown that a sustainable value chain is key to alleviating paradoxical tensions in sustainability. Therefore, cluster coordinators can apply our research as best practices to build a value chain comprising complementary resources of member companies. Moreover, entities responsible for cluster policy should consider support for activities leading to the development of cooperation within such a chain, whereas other practices identified in the study, especially those aimed at creating favorable solutions for the development of the energy industry, can be supportive for relieving paradoxical tensions and achieving sustainable development goals. Also, in the case of sustainable value chain development, this may prove relevant to both coordinators managing cluster cooperation and policymakers at various levels responsible for shaping socioeconomic policy.

### *10.7.3 Research Limitations and Further Studies*

The study has mainly highlighted the sustainable value chain to counter paradoxes, while other methods, such as meta-capabilities, have been omitted from the coordinators' accounts. Future research may expand on this. Similarly, based on the interviews, the authors have identified mainly two basic tensions (performing and organizing), with the identity and learning tensions needing to be sufficiently addressed, and this may be the subject of further research. The study discusses organizing tension as an opposition between cooperation and competition. At the same time, its other features have not been documented, and other researchers may try to develop this path. The research was conducted on a small sample of clusters purposively selected from different countries, but at three points in time, it was verified in document analysis. Future research should confirm the observation with other cluster stakeholders and in other energy clusters to overcome the subjectivity of this study. Finally, our study focuses on clusters operating in the energy industry. However, carrying out similar studies in other energy-related cluster structures, such as energy cooperatives, is worthwhile.

## Note

1 A search of the Scopus database with the keyword "energy clusters" in the article title, abstract, and keywords conducted on July 31, 2024, showed that just a few were linked to the subject area of Business, Management, and Accounting.

## References

Altenburg, T., & Vrolijk, K. (2020). Greening structural transformation: What role for industrial hubs? In A. Oqubay & J. Y. Lin (Eds.), *The Oxford Handbook of Industrial Hubs and Economic Development* (p. 0). Oxford: Oxford University Press. https://doi.org/10.1093/oxfordhb/9780198850434.013.25

Battaglia, M., Bianchi, L., Frey, M., & Iraldo, F. (2010). An innovative model to promote CSR among SMEs operating in industrial clusters: Evidence from an EU project. *Corporate Social Responsibility and Environmental Management, 17*(3), 133–141. https://doi.org/10.1002/csr.224

Berkowitz, H. (2018). Meta-organizing firms' capabilities for sustainable innovation: A conceptual framework. *Journal of Cleaner Production, 175*, 420–430. https://doi.org/10.1016/j.jclepro.2017.12.028

Brix-Asala, C., Geisbüsch, A. K., Sauer, P. C., Schöpflin, P., & Zehendner, A. (2018). Sustainability tensions in supply chains: A case study of paradoxes and their management. *Sustainability (Switzerland), 10*(2). https://doi.org/10.3390/su10020424

Brosnan, S., Doyle, E., & O'Connor, S. (2016). From Marshall's Triad to Porter's Diamond: Added value? *Competitiveness Review, 26*(5), 500–516. https://doi.org/10.1108/CR-05-2015-0037

Carmine, S., & De Marchi, V. (2023). Reviewing paradox theory in corporate sustainability toward a systems perspective. *Journal of Business Ethics, 184*(1), 139–158. https://doi.org/10.1007/s10551-022-05112-2

Casarotto Filho, N., Santa Catarina, A., Ferasso, M., & Cunha, I. J. (2020). Becoming an eco-innovative industrial cluster through de-regionalization: Lessons from Italian and Brazilian clusters. *Latin American Business Review, 0*(0), 1–31. https://doi.org/10.1080/10978526.2020.1788392

Czaplicka-Kotas, A., Kulczycka, J., & Iwaszczuk, N. (2020). Energy clusters as a new urban symbiosis concept for increasing renewable energy production - a case study of Zakopane city. *Sustainability (Switzerland)*, *12*(14), 5634. https://doi.org/10.3390/su12145634

Daddi, T., Ceglia, D., Bianchi, G., & de Barcellos, M. D. (2019). Paradoxical tensions and corporate sustainability: A focus on circular economy business cases. *Corporate Social Responsibility and Environmental Management*, *26*(4), 770–780. https://doi.org/10.1002/csr.1719

De Angelis, R. (2021). Circular economy and paradox theory: A business model perspective. *Journal of Cleaner Production*, *285*, 124823. https://doi.org/10.1016/j.jclepro.2020.124823

Hessevik, A. (2022). Green shipping networks as drivers of decarbonization in offshore shipping companies. *Maritime Transport Research*, *3*(January), 100053. https://doi.org/10.1016/j.martra.2022.100053

Ivory, S. B., & Brooks, S. B. (2018). Managing corporate sustainability with a paradoxical lens: Lessons from strategic agility. *Journal of Business Ethics*, *148*(2), 347–361. https://doi.org/10.1007/s10551-017-3583-6

Jnr, B. A. (2019). Sustainable value chain practice adoption to improve strategic environmentalism in ICT-based industries. *Journal of Global Operations and Strategic Sourcing*, *12*(3), 380–409. https://doi.org/10.1108/JGOSS-06-2018-0022

Kajikawa, Y., Tacoa, F., & Yamaguchi, K. (2014). Sustainability science: The changing landscape of sustainability research. *Sustainability Science*, *9*(4), 431–438. https://doi.org/10.1007/s11625-014-0244-x

Kamath, R., Sun, Z., & Hermans, F. (2022). Policy instruments for green-growth of clusters: Implications from an agent-based model. *Environmental Innovation and Societal Transitions*, *43*(March), 257–269. https://doi.org/10.1016/j.eist.2022.04.003

Koliousis, I. G., Papadimitriou, S., Riza, E., Stavroulakis, P. J., & Tsioumas, V. (2018). Scarcity theory and maritime clusters: From paradox to modelling. *Marine Policy*, *93*(April), 40–46. https://doi.org/10.1016/j.marpol.2018.03.029

Lis, A. M., & Lis, A. (2021). *The cluster organization: Analyzing the development of cooperative relationships*. New York: Routledge.

Maher, R., Maher, M., McAlpine, C. A., Mann, S., & Seabrook, L. (2018). Overcoming barriers to sustainability by combining conceptual, visual, and networking systems. *Sustainability Science*, *13*(5), 1357–1373. https://doi.org/10.1007/s11625-018-0576-z

Marra, A., Carlei, V., & Baldassari, C. (2020). Exploring networks of proximity for partner selection, firms' collaboration and knowledge exchange. The case of cleantech industry. *Business Strategy and the Environment*, *29*(3), 1034–1044. https://doi.org/10.1002/bse.2415

McCauley, S. M., & Stephens, J. C. (2012). Green energy clusters and socio-technical transitions: Analysis of a sustainable energy cluster for regional economic development in Central Massachusetts, USA. *Sustainability Science*, *7*(2), 213–225. https://doi.org/10.1007/s11625-012-0164-6

Mousavi, S., Bossink, B., & van Vliet, M. (2018). Dynamic capabilities and organizational routines for managing innovation towards sustainability. *Journal of Cleaner Production*, *203*, 224–239. https://doi.org/10.1016/j.jclepro.2018.08.215

Niesten, E., Jolink, A., Lopes de Sousa Jabbour, A. B., Chappin, M., & Lozano, R. (2017). Sustainable collaboration: The impact of governance and institutions on sustainable performance. *Journal of Cleaner Production, 155*(2017), 1–6. https://doi.org/10.1016/j.jclepro.2016.12.085

Rey-Garcia, M., Mato-Santiso, V., & Felgueiras, A. (2020). Transitioning collaborative cross-sector business models for sustainability innovation: Multilevel tension management as a dynamic capability. *Business and Society, 60*(5), 1132–1173. https://doi.org/10.1177/0007650320949822

Rozkwitalska, M., & Lis, A. (2020). Social learning in cluster initiatives. *Competitiveness Review, 32*(1), 8–34. https://doi.org/10.1108/CR-10-2019-0099

Saldana, J. (2021). *The Coding Manual for Qualitative Researchers* (4th ed.). SAGE Publications Ltd.

Stephens, J. C., & Mccauley, S. M. (2013). Clusters in transition: Analysis of a sustainable energy- cluster initiative. In M. J. Cohen, H. Szejnwald Brown, & P. J. Vergragt (Eds.), *Innovations in Sustainable Consumption New Economics, Socio-technical Transitions and Social Practices* (pp. 179–206). Cheltenham: Edward Elgar Publishing.

Tvedt, H. L. (2019). The formation and structure of cleantech clusters: Insights from San Diego, Dublin, and Graz. *Norsk Geografisk Tidsskrift, 73*(1), 53–64. https://doi.org/10.1080/00291951.2019.1568295

Von Geibler, J. (2013). Market-based governance for sustainability in value chains: Conditions for successful standard setting in the palm oil sector. *Journal of Cleaner Production, 56*, 39–53. https://doi.org/10.1016/j.jclepro.2012.08.027

Walker, K., Yu, X., & Zhang, Z. (2020). All for one or all for three: Empirical evidence of paradox theory in the triple-bottom-line. *Journal of Cleaner Production, 275*, 122881. https://doi.org/10.1016/j.jclepro.2020.122881

# 11 Energy Transition through the Energy-based Industrial Clusters

## Paradoxes and Their Solutions

*Chen Xiu*

### 11.1 Introduction

The 2015 Paris Climate Conference established the goal of keeping the global average temperature increase within 2 degrees Celsius above pre-industrial levels, with efforts to limit the increase to 1.5 degrees Celsius. This marked a new phase in global efforts to address climate change. By the second quarter of 2023, the European Union (EU) had reduced its economy's greenhouse gas emissions by 5.3% compared to the same quarter in 2022, totaling 821 million tons of $CO_2$-equivalents. The proportion of renewable energy sources in EU energy consumption had risen from 12.5% in 2010 to 21.8% in 2021. This increase played a crucial role in energy conservation and emissions reduction. Therefore, coordinating the development strategies among multiple energy sources is essential to ensure the gradual transition from traditional energy sources to renewable energy (Xiu & Lis, 2024). The emergence of multi-energy systems integration (MESI) partially addresses this challenge (Ngwaka et al., 2023). Essentially, MESI represents a distinctive industrial cluster structure comprising energy-based enterprises (O'Malley et al., 2016) and a framework with great potential to achieve efficiency in energy management, reduce environmental impact, and reduce costs. MESI's ultimate strategic goal is to develop methods for the optimal design and operation of unified energy systems, as well as systems that make infrastructure flexible, efficient, and reliable (Guelpa et al., 2019; Ngwaka et al., 2023). Research in this area focuses on techno-economic and environmental assessment, including the use of systematics combined with artificial intelligence techniques to determine optimal system sizing and MESI components to minimize emissions, costs, and energy consumption. Against this backdrop, the increasing demand for MESI modeling tools to support evidence-based analysis of capital investments and emission reductions highlights the need for advanced industrial energy management systems to address integration challenges (Guelpa et al., 2019).

Energy-based industrial clusters (EBICs) consist of companies, technologies, and resources related to the energy industry, often jointly producing similar and interrelated energy products (Rosenfeld, 1997). These clusters focus on seeking local solutions to reduce costs and stimulate ongoing innovation rather than

DOI: 10.4324/9781003541394-16

outsourcing capital, goods, labor, and technology. MESI falls within the scope of EBICs, representing a form of energy cooperation. The essence of EBICs lies in researching its development model and indicators. Ngwaka (2023) have modeled, simulated, and controlled industrial clusters through transfer functions, introducing important contributions to modeling energy systems for achieving energy conservation and emissions reduction. Zhang (2021) analyzed the necessary components of energy systems and optimization methods from a digital tools perspective. Bechara and Alnouri (2022) utilized mathematical methods like nonlinear programming to optimize internal characteristics of industrial clusters, aiming for cost maximization while reducing emissions. Patrizia et al. primarily focused on small and medium-sized energy flows, proposing a decision-support methodology based on performance indicators and Pareto multi-objective optimization methods (Simeoni et al., 2018). Li et al. discussed industrial symbiosis as an energy optimization method, where multiple enterprises share resources and materials through proximity (Meneghetti & Nardin, 2012). McCauley and Stephens (2012) introduced cluster strategies for regional economic development, specifically in sustainable energy fields, highlighting the need for further integration of regional policies. Besides, concepts such as cleantech clusters (McCauley and Stephens, 2012; Tvedt, 2019), energy clusters (He et al., 2016), and EBICs (Cornett and Sørensen, 2011; Wang et al., 2017), are to focus on combining energy sources with industrial clusters to achieve sustainable development of energy (Bridge et al., 2013; Lowitzsch, 2019; Lowitzsch et al., 2020).

While previous research has primarily focused on the concept of industrial clusters and optimization methods, this chapter examines EBICs through the lens of paradoxical tensions inherent in the energy transition. Specifically, it explores how these clusters navigate the competing demands of environmental sustainability and economic development. From micro and macro perspectives, the chapter investigates the mechanisms and influencing factors driving the development of EBICs, particularly in coastal regions where energy-based industries and their ancillary sectors converge. Although cooperation and competition coexist within clusters, they collectively strive to advance sustainable energy development in these areas (Cornett & Sørensen, 2011; Wang et al., 2017). This chapter addresses several critical gaps in the literature. First, while much research emphasizes the development of single offshore energy sources or specific energy strategies, there is limited attention to the systemic dynamics of energy clusters and the paradoxes they embody. Second, previous studies have often overlooked the key indicators shaping cluster development and the interplay between energy clusters and economic growth. This has resulted in fragmented development patterns across energy-based enterprises.

To address these gaps, the chapter offers ideas by employing a quantitative economic model to analyze the inherent factors influencing EBIC development. It proposes a theory of complementary multi-energy development in coastal regions, demonstrating how such an approach can reconcile the tensions between environmental and economic priorities. The chapter aims to provide both theoretical insights and practical strategies for achieving a sustainable and economically viable energy future. Through this exploration, it highlights the importance of balancing these paradoxical tensions as a cornerstone of effective energy cluster development. It also explores challenges in EBIC development in one of the Central and East European countries (CEE), i.e., Poland. It compares it with the functioning of well-established EBICs in the Netherlands and Denmark.

## 11.2 Paradox of Energy and Economic Development

### *11.2.1 Paradox Theory of Energy*

The paradox of energy and economic development refers to the contradictory relationship between economic growth and environmental sustainability. Economic development often relies on a large amount of energy consumption. Energy input can bring about productivity improvement and wealth increase, driving rapid economic development. For the sake of sustainable development, energy use must be restricted. This conflict between the dual needs of economic development and environmental protection constitutes a paradox. Within the framework of paradox theory, this contradiction is seen as a dynamic tension, that is, rather than making a simple trade-off between the two, a balance can be found through management, innovation, and coordination. Therefore, paradox theory encourages us to view this seemingly opposing relationship as an interdependent duality to achieve more resilient and sustainable solutions (Smith & Lewis, 2011).

The transition to renewable energy sources represents one of the most pressing challenges in addressing climate change and promoting environmental sustainability. However, this transition presents a significant paradox when viewed from the perspective of economic development, particularly in regions heavily reliant on traditional energy industries. The essence of this paradox lies in the conflict between achieving environmental goals and maintaining economic stability. On the one hand, the shift toward renewable energy and promoting sustainable practices within coastal EBICs can have significant environmental benefits. It aids in reducing carbon emissions, mitigating climate change, and fostering a cleaner and more sustainable use of resources. Coastal regions, with their access to offshore wind, tidal, and other marine renewable energy sources, are particularly well-suited to drive this transition. Therefore, EBICs are often seen as critical players in the global movement toward a greener future.

Jevons's paradox is the classical paradox between energy and economic development. There is considerable debate about the size of the energy efficiency rebound and the relevance of the Jevons paradox to energy conservation. Some have refuted the paradox, while others worry that pursuing sustainable development through energy efficiency improvements may be self-defeating

(Alcott, 2005). Environmental economists have proposed that conservation policies that increase efficiency and keep utility costs the same (or higher) avoid the Jevons paradox (Wackernagel & Rees, 1997). Conservation policies (such as cap and trade) do not exhibit the paradox and can be used to control rebound effects (Lez & Puig-Ventosa, 2015).

The transition from traditional energy sources such as coal, oil, and gas presents a complex economic paradox, especially in regions and communities that have long relied on these industries to prosper. In regions such as Poland's Pomerania region, where traditional energy sectors form the backbone of economic activity, the shift to renewable energy has the potential to trigger economic decline, unemployment, and social unrest. The decline of traditional power plants and the decline of the fossil fuel industry could lead to widespread unemployment and a decline in regional economic output. These dynamics highlight a core paradox: While the transition to renewable energy is essential for long-term environmental health, it simultaneously undermines short- to medium-term economic development, especially in regions that are closely intertwined with traditional energy sectors. This paradox is further complicated by the large investments required for renewable energy infrastructure. The development of clean energy sources such as offshore wind farms and solar parks requires large amounts of upfront capital, often leading to short-term economic pressures before long-term benefits are realized. This is further complicated by the Jevons paradox, which states that increasing energy use efficiency does not necessarily lead to a reduction in overall energy consumption. As renewable energy becomes more efficient and affordable, energy demand may rise while increasing environmental impacts if not managed well. This creates additional challenges in balancing energy use with environmental and economic goals.

Furthermore, rapid policy changes and infrastructure development can create market uncertainty, creating difficulties for businesses, investors, and workers trying to adapt. As a result, the energy transition can become a disruptive force that initially leads to economic instability rather than stable development. This tension is reflected in the experience of the Pomeranian region, where the urgent need to promote renewable energy to protect the coastal environment and reduce emissions has collided with economic issues related to the traditional energy industry.

Another aspect of this paradox is the "green growth paradox," which questions whether pursuing sustainable development through renewable energy will reduce environmental impacts. Economic growth driven by the renewable energy industry may lead to increased production, consumption, and resource extraction, offsetting some of the environmental benefits of the transition from fossil fuels. Similarly, the "energy transition paradox" occurs when efforts to develop renewable energy infrastructure, such as wind farms or solar parks, are met with resistance due to their environmental footprint or damage to local communities, thereby hindering the transition.

The Pomeranian region's experience reflects similar friction points in other European countries, suggesting that this paradox is not isolated but a recurring theme in the global energy transition narrative. Addressing these paradoxes requires comprehensive planning, strategic investments, and policies that strike a delicate balance between environmental goals and economic needs. This includes creating pathways to retrain the workforce, supporting the development of new industries around renewable energy, and ensuring a gradual and inclusive transition process. Recognizing and managing these tensions is critical to fostering a successful energy transition that does not sacrifice economic well-being for environmental progress. As such, these paradoxes – the Jevons paradox, the green growth paradox, and others – underscore the complex journey toward a truly sustainable future.

### *11.2.2 The Characteristics of Industrial Clusters*

Regarding the hierarchical division of industrial clusters, we generally use the method described in Roelandt and den Hertog (1999) to divide them into macro-level (from the perspective of the country), meso-level (industry), and micro-level (specifically enterprise). Porter's diamond model is commonly employed in the structure of industrial clusters, consisting of three parts: Trade, related departments, and institutions. Within the same cluster, the status of different enterprises varies, and there exists both cooperation and competition between them. Additionally, in different countries, the structure and driving factors of industrial clusters in various industries differ due to their distinct historical and cultural backgrounds. While some factors are specific to regions, others are more general. Furthermore, the performance of the same industrial cluster and the degree and mode of connection also exhibit significant variations, which contribute to the diversity of industrial cluster research. Table 11.1 presents the general characteristics of industrial clusters and representative literature studies.

Classifying industry clusters takes on various formats because of different research purposes and classification criteria, as well as the fact that industry clusters are likely to have overlapping characteristics or be based on distinct regional backgrounds or criteria used by policymakers. The following are the common types and classifications of clusters:

- Specialization-based clusters

Specialization-based clusters focus on a specific industry or sector, such as vegetable and agricultural production sites, the aerospace sector, the renewable energy sector, or the automotive sector. A model of integrated services that combines the resources of a specific sector or a wide range of sectors to enable the exchange and collaboration of inputs and outputs for the whole industry.

*Table 11.1* The Characteristic of Industrial Clusters and Case Studies

| *Characteristics* | *Description* | *Literature* |
|---|---|---|
| Regional characteristics (Geographical proximity) | Clusters exhibit characteristics of geographical proximity and spatial concentration, as industrial clusters tend to be relatively concentrated in specific areas. Although there is no consensus on the ideal geographical scope of clusters, different industrial clusters encompass the geographical location and spatial extent of the cluster. This highlights the significance of geography and spatial considerations in the formation of clusters. | (Biggiero & Sammarra, 2010; Boschma, 2005; De Dominicis et al., 2013; Geldes et al., 2015; Letaifa and Rabeau, 2013; Lis & Lis, 2021, 2023) |
| Innovative | Industrial clusters can enhance their competitive advantages by promoting accelerated technological progress and diffusion within the cluster. The cluster's unique innovation environment and knowledge dissemination mechanisms contribute to the improved innovation capabilities and synergies among its constituent enterprises. Innovation plays a crucial role as a driving force in the process of cluster development. | (Audretsch & Feldman, 1996; Fundeanu & Badele, 2014; Simmie & Sennett, 1999) |
| Cooperative and competitive | Within an industrial cluster, each enterprise develops close relationships through the division of labor and cooperation. They establish a production network and prioritize it as their main competitive strategy despite facing numerous competitors in the market. Through cooperation, enterprises share valuable information and efficiently allocate scarce resources they acquire, fostering economic growth while promoting both cooperation and competition. This cooperative and competitive relationship between enterprises has emerged as a significant characteristic of the industrial cluster model, constituting a major focus of theoretical research on industrial clusters. | (Bengtsson & Sölvell, 2004; Cooke, 2002; Karaev et al., 2007; Newlands, 2003) |

(*Continued*)

*Table 11.1* (*Continued*)

| *Characteristics* | *Description* | *Literature* |
|---|---|---|
| Coordination | A cluster is an organic whole. It is not just a simple sum of several individual enterprises but a continuous, stable, and orderly ecological organization formed through organic connection so as to gain competitiveness, attractiveness, integration, and influence, etc., overall competitive advantage. In a particular field, companies in an industry cluster usually gather together. This field covers many participants, such as product manufacturers, upstream and downstream suppliers and sales channels, providers of complementary products, and service intermediaries. These participants maintain close contact and strong coordination in the division of labor and cooperation. | (Lorenzen, 2001; Lorenzen & Foss, 2003) |
| Regional influence | Industrial clusters take root in specific local communities and are closely related to the local economic, social, cultural, and political environments. Embedded means that economic activity is deeply embedded in local social relations. From the perspective of regional economic theory, the most important feature of industrial clusters is their geographical rooting, that is, a large number of related industries are concentrated in a specific geographical range. | (Feldman et al., 2005; John St & Pouder, 2006; Padmore & Gibson, 1998, 1998; Porter, 2012; Wolfe & Gertler, 2004) |

- Geographical-based clusters

The scale of development of clusters varies based on localization, regionalization, nationalization, and globalization. The localized model relies on local networks and collaboration as a guarantee. Regionalized clusters are relatively more expansive and are able to span multiple provinces and cities with interconnected businesses and supporting infrastructure. Nationalized clusters are often able to connect the resources and development of an entire country and have a significant impact on the national economy as a whole. Clusters with a global impact enable multiple national and regional institutions to operate jointly, making excellent use of global networks and the development of a global marketing economy.

- Policy-based clusters

The initial establishment of industrial clusters is usually accompanied by certain policy benefits, such as special economic zones and free trade zones, to maximize domestic and foreign investment, reduce tariffs and taxes, eliminate trade barriers, and create incentives to encourage the development of enterprises to promote the benefits of clustering, thus helping to increase economic growth and international trading.

- Innovation-based clusters

In fact, EBICs are also an innovative cluster. In order to vigorously develop high technology and increase the capacity for independent research and development (R&D) and innovation. The establishment of R&D clusters and innovation centers is now a common practice in technological innovation-based clusters. They are usually associated with universities, research institutes, and high-tech enterprises. To promote technological innovation and cooperation between industry, academic, and research institutions, and to provide opportunities for exchanges such as incubators, accelerators, and venture financing. This enables technology development to be implemented as speedily as possible and enhances practical implementation support.

## 11.3 Coastal Energy-based Industrial Clusters

### *11.3.1 Energy-based Industrial Clusters Theory*

The author conducted an exploratory qualitative study in selected industrial clusters in the energy sector to identify the main paradoxical tensions in clusters and their consequences for sustainable development cooperation. The activities of the energy clusters are closely related to sustainable development and are aimed at promoting renewable energy sources and raising energy awareness. The energy clusters provide a platform for cooperation, bringing together stakeholders from various sectors, including businesses, the R&D sector, and public administration, to implement joint projects, stimulate innovation, develop environmentally sustainable solutions, and improve business models. In this way, they contribute to forming a sustainable economy and society.

Energy-based industrial clusters comprise enterprises engaged in energy production and utilization. This category of cluster structures mainly focuses on more effectively developing and optimizing energy in coastal areas. This refers to the spatial and geographical agglomeration of enterprises whose main purpose is to develop inshore and offshore energy. These enterprises collaboratively aim to improve energy production efficiency, minimize waste, and promote sustainability through persistent investment in innovation. Coastal energy-based industrial clusters are distinct from traditional industrial clusters. Their characteristics contribute to the unique advantages of coastal energy clusters and reveal their potential as drivers of sustainable economic development. The following are some of the key characteristics of coastal energy clusters.

- Coastal location

The convenient coastal location makes it easier to use coastal resources such as waves, tides, and wind energy, and the port terminal for easy access to shipping. Local renewable energy sources can be utilized without the need for additional investment and transport costs. These coastal resources become the basis on which sustainable energy generation and exploitation can be obtained.

- Convergence of multi-energy technologies

The development of coastal energy clusters is not limited to a single traditional energy source, where it is frequently possible to develop multiple energy technologies. This is, for instance, the case with offshore wind, wave and tidal energy, offshore hydrogen production technologies, technologies for powering oil rig platforms, and many other methods. This promotes the development of technological innovation and the efficient use of energy flexibility within the clusters, optimizing the allocation of resources and reducing carbon emissions for a greener environment.

- Synergies and value chain integration

The coastal energy cluster development model is not limited to energy production but can also facilitate supply chain services related to renewable energy projects, such as the supply of basic cables, the construction of transmission facilities, turbine manufacturing, maintenance services, etc. It is possible to collaborate with multiple parties to facilitate the aggregation of the stakeholders in the cluster and to reduce costs.

- Research and innovation focus

In coastal energy industrial clusters, the development centers usually have a strong focus on research and innovation. They attract a large number of research institutes, universities, and technology development centers that promote research in renewable energy technologies, environmental monitoring, and the advancement of sustainable practices. The scientific research institutions develop in a synchronous way based on the industrial practices within the clusters, encouraging collaboration and helping with technology transfer, providing technological support, and promoting continuous improvement and innovation in the field of traditional and renewable energy sources.

### *11.3.2 Energy-based Industrial Clusters' Development Path*

The development models of energy industry clusters can be divided into two main models: Market-led and government-dominated. The development of most of these energy industry clusters is based on a mixture of various models. The market-led model can be subdivided into foreign capital-driven and local enterprises. Many energy issues involve national security, so only some of them are open to foreign capital, such as wind energy, solar energy, and some natural gas energy. This type of development is relatively conservative, and the correlation between industries is not strong. The spillover effect of technology in this model is not obvious, so the marketization effect of this mode of energy development is relatively poor. In Poland and even the EU, local enterprises form the majority of industrial clusters spontaneously, and traditional energy accounts for a relatively high proportion. The new energy field is relatively open, and most new energy clusters involve investment of various types of capital. The entire construction cycle of coastal energy clusters takes a long time, and it is still at a disadvantage compared to the current construction of traditional energy clusters. It is mainly limited to the current level of new energy technology, and this type of cluster is currently in its infancy (suitable for labor-intensive products with low technical content). However, in the long run, basic innovation, research, and development are still obstacles to the sustainable development of EBICs. Only when the awareness of environmental protection in the whole society is strong, the low-carbon concept is deeply rooted in the hearts of the people, and the core technology of new energy has been through can it be possible to form a highly competitive energy industry cluster.

In the initial stage of the formation of a sound energy industry cluster, the government's policy support should replace the market mechanism and occupy a dominant position. This leading role can provide funds and support for the development of the cluster. The government formulates a series of laws, regulations, and policies to guide and regulate the development of energy clusters, such as providing financial subsidies, tax incentives, land transfer fee reductions, building technological innovation platforms, rationally arranging financial systems, and improving energy infrastructure construction.

The development cycle of EBICs is generally divided into four stages. According to the time cycle of cluster development, the author divides the stages of EBICs into the initial stage, development stage, stable stage, and long-term stage based on the industrial cluster life cycle theory. The development cycle of energy clusters follows the logistic growth law of general innovative clusters, as shown in Figure 11.1.

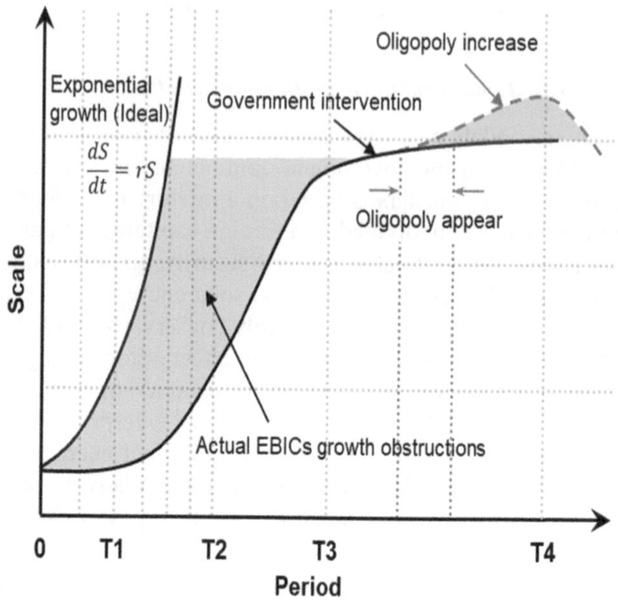


*Figure 11.1* Diagram of Oligopoly Phenomenon and Government Intervention in the Process of EBICs Growth.

An energy industry cluster is a cluster network formed by the geographical concentration and functional connection of energy companies and other related actors. It possesses the characteristics of high technology and high risk. Therefore, the role of the government and the market is crucial in promoting the evolution of EBICs. The following analysis focuses on the characteristics of the evolution stage of the EBICs and the role of the government and the market in each stage.

#### *11.3.2.1 Initial Stage of EBICs Development*

As mentioned earlier, the development of EBICs in the initial stage tends to be labor-intensive, with labor being an important driving force for early stage development. During this period, energy companies begin to concentrate geographically in specific areas, but there is little cooperation and communication among them beyond the logistics relationship in the industrial chain. Universities, scientific research institutes, governments, and intermediary service agencies have not yet fully joined the cluster network, and collaborative innovation in technology has not been established. Therefore, at this stage, the government should assume a leading role, with the labor force dominating the market. The government should actively research and formulate development plans for the energy-based industry, increase infrastructure construction, establish a common technology research platform, and invest in R&D. EBICs relying on labor force can develop relatively rapidly during this stage.

#### *11.3.2.2 Development Period of EBICs' Development*

During this period, noticeable differences in cluster development emerge. Innovative clusters achieve full automation, the marginal cost of unit production continues to decline, and they gradually gain control of the entire market. The enterprises that survive the third stage also become subsidiary clusters of the oligopolistic cluster. Therefore, in the long run, the government should continue to regulate the market to prevent oligopoly in cluster development. Due to the relatively rapid development of some EBICs, based on cluster development theory, the number of related energy companies continues to increase. Universities, research institutes, and service organizations begin to join the cluster network, and enterprises within the cluster start developing their own R&D capabilities, leading to gradual changes in the cluster's structure. Learning exchanges and cooperative innovation among energy companies, as well as between energy companies and universities, research institutes, and governments, become more frequent, leading to the formation of collaborative innovation. However, due to the surplus of labor in the early stages of EBICs, labor-intensive cluster development remains dominant during this period. Nonetheless, with ongoing investment in R&D, the cluster's automation level increases, resulting in decreasing unit production costs and increased efficiency.

#### *11.3.2.3 Stable Period of EBICs' Development*

During this period, energy-based companies' R&D capabilities continue to strengthen, and enterprise automation reaches its peak. The number of related enterprises (the number of enterprises in EBICs) reaches its maximum scale, and all innovation subjects truly join the cluster innovation network. The culture of collective learning and innovation becomes more mature, and collaborative innovation becomes more perfect. The energy industry cluster occupies a higher value-added position in the value chain, becoming a genuine innovation cluster. Cluster development during this stage is relatively stable. However, labor-intensive clusters that fail to keep up with technology and innovation at this stage gradually decline or disappear, while clusters focused on innovative technologies gain dominant market positions. Therefore, to prevent the decline or disappearance of certain clusters, the government should encourage innovation through macro-control, further upgrading energy industry clusters lacking a sufficient innovation driving force.

#### *11.3.2.4 Final Period of EBICs' Development*

During this period, due to the vigorous development of innovative industrial clusters in the early stages, they have already established dominance in the market. Some remaining enterprises also become subsidiary enterprises of the oligopoly. Therefore, at this stage, the government should continue to regulate the market to avoid the formation of oligopoly clusters. This stage represents a period of rapid development. The production capacity of EBICs rapidly increases, but it also brings along some issues, such as severe environmental pollution and internal management contradictions within the cluster. These factors increase resistance to the development of energy industry clusters. When the resistance surpasses the driving force, EBICs enter a recession period. At this point, the number of energy-based companies begins to decrease, and the cluster innovation network starts to disintegrate. Therefore, the government should dynamically monitor changes in the development of energy industry clusters during this stage to ensure their long-term stable development.

Energy-based industrial clusters have many advantages that cluster development does not have, such as location advantages, energy development advantages, and transportation conditions, among others. EBICs encompass both traditional energy and new energy sectors. During the development process, the collaboration and innovation between these two types of energy can reduce the reliance on traditional sources and decrease the emission of environmental pollutants. The new energy industry, including photovoltaic and wind power industries, is given priority in EBICs development, representing a unique advantage within coastal energy industry clusters.

Energy-based industrial clusters are typically established in coastal regions known for their developed economies and convenient transportation networks. Compared to other cluster types, the synergy between regions and clusters in terms of innovation is stronger, leading to a more significant flow of knowledge. Innovation knowledge is effectively transferred, recombined, and optimized among various actors within the cluster, thus enhancing the efficiency of knowledge utilization and fostering technological innovation through the integration of production. Consequently, each innovation subject within the energy industry cluster gains a wealth of knowledge through network connections, surpassing what can be achieved through independent innovation. The quantity of knowledge acquired depends on the learning ability of the innovation subject. Energy industry clusters serve as innovation hubs where energy companies, universities, research institutes, governments, and intermediary service agencies are geographically and organizationally interconnected.

The geographical location advantages of energy industry clusters are evident. Many energy industry clusters have flourished due to their unique geographical positions, which serve as the primary driving force behind their establishment. Additionally, coastal areas generally benefit from comprehensive policy support.

For instance, policies promoting sustainable development and reducing carbon emissions greatly favor the development of coastal and offshore wind energy. These policy advantages have significantly accelerated the rapid growth of EBICs.

## 11.4 Methodology and Analysis

The research question of this chapter focuses on how energy clusters have been effectively built in coastal areas, which is of great significance for achieving sustainable economic development but faces many complexities in practice, especially in CEE, e.g., in Poland.

This study adopts a case study method and document analysis for collecting data. It selects three typical port energy cluster cases: The Port of Rotterdam in the Netherlands, the Port of Esbjerg in Denmark, and the Port of Gdańsk in Poland. Each case represents a unique integration model of port and energy clusters and can provide a comparative analysis perspective for clusters at different stages of development. The reason for case selection is that the Port of Rotterdam and the Port of Esbjerg, as successful cases in Western Europe, embody advanced models of energy cluster integration and sustainable innovation, while the Port of Gdańsk in Poland represents the background of CEE. As a CEE country, Poland has its own unique challenges and opportunities in achieving alignment with the EU's sustainable development goals and overcoming paradoxes related to energy transition. The case of Gdańsk, therefore, allows us to compare the adaptability of these strategies directly in the CEE context.

The energy cluster, the construction and development of coastal resources, and the development of ports and shipping have a long history in Europe. Among them, the London Port Cluster and its nearby energy cluster, and the Rotterdam Port Cluster, combined with the development of a new energy cluster in the Netherlands, are the most representative EBICs. They combine the advantages of port and shipping and integrate new coastal energy industries and world-renowned traditional energy companies. Currently, they are relatively fast-growing energy clusters. Here are some key points about the development of industrial clusters in the EU:

- *Path dependence and historical accumulation*: The development of the European energy industry has gone through a very long process of path dependence. The early coastal energy industry clusters gathered near coastal ports, relying heavily on the ports' shipping and trade advantages, and the developed energy industry mainly focused on traditional energy. However, with the recovery of the European economy and the continuous development of new energy technologies, traditional energy industry clusters have gradually transformed into a development method that combines new energy with traditional energy. They have also begun to gradually break away from the dependence on ports and develop into an independent cluster format. Through continuous development and innovation improvement, these energy industry clusters have gradually formed regional energy construction plans that affect the entire country and the world.

- *Promoted by national policies and enterprise innovation*: The development of energy industry clusters benefits from the support of national policies and the innovation of energy enterprises. The government promotes the development of the energy industry by providing financial, policy, and infrastructure support. At the same time, enterprises improve the quality and efficiency of energy development services through continuous innovation and improvement.
- To promote the development of energy industry clusters, the key is to create a good development environment and accumulate professional knowledge. This requires the government to provide a stable policy environment and legal system while cultivating talent and professional skills. Many European countries have established new energy and coastal energy development and research units to promote energy innovation and development.
- *Multi-departmental and multi-level cooperation*: The development of energy industry clusters requires multi-departmental and multi-level cooperation. This includes the collaboration and cooperation of governments, research institutions (providing R&D and technology development), shipping companies (port and ship transportation teams), logistics service providers (land transportation), etc. A complete internal and external service system can be formed by establishing a good cooperative relationship.
- *Market innovation and resource allocation capabilities*: The development of clusters also requires improving market innovation and resource allocation capabilities. Innovative EBICs should pay more attention to the development of hardware resources, such as R&D, when developing energy, which is more effective in increasing cluster output than the development of software resources. This is because the energy cluster is essentially a cluster with high requirements for innovation, and it is necessary to continuously improve the R&D quality of the enterprises within the cluster to adapt to different market demands and solutions. At the same time, clusters need to allocate resources reasonably to meet the needs of different industries and customers.

Based on these key points, the construction of energy clusters in Europe is constantly improving, and today a complete energy development and management system has basically been established. As pointed out in this chapter, a good energy industry cluster should make reasonable use of various resources, focus on internal R&D, exert macro-control, and continuously improve the energy service and logistics system. Such EBICs are more complex with the current international cluster construction direction. The following three examples will analyze the current construction plan of the energy cluster from the construction of enterprises within the cluster, the configuration, and the development status of the cluster, as described in Table 11.2.

*Table 11.2* Parameter Values of the Cobb-Douglas Function for Three Clusters

| *Port* | *Location* | *Energy-Based Cluster* | *Notable Energy Companies* |
|---|---|---|---|
| Rotterdam Port | Rotterdam, Netherlands | It is one of the largest and busiest ports globally, playing a vital role in energy imports, exports, refining, and distribution. | Royal Dutch Shell: Multinational energy company engaged in oil and gas exploration, production, refining, and marketing.<br>ExxonMobil: Global energy company involved in refining and petrochemical production.<br>Eneco: An energy company focused on sustainable energy solutions, including wind power, with operations and facilities in the port area.<br>Vopak: A global tank storage company that provides storage and handling services for various energy products, including crude oil and petroleum. |
| Gdańsk Port | Gdańsk, Poland | Handles various energy commodities, including oil, liquefied natural gas (LNG), coal, and other energy products. | Lotos Group: Polish oil and gas company engaged in the exploration, production, refining, and marketing of petroleum products.<br>PGNiG: Polish state-owned oil and gas company involved in exploration, production, and distribution of natural gas and crude oil.<br>Baltic Gas Company: Baltic Gas Company operates a liquefied natural gas (LNG) terminal in the Port of Gdańsk. The terminal provides import, storage, and regasification services for LNG. |

(*Continued*)

*Table 11.2 (Continued)*

| *Port* | *Location* | *Energy-Based Cluster* | *Notable Energy Companies* |
|---|---|---|---|
| Esbjerg Port | Esbjerg, Denmark | A major hub for offshore wind farm installations, maintenance operations, and oil and gas activities in the North Sea. | Ørsted (formerly DONG Energy): Global leader in offshore wind development.<br>Vattenfall: Swedish energy company that operates wind energy projects.<br>Maersk Drilling: Provider of drilling services to the offshore energy industry. |

### *11.4.1 Rotterdam Port Analysis*

The Port of Rotterdam is recognized as the main port related to the Dutch energy cluster, bringing together the largest energy companies in the Netherlands. The Rotterdam energy industry cluster is considered a well-established energy cluster solution. Table 11.2 shows that the Rotterdam Port brings together traditional energy companies, new energy companies, shipping, logistics, and energy storage industries. It provides many innovative solutions. The port has an international reputation as one of the world's largest and busiest ports, playing a pivotal role in the energy industry. It is an important hub for importing, exporting, and storing various energy resources, including crude oil, natural gas, coal, and petroleum products. Additionally, it is a major hub for oil refining, petrochemical production, and energy distribution throughout Europe. The prominence of the energy cluster in the Port of Rotterdam is also attributed to its strategic location, extensive infrastructure, and close links to the global energy market. The port is trying to attract new innovative developments, such as the production of green products such as hydrogen, biofuels, and recycling activities. It has also created infrastructure such as heating, hydrogen, and carbon dioxide pipelines. In addition, the port also has shipping conditions. Meanwhile, the Port of Rotterdam is the first EBICs in the world's energy clusters to build hydrogen production capacity. The Rotterdam Port Authority and its partners are researching hydrogen systems. The use of hydrogen in industry and transport, especially green hydrogen (hydrogen produced by green means), contributes to the goal of $CO_2$-neutral ports since green hydrogen does not release any emissions. Currently, half of the hydrogen projects in the Netherlands are taking place in Rotterdam. These factors firmly establish its position as an energy center of excellence in the Netherlands and Europe. As an important part of the energy supply chain, the development of the cluster has also attracted many energy groups from other countries, making important contributions to the development of the national energy industry cluster.

### *11.4.2 Gdańsk Port Analysis*

The Port of Gdańsk is the port with the most significant development in Poland. It is home to many energy companies, including oil, LNG, coal, and other energy products, with a large proportion of traditional energy playing an important role in Poland's energy market. Although the energy cluster construction of the Port of Gdańsk is not as complete as other clusters, the port serves as an important energy import and export portal in Poland. It possesses strong energy transportation and storage capabilities and has the potential to develop into a large energy cluster. The construction of an offshore wind farm in the Baltic Sea, currently promoted by the city of Gdańsk, serves as a powerful driving force for Poland's economic development based on modern technology and the realization of sustainable energy development. Investments in the offshore wind industry are essential for strengthening national energy security and creating a supply chain involving Polish industrial and technological companies, universities, research institutions, and professionals. Therefore, as more energy clusters enter the Gdańsk market, the construction of energy clusters in Poland will experience rapid development in the short term. About 70% of Poland's electricity is imported to Gdańsk, making the Pomeranian Voivodeship one of the largest recipients of domestic energy. Despite having great potential, the region has the smallest electricity industry. This situation creates a significant demand, especially for low-emission power plants that comply with EU standards. As an EU member state, Poland was required to produce 15% of its energy from renewable sources (RES) by 2020. Therefore, there is a clear demand for electricity produced by renewable energy investors. Additionally, the implementation of investment plans for transmission and distribution lines in the region significantly increases the possibilities for connecting green energy producers. Gdańsk is also the most promising place for wind power investments in Poland. Offshore wind energy has enormous economic potential in the region. By 2025, installed capacity is expected to reach 2.2 gross weight (GW), and by 2030, it will reach GW. Furthermore, the Pomeranian Voivodeship has been identified as the optimal location for a new nuclear power plant, with initial investment plans already underway since 2020. Gdańsk University of Technology has started cultivating students in the field of nuclear energy. This is a typical example of diversified complementary energy sources, with universities and research institutions providing innovation and talent for energy development. The Pomeranian Voivodeship has significant potential in biomass production, with arable land accounting for 42.6% and forests covering 37% of the region. Poldanor S.A., located in the Pomeranian Voivodeship, is a leading example of effectively utilizing this potential in Polish agricultural biogas plants (data and information come from the Invest in Pomerania Agency website). Furthermore, Gdańsk is actively developing offshore wind energy, leveraging its excellent geographical location. To make the Pomeranian region an ideal location for establishing a marine industry production center, wind towers are manufactured in Gdańsk shipyards. Some local shipyards have also joined in manufacturing special units used to install offshore wind turbines. This integration of production technology and transportation equipment demonstrates the combination of energy equipment research, manufacturing, production, and transportation. In addition, the energy departments of universities in the Pomeranian Voivodeship cultivate approximately 9,500 students, and about 1,500 students graduate annually. Gdańsk University of Technology collaborates with many energy companies such as Grupa Energa, Grupa Lotos, PGE Nuclear Energy Ltd., and GE Nuclear Power, fostering highly skilled energy professionals and providing support for the development of the energy sector.

In summary, the current development of the Gdańsk energy cluster within the Port of Gdańsk has brought about many positive outcomes and implications for the development and sustainability of the port. At the same time, the development model of the cluster is also based on the mutual promotion of multiple energy sources, and universities provide innovation for energy construction. The establishment of energy clusters has made the Port of Gdańsk more energy-efficient and environmentally friendly. By utilizing innovative technologies and implementing renewable energy sources such as solar panels and wind turbines, the port has reduced its carbon footprint and decreased its reliance on conventional energy sources. This shift has improved the port's environmental performance and made it a leader in sustainable port operations. In addition, the Gdańsk energy cluster facilitates cooperation among various stakeholders within the port community, including port authorities, energy companies, research institutions, and technology providers. This collaboration facilitates the exchange of knowledge, expertise, and best practices, leading to the implementation of cutting-edge energy solutions within the port. The cluster's collaboration also enhances the port's elasticity through multi-energy sources and the establishment of backup systems to ensure uninterrupted operations. Furthermore, the energy cluster development has attracted investment and business opportunities for the Port of Gdańsk. The adoption of sustainable energy practices and the availability of clean energy infrastructure make the port an attractive destination for companies seeking environmentally conscious transportation and logistics solutions. The cluster of investments has boosted the port's economic growth, created jobs, and increased competitiveness in the global maritime industry. The development of the Gdańsk energy cluster within the Port of Gdańsk has yielded significant benefits. It enhances the port's sustainability, promotes cooperation and knowledge exchange, attracts investment, and strengthens its position as the leading port in the region. The cluster's efforts not only transform the port's energy landscape but also position it as a model for other ports to adopt sustainable practices and contribute to a greener future.

### *11.4.3 Denmark Port Analysis*

Denmark's energy cluster differs slightly from the above two. Denmark excels in the development of wind energy, making it a pioneer in the field of new energy globally. The Danish EBICs development model is primarily based on new energy sources, supplemented by traditional energy sources. One of the most renowned clusters is Denmark's Esbjerg energy industry cluster. Esbjerg is well-known for its developments in offshore wind power and natural gas industries, making it the largest energy city in Denmark and providing a substantial amount of clean energy for the country. The cluster encompasses offshore wind energy, onshore wind energy, offshore oil development, natural gas, and hydrogen development. Offshore wind energy construction holds a larger proportion in Esbjerg compared to the other two ports, and the cluster is currently developing renewable resources in the Danish North Sea and the German Sea. Energy grids, particularly offshore wind power projects, serve as demonstrations for the renewable energy industry. The energy supply of Esbjerg's energy cluster follows the strategy of multi-energy recycling. The port of Esbjerg, within the cluster, serves as an important transportation channel for wind turbines, wind power equipment, and hydrogen production equipment to the North Sea. It also acts as a crucial gateway for the operation and maintenance of offshore wind power products. The port offers specialized facilities for handling and storing wind turbine components, as well as servicing vessels and crew transfers. Furthermore, it houses numerous R&D institutions, such as the world-renowned Danish University of Technology, continuously injecting new energy into the development and providing new vitality. Companies like Ørsted, a globally recognized energy company, and Vattenfall, a Swedish energy company, along with several oil exploration and product manufacturing companies, engage in local energy business, fostering cooperation and mutual benefit to promote the construction of the Danish coastal energy cluster. Esbjerg has thus become an important leading port in the offshore wind sector for Denmark and the entire Europe; Esbjerg Port has held a prominent position in the offshore wind industry since its involvement in the construction of Denmark's first large-scale offshore wind farm in 2002. Approximately 80% of Europe's offshore wind capacity passes through this port. As the world seeks to reduce its reliance on fossil fuels, offshore wind power is expected to play an increasingly significant role in providing renewable energy. Esbjerg Port is the only place in the world with the entire value chain of wind energy companies, supporting comprehensive development processes, including R&D, manufacturing, transportation, pre-assembly, and technical maintenance. This has made Esbjerg Port a crucial hub for communication and collaboration in the global wind energy sector.

According to data from 2020, Denmark's offshore wind capacity reached 1,700 megawatts, accounting for approximately 31% of the country's total wind energy capacity. Denmark's net-zero commitments and progress in renewable energy have positioned it as a leader in the energy transition. The country aims to reduce greenhouse gas emissions by 70% from 1990 levels and have renewable energy account for at least 50% of its total energy consumption by 2030. Denmark's 2050 energy strategy aims to achieve 100% independence from fossil fuels in the national energy structure by 2050 (data comes from Europa, EU and International Energy Agency websites).

As part of the European green energy transition, Esbjerg Port is also in a favorable position to lead Denmark's hydrogen economy. The port plans to develop hydrogen energy infrastructure, including hydrogen production and storage facilities, as well as hydrogen refueling stations. The construction of these infrastructure elements will provide a supply and distribution system for hydrogen energy in Esbjerg Port and its surrounding areas. It will drive the adoption of hydrogen in the transportation sector, such as promoting fuel cell vehicles and hydrogen-powered buses. Additionally, it can facilitate the diversification of industrial energy sources and play a critical role in energy storage. The research institutions and universities in Esbjerg Port and its surrounding region actively engage in hydrogen energy research and innovation. They are dedicated to improving hydrogen production technologies, hydrogen storage techniques, and the efficiency and sustainability of hydrogen energy systems.

### *11.4.4 Cases Comparative Analysis*

CEE and Western European countries significantly differ in energy transition and industrial cluster development. These differences are mainly due to each country's different economic structures, resources, and policy orientations. In terms of energy transition, some CEE countries, such as Poland, still rely on traditional energy industries, especially coal mining and thermal power generation. This reliance on fossil fuels provides a stable source of jobs and tax revenue for these countries' economies, but it also poses numerous challenges for the energy transition. Taking Poland's Pomeranian region as an example, although the region's energy-based industrial clusters are actively exploring the transition to renewable energy, they have also exposed many contradictions, such as social problems caused by cuts in the traditional energy industry. Western European countries, such as Germany, the Netherlands, and Denmark, started their energy transition earlier and have made significant progress in renewable energy. Most EBICs in Western Europe have established complete industrial chains covering wind energy, solar energy, biomass energy, and other fields and have formed close cooperation with advanced manufacturing, high-tech enterprises, and research institutions. The maturity of this industrial cluster and the support of efficient policy gives Western Europe an advantage in the energy transition.

However, CEE also has its own advantages. For example, many CEE countries have abundant natural resources, such as wind energy resources on the Baltic Sea coast and solar energy resources on the Eastern European plains, which provide potential opportunities for the development of local renewable energy industries. At the same time, the economic development stability of CEE is relatively high, and a large number of social labor forces have brought broad space for energy development. At the same time, through the guidance of government policies, the support of EU funds, and regional cooperation, energy transformation and cluster development have gradually found their own path. Therefore, in the long term, the gap in energy development between CEE and Western Europe is gradually narrowing, especially with the EU's continuous investment in new energy and the strengthening of policies in recent years.

## 11.5 Conclusions

This study has examined the intricate dynamics of EBICs in the context of the energy transition, with a particular focus on the paradoxical tensions that arise during this process. Central to the findings is the realization that while EBICs are uniquely positioned to drive renewable energy adoption and environmental sustainability, they simultaneously grapple with economic challenges that threaten the stability of regional development. The transition to renewable energy sources in EBICs, exemplified by the three cluster case studies, underscores the tension between achieving long-term sustainability and addressing short-term economic impacts. As established energy industries decline, the resulting job losses and regional economic downturns create resistance to change, complicating the path toward a green energy future. Energy-based industrial clusters rely on symbiotic relationships among businesses to share resources and optimize renewable energy solutions. However, competition for limited resources, such as investments and technological leadership, can hinder collective progress. Coastal EBICs often serve regional development goals while contributing to global carbon reduction efforts. This dual responsibility introduces additional layers of complexity, as local communities may prioritize immediate economic benefits over broader environmental objectives. These findings align with the theoretical frameworks proposed in previous literature (e.g., Xiu & Lis, 2024; Lez & Puig-Ventosa, 2015, Wang et al., 2017), which highlight the dual role of industrial clusters in fostering innovation and mitigating economic risks. By synthesizing the results with insights from the literature, this chapter contributes to the broader understanding of how EBICs can serve as both catalysts for and subjects of paradoxical tensions during the energy transition. Addressing these tensions is essential for ensuring that EBICs fulfill their potential as models for sustainable and economically viable energy development, both regionally and globally.

By comparing the three energy clusters in the EU, the chapter highlights that the paradoxes identified are not isolated but reflect broader, systemic challenges within the global energy transition. The findings emphasize that managing this transition requires more than just technological advancements. While the energy transition is universally challenging, regions in CEE often face additional complexities due to their reliance on traditional energy sectors and slower adoption of renewable technologies. The study suggests that paradoxical tensions, such as the trade-off between environmental goals and economic stability, can be managed through a balanced and inclusive approach. This includes promoting new economic opportunities around renewable energy, re-skilling the workforce, and ensuring gradual transitions that minimize social and economic disruptions. By leveraging the strengths of EBICs as industrial clusters, fostering collaboration, and utilizing coastal resources, regions can build a pathway toward a sustainable and economically viable energy future.

There are several limitations to studying EBICs from a paradoxical perspective. For example, in CEE, the complexity of energy policies and market mechanisms may limit the simple balance of paradoxes, especially in the short term. Therefore, it may be difficult to fully capture the complex external constraints when applying paradox theory to the study of EBICs. In addition, paradox theory focuses on high-level dualities but provides limited operational guidance on actual management details, posing certain challenges to analyzing specific energy cluster projects. Future research can explore how to combine the paradoxical perspective with practice-oriented frameworks, such as technological innovation management and policy adaptation, to support better the promotion and implementation of EBICs in different regions. This study expands the application of paradox theory through a case study of energy clusters, especially in the management paradox of resource and environmental sustainability. The dual needs of economic development and environmental protection in energy clusters provide a new perspective for the empirical application of paradox theory. At the same time, this study emphasizes the differences in paradoxes in different geopolitical and economic contexts, allowing paradox theory to more effectively consider regional constraints and diverse needs. This analysis is of great significance in broadening the explanatory power of paradox theory. Furthermore, the empirical findings of this study indicate that the diversity of stakeholders in energy clusters requires a dynamic and flexible management approach, providing important management implications for the application of paradox theory in complex systems.

## References


Alcott, B. (2005). Jevons' paradox. *Ecological Economics*, *54*(1), 9–21. https://doi.org/10.1016/j.ecolecon.2005.03.020

Audretsch, D. B., & Feldman, M. P. (1996). Innovative clusters and the industry life cycle. *Review of Industrial Organization*, 253–273.

Bechara, C. A., & Alnouri, S. Y. (2022). Energy assessment strategies in carbon-constrained industrial clusters. *Energy Conversion and Management*, *254*, 115204. https://doi.org/10.1016/j.enconman.2021.115204

Bengtsson, M., & Sölvell, Ö. (2004). Climate of competition, clusters and innovative performance. *Scandinavian Journal of Management, 20*(3), 225–244.
Biggiero, L., & Sammarra, A. (2010). Does geographical proximity enhance knowledge exchange? The case of the aerospace industrial cluster of Centre Italy. *International Journal of Technology Transfer and Commercialisation, 9*(4), 283–305.
Boschma, R. (2005). Proximity and innovation: A critical assessment. *Regional Studies, 39*(1), Article 1.
Bridge, G., Bouzarovski, S., Bradshaw, M., & Eyre, N. (2013). Geographies of energy transition: Space, place and the low-carbon economy. *Energy Policy, 53*, 331–340. https://doi.org/10.1016/j.enpol.2012.10.066
Cooke, P. (2002). *Knowledge economies: Clusters, learning and cooperative advantage*. London: Routledge.
Cornett, A. P., & Sørensen, N. K. (2011). Regional economic aspects of the Danish Windmill Cluster: The case of the emerging off shore wind energy cluster on the west coast of Jutland. *Paper for the Special Session'Cluster Development and Regional Transformation in an Economic Perspective*, 16–18.
De Dominicis, L., Florax, R. J., & de Groot, H. L. (2013). Regional clusters of innovative activity in Europe: Are social capital and geographical proximity key determinants? *Applied Economics, 45*(17), 2325–2335.
Feldman, M., Francis, J., & Bercovitz, J. (2005). Creating a cluster while building a firm: Entrepreneurs and the formation of industrial clusters. *Regional Studies, 39*(1), 129–141.
Fundeanu, D. D., & Badele, C. S. (2014). The impact of regional innovative clusters on competitiveness. *Procedia-Social and Behavioral Sciences, 124*, 405–414.
Geldes, C., Felzensztein, C., Turkina, E., & Durand, A. (2015). How does proximity affect interfirm marketing cooperation? A study of an agribusiness cluster. *Journal of Business Research, 68*(2), 263–272.
Guelpa, E., Bischi, A., Verda, V., Chertkov, M., & Lund, H. (2019). Towards future infrastructures for sustainable multi-energy systems: A review. *Energy, 184*, 2–21. https://doi.org/10.1016/j.energy.2019.05.057
He, Z., Xu, S., Shen, W., Long, R., & Yang, H. (2016). Overview of the development of the Chinese Jiangsu coastal wind-power industry cluster. *Renewable and Sustainable Energy Reviews, 57*, 59–71. https://doi.org/10.1016/j.rser.2015.12.187
JOHN ST, C. H., & Pouder, R. W. (2006). Technology clusters versus industry clusters: Resources, networks, and regional advantages. *Growth and Change, 37*(2), 141–171.
Karaev, A., Lenny Koh, S. C., & Szamosi, L. T. (2007). The cluster approach and SME competitiveness: A review. *Journal of Manufacturing Technology Management, 18*(7), 818–835.
Letaifa, S. B., & Rabeau, Y. (2013). Too close to collaborate? How geographic proximity could impede entrepreneurship and innovation. *Journal of Business Research, 66*(10), 2071–2078.
Lez, J. F.-G., & Puig-Ventosa, I. (2015). Energy efficiency policies and the Jevons paradox. *International Journal of Energy Economics and Policy, 5*(1), 69–79.
Lis, A. M., & Lis, A. (2021). *The Cluster Organization: Analyzing the Development of Cooperative Relationships*. New York: Routledge.

Lis, A. M., & Lis, A. (2023). *Proximity and the Cluster Organization.* New York: Taylor & Francis.

Lorenzen, M. (2001). Ties, trust, and trade: Elements of a theory of coordination in industrial clusters. *International Studies of Management & Organization, 31*(4), 14–34.

Lorenzen, M., & Foss, N. J. (2003). Cognitive coordination, institutions and clusters: An exploratory discussion. In D. Fornahl, T. Brenner (Eds.), *Cooperation, networks and institutions in regional innovation systems* (pp. 82–104). Cheltenham: Edward Elgar Publishing.

Lowitzsch, J. (2019). Investing in a Renewable Future – Renewable Energy Communities, Consumer (Co-)Ownership and Energy Sharing in the Clean Energy Package. *Renewable Energy Law and Policy Review, 9*(2), 14–36. https://doi.org/10.4337/relp.2019.02.02

Lowitzsch, J., Hoicka, C. E., & van Tulder, F. J. (2020). Renewable energy communities under the 2019 European Clean Energy Package – Governance model for the energy clusters of the future? *Renewable and Sustainable Energy Reviews, 122*, 109489. https://doi.org/10.1016/j.rser.2019.109489

McCauley, S. M., & Stephens, J. C. (2012). Green energy clusters and socio-technical transitions: Analysis of a sustainable energy cluster for regional economic development in Central Massachusetts, USA. *Sustainability Science, 7*(2), 213–225. https://doi.org/10.1007/s11625-012-0164-6

Meneghetti, A., & Nardin, G. (2012). Enabling industrial symbiosis by a facilities management optimization approach. *Journal of Cleaner Production, 35*, 263–273. https://doi.org/10.1016/j.jclepro.2012.06.002

Newlands, D. (2003). Competition and cooperation in industrial clusters: The implications for public policy. *European Planning Studies, 11*(5), 521–532.

Ngwaka, U., Khalid, Y., Ling-Chin, J., Counsell, J., Siddiqui, F., Pinedo-Cuenca, R., Dawood, H., Smallbone, A., Dawood, N., & Roskilly, A. P. (2023). Industrial cluster energy systems integration and management tool. *Energy Conversion and Management, 297*, 117731. https://doi.org/10.1016/j.enconman.2023.117731

O'Malley, M., Kroposki, B., Hannegan, B., Madsen, H., Andersson, M., D'haeseleer, W., McGranaghan, M. F., Dent, C., Strbac, G., & Baskaran, S. (2016). *Energy systems integration. Defining and describing the value proposition.* National Renewable Energy Lab.(NREL), Golden, CO (United States). https://www.osti.gov/servlets/purl/1257674

Padmore, T., & Gibson, H. (1998). Modelling systems of innovation: II. A framework for industrial cluster analysis in regions. *Research Policy, 26*(6), 625–641. https://doi.org/10.1016/S0048-7333(97)00038-3

Porter, M. E. (2012). The economic performance of regions. *Regional Competitiveness, 37*(6-7), 137–166.

Roelandt, T. J., & den Hertog, P. (1999). Cluster analysis and cluster-based policy making: The state of the art. In *Boosting Innovation: The Cluster Approach* (pp. 413–427). Paris: OECD Publishing.

Rosenfeld, S. A. (1997). Bringing business clusters into the mainstream of economic development. *European Planning Studies, 5*(1), 3–23. https://doi.org/10.1080/09654319708720381

Simeoni, P., Nardin, G., & Ciotti, G. (2018). Planning and design of sustainable smart multi energy systems. The case of a food industrial district in Italy. *Energy*, *163*, 443–456. https://doi.org/10.1016/j.energy.2018.08.125

Simmie, J., & Sennett, J. (1999). Innovative clusters: Global or local linkages? *National Institute Economic Review*, *170*, 87–98.

Smith, W. K., & Lewis, M. W. (2011). Toward a theory of paradox: A dynamic equilibrium model of organizing. *Academy of Management Review*, *36*(2), 381–403. https://doi.org/10.5465/amr.2011.59330958

Tvedt, H. L. (2019). The formation and structure of cleantech clusters: Insights from San Diego, Dublin, and Graz. *Norsk Geografisk Tidsskrift-Norwegian Journal of Geography*, *73*(1), Article 1.

Wackernagel, M., & Rees, W. E. (1997). Perceptual and structural barriers to investing in natural capital: Economics from an ecological footprint perspective. *Ecological Economics*, *20*(1), 3–24. https://doi.org/10.1016/S0921-8009(96)00077-8

Wang L., Wu X., & Li Q. (2017, February). *Research on* industrial cluster development of liaoning coastal economic belt. *2016 7th International Conference on Education, Management, Computer and Medicine* (EMCM 2016). https://doi.org/10.2991/emcm-16.2017.182

Wolfe, D. A., & Gertler, M. S. (2004). Clusters from the inside and out: Local dynamics and global linkages. *Urban Studies*, *41*(5–6), 1071–1093.

Xiu, C., & Lis, A. M. (2024). Collaborative development model and strategies of multi-energy industry clusters: Multi-indicators analysis affecting the development of coastal energy clusters. *Energy*, *295*, 131036. https://doi.org/10.1016/j.energy.2024.131036

Zhang, M., Wu, Q., Wen, J., Lin, Z., Fang, F., & Chen, Q. (2021). Optimal operation of integrated electricity and heat system: A review of modeling and solution methods. *Renewable and Sustainable Energy Reviews*, *135*, 110098. https://doi.org/10.1016/j.rser.2020.110098

# Index

Page numbers in *italics* indicate figures while page numbers in **bold** indicate tables.

For Product Safety Concerns and Information please contact our EU representative GPSR@taylorandfrancis.com Taylor & Francis Verlag GmbH, Kaufingerstraße 24, 80331 München, Germany